EMPLOYMENT EQUALITY IN NORTHERN IRELAND

SERIES EDITOR **Eithne McLaughlin**

POLICY ASPECTS OF EMPLOYMENT EQUALITY IN NORTHERN IRELAND

Edited by Eithne McLaughlin and Pádraic Quirk

This volume is one of a series arising from a review of fair employment legislation and other social and economic policies relevant to employment equality carried out by The Standing Advisory Commission on Human Rights, at the request of the Secretary of State for Northern Ireland. The review took place throughout 1995 and 1996 and this book series summarises research commissioned by SACHR from experts across a range of fields.

ALSO PUBLISHED IN THIS SERIES

Fair Employment Law in Northern Ireland: debates and issues
Edited by Denise Magill and Sarah Rose
ISBN 0 9527528 0 8

Public Views and Experiences of Fair Employment and Equality Issues in Northern Ireland
Edited by John McVey and Nigel Hutson
ISBN 0 9527528 2 4

Published by
The Standing Advisory Commission on Human Rights,
Temple Court, North Street, Belfast

ISBN 0 9527528 1 6 (paper)

Printed by ColourBooks Ltd.
105 Baldoyle Industrial Estate
Baldoyle, Dublin 13.

EMPLOYMENT EQUALITY IN NORTHERN IRELAND

SERIES EDITOR Eithne McLaughlin

POLICY ASPECTS OF EMPLOYMENT EQUALITY IN NORTHERN IRELAND

Edited by

Eithne McLaughlin and Pádraic Quirk

CONTENTS

LIST OF TABLES

LIST OF FIGURES AND MAPS

NOTES ON CONTRIBUTORS

Professor Vani Borooah has held the Chair of Applied Economics at the University of Ulster since 1987. He was previously Senior Research Officer on the Cambridge Growth Project and concurrently Fellow of Queen's College, Cambridge and Director of Cambridge Econometrics Limited. Professor Borooah is a past President of the European Public Choice Society and the current president of the Irish Economic Association. He is the author of *Political Aspects of the Economy* (with F. van der Ploeg); *The Structure of Consumption Decisions*; and *Regional Income Inequality and Poverty in the United Kingdom* (with P. McGregor and P. McKee).

Dr Leslie Caul is Senior Tutor for Education and Professional Studies at Stranmillis College of Education, Belfast. He has co-ordinated research into absenteeism, classroom processes and school effectiveness in Northern Ireland. He has served as a member of a number of public bodies including the Probation Board for Northern Ireland, Youth Committee for Northern Ireland, Northern Ireland Council for Educational Research and the Northern Ireland Council for Educational development and retains an active interest in local schools as a school governor.

Professor Robert Cormack is Pro-Vice-Chancellor of the Queen's University of Belfast. He has written widely on aspects of education, employment and equal opportunities including a series of books on discrimination in Northern Ireland with Professor Robert Osborne, such as *Discrimination and Public Policy in Northern Ireland* (1991) and *Religion, Education and Employment* (1983).

Dr Tony Dignan is a Consultant in the Economics and Public Policy Division at Coopers and Lybrands Belfast office. His previous publications include the EOC (NI) funded study *Labour Availability and Demographic Trends.* He has also worked in regional economic forecasting and is currently assisting in the preparation of an employment forecasting model for Greater London. His other publications include a review of regional disparities and policy in the European Union.

Dr Anthony Gallagher is a Reader in the School of Education, Queen's University of Belfast. He has published on the role of education systems in ethnically divided societies, and has experience in the policy and practice of equality of opportunity measures, education and social programmes.

Norman Gillespie is a Research Fellow in the Department of Sociology and Social Policy at the Queen's University of Belfast and was formerly Research

Officer with SACHR. He previously worked on the Third European Anti-Poverty Programme in Northern Ireland. His research interests include employment and unemployment, aspects of social disadvantage and exclusion, and social and economic regeneration strategies.

Kathleen Hoye is a Visiting Researcher at the Northern Ireland Economic Research Centre (NIERC) and an Atlantic Fellow. Before coming to Northern Ireland she worked for five years with the Chicago Association of Neighbourhood Development Organisations (CanDo), latterly as an Associate Finance Director.

Darren McKinstry is a Research Assistant in the School of Geosciences at the Queen's University of Belfast. He has research interests in computing applications in Geography and in the use of Geographical Information Systems (GIS) in social analysis.

Professor Eithne McLaughlin holds the Chair in Social Policy at the Queen's University of Belfast. She was previously Reader and lecturer in Social Policy at Queen's, Research Fellow at the University of York and Research Officer at the University of Ulster. She is a member of SACHR and has previously served on the UK Commission on Social Justice. She has published across a range of areas including labour supply, unemployment, equal opportunities policies, family and community care policies: for example, *Understanding Unemployment* (1992); *Flexibility in Work and Benefits* (1994); *Women, Employment and Social Policy in Northern Ireland* (with C. Davies, 1991); and *Paying for Care - Lessons from Europe* (with C. Glendinning, 1994).

Dr Anthony Murphy is a College Lecturer in the Department of Economics, University College, Dublin. His main research interests are in the areas of labour markets, regional migration, housing markets and econometrics. His recent research publications include a number of studies related to the Northern Ireland labour market, notably, *A Picture of Catholic and Protestant Male Unemployed* (1991, with D. Armstrong).

Professor Robert Osborne holds the Chair in Applied Policy Studies at the University of Ulster. His previous publications include: *Higher Education in Ireland: North and South* (1966); *After the Reforms: Education and Policy in Northern Ireland* (joint editor, 1993); and *Discrimination and Public Policy in Northern Ireland* (joint editor, 1991). His research interests lie in equality policies, education and higher education policy.

Pádraic Quirk is a Research Officer in the School of Public Policy, Economics and Law at the University of Ulster, and has previously held similar posts with SACHR, Making Belfast Work and the University of Ulster. His main research interests are in local government and the politics of divided societies, and he is currently examining conflict resolution strategies in Israel, South Africa and Northern Ireland.

Ronnie Scott is a Senior Research Officer with the Northern Ireland Economic Research Centre (NIERC). He was formerly an economic advisor in the Departments of Finance and Economic Development and a Senior Consultant in Coopers and Lybrand. His main research interests are in regional economic development and policy evaluation.

Dr Peter Shirlow is a Lecturer in Geography in the School of Geosciences at the Queen's University of Belfast. He has interests in cultural change, economic restructuring and labour market and has recently edited a book on the economy of Ireland entitled *Development Ireland: Contemporary Issues* (1995).

Dr Ian Shuttleworth is a Lecturer in Geography in the School of Geosciences at the Queen's University of Belfast. He has research interests in migration, census analysis and the economic fortunes of young people and recently published in these areas.

Dr Maura Sheehan is a Lecturer in Economics at the Queen's University of Belfast. Her current research interests are in industrial policy and labour markets in relation to equal opportunities. She is a member of the West Belfast Economic Forum for which she recently completed a study of the International Fund for Ireland.

John Simpson writes on business issues for *The Belfast Telegraph* and was recently the specialist adviser to the Northern Ireland Affairs Select Committee, House of Commons, on employment creation in Northern Ireland. Until 1989, he was a Lecturer in Economics at Queen's University, Belfast. He is at present one of the UK members of the Economic and Social Committee of the European Communities, Chairman of the Executive Committee of the Northern Ireland Small Business Institute, Chairman of Industry Matters and a member of the Citizens Charter Advisory Panel in Northern Ireland and the Council for Catholic Maintained Schools.

Mike Tomlinson is a Lecturer in Social Policy at the Queen's University of Belfast. He is co-author of *Northern Ireland: Between Civil Rights and Civil War* and *Unemployment in West Belfast*. His main work is in areas of criminal justice issues and the social policy of marginalised groups. He is a founder member of the West Belfast Economic Forum through which he has developed a particular interest in the political economy of the Northern Ireland conflict.

PREFACE

The Standing Advisory Commission on Human Rights (SACHR) was established by Parliament under section 20 of the Northern Ireland Constitution Act 1973 for the purpose of:

> advising the Secretary of State on the adequacy and effectiveness of the law for the time being in force in preventing discrimination on the ground of religious belief or political opinion and in providing redress for persons aggrieved by discrimination on either ground.

In January 1985 the Commission informed the then Secretary of State, the Right Honourable Douglas Hurd MP, of its intention to undertake a review of the adequacy and effectiveness of existing laws and institutions in securing freedom from discrimination and furthering equality of opportunity in Northern Ireland. This review culminated in the publication of two reports on religious and political discrimination and equality of opportunity in Northern Ireland (SACHR, 1987[1]; SACHR, 1990[2]). The debates surrounding the reports were influential in the development of fair employment legislation leading to the Fair Employment (Northern Ireland) Act 1989, amendments to the 1976 Fair Employment Act and related government policies.

It was therefore appropriate that the Secretary of State should ask the Commission to review employment equality five years after the introduction of the 1989 Fair Employment (Northern Ireland) Act. The terms of the review were:

> In the context of the commitment given by Peter Viggers MP in Parliament on 16 March 1989, to undertake a comprehensive review of employment equality, after five years' experience of the operation of the Fair Employment (Northern Ireland) Act 1976 as amended. The review should consider the effectiveness of those enactments and the institutions and procedures which they established in promoting equality of opportunity in employment and fair participation in employment between the Protestant and Catholic communities in Northern Ireland. The review should consider all aspects of fair employment (including the cost of compliance effects on employers and employees) but notably the legal, social and economic dimensions and the impact of relevant Government policies. The Commission may include additional relevant matters in its report.[3]

By March 1995, the Commission had agreed a basic strategy for the review and began to develop mechanisms to set this strategy in motion. In May 1995 a two-day seminar was held at which a cross-section of interested parties discussed areas of research which it would be necessary to pursue in order to fulfil the terms of reference. This, together with an earlier paper by Cassidy and Jones (1994)[4], resulted in the body of research which is presented in summarised form in the three volumes of this book series. The research has been published as quickly as the information has become available so that all those with an interest in equality issues may have access to the information which the Commission has considered. The views expressed in these books are those of the contributors themselves, writing as individuals, not as members or staff of the Standing Advisory Commission on Human Rights. The Commission's views will be set out in a separate later Final Report. It is the hope of the Commission that the books will stimulate and contribute to debate on the many aspects of employment equality in Northern Ireland.

This volume of the series focuses on the social and economic context in which fair employment legislation operates and reviews the public policy approach taken by Government in recent times. Volume I (Magill and Rose, 1996[5]) provided information on the law itself and debates surrounding some of the central concepts in the legislation, such as the 'merit principle' and 'fair participation'. It also included analysis of some specific aspects of the law, the enforcement mechanisms and the case law arising, together with a comparative study of equality measures elsewhere. Volume III (McVey and Hutson, in print[6]) focuses on public perceptions of fair employment and the 'machinery' of fair employment law in Northern Ireland today. Taken together, the work in these three volumes has assisted the Commission in drawing conclusions and making recommendations about 'the effectiveness of those enactments and the institutions and procedures which they established [to promote] equality of opportunity and fair participation in employment between the Protestant and Catholic communities in Northern Ireland'.

The Commission wishes to record its thanks to all those who have made the publication of this book series possible. In particular it is grateful to those academics and other professionals concerned who completed the complex research required within very demanding deadlines. To the Commission's own staff many thanks are due for their commitment and enthusiasm.

Mr Michael Lavery, QC, Chairman
Mrs Joan Harbison, CBE, Vice-Chairman (Public Participation)
Professor Eithne McLaughlin, Vice-Chairman (Research and Series Editor)

ENDNOTES

1 Standing Advisory Commission on Human Rights (1987) *Religious and Political Discrimination and Equality of Opportunity in Northern Ireland*, Cm 237, London: HMSO.

2 Standing Advisory Commission on Human Rights (1990) *Religious and Political Discrimination and Equality of Opportunity in Northern Ireland*, Cm 1107, London: HMSO.

3 Statement by Sir Patrick Mayhew, QC, MP, Secretary of State for Northern Ireland, 15 November 1994.

4 Cassidy, F. and Jones, B. (1994) 'Fair Employment Legislation - Issues arising from the First and Second Reports of the Standing Advisory Commission on Human Rights', Annex M(i), *Standing Advisory Commission on Human Rights 19th Annual Report 1993-4*, London: HMSO.

5 Magill, D. and Rose, S. (1996) (eds.) *Fair Employment Law in Northern Ireland: debates and issues*, Belfast: Standing Advisory Commission on Human Rights.

6 McVey, J. and Hutson, N. (forthcoming, 1996) (eds.) *Public Views and Experiences of Fair Employment and Equality Issues in Northern Ireland*, Belfast: Standing Advisory Commission on Human Rights.

Chapter One

EMPLOYMENT, UNEMPLOYMENT AND EQUALITY OF OPPORTUNITY: AN INTRODUCTION

Norman Gillespie

INTRODUCTION

The parameters of a review of employment equality stretch much wider than fair employment legislation. They include the diverse and extensive realms of economic policy, labour market interventions, training and education developments, social policy initiatives and strategic prioritisation in a whole range of service provision and planning. This is inevitable because inequality of opportunity and social and economic disadvantage are complex issues. An understanding of their nature, and subsequent implementation of measures aimed at redress, therefore require a comprehensive and systematic analysis of many factors. This chapter provides an introduction to the main issues of concern in the policy aspects of employment equality which are then explored further in the rest of this book.

The first section of this chapter will deal with patterns of employment and unemployment as experienced by the two main communities in Northern Ireland, followed by an outline of the debate on the role of structural factors in accounting for disparities in unemployment and equality of opportunity. These sections are set against the background of a changing economic climate. This will then be followed by a section on the role and record of job creation and economic development agencies in addressing unemployment and inequality. The final section details recent debates and developments in education and policy related measures, much of it informed by work commissioned by the Standing Advisory Commission on Human Rights (SACHR). Throughout these sections, brief outlines of the context of, and the issues raised by, subsequent chapters are presented.

PATTERNS OF EMPLOYMENT AND UNEMPLOYMENT: 1971-1996

Patterns of Unemployment: 1971-1996

Since the previous SACHR Review of Fair Employment in 1987, and indeed for some time before that, the unemployment rate in Northern Ireland has tended to be between 1.5 and 2.3 times higher than the rate in the United Kingdom. Given the regional nature of unemployment throughout the UK this might not be thought to be surprising. Yet over the past 20 years, the unemployment rate in Northern Ireland has been consistently higher than that of any other region in the UK. Although the unemployment rate, based on the claimant count, dropped below 12% in December 1995 from 18.6% in July 1987, it remains high and is characterised by long-term joblessness. Fifty seven per cent of the unemployed in Northern Ireland have been out of work for more than a year compared to a UK average of 38%. This discrepancy is a recent phenomenon; the figures for long-term unemployment in Northern Ireland and the UK in 1979 were 28% and 25% respectively (NIERC, 1993:86).

In 1987, the number of unemployed claimants in Northern Ireland was 127,927 (92,014 males and 35,913 females) (DED, 1987). Since then unemployment in Northern Ireland has continued to fall steadily. In December 1995, the overall number of unemployed claimants was 86,400 (67,400 males and 19,000 females), representing 11.4% of the workforce, and the seasonally adjusted figure[1] for 1995 had reached its lowest level for 14 years. Indeed, over the previous two years, unemployment had fallen by over 20,000 (Northern Ireland Information Service, 1995; DED, 1996).

Official records also showed that there had been a significant increase in the number of vacancies. In December 1995, there were 7253 vacancies for adults and 659 for young persons on offer at Training and Employment Agency offices (DED, 1996) compared with 2130 unfilled vacancies for adults and 814 for young persons at Employment Service Jobmarkets in July 1987 (DED, 1987). It should, however, be noted that the proportion of unemployed claimants to vacancies is much higher in Northern Ireland than the UK. In 1990, almost 1.7 million people in the UK were registered unemployed while average vacancies at Job Centres stood at 173,500, giving a ratio of 9.6 claimants for each vacancy (McLaughlin, 1992:3). The corresponding ratio, however, for Northern Ireland in 1990 was 22.6:1 (PPRU, 1995).

Within these trends there have been variations in the overall fall in unemployment at the sub-regional level with Northern Ireland as shown in Table 1.1. There was quite a significant fall in the unemployment rate of 45.6% between 1987 and 1995. Significantly, the only Travel to Work Areas[2] (TTWAs) showing a smaller decrease have been Belfast (45%),

Londonderry (43%), Coleraine (43%) and Newry (45%). Given that Belfast and Londonderry between them accounted for over 60% of the unemployed in July 1987, and just under it in December 1995, emphasises the particular problems of acute unemployment in urban settings. In contrast, unemployment rates in the Magherafelt, Cookstown, Craigavon, Enniskillen and Dungannon Travel to Work Areas more than halved (by 58.7%, 52.8%, 51.8%, 51.2% and 51.1% respectively). Despite these changes, unemployment rates continue to be significantly higher in areas west of the Bann where there is a higher concentration of the Catholic population.

Table 1.1: Unemployment Rates by Travel to Work Area, 1987 (July) and 1995 (December).

Travel to Work Area	N unemployed		N 1995 as % of 1987	%	unemploy -ment	% decrease in unemploy-ment rate 1987-95
	1987 N	1995 N	1987 %	1987 %	1995 %	%
Ballymena	3576	2271	63.5	14.4	7.4	48.6
Belfast	63,363	41,109	64.9	18.2	10.0	45.1
Coleraine	7392	5082	68.7	22.9	12.7	44.5
Cookstown	2676	1685	63.0	31.6	14.9	52.8
Craigavon	11,547	6623	57.3	19.1	9.2	51.8
Dungannon	3946	2612	66.2	26.6	13.0	51.1
Enniskillen	44,79	3011	67.2	25.0	12.2	51.2
Londonderry	12,577	9191	73.1	27.5	15.7	42.9
Magherafelt	3034	1872	61.7	29.3	12.1	58.7
Newry	7638	5679	74.3	29.8	16.4	45.0
Omagh	3770	2561	67.9	23.3	12.0	48.5
Strabane	3929	2431	61.9	34.7	17.7	49.0
NI totals	125,550	84,127	67.0	20.4	11.1	45.6

Source: DED, August 1987 and January 1996

Unemployment, therefore, remains politically contentious because it continues to be disproportionately experienced throughout the population. Table 1.2 shows unemployment rates by sex and religion in the last three Census of Population. The ratio of Catholic to Protestant unemployment has decreased somewhat over the 20 year period from 2:6 to 2:2 for men and from 1:9 to 1:8 for women. Close inspection of the 1991 Census shows large pockets of high unemployment throughout Northern Ireland. In 107 out of

566 electoral wards male unemployment exceeded 30% (1991 NI Census of Population).

Table 1.2: Unemployment Rates for Protestants and Catholics in 1971,1981 and 1991

	Men			Women		
Census of Population	Protestant (a)	Catholic (b)	Ratio of (a) to (b)	Protestant (c)	Catholic (d)	Ratio of (c) to (d)
1971	6.5%	17.3%	2.6	3.6%	7.0%	1.9
1981	12.4%	30.2%	2.4	9.6%	17.1%	1.8
1991	12.7%	28.4%	2.2	8.0%	14.5%	1.8

Catholics are still more than twice as likely to experience unemployment than Protestants despite relative improvements. Significantly, this differential is particularly marked in younger age groups. Furthermore, Catholics are also overrepresented in the long-term unemployed. In 1991, 65% of the 50,000 people who had not been in paid employment in the previous decade were Catholic compared with 35% Protestant, an overrepresentation of Catholics of 25% (FEC, 1995:40).

Research projects commissioned by the Fair Employment Commission (FEC) and using the 1991 Census identified a number of key aspects relevant to the issues of employment and unemployment. For example, the majority of unemployed workers in 1991 were Catholic (58.4%) compared to a share of the workforce figure of 39.8%. In terms of geography, Catholics were more likely to be unemployed than Protestants living in the same council area in 25 out of the 26 Districts. Catholics experienced higher levels of unemployment than Protestants with similar levels of qualifications and this was found to be the case at each level of qualification and regardless of the overall rate of unemployment. So while the total rate of unemployment decreased as the level of qualification increased, Catholics were still more likely not to have a job. In fact, Catholics were more than twice as likely as Protestants to be unemployed at every level of qualification excepting degree level, where a Catholic was 1.5 times more likely to be unemployed than a Protestant. For Catholics without qualifications, the unemployment rate was over 30%, or almost one in three, while the rate was less than 15% for Protestants, or just under one in seven (FEC,1995:13-14).

Economic Activity and Joblessness

One of the most dramatic changes in the UK labour market during the last 20 years has been the increase in the proportion of people classed as jobless. Joblessness relates to those of working age who do not have a job. In 1975, only 3% of working age males were economically inactive and virtually all the rest were either unemployed and searching for a job or employed. This situation has changed as the number of those classed as inactive now contributes as much to the jobless total as those who are looking for work. This rise in inactivity has been mirrored in the regions. In 1971, 19.9% of the total working age population in Northern Ireland were unemployed compared with only 7.8% who were inactive. By 1993, however, almost half of the jobless were not searching for work or were otherwise inactive (Borooah, 1995).

The main cause of the rise in inactivity relates to the fact that considerably more people are leaving the labour market and registering as long-term sick. In 1984, 48% of inactive persons were long-term sick or were 'discouraged' workers, while only 3% were simply not looking for jobs. By 1993, however, 60% of inactive persons were long-term sick, the figure for 'discouraged' workers had fallen from 31% to 14% and the figure for those not looking for work was between 3% and 5% (Borooah, 1995). A rise in inactivity had therefore been accompanied by an increase in long-term illness and a fall in the proportion of 'discouraged' workers. However, long-term illness may have become a mask for 'discouraged' workers. Lower probabilities of finding a job, rather than epidemics, may have resulted in substantial numbers of people moving from actively searching for work to being jobless and not searching (Borooah, 1995). Table 1.3 illustrates the change in male economic inactivity rates (excluding the retired and students) as experienced by the two communities between 1981 and 1991.

Table 1.3: Economic Inactivity Rates for Protestants and Catholics in 1981 and 1991

	1981		1991	
	N	%	N	%
Protestant	9557	58.3	19,288	52.9
Catholic	6846	41.7	17,146	47.1
Total	16,403	100.0	36,434	100.0

Source: NI Census of Population, 1981 and 1991.

Table 1.3 shows that there has been a marked increase in economic inactivity between 1981 and 1991. However, although the incidence doubled for the Protestant community, it rose by above 250% for the Catholic community. Thus, the factor of the 'discouraged' worker is being disproportionately experienced between the two communities and the implications that this has in relation to disparities in employment and unemployment need to be addressed.

Ongoing research at the NIERC (forthcoming) has shown that when employment has been created in a given (council) area in Northern Ireland in the last few years, this has usually had no impact on the level of (registered) unemployment in that area. Given (a) the persistence of large differentials in unemployment between Protestants and Catholics in Northern Ireland, and (b) the argument that what is required to redress these differentials is job creation in local labour markets with high levels of registered unemployment, Shuttleworth *et al* (Chapter Two, this volume) examine labour market processes, barriers which may negatively affect unemployed people's access to jobs and employers' attitudes to the long-term unemployed in the recruitment process.

Despite the high concentration of long-term unemployed people in the UK, there has been a distinct lack of research on issues concerned with long-term unemployment and related problems in Northern Ireland, such as the attitudes, feelings, behaviour and needs of long-term unemployed people. This is unusual given the nature and extent of the problems associated with long-term unemployment. These include loss of financial security, social status and friendships. Skills can become outdated and frequently unemployment is correlated with stress and ill-health. As a result a cycle of exclusion can be created whereby those experiencing unemployment over lengthy periods become increasingly marginalised from the world of work through an accumulation of redundant skills, lack of recent work experience, loss of self-esteem and failing health. The attitude of employers to the long-term unemployed is often negative and this may intensify feelings of alienation and powerlessness. Such problems have been exacerbated by the political crisis and 'troubles' over the past 27 years. The dearth of research in this field is even more noticeable given the attention directed at the causes of unemployment in political debate and the focus on employment creation programmes in Northern Ireland. Added to this there has been a plethora of studies concerned with various aspects and interpretations of the political conflict which in itself has not been entirely divorced from the economic situation and high incidence of long-term unemployment. Sheehan and Tomlinson's chapters (Chapters Three and Four, this volume) go some way to addressing these issues through a case study of West Belfast.

Patterns of Employment: 1990-1995

In the past Catholics were disadvantaged not only by their overrepresentation among the unemployed but also their underrepresentation in employment. This section draws on recent FEC data in order to illustrate the nature of disparities in employment and changes in recent years.[3] When the first analysis of employers' returns was conducted in 1990, the composition of the monitored workforce was 65.1% Protestant and 34.9% Catholic. The most recent report records a composition of 62.7% Protestant and 37.3% Catholic, an increase in the Catholic proportion of 2.4 percentage points since 1990 (FEC, 1996). It is estimated that, at present, the Catholic share of the economically active population, that is, those available for work, is 40% (FEC, 1996:9). It is important to note that since there has been an annual increase in the Catholic share of those available for work, then one would expect to find an increase in the Catholic share of employment, even if there had been no underrepresentation in the first place.

In 1994, the composition of male employees was 65.3% Protestant and 34.7% Catholic. For females, the composition was 59.7% Protestant and 40.3% Catholic, which is very close to their share of the economically active population. The overall Catholic compositions of the public and private sectors in 1994 were respectively 37.2% and 37.4% and the Catholic increases in share over the period 1990-4 were 1.8% in the case of the public sector and 2.6% for private sector concerns (FEC, 1996:10). Table 1.4 gives a break down of the change in the Catholic percentage of the Northern Ireland workforce by Standard Occupational Classification (SOC) between 1990 and 1994.

Table 1.4: Change in the Catholic Percentage of the Northern Ireland Workforce (Public and Private Sector Concerns with 26 or More Employees) by SOC 1990-1994.

	1990 %	1991 %	1992 %	1993 %	1994 %	Overall Change %
SOC1 (Managers & Administrators)	30.50	31.30	32.50	33.60	34.40	3.90
SOC2 (Professional Occupations)	33.40	34.40	35.90	36.80	38.80	5.40
SOC3 (Associate Professional & Technical Occupations)	40.10	40.10	40.60	41.20	41.80	1.70
SOC4 (Clerical & Secretarial Occupations)	34.20	34.60	35.20	36.40	37.10	2.90
SOC5 (Craft & Skilled Manual Occupations)	34.30	33.20	33.40	34.10	34.50	0.20
SOC6 (Personal & Protective Services)	28.50	29.60	30.20	30.50	30.40	1.90
SOC7 (Sales Occupations)	33.30	34.00	35.00	35.60	36.70	3.40
SOC8 (Plant & Machine operatives)	38.50	39.00	39.70	40.70	41.50	3.00
SOC9 (Other Occupations)	38.80	39.80	39.50	39.20	40.30	1.50
Total	34.90	35.30	35.80	36.50	37.20	2.30

Source: FEC, 1996.

Historically, Catholics were significantly underrepresented in prestigious occupations SOC 1-3. However, according to Table 1.4, the Catholic proportion in every occupational group between 1990 and 1994 increased with the largest increase being in managerial and professional occupations. Catholic managers and administrators have increased from 30.5% to 34.4%, while the proportion of Catholic professionals increased from 33.4% to 38.8%, an increase of 5.4 percentage points (FEC, 1996:10). These figures suggest that between 1990 and 1994 more than half the Catholic underrepresentation in the top two Standard Occupational Classifications (SOCs) has been eliminated. In addition, between 1991 and 1994 in both the public and private sectors (concerns with 251+ employees) the share of Catholic applications was 41.5% and 42.9% and the composition of appointees was 41.1% and 44.0% respectively.

Despite these changes, the FEC identifies a number of areas of concern which we have already mentioned: that the majority of unemployed workers continues to be Catholic; Catholics experience higher levels of unemployment than Protestants with similar qualifications; and those with no formal qualifications were the most likely to be unemployed. Two areas in particular are highlighted. Firstly, existing progress needs not only to be maintained, but increased, as the Catholic share of the economically active population under 35 is now 44%. Secondly, a central failure of equality legislation the world over is that the benefits of increased opportunity are felt by the most advantaged sections of minority communities, but the most disadvantaged are left largely untouched (FEC,1995:12).

It is for the second reason that employment inequality can only be effectively tackled by a range of social and economic policies and practices in addition to effective fair employment legislation. While the latter was the primary focus of concern for the previous book in this series (Magill and Rose, 1996), the former is the focus for this volume. However, what we need to do now is consider recent developments in the debate on the role of various factors in accounting for the discrepancies in unemployment rates, as perceptions of the relative strengths attributed to these are likely to influence the nature and extent of future action for promoting equality of opportunity.

FAIR EMPLOYMENT AND EQUALITY OF OPPORTUNITY: THE ROLE OF STRUCTURAL FACTORS

The Changing Economic Climate: 1971-1995

The establishment of the Fair Employment Agency in 1976 coincided with the beginning of the most dramatic period of economic transformation in Northern Ireland since the Second World War. Manufacturing jobs declined by 40% between 1973 and 1990 (Whyte, 1990:52) and attempts to start up new industries to compensate for the decline of old ones met with only limited success. Rowthorn and Wayne (1988:82-3) have pointed to a number of factors peculiar to the Northern Ireland situation, such as: the slump in the world economy following 1973, which had a particularly adverse effect on the Northern Ireland economy due to its dependence on exports; the dependence of Northern Ireland on the British economy; the preponderance of problem industries in the Northern Ireland economy; and the concentration of multinational 'branch plants' that are particularly vulnerable to recession. The economy as a result became heavily dependent on the public sector which was maintained by massive subsidies from the rest of the UK. Indeed, there has recently been some concern expressed about the impact that changes in public sector employment may have had on efforts to create more favourable conditions for equality of employment opportunity in Northern Ireland. With approximately 5000 jobs lost in the public sector (excluding those lost by the privatisation of Northern Ireland Electricity) since 1990 (FEC, 1994), the question to be addressed is whether these losses have affected Catholics and Protestants equally. Given the importance of the public sector for redressing community differentials in employment. Dignan and Murphy analyse the impact of key trends in public sector employment on community differentials in Chapter Eight, this volume.

The late 1980s and early 1990s were dominated by recession in the UK as a whole with the gradual recovery beginning in 1993. In the Northern Ireland economy during this period, there is evidence to support the view that the effects of recession were not only less severe but that the local economy actually improved its position relative to national trends. For instance, Northern Ireland employment levels (employees in employment) by mid-1995 stood at 2.7% above the 1990 figure and, although manufacturing employment dropped by 8% during the recession, recently there has been a trend upwards with an increase of 3% since mid-1993 (DED, 1995(a):8). Manufacturing output also performed well with an increase in output of 5% in the year ending the third quarter of 1995 (*Belfast Telegraph*, 17/1/96).

There is a consensus among local economic commentators that this better performance reflects three factors: (i) a material improvement in the underlying competitiveness of Northern Ireland manufacturing; (ii) the absence of the 1980s boom (and hence the worst of the subsequent downturn); and (iii) the relatively higher levels of public expenditure and public sector employment (DED, 1995(a):8-9).

Explaining High Unemployment

Against this, as the previous section showed, unemployment, and especially long-term unemployment, has remained high. Competing views have been postulated for the continuation of high unemployment. On the one hand there are those who see the problem as basically demographic in that a fast-growing population needs more jobs than the economy can create (Gudgin and O'Shea, 1993:3). Others have argued that the rise in unemployment has been very much greater than can be accounted for by the demographic changes (Eversley,1989:90).

Of particular concern is the fact that there was little change in the unemployment differential between Protestants and Catholics. Catholic males continue to be over twice as likely to be unemployed as Protestant males. Although the differential in respect of women is less, it should be noted that, for technical reasons, unemployment rates for women are always more difficult to quantify accurately (McLaughlin, 1992; see also Shuttleworth *et al*, Chapter Two, this volume).

Explaining Unemployment Differentials

There has been a great deal of controversy surrounding the various explanations of the unemployment differential. Much of this has concentrated on the relative weight that should be attached to what are sometimes referred to as 'structural' factors as against religion (including discrimination). The 1987 SACHR report on fair employment summarised the main factors identified by the protagonists in this debate as:

(i) regional factors: because Catholics are concentrated in areas of higher unemployment in the west of Northern Ireland this contributes to the continuing differential;
(ii) different labour markets: there are two separate labour markets in Northern Ireland, one catering primarily for Protestants and the other for Catholics, and this contributes to the differential in unemployment;
(iii) class differences: class differences between Protestants and Catholics, since it is generally found that unemployment is greater in lower socio-economic classes;
(iv) differences in education: differences in educational attainment and in subject choice and availability have contributed to the greater difficulty for Catholics in obtaining employment;
(v) differences in attitude to work: Catholics tend to have a lower commitment to work than Protestants;
(vi) age: differences in the age distribution of the Catholic and Protestant sections of the community have contributed to the differences in unemployment;
(vii) family size: Catholics tend to have larger families which contributes to the differences in unemployment;
(viii) the chill factor: the reluctance of Catholics and Protestants to apply for jobs or to travel to work in areas which lie outside their 'own areas', or to work in workplaces which they regard as hostile, or to apply for jobs

with employers whom they think will not employ them, contributes to the differentials in unemployment;

(ix) security occupations: Catholics have excluded themselves from certain types of employment, the most obvious example being the security forces, which are open to them but which for various reasons they do not wish to undertake;

(x) the black [*sic*] economy: the extent of unemployment has been exaggerated and there is a substantial hidden economy in which many 'unemployed' have both occasional and permanent paid employment; and

(xi) religion: differences in unemployment rates for Catholics and Protestants are largely due to direct or indirect discrimination on religious grounds (SACHR, 1987:25).

SACHR (1987) made no attempt to give a full account of the evidence in respect of these various possible explanations, which in some cases involved complex statistical and analytical techniques. It proceeded instead to concentrate on setting out the nature of the proposed explanations, the most important evidence in respect of each and an estimate of the extent to which they may or may not contribute to the differentials in employment and unemployment. It then proceeded to suggest ways in which action could be taken to address the relevant contributory factors. Some of these, it was felt, necessitated legislation and administrative action to promote equality of opportunity. Others required 'other measures', while others could not readily be dealt with in any other way than by 'drawing attention to their existence' (SACHR, 1987:26). The relative strengths and weaknesses of this position subsequently engendered considerable debate.

Structural v. Religious Discrimination: Academic Arguments

Two recent studies commissioned by government - Murphy and Armstrong (1994) and Gudgin and Breen (1996) - have continued the debate over the relative importance of 'structural factors' versus direct or indirect discrimination on the grounds of religion. Murphy and Armstrong concluded that about half the unemployment differential between Catholics and Protestants can be accounted for by factors such as age, number of children, housing tenure, qualifications and area of residence. The other half is attributed to personal characteristics or other factors such as discrimination. Differences in labour force growth (that is, demographic differences between the two communities) were only found to have an effect on the unemployment differential when they were coupled with a range of assumptions about labour turnover rates, zero or negative employment growth rates and segregation in employment. They also found that Catholic men are significantly more likely to be economically inactive and again half of this difference is attributed to religion, and there were also differences in job search activities between Catholic and Protestant men.

Although this was an elaborate econometric study of the unemployment differential, the authors themselves admitted that their findings 'must be interpreted carefully' (Murphy and Armstrong, 1994:65). They suggest that a large and significant Catholic/religion effect may be explained by a range of factors that were not included in their analysis. Such factors might include differences in labour force growth, subject mix at school or college, motivation, direct and indirect discrimination, or the 'chill factor'. However, they point out that there is little evidence that educational subject mix in Northern Ireland or elsewhere has a large effect on the incidence of unemployment. They further add that the limited evidence available does not suggest that Catholics are less motivated, less flexible or have a poorer attitude to work than non-Catholics. This is supported by the results presented by Sheehan and Tomlinson on the job search activity of the long term unemployed in West Belfast in Chapter Three, this volume. However, past unemployment increases the risk of current unemployment due to the loss of human capital or 'stigma' or 'scarring' effects (Murphy and Armstrong, 1994:65-66; see also Chapters Two, Three and Four, this volume).

Gudgin and Breen (1996) set out to explain why the Catholic/Protestant differential has stayed at a constant ratio of roughly 2:5 for over 20 years despite significant variations in labour conditions. For instance, in 1991 the male unemployment rate was 21% compared to 7% in 1971 yet the unemployment differential remained largely unaffected. They attempt to explain the stubbornness of this ratio by emphasising flows 'in' and 'out' of employment and unemployment. Four factors are given to explain this differential. Firstly, there has been a differential labour force growth between the two communities. Gudgin and Breen estimate that between 1971 and 1991 the Catholic population of working age increased by 61% (2.4% per annum) compared with 22% (1% per annum) for Protestants. This meant that with more Catholics entering the labour market, they had a higher probability of not finding a job given the relatively low level of employment growth. Secondly, the different migration rates of the two communities suggests that Catholics are less likely to respond to unemployment by emigrating than Protestants. They argue that, although between 1971 and 1991 roughly 33,000 Catholics left Northern Ireland against 17,000 Protestants, the Protestant propensity to migrate in the face of a given level of unemployment is more than 2.5 times higher than for Catholics. Thirdly, Catholics have higher levels of 'quit' rates from jobs than Protestants and, fourthly, Protestants are in a better position to obtain a job given the number of disadvantages experienced by Catholics such as location, age and qualifications.

In short, Gudgin and Breen suggest that these four factors taken together fully account for the 2.5 times differential between Catholic and Protestant unemployment rates. It would, therefore, follow from this position that discrimination on the grounds of religion in recruitment plays little or no part in accounting for this discrepancy and that there is, therefore, no need for fair employment legislation.

The Gudgin and Breen study has precipitated considerable controversy and debate, not least because of the implications it has in relation to raising certain underlying assumptions about 'cultural' distinctions between the two communities. One problem with the study is that it does not account for the causal factors whereby Catholic 'quit' rates are higher than for Protestants (for example, that Catholics predominate in employment sectors and occupations that are more prone to lay-offs and 'quit' rates). They also offer no explanation as to why the migration propensity for Protestants may be higher than for Catholics. One possibility is that Protestants who lose their jobs are more qualified and experienced and therefore in a stronger position to move elsewhere. In other words, recent migration propensities may be the product of the religious complexion of the employment structure in the past and Protestant overrepresentation in better occupations.

A critical flaw in the whole debate surrounding these studies is that most of the work sets out to 'prove' (or is taken to 'prove') whether or not Catholics have been discriminated against in recruitment. While those with nationalist inclinations will tend to reject such studies as Gudgin and Breen as inconsequential in accounting for unemployment differentials, those with unionist leanings will tend to accept them. However, a broader perspective would acknowledge the importance of historical disadvantage as well as, or instead of, 'direct' discrimination in recruitment to jobs. For example, higher levels of unemployment are common among those with larger families in Great Britain as well as in Northern Ireland. It may be that experience of unemployment (in past as well as present generations) and low expectations of employment prevent the kind of 'self-limitation' of fertility which people with jobs, especially dual-earner couples, have increasingly engaged in. As such, levels of fertility (and hence, in the long-term, differential labour force growth between the two communities) may not be unrelated to the historical experience of employment opportunities. Equally, motivations to succeed at school and in post-16 educational and training provision are likely to be affected by the young person's and their friends', families' and relations' expectations of the probability that attainment will result in employment. Such differences as there are in attainment also then may be related to the historical positions of the two communities in Northern Ireland. In addition, poorer socio-economic circumstances may also affect an individual's abilities to achieve through their effects on physical health and mental well-being (Fryer, 1992).

In essence, the issue is the extent to which one wishes to adopt a position which includes all the possible impacts a history of high unemployment and low employment might have on a community, and which assumes that these, as well as, or instead of, religious discrimination at the point of recruitment by employers, are matters of public policy interest, concern and potential action. The alternative position - that it is only discrimination at the point of recruitment which is at issue - inevitably leads to an increasingly technical debate about how much discrimination there is or has been. In this regard, it may be worth noting that views differ as to whether the methodologies commonly adopted in studies such as those of Murphy and Armstrong and Gudgin and Breen are actually capable of ever delivering a clear and unambiguous answer to the question of whether there is or has been discrimination by employers at the point of recruitment. Whatever position is adopted, few would disagree that employment creation is vital if unemployment generally is to be reduced, and it is to this that we now turn.

JOB CREATION AGENCIES AND ECONOMIC DEVELOPMENT: 1989-1995

Employment Creation: The Policy Context

Recent research for the 1987-1991 period has shown an 18% growth in manufacturing employment in Catholic wards. This was about three times the level of growth in mainly Protestant wards, excluding Belfast. There was a strong shift away from the city in terms of employment location over this period (NIERC, forthcoming). This research also showed that the contributions of the Industrial Development Board (IDB) and Local Enterprise Development Unit (LEDU) to the share of manufacturing employment growth in each area was similar. Of those wards that increased their share of new jobs during this period, the overall increase in Catholic areas was about 50% more than would be normally expected based on overall manufacturing growth (*ibid*). Such figures describe movements within and between areas but they do not address the role of employment creation in tackling unemployment or the unemployment differential. While no similar study to that described above exists for the more recent period, 1991-1995, it is possible to review policy shifts which have occurred since then and the performance of relevant agencies, and these are the tasks undertaken by Simpson in Chapter Ten, this volume. Simpson compares the performance of the IDB with its counterparts in the Republic of Ireland and Scotland, the geographical location of jobs created and the structure and level of financial assistance to industry in the context of other countries' systems of aid. He also considers the historical and economic context for the performance of the DED and its agencies in terms of job creation since the late 1980s. In 1992, changes in local government legislation provided local authorities in Northern

Ireland with the statutory authority to set aside funds to promote economic development. This measure was complemented by the encouragement and opportunity offered by the European Structural Funds (1994-1999), under which councils are encouraged to stimulate local economic development adopting a strategic, integrated approach. Scott and Hoye, in Chapter Nine, this volume, provide a review of what councils are doing with the additional resources available for economic development and what effect, if any, this is likely to have on employment equality, given the unequal distribution of unemployment between and within local council areas.

ACTIVE LABOUR MARKET POLICES

Current Department of Economic Development policy is set out in 'Competing in the 1990s: The Key to Growth' (DED, 1990), which built on an earlier strategy outlined in the 'Pathfinder Process' (DED, 1987). As Simpson (Chapter Ten, this volume) discusses, the implementation of the more recent approach resulted in significant changes in both the objectives of industrial policy and the DED's organisational structure. An interim document reviewing the implementation of this strategy to date was launched recently (DED, 1995(b)), setting out how the DED intends to 'improve delivery of its services and target them more effectively' (*ibid*). The most significant departure from the point of view of employment equality was that the DED and its economic development agencies agreed a 'renewed commitment to the policy of Targeting Social Need (TSN) (see Quirk and McLaughlin, Chapter Seven, this volume). The following sections review the overall performance of the DED agencies against the background of unemployment rates. The next section is a summary of the overall performance of these agencies in recent years.

The IDB

Employment in IDB client companies as at 31 March 1995 totalled 82,940. Table 1.5 gives a break down of the distribution of these jobs by Travel to Work Area, along with the corresponding unemployment distribution for 13 April 1995. While the table cannot be regarded as in any way definitive, it may shed some light on discussions concerning assisted employment. There are, of course, a whole range of other factors to consider, for instance, the number of actual jobs created (for which see Simpson, Chapter Ten, this volume) and expenditure per area. There are also local disparities in existing infrastructure and geographical proximity. Nevertheless, the table does suggest some local disparities which may need consideration. The Ballymena and Craigavon Travel to Work Areas contain almost twice the proportion of total assisted jobs as these areas' share of unemployment. On the other hand, in the Newry and Omagh areas, the trend is reversed.

Table 1.5: IDB Assisted Employment and Unemployment Distribution by Travel to Work Area, March/April 1995

Travel to Work Area	Employment in IDB Client Companies	% of Employment in IDB Client Companies	Total % Distribution of Total Unemployment
Ballymena	4419	5.3	2.8
Belfast	37,149	44.8	49.8
Coleraine	4338	5.2	6.1
Cookstown	031	1.2	2.0
Craigavon	12,142	14.6	7.8
Dungannon	3590	4.3	2.9
Enniskillen	2833	3.4	3.7
Londonderry	9193	11.1	10.3
Magherafelt	1906	2.3	2.2
Newry	2932	3.5	6.5
Omagh	990	1.2	3.0
Strabane	2417	2.9	2.8
Total	82,940	100.0	100.0

Source: DED, April 1995 and IDB, 1995

LEDU

Between 1991 and 1994, Northern Ireland had the most successful record of any region in the UK in increasing the number of small businesses. In addition, Northern Ireland has achieved a 'better balance' between business start-ups and the prospects of survival. While a number of explanations may be forwarded for this trend, it has been noted that 'LEDU and the 30 Local Enterprise Agencies, might reasonably claim credit for their efforts to stimulate more soundly based businesses' (Simpson, 1996:6). LEDU client companies now claim almost 40,000 jobs (LEDU, 1995:8), but there remain questions as to the capacity of this form of job creation to target areas of greatest need. Simpson (*op. cit*) argues that people who are unemployed do not offer the best prospects for launching more than single person businesses. This, of course, is a problem widely associated with areas where high and long-term unemployment rates are endemic. In order to redress this, LEDU has committed itself to TSN as a policy priority, adopting as a principal target the:

> improvement of equality of economic opportunity throughout Northern Ireland with particular emphasis on supporting businesses in the areas of deprivation ... data indicates that employment growth amongst surviving

client businesses in 215 (out of 566) of the most deprived District Council wards was 6% compared with 7.2% for businesses in the remaining 351 wards (LEDU, 1995:15).

Work on measuring the impact of LEDU's work on the two communities has focused on the two communities in terms of access to pre-start-up and start-up schemes. A study of this by the Institute of Enterprise Strategies (1993), commissioned by LEDU, concluded that its provision had been balanced in community terms.

Whatever attempts are made at redressing regional inequalities in job creation, they are unlikely by themselves to make a substantial impact in reducing unemployment given that there are some 8000 entrants to the labour force each year, yet only about 4000 new jobs being created (Opsahl Report, 1993:287). Other commentators have added that, even after a record level of job generation between 1986 and 1990, in which 52,000 additional jobs were created, unemployment was never below 13.5% (Gudgin and O'Shea, 1993:3). It has been argued that one of the most difficult aspects of Northern Ireland's unemployment problem is that job creation has to be 'massive' in order to make any significant difference. Current evidence suggests that every two jobs created in manufacturing or public service leads to only one person coming off the unemployment register (Gudgin and O'Shea, 1993).

The Training and Employment Agency (T&EA)

Given the nature of the unemployment differential and the tendency for young Catholic males to have higher rates of participation in government training, the nature of such training and its availability to disadvantaged areas and those most in need is an important issue in the equality debate, as Caul discusses in Chapter Five, this volume. Since its inception, the T&EA has allocated some 75% of its programme budget of around £170 million to programmes which 'whilst economically significant, also address various problems of social need' (DED, 1995(b):27). Every 16 and 17 year old who, on leaving full-time education, does not enter employment is guaranteed up to two years training in the Jobskills programme. This is open to long-term unemployed adults and is designed to enhance the quality of vocational training in Northern Ireland and improve trainees' prospects of achieving qualifications and employment. Jobskills replaced the Youth Training and Job Training Programmes (YTP and JTP). In the years 1990/91 to 1993/94, there was an average of some 12,000 young people in YTP, representing about a quarter of school-leavers - an important part of the potential workforce. The T&EA reports that in 1993/94, 68% of participants in YTP achieved a positive outcome in the form of a job (56%) or continuing education (12%). Although only 20% of YTP trainees now achieve recognised vocational qualifications at NVQ level 2 or above, this is compared with 2% in 1990. An average of 4500 long term unemployed adults participated in the Job Training Programme in 1993/94, and of these 43% achieved a positive outcome in terms of a job or continuing education (DED, 1995(b):28).

What happens to the 32% of YTP trainees who do not achieve a 'positive outcome' remains a considerable concern. Presumably, these are most likely to be those who 'under achieved' at school, have no recognised vocational or other qualifications and seem destined at the age of 18 to a future of long-term unemployment or stopgap, meaningless jobs. Similarly, those 57% of adults who did not achieve a 'positive outcome' from JTP were most likely those coming from longer term unemployment and most likely to return to it. These adults and young people alike are also most likely to be concentrated in disadvantaged areas, be right at the bottom of the occupational and social classifications and be overrepresented in the Catholic community.

Since 1993, participation in T&EA programmes has been monitored by reference to religion, gender and disability. This information is said to be used to promote equality of opportunity within the agency's programmes, in order to 'give full effect to the Government's policies of Targeting Social Need (TSN) and ensuring fair treatment' (DED, 1995(b):29). TSN (examined by Quirk and McLaughlin in Chapter Seven, this volume) and the more recent PAFT guidelines (examined by Osborne *et al*, in Chapter Six, this volume) have become, politically at least, cornerstones of government attempts to promote equality of opportunity.

Long-term Unemployment: Targeted Programmes

Given the extent and nature of long-term unemployment in Northern Ireland, this has been described as a 'priority area' by the DED. The Department argues that demographic trends and rising labour market participation rates imply that unemployment is likely to remain a significant problem for the foreseeable future. As regards long-term unemployment, the Department notes the common problem that long-term unemployed people are the least likely to gain employment even when relatively substantial numbers of additional jobs are created. The Department explains this in terms of the way in which time can erode experience and motivation thereby reducing their attractiveness to employers. Whether this is an adequate explanation in terms of Northern Ireland will be addressed in Chapters Two and Three of this volume.

Whatever the reason, a number of measures have been taken in order to address the problems associated with long-term unemployment.

Restart

Under this programme unemployed persons entering their sixth month of unemployment are offered a counselling interview with the objective of facilitating their entry into employment or training. Those unemployed for more than six months are invited back for further counseling interviews at six monthly intervals. An 'offer' (a referral to one of a number of options, such as job search, training and employment scheme places) is usually made to the interviewee at the session. However, it has been noted that, due to the short duration and lack of depth of the interview and the limited menu of 'offers' available, it 'would be surprising if more than a small proportion of those counselled actually ended up in such a placement' (Scott, 1993:94).

Action for Community Employment

The aim of Action for Community Employment (ACE) is to provide employment of up to one year's duration for long-term unemployed adults in a range of projects of 'community benefit'. Although it has proved to be a reasonably effective direct employment scheme for the temporary relief of unemployment, it has encountered a number of drawbacks. The high level of part-time posts has led some to question whether the scheme is being targeted at those long-term unemployed people in most need of assistance and whether those working part-time would otherwise be available for full-time work. Furthermore, placement rates into employment and training from the scheme, around 27%, are only slightly better than the normal outflow rate from long-term unemployment (Scott, 1993:94-5). However, the introduction of a training requirement to ACE had been accompanied by a 20% increase in the proportion of former ACE participants finding employment (DED, 1995(b):28).

Recent concern has, however, been expressed at the T&EA's decision to reduce the number of Action for Community Employment (ACE) posts from 9600 to 7200. A high percentage of the Agency's expenditure on Jobskills and ACE is concentrated, by the nature of these programmes, in areas of social need. ACE jobs, for example, are in general distributed according to the pattern of long-term unemployment and over 30% of all ACE jobs are in Making Belfast Work areas. The introduction of the Community Work Programme (CWP) has failed to alleviate the fears of political and voluntary sector leaders that the unemployed will lose out if ACE provision is reduced (see Quirk and McLaughlin, Chapter Seven, this volume).

Community Work Programme

Through the Community Work Programme currently being piloted in Strabane, Fermanagh and West Belfast, the DED intends to provide 'stimulating and meaningful employment of benefit to the community' for a significant proportion of the long-term unemployed. In return for a three year placement they receive a payment equivalent to their benefit, plus an additional small weekly cash incentive. Although designed to alleviate the worst effects and extent of long-term unemployment throughout the population, the fact that Catholics are much more likely to be long-term unemployed than Protestants means that this programme could have significant implications for employment equality. The potential viability of the Programme is assessed by Sheehan and Tomlinson in Chapter Four, this volume, who also examine the attitudes of unemployed people and employers to schemes targeted at the long-term unemployed in general.

Although the improvement of vocational training standards has been advocated as a means of reducing unemployment, the supply of skilled labour would continue to exceed demand (Gudgin and O'Shea, 1993:6) as training programmes need to be accompanied by a substantial increase in appropriate employment opportunities.

EDUCATION

As noted in Chapters Five and Seven, this volume, the effectiveness of training programmes targeted at unemployed adults depends to a considerable extent on prior achievement at school. Equity in educational outputs (levels of attainment) and inputs (funding levels, for example) have been a major focus in the equality debate in Northern Ireland. SACHR's second report on religious and political discrimination and equality of opportunity (SACHR, 1990) recommended that funding of education should be debated and that there should be a statutory duty on all public bodies to monitor the way in which the two main sections of the community are affected by their activities. The latter of these comes under the remit of PAFT, discussed in Chapter Six, this volume. As regards the former, SACHR commissioned a number of papers in the early 1990s which contributed to the wide debate on educational funding in Northern Ireland. These studies, on school size (Cormack *et al*, 1991(a)), secondary analysis of the School Leavers Survey (Cormack *et al*, 1989) and grammar school provision (Cormack *et al*, 1991(b)), generated a considerable number of observations leading to a number of SACHR recommendations. These included: comprehensive monitoring of recurrent and capital expenditure between Catholic, Protestant and integrated schools; abolition or substantial reduction of the voluntary contribution towards capital projects; and that grammar school provision should be reviewed and equity of access made a priority. The publication of the research, particularly that part concerned with financial issues 'provoked substantial public comment and debate which might, as far as the Catholic community and educational authorities were concerned, be described as an outcry' (Osborne, 1993:472).

In February 1992, eight months after the report covering finance had been published, the Department of Education for Northern Ireland (DENI) issued a discussion paper on the proposed comprehensive monitoring of recurrent and capital expenditure in the different school sectors and a final version was published in June 1992 (DENI, 1992). The DENI is now committed to monitoring all recurrent and capital expenditure on an annual basis and publishing the results. In July 1992, it was announced that a new Catholic grammar school was to be established in Belfast, the first for fifty years, and similar provision was subsequently announced for Londonderry. In November 1992, it was announced that following discussion with relevant authorities a new category of voluntary school was to be established which, in return for adjustments in the composition of the board of governors, would receive 100% capital funding. This development, which meant that there would be 'little likelihood of any loss of effective control by the Catholic authorities' (Osborne, 1993:474) was welcomed by the Catholic education authorities. Chapter Five continues this debate on aspects of equity and equality in the Northern Ireland educational and training systems, as do Chapter Six and Seven, this volume.

TARGETING SOCIAL NEED

Quirk and McLaughlin, in Chapter Seven, show that there is still room for concern on the equity with which school funding is distributed, though in their case they are focusing on how well school funding reflects social need as part of a review of Targeting Social Need. TSN was introduced in 1991, alongside economic development and law and order, as a principle to guide the allocation of public funds in Northern Ireland. Several government statements on TSN have suggested that it is seen as an issue of targeting special additional resources on specific areas, for example:

> Through the Targeting Social Need initiative the Government are working to eradicate the significant inequalities which persist in the social and economic conditions experienced by Protestants and Catholics. By identifying where the highest levels of disadvantage and deprivation exist, by analysing the precise extent to which their whole range of policies has a differential impact on each side of the community and by targeting the programmes and resources much more sharply on those areas suffering the highest levels of social and economic disadvantage, the Government are genuinely and constantly seeking to remove differentials and rectify injustices (Lord Belstead, House of Lords, 13 February 1992).

As Quirk and McLaughlin in Chapter Seven argue, however, TSN should, in terms of its own logic, extend beyond locality-based special programmes - which, by their nature, consume only a small proportion of total public expenditure in Northern Ireland - to focus on particular social groups. While some literature exists reviewing the effectiveness of locality-specific programmes, such as MBW, there has been no previous research examining the extent to which TSN has indeed guided public expenditure patterns, decisions and provisions in general.

Examination of the extent to which TSN has been operationalised and influential in public expenditure patterns, public provision and policy making is important in any discussions of equality in Northern Ireland for two reasons. First, the importance attached to TSN by government ministers in terms of publicising their efforts to reduce social and economic differentials between the two communities in Northern Ireland make its effective implementation an important matter of accountability. Secondly, 'pre-employment' measures, such as enhanced participation in voluntary action, education and training programmes and improvements in physical and social environments, are widely acknowledged to play an important role in preparing disadvantaged individuals and local communities for participation in employment. Chapter Seven of this volume, however, provides little comfort on either of these two counts.

POLICY APPRAISAL AND FAIR TREATMENT (PAFT)

Just as TSN has become a high-profile 'example' of government commitment to equality, so too PAFT, introduced in January 1994, has been cited as evidence of the commitment of government in Northern Ireland to equitable public policy making and implementation and equality of opportunity. The PAFT guidelines state that all government departments and 'next step' agencies must be proactive in securing the elimination of discrimination and actively promote fair treatment through government policy making and implementation in respect of religion, political opinion, gender, marital status, disability, ethnicity, age and sexual orientation. PAFT is envisaged as an integral part of all policy formulation, monitoring and review, rather than being something which is done retrospectively. Osborne *et al*, Chapter Six, this volume, provide an overview of the implementation and potential of PAFT for equality of opportunity and, as with the review of TSN, raise important questions about the extent to which political commitment has translated into real achievements which might set Northern Ireland on the road to social and economic justice for all.

CONCLUSIONS

The problems of creating employment equality and reducing unemployment surveyed in this opening chapter are pursued in greater depth in subsequent chapters. As this chapter has shown, the context is that some progress has been made in increasing the proportions of employees who are Catholic, and in attracting jobs to some Catholic areas. But the base from which such progress has occurred was low, with the result that high levels of unemployment and especially long-term unemployment remain disproportionately experienced by Catholics. It is for this reason that employment inequality can only be effectively tackled by a wide range of social and economic policies and practices, acting on a floor of effective fair employment legislation. Such social and economic policies must operate at both macro- and micro-economic and social levels. The various chapters which follow challenge the adequacy of current educational, training and unemployment policies. Are such policies sufficiently ambitious and well-integrated with other policies to achieve improvements in employment opportunities? Are economic growth and development policies sufficiently ambitious and well-targeted to meet the serious challenge posed by high levels of long-term unemployment? And how far have such policies been developed with issues of equality and equity as serious objectives? It is all of these questions, to varying extents, which are addressed by the subsequent chapters of this volume address. It is clear from the research reported in this volume that a fresh approach to both policymaking on, and research into, these issues is required in the future and the final chapter of this volume provides some indications of directions for the future.

ENDNOTES

1. The seasonally adjusted figure represents the average monthly change over a period of three months in order to give a more balanced view of movement in vacancies and placings as it smooths out some of the monthly fluctuations.
2. Travel to Work Areas (TTWAs) are local labour markets - areas within which the majority of people both live and work - that are based on journey to work patterns indicated by the Census of Population.
3. This analysis can only be undertaken across the given time period due to the availability of FEC monitoring data since 1990.

REFERENCES

Borooah, V. (1995) *Economic Inactivity - Change and Causes,* Proceedings of SACHR Research Conference - May 1995, Belfast: SACHR.

Cormack, R., Gallagher, T. and Osborne, R. (1991(a)) 'Report on School Size', *The 16th Annual Report of the Standing Advisory Commission on Human Rights,* London: HMSO.

Cormack, R., Gallagher, T. and Osborne, R. (1991(b)) 'Access to Grammar Schools', *The 16th Annual Report of the Standing Advisory Commission on Human Rights,* London: HMSO.

Cormack, R., Gallagher, T., Osborne, R. and Fisher, M. (1989) 'Secondary Analysis of the School Leavers Survey, *The 14th Annual Report of the Standing Advisory Commission on Human Rights,* London: HMSO.

DED (1996) Press Notice, January, Belfast: DED.

DED (1995(a)) Press Notice, May, Belfast: DED.

DED (1995(b)) *Growing Competitively: A Review of Economic Development Policy in Northern Ireland,* Belfast: DED.

DED (1990) *Competing in the 1990s - The Key to Growth,* Belfast: DED.

DED (1987) Press Notice, August, Belfast: DED.

DENI (1992) *Monitoring of recurrent and capital expenditure on the education service in terms of targeting social needs: report on current systems and proposals for action,* Bangor: DENI.

Eversley, D. (1989) *Religion and Employment in Northern Ireland,* London: Sage.

FEC (1996) *Indicators of Change: 1990-1995,* Belfast: FEC.

FEC (1995) *The Key Facts: Religion and Community Background in Northern Ireland,* Belfast: FEC.

FEC (1994) *Monitoring Returns,* Belfast: FEC.

Fryer, D. (1992) 'Psychological or Material Deprivation: Why Does Unemployment Have Mental Health Consequences?' in McLaughlin, E. (ed.) (1992) *Understanding Unemployment,* London: Routledge.

Gudgin, G. and Breen, R. (1996) *Evaluation of the Ratio of Unemployment Rates as an Indicator of Fair Employment,* Belfast: CCRU.

Gudgin, G. and O'Shea, G. (1993) *Unemployment Forever?* NIERC Report No. 13, Belfast: NIERC.

IDB (1995) *Annual Report:1994/1995,* Belfast: IDB.

Institute of Enterprise Strategies (1993) *Assessing Equity,* Belfast: LEDU.

LEDU (1995) *Annual Report:1994/1995,* Belfast: LEDU.

McLaughlin, E. (ed.) (1992) *Understanding Unemployment: new perspectives on active labour market policies,* London: Routledge.

Magill, D. and Rose, S. (eds.) (1996) *Fair Employment Law in Northern Ireland: debates and issues,* Belfast: SACHR.

Murphy, A. and Armstrong, D. (1994) *A Picture of the Catholic and Protestant Male Unemployed,* Belfast: CCRU.

NIERC (forthcoming) *Spatial Patterns of Employment Change in Northern Ireland for the period 1987-1991 in the Context of Fair Employment,* Report to PPRU/CCRU, Belfast: NIERC.

Northern Ireland Information Service (1995) Press Notice, October, Belfast: NIIS.

Opsahl Report (1993) *A Citizens' Inquiry,* Dublin: Lilliput.

Osborne, R. (1993) 'Research and Policy: a Northern Ireland Perspective', *Environment and Planning C: Government and Policy,* 11:465-477.

PPRU (1995) *Northern Ireland Annual Abstract of Statistics*: No. 13, Belfast: PPRU.

Rowthorn, B. and Wayne, N. (1988) *Northern Ireland: The Political Economy of Conflict,* Cambridge: Polity.

SACHR (1990) *Religious and Political Discrimination and Equality of Opportunity in Northern Ireland:* Second Report, Cm 1107, London: HMSO.

SACHR (1987) *Religious and Political Discrimination and Equality of Opportunity in Northern Ireland,* London: HMSO.

Scott, R. (1993) 'Long-Term Unemployment and Policy Response in Northern Ireland' in Gudgin, G. and O'Shea, G. (1993) *Unemployment Forever?,* Belfast: NIERC.

Simpson, J. (1996) 'Small firm start-up and the enterprise economy', *Belfast Telegraph,* 16 January 1996.

Whyte, J. (1990) *Interpreting Northern Ireland,* Oxford: Clarendon.

Chapter Two

VACANCIES, ACCESS TO EMPLOYMENT AND THE UNEMPLOYED: TWO CASE STUDIES OF BELFAST AND LONDONDERRY

Ian Shuttleworth, Peter Shirlow and Darren McKinstry

INTRODUCTION

This chapter presents the results of ongoing research on the uptake of jobs by the unemployed, and by the long-term unemployed in particular.[1] This theme is important for the employment equality debate on several counts. Firstly, although an issue of general social disadvantage that affects all sections of the Northern Ireland population, unemployment is disproportionately higher amongst the Catholic community (Murphy and Armstrong, 1994) and unemployment differentials are the most common indicator of religious inequality in the labour market. Secondly, given general economic policy to create jobs, it is important that any job creation translates directly to a reduction in unemployment if social disadvantage is to be lessened. For job creation policy to be effective in terms of the social objectives of lessening inequality, then the unemployed, and specifically the long-term unemployed, ought to gain many or all of the new jobs that have been created. Moreover, if new jobs are taken by the unemployed, and the long-term unemployed especially, then there should be an indirect benefit to the Catholic community that would begin to redress differentials in the labour market.

Empirical evidence from Britain and Northern Ireland suggests, however, that job creation is unlikely to result in substantial reductions in registered unemployment, and that the long-term unemployed have significant problems in making the transition back to work (Daniel, 1990; Murphy and Armstrong, 1994; Nickell, 1980). This has important social and policy implications especially with regard to religious differentials in the Northern Ireland labour market. In effect, employment creation on its own is implausible as the major mechanism for the reduction of unemployment. This apparent paradox, that employment gains do not necessarily mean decreases in unemployment, has been explained in terms of barriers that prevent the unemployed getting work (see also Chapter Three, this volume). This implies that measures are needed to help the unemployed to gain work to ensure the maximum social benefit from employment growth. Before implementing policies to help overcome these postulated labour market barriers it is necessary to understand what these might be in the local labour market conditions prevailing in Northern Ireland. The chapter will therefore discuss whether there are significant barriers to the unemployed gaining work, and what these barriers might be, by analysing the local labour markets of Belfast and Londonderry,[2] the behaviour of applicants and the policies of major employers.

The discussion begins by providing background on the social and spatial incidence of unemployment in western economies, the nature of labour market flows and the barriers that have been identified elsewhere as contributing to the exclusion of the unemployed from work. The chapter then commences its empirical reporting by considering the extent to which the incidence of unemployment in Belfast and Derry is like that noted elsewhere; it also profiles the social background of the unemployed using data from a survey undertaken by the authors. The central question to which we seek an answer here concerns the definition of unemployment. This is not necessarily a straightforward matter but it is necessary to show the extent to which concentration on the registered unemployed as the focus of policy attention ignores the social reality of unemployment and thereby leads to potentially misleading conclusions.

We then proceed to examine how realistic it is to say that there are barriers to the unemployed in Northern Ireland gaining work. The discussion encompasses a variety of dimensions looking at employers' perceptions and practices, the role of government agencies and the perceptions of the unemployed themselves. Special attention is paid to why the unemployed have turned a job down and the extent to which a 'chill factor' diminishes the likelihood that the unemployed will be prepared to travel to a job (or will only seek work in certain areas).

We then conclude the empirical part of the chapter by analysing data on applications to major employers in Derry and Belfast. These employers are based in a variety of different areas and industrial sectors so as to provide contrasting case studies of labour market behaviour. By considering data on applicants spatially we seek to answer the question of whether bringing jobs to an area necessarily leads to jobs in that area, or instead to applications from other areas that result in employment gains being more widely spread. Associated with this we also examine the spatial distribution of applicants to provide tentative comments on the extent to which applications are received from all sections of the community and all locales. The chapter concludes by summarising the evidence and evaluating it in terms of the extent to which it is possible to say that there are barriers that deny the unemployed access to employment.

BACKGROUND

An examination of the definition and incidence of unemployment is useful as a starting point for an investigation of the uptake of new jobs because it shows to whom new jobs should be targeted. Unemployment is usually defined uncritically and simplistically as those who are registered as unemployed and/or those who are seeking work. In practice, however, the notion of unemployment is complex and embodies a number of statistical and social conventions and, as Metcalf (1992:160) argues, 'if the definitions of unemployment and non-participation are flawed, analysis and policy may also be flawed.' Claimant counts, or even counts of those who state they are seeking work, do not account for the 'hidden unemployed' who may not be registered but who may still be searching for work and are in competition with the registered unemployed. Many more people may describe themselves as being unemployed than are registered and these conceptual problems make the real extent and nature of unemployment hard to evaluate. We will return to this point later but will now concentrate, for the moment, on the profile of the registered unemployed.

The social and spatial incidence of unemployment has been relatively well researched. The unemployed in Britain are generally characterised by poor educational attainment, by having previously been in semi-skilled or unskilled work, as living in public authority housing and as being in socially vulnerable positions such as membership of an ethnic minority group (Nickell, 1980; Pissarides and Wadsworth, 1992; Ward and Cross, 1991). These sections of the population are also those which are more likely to become long-term unemployed (often defined as an unemployment duration greater than one year) or vulnerable to recurrent unemployment. In Northern Ireland, similar observations hold true, with analyses of the Labour Force Survey (LFS) by Murphy and Armstrong (1994) demonstrating social inequalities in the experience of unemployment, with the unqualified, younger and older people, those who are unmarried and those who have just entered the labour force having higher rates of unemployment. Increasingly it appears that unemployment is concentrated in certain households since the unemployed are likely to live with other household members who are also unemployed (Borooah *et al*, 1995). In Northern Ireland the duration of unemployment is also influenced by occupation with the unskilled having higher durations than other groups. The already low chances of unemployed people making the transition to work (relative to groups in other labour market statuses) are not enhanced by unemployment duration. As duration increases, the probability of entering employment decreases.

Unsurprisingly, these marked social inequalities in the incidence of unemployment are also mirrored spatially, with pockets of high unemployment noted by many observers at the local scale (Green and Owen,

1989; Haughton *et al*, 1993). There appear to be strong spatial associations in many British cities between long-term unemployment, non-car ownership, social class, mode of travel to work and housing tenure. No single explanation of the spatial concentration of unemployment exists but industrial restructuring, supply-side problems such as a lack of training, physical infrastructure, problems like a lack of transport, institutional failures such as 'poverty traps' and discrimination and inequalities in the operation of the housing market have all been suggested as potential causes (Haughton *et al*, 1993).

Explanations of the social and spatial unevenness of unemployment have stressed labour market barriers as reasons for the failure of the unemployed to gain work. Barriers exist in many forms. Firstly, they may include supply-side factors such as education and training, where poor skills may lessen employability. Secondly, they may be a function of the type of work offered, where temporary contracts, low wages and unsuitable hours can be significant disincentives. Thirdly, recruitment practices might also be major barriers, especially in cases where the unemployed are stereotyped by gender, age, current labour market status, ethnicity or address (Meager and Metcalf, 1987). Finally, institutional or physical barriers might also be significant. Transport is an important issue which is given more weight by the lack of access of many unemployed people to private transport, and childcare provision might also be a significant factor for many women or single parents of either gender.

The experience of other areas, and of Northern Ireland, suggests that the incidence of unemployment is highly uneven socially and spatially, that there are definitional problems in deciding who the unemployed are and that certain social and institutional factors might explain the persistence of unemployment and the failure of the unemployed to gain work. These themes are relevant to understanding the factors that determine access to employment and in suggesting why the count of registered unemployed is not readily responsive to job growth. They will therefore be discussed in turn in the next sections of the chapter.

WHO ARE THE UNEMPLOYED IN BELFAST AND DERRY?

As suggested earlier, this question is not easily answered in conceptual terms. At the local level, the situation is further complicated by data difficulties. The Census of Population can give disaggregations of the unemployed by age, religion, sex, occupation and education at small spatial scales. The data, however, are now somewhat dated and economic status is self-reported. Because of this, the census definition of unemployed will not match exactly with that reported in the claimant count as it may include some of the 'hidden unemployed' who would otherwise be reported as economically inactive. Claimant data, on the other hand, are up to date but cannot be desegregated except by age and sex. By their very nature they deal only with claimants and will discount many 'hidden unemployed', particularly women, who receive no benefit from registering. Because of these limitations only the salient points noted in these data will be reported to give an overall picture of the unemployed and the nature of flows to and from the unemployed register in Belfast and Derry, and the main results will be presented from a survey undertaken by the authors.

In general, census data shows that the social incidence of unemployment in Belfast and Derry is like that noted in Northern Ireland and Britain as a whole. A high proportion of the unemployed were previously employed in semi-skilled or unskilled work and were poorly educated, and more likely to be Catholic. Those who stated they were unemployed were evenly spread through the age groups between 16 and 65 although there was some bunching in the 20-34 year old age class. The data on claimant counts show that males far outnumber females as claimants and that over 50% of the unemployed have been out of work for more than one year (largely explained by the long durations of male unemployment spells). Two points worth noting are that flows off and on the register are disproportionately concentrated in the 20-29 age group (some 30% of on-flows are for 20-24 year olds and about 20% of off-flows are in this age group) and that the strongest effect noted in a time series of on-flows and off-flows in Belfast and Derry was seasonal. No long-term trend was observable in the series in which the major effect was a peak of on-flows in July and a peak of off-flows in October. This may reflect the role of institutional factors in determining the level of registered unemployed.

To get further insights into unemployment and economic inactivity beyond those provided by these data sets, we surveyed 552 unemployed and inactive people via community groups in Belfast and Derry. The choice of this method was made so as to gain access to as wide a selection of the unemployed as possible. The survey was not conducted using a random sample so wider generalisations may be problematic. However, since the purpose of the exercise was to consider the unemployed in the broadest sense, of whom many are hidden from official data sources and thus not included in sampling populations, this weakness was considered to be relatively minor. The profile of the unemployed who responded to the survey was very much as might have been expected given what is known about the unemployed in Northern Ireland and Britain. Over a third (in Belfast over 40%) had no qualifications and the majority (in both Belfast and Derry about 70%) resided in Housing Executive accommodation. Most of the unemployed also lived in households were there were other people unemployed. Therefore, in these aspects, the social incidence of unemployment conforms to prior expectations.

The analysis of claimant status is more interesting and throws some light on 'hidden unemployment' and competition between the registered and other unemployed. About 65% of respondents claimed that they were unemployed and seeking work, just over 8% stated they were unemployed and not seeking work, around 3% were waiting to start a job or a government scheme, 19% were on home duties and the remainder (about 3%) were caring for a relative. Of these respondents, 70% stated that they were signing on and were thus presumably registered as being unemployed. These data on their own do not reveal the relationship between signing on and labour market status. This relationship, however, is important as a way of understanding the means by which signing on does not necessarily equate with unemployment, and so Table 2.1 tabulates along labour market status, job search activity and signing on.

Table 2.1: Signing on and Labour Market Status (percentage rates), 1995, Belfast and Derry

Status	Signing on %	Not signing on %	N
Unemployed and seeking work	85.7	14.3	342
Unemployed and not seeking work	47.7	52.3	44
Waiting to start a job	66.7	33.3	15
Waiting to start a scheme	45.5	54.5	11
Looking after the home	34.3	65.7	99
Caring for a dependent	35.7	64.3	17
Looking for a job			
Yes	86.6	13.4	322
No	43.5	56.5	209

Source: Survey of the Belfast and Derry unemployed.

Although some of the categories, such as waiting to start a job or scheme, are small and estimates may therefore be unreliable, the key point to note is that 14% of those who claim that they are seeking work are not signing on and are therefore likely to be part of the hidden unemployed. Furthermore, many of those who are signing on, and presumably are registered as being unemployed, are not seeking work either through discouragement or because they have other (home) duties. This mismatch is reinforced when active job search is considered. In this case about 13% of those looking for a job are not signing on and over 40% who are signing on did not look for a job in the previous month. The contradictory nature of respondents' answers and their assessment of their labour market position is shown in Table 2.2, which tabulates active job search by the labour market status which people reported.

Table 2.2: Active Job Search by Labour Market Status (percentage rates) 1995, Belfast and Derry

Status	Sought work in last month %	Did not seek work %	N
Unemployed and seeking work	80.1	19.9	346
Unemployed and not seeking work	18.2	81.8	44
Waiting to start a job	78.6	21.4	14
Waiting to start a scheme	58.3	41.7	12
Looking after the home	16.0	84.0	100
Caring for a relative	26.3	73.7	19

Source: Survey of the Belfast and Derry unemployed.

These simple tabulations suggest some reasons why unemployment does not fall in a one to one relationship with job creation. Firstly, people who are signing on do not always actively seek work, and on the contrary, those who are not signing on are sometimes active in the labour market. Therefore, even before we take account of labour market barriers that act against the unemployed, there is sufficient complexity of behaviour to imply that the registered unemployed would not get all the jobs even in the hypothetical situation in which all new jobs were reserved for those who said they were out of work. Secondly, given the complex and often contradictory ways in which the unemployed view their labour market status it might well be that the focus on registered unemployment by policymakers is misleading. A measure of 'non-employment' might well be more useful given that some of those who are nominally economically inactive are job seeking and that new flexible types of employment draw on the pool of the inactive (Haughton *et al*, 1993). Furthermore, since the nature and incidence of unemployment has changed so markedly in the past 30 years, and economic inactivity has also grown, registered unemployment may no longer be a useful labour market indicator. Finally, the results also show something of the complexity of unemployment. It seems that the only sure and sharp definitions of unemployment come from the use of official statistics which rectify the concept. On the ground, however, it appears that there is a continuum of self-perceptions and orientations to the labour market that range from someone signing on and seeking week to somebody nominally inactive but who is prepared to take any available job. These orientations and attitudes may change even over the short term, but the appearance that the unemployed do not behave in a binary, clear cut way towards the labour market means that the full impact of job creation on the unemployed cannot be estimated by registered unemployment alone.

These definitional problems reduce the scope of the registered unemployed to find work. Beyond these, however, there are barriers, either self-imposed or external, that also reduce the effectiveness of job creation as a means to reduce unemployment. These themes are developed in the next section.

LABOUR MARKET BARRIERS IN BELFAST AND DERRY: EMPLOYERS' PERCEPTIONS, GOVERNMENT AGENCIES AND PERCEPTIONS

We begin the analysis of potential barriers to employment with Table 2.3 and a brief commentary on the applicant data generated by this study. Table 2.3 summarises the previous labour market statuses given by appointees from our five case study companies[3] (which had, in total, locations at 12 sites in Belfast and Derry). The companies were selected so as to provide examples from several industrial sectors. The table is important because it shows that most appointees came from other jobs or from education. The proportion of appointees who stated they came from unemployment is about what might be expected given the percentage share of unemployed people in the labour force. Note, however, that these data are self-reported and the unemployed in the table are not necessarily the registered unemployed. Indeed, given the ways in which people classify their status, some of the unemployed here may previously have been on government training schemes or have been economically inactive. The figure of 18.5%, therefore, is likely to overestimate the uptake of employment by the unemployed. Moreover, this proportion is also an overestimate for four of the companies since one company in particular employed a relatively high proportion of the previously unemployed.

Table 2.3: Previous Labour Market Statuses of Case Study Appointees 1995, Belfast and Derry

Status	Percentage share %	N
Employment	54.2	193
Government scheme	1.7	6
Unemployment	18.5	66
Education	0.8	3
Other inactivity	24.7	88

Source: Sample of Appointees.

There are, of course, other factors that suggest that there are socially constructed barriers in the labour market and that applicants and employers have strong perceptions about who should apply for a job and who should get a job. One such dimension is age. The mean age of all applicants to our case study companies was about 26. This implies that only relatively young people applied for jobs in these companies. At all sites, except one, appointees were one or two years younger than unsuccessful applicants which appears to mean that age, among other things, might be a significant criteria in recruitment. Access to employment, therefore, appears to be dependent, among other things, on previous labour market status and age. These and other factors will be explored now with reference to employers' attitudes, institutional factors such as government agencies and the attitudes of the unemployed themselves.

To investigate employers' attitudes, interviews were conducted with personnel managers in the five case study companies. The main focus of the interviews was on attitudes to the unemployed and on the nature of recruitment practices. The interviews showed that practices and attitudes varied markedly between employers, though whether this reflected company culture, the type of employment offered, the character of the interviewee or the locale in which the company was located, was difficult to say.

Most of the companies in which we interviewed recruited only a relatively low proportion of previously unemployed people. To a large extent this was because of the labour preferences of employers and negative attitudes toward the unemployed. One company in particular preferred to recruit school-leavers, and many of the jobs it offered were largely seen both by neighbouring communities and the employer itself as being female-oriented. This introduced a barrier to the recruitment of the male unemployed. A second company, in the retail sector, offered mainly part-time work which was again considered to be mainly female-oriented. Further, the company considered that motivation was a problem, with the unemployed lacking the discipline to work and the personal characteristics necessary to successfully meet customers. Attitudes toward the unemployed generally were a vexed area. It was difficult to know whether the attitudes of the interviewee were being voiced, or if (unofficial) company policy was being expressed. Some interviewees held very firmly to an official line that nobody was being excluded from employment, perhaps because of the obvious dangers of admitting to discriminatory practices (despite strong impressions that they had very firm tastes for certain types of labour). Other personnel staff were happier to speak strictly 'off the record' about the unemployed.

In these instances, it appeared that stereotypes about the unemployed noted elsewhere (see, for example, Dawes, 1993) were very much alive. The unemployed were seen as being bad risks because of a lack of work discipline, a perceived laziness and their length of unemployment. The main criticisms were that recruits from the unemployed had proved unreliable and unable to perform satisfactorily in their posts. The fact that they were unemployed was also seen as something of a stigma. Gaps in work histories raised awkward questions about motivation, and unemployment was generally seen as being a result of a personal failing of the unemployed person. Although opinions can be dismissed as ill-informed stereotypes, most employers holding them claimed they could be supported by experience. They argued that the unemployed had been recruited but that they had proved to be poor risks in very competitive economic environments. Two employers noted sectarian dimensions which influenced their recruitment habits. One commented that the company site might potentially restrict the range of applicants and was very conscious of the politics of employment creation in a divided society. A second made efforts to reach into Protestant and Catholic areas to seek recruits, but again was aware of the local political environment which had the potential to cause difficulties.

Some of the factors which restricted the recruitment of the unemployed in Belfast and Derry were, therefore, perceptions of the unemployed and the social construction of the labour market in terms of gender and occupation. Firm location was also identified as being a potential problem in 'off the record' remarks by some politically aware personnel managers. To understand how these barriers may be overcome, and to show how the unemployed can find places in the workforce, it is useful to look in more detail at one case study where the unemployed did appear to be relatively successful.

This employer is a non-Northern Ireland owned company which recruited about 50% of its workforce from the unemployed. The employer has been expanding its workforce in the years since it was established in Northern Ireland and its workforce is set to grow in the immediate future. Competing with companies on a Europe-wide scale, it operates in a highly competitive environment but feels that locating in Northern Ireland is not a disadvantage because of the availability of labour. It recruits for a wide variety of vacancies, ranging from managerial and technical jobs to shop-floor and warehouse work. For the higher-skilled jobs employees have been known to travel a considerable distance but most other jobs are filled from people in the locality. It offers above average wages and claims that it has relatively low labour turnover.

This company has a relatively sophisticated view of the labour market, and in part this translates into a willingness to recruit the unemployed. Personnel managers in the company were well aware of the advent of flexible work and labour market insecurity. Because of this, they did not see unemployment as being a stigma because many people now have at least one period of unemployment in their working life. The unemployed were, therefore, not rejected out of hand as being deficient, because unemployment was seen as something that the majority of people will experience. This, however, is insufficient to explain why the unemployed were given work in relatively large numbers by this employer.

Other factors concerned, firstly, the type of work offered and, secondly, the institutional links that this employer has made with government agencies. The unemployed generally entered shop-floor jobs. No specific skills were required from them except general industrial experience. Many of the unemployed have this background, or if they have not, it can be developed. Links with ACE schemes and government training centres have also proved to be useful. These gave the employer a chance to employ on trial and to see if the unemployed person would make a suitable employee. A further strategy concerned the firm's organisation of its labour force. This was very nearly a classic primary/secondary dual labour market where the primary sector jobs are long-term and secure, and the secondary sector jobs are often short term contracts. Most employment growth initially takes place in the secondary sector into which the unemployed are generally taken into short-term employment. This gave the company a further chance to assess them and, as the workforce expanded, integrate them into the workforce. The completion of a contract gave the employer the chance to dismiss unsuitable employees though most contracts were renewed and made permanent, except in cases of sudden cyclical downturns in the firm's business.

This case study suggests how the unemployed may gain employment. Of course, not all the unemployed who applied to this employer gained work, but the mere fact that someone was unemployed was insufficient to stigmatise them. Whilst with this employer a record of unemployment did not necessarily stigmatise, the employer was very much like the other case study companies in stressing motivation. Thus, unemployed people who had been active whilst out of work were favoured. 'Activity' included voluntary work or 'doing the double', because such activity showed that the unemployed person had a positive attitude. The willingness to employ those out of work was partly because of the labour market awareness of the personnel staff, but also because the structure of the workforce and the relationships with training providers gave the company a chance to sift their applicants thoroughly. Government agencies might therefore be expected to be important in re-integrating the unemployed into the workforce.

Accordingly, Job Centre staff in Belfast and Derry were interviewed to discover their attitudes toward the unemployed and the labour market in general. Job Centres have a large potential influence on the integration of the unemployed into the workforce, since many large employers use them as the first stage of screening for many posts. However, formal criteria to benefit the long-term unemployed, or the unemployed as a whole, did not appear to have been applied, in some cases at least. For example, for one vacancy which was discussed, the first 40 people to show an interest were introduced to the company in question simply because the sheer numbers of potential applicants made more considered screening highly problematic. This stage of the recruitment procedure might be profitable for interventions to benefit the long-term unemployed (though careful consideration of legal complications would be needed).

Some issues raised in interviews with Job Centre Staff confirm the perceptual information on labour market barriers given by some of the employers. Firstly, the unemployed were seen as being blamed by employers for their status and, to some extent, as being indirectly discriminated against. Secondly, significant barriers to employment were noted in textiles and hospitality, such as poor conditions, poor perceptions of the industries and insecurity. These difficulties are significant especially with regard to hospitality since this cover-all label encompasses the growth sectors of catering, hoteling and tourism. Unemployed people, it was noted, were refusing jobs in these sectors. Finally, and allied to this, was the problem of low wages and the perception of a low wage economy. It was remarked that some jobs were advertised with wages 'to be arranged'. Job Centre Staff considered that these were likely to be poorly paid, unprotected and would involve bargaining to set a wage rate. Hardly surprisingly, they reported that these posts were unattractive to the unemployed.

Barriers to employment in terms of spatial behaviour and transport were also suggested as being important. A lack of transport was identified as causing substantial problems for the unemployed in their search for work and it was also argued by some Job Centre interviewees that a religious 'chill factor' restricted the mobility of some people in their search for work. A substantial minority wished to remain in 'their own areas' because 25 years of the troubles made them feel unsafe elsewhere (see also Chapter Three, this volume). It was also suggested that some employers were reluctant to take people from outside their own areas and, in cases where they had tried, that unwillingness to travel had frustrated them. These topics are very difficult to research. Few employers would admit to an overt spatial bias in recruitment practice and fewer still to bias against any religious denomination. However, analysis of the spatial patterns of applicants can go some way to addressing these issues and we will turn to this later.

The final perspective from which barriers to employment can be discussed is from the viewpoint of the unemployed themselves. About 35% of respondents to the survey of the unemployed in Belfast and Derry stated that they had turned down a job whilst out of work. The reasons that they gave are presented in Table 2.4 and, in essence, confirm the impressions of Job Centre staff. The most important reason for turning a job down was simply that it was low wage, followed by insecurity in terms of contract and condition. For women, a lack of childcare facilities was also important. It therefore seems the work that is open to the unemployed in terms of their qualifications, background and experience is precisely the sort of work which offers few prospects and is not very attractive.

Table 2.4: Overt Reasons for Turning Down a Job Offer, 1995, Belfast and Derry

Reason	%	N
Low wage	77.0	147
Insecurity	26.7	51
Childcare	24.6	47
Bad quality work	16.8	32
Transport	11.0	21
Effect on partner	7.9	15

Note: Percentages do not add to 100 as respondents were allowed to tick more than one choice

Source: Survey of Belfast and Derry unemployed.

Besides the factors that have led to offered jobs being turned down are a range of perceptions, opinions and beliefs that act as less direct barriers to employment, and which show what factors the unemployed feel are the main hindrance to their gaining work. These are tabulated in Table 2.5.

Table 2.5: Reasons Given for Being Unemployed, 1995, Belfast and Derry

Reason	Percentage	N
Not "right" skills	48.9	270
No qualifications	43.1	238
Not relevant experience	34.2	189
Not "right" contacts	23.0	127
Wrong religion	20.7	114
Too old	15.7	84
Wrong part of town	14.1	78
History of unemployment	12.7	70
Because a woman	10.3	56
Political affiliation	10.0	55

Note: Percentages do not add to 100 as respondents were allowed to tick more than one choice.

Source: Survey of Belfast and Derry unemployed.

These data are interesting on three counts. Firstly, they suggest that the unemployed feel they are suffering from a skills and qualification mismatch in relation to available vacancies. Secondly, there is some evidence for the presence of social barriers to employment; that is, some respondents indicated that being of the wrong religion, or not having the right contacts, were reasons for their joblessness. Thirdly, the weight attached to age is intriguing in light of the data on applications and flows off and on to the unemployment register. This leads us to think that a substantial body of the unemployed are excluded by reason of their age. Interestingly, unemployed people did not appear to believe that a history of unemployment is important, although this stigma effect was advanced both by employers and Job Centre staff.

A question about religion was also asked to try to get some idea of the extent to which sectarian factors were an issue in restricting access to jobs. The question was expressed in terms of travelling through or working in an area of the opposite religion. About 34% of respondents said they would not be prepared to travel through an area of the opposite religion and 55% stated they would not work in a workplace predominantly of the opposite religion (see also Chapter Three, this volume). If these intentions translate to the behaviour of applicants for jobs, then there are significant implications for the location of new jobs and for the targeting of social need via job creation (see also Chapter Six, this volume).

The views that the unemployed held of their prospects in the labour market were very bleak. Over 90% thought they would be unable to get a job in the next few months and over 90% thought that 'people like them' could not get jobs. This pessimism did not appear to be based on ignorance of areas, as respondents correctly characterised their local labour markets as being dominated by jobs for professionals, the young, who could work part-time and, in Belfast, by commuters.

In explaining why the registered unemployed fail to gain work, the data presented so far point to two sets of non-spatial factors. Firstly, it is not just the registered unemployed who seek work. In many cases they are in competition with the 'hidden unemployed'. Secondly, a number of barriers mean that all the unemployed tend to lose out as a group. These obstacles to employment include the stigma of unemployment, the preference of some employers for other sections of the population such as school-leavers, the lack of formal criteria to help the unemployed into work and the poor quality of some jobs and their associated low wages. In addition, there are religious and job search themes relating to applicants, specific to Northern Ireland, which, if it cannot be proved that they cause harm, at least could not be assumed to benefit many unemployed job seekers.

The theme of applicant behaviour introduces a spatial dimension to the discussion. In reducing pockets of registered unemployment, and targeting social need, it is useful to understand not only something of the types of people who apply for jobs but also where they live. In the media, for example, there are often statements about jobs being brought to Belfast or Derry. The question of whether many applicants for such jobs live in these areas is important not only because it could indicate whether residents will benefit, but could also be used to evaluate whether applicants come equally from all communities. This might have important implications for equality of opportunity.

SPATIAL DIMENSIONS TO JOB CREATION

To investigate this type of question we collected detailed information on the addresses of applicants for a variety of posts over the period 1993-95 in our five case study companies. Since some of these companies were multi-site, this generated data on 13,000 applicants for jobs at 12 sites. Data were collected on the age and gender of applicants and the type of jobs for which they were applying. Although not an exhaustive range of case studies, the companies chosen differed widely in the type of employment offered. Some, for example, were traditional male employers, or had a high proportion of high-skill jobs, whereas others were mainly female or low-skill. This enabled us to compare the spatial profile of applicant behaviour in contrasting situations.[4] The results presented here are not yet complete and merely map the point distribution of all applicant postcodes. More sophisticated analysis, desegregating by gender and occupation and linking applicant data to information from the Census of Population, will be possible in the future. This will allow us to estimate spatial variations in applicant behaviour and to investigate if these variations can be meaningfully related to spatial differences in social and demographic context and physical constraints such as travel time. Behaviour at small scales, for example at intra-urban scales within Belfast and Derry, is also likely to prove interesting. However, the patterns that have been revealed so far at less aggregated levels of analysis are suggestive and point to a variety of policy choices.

Maps 2.1 and 2.2 show the applicant postcode locations of two contrasting employers, one manufacturing and in Derry, and the other a Belfast-based retailer. The first point that emerges from a comparison of the two maps is that applicant behaviour and, by implication, catchment areas, vary widely by the type of job offered and the industrial sector of the employment. In focusing on the Travel to Work Area (TTWA), the District Council Area (DCA) or the local labour market as the scale at which interventions to reduce unemployment can be measured, the maps pose questions about how labour markets should be defined. In the case of the Derry-based manufacturer, the boundary of Derry DCA underbounds the catchment area. In this instance, it is not so much a case of jobs coming to the people, but of people coming to the jobs. On the other hand, the applicant pool for the Belfast-located retailer is much more spatially restricted. But again, it is not congruent with the boundaries used to collect labour market data. Therefore, in investigating the labour market impact of these employers on their respective localities, the conclusion must be that standard accounts that seek to relate job creation in an area to unemployment reduction cannot account for the complexity of applicant behaviour. This suggests that area-based evaluations of job creation using the framework of DCAs (or other units) is too limited to achieve success.

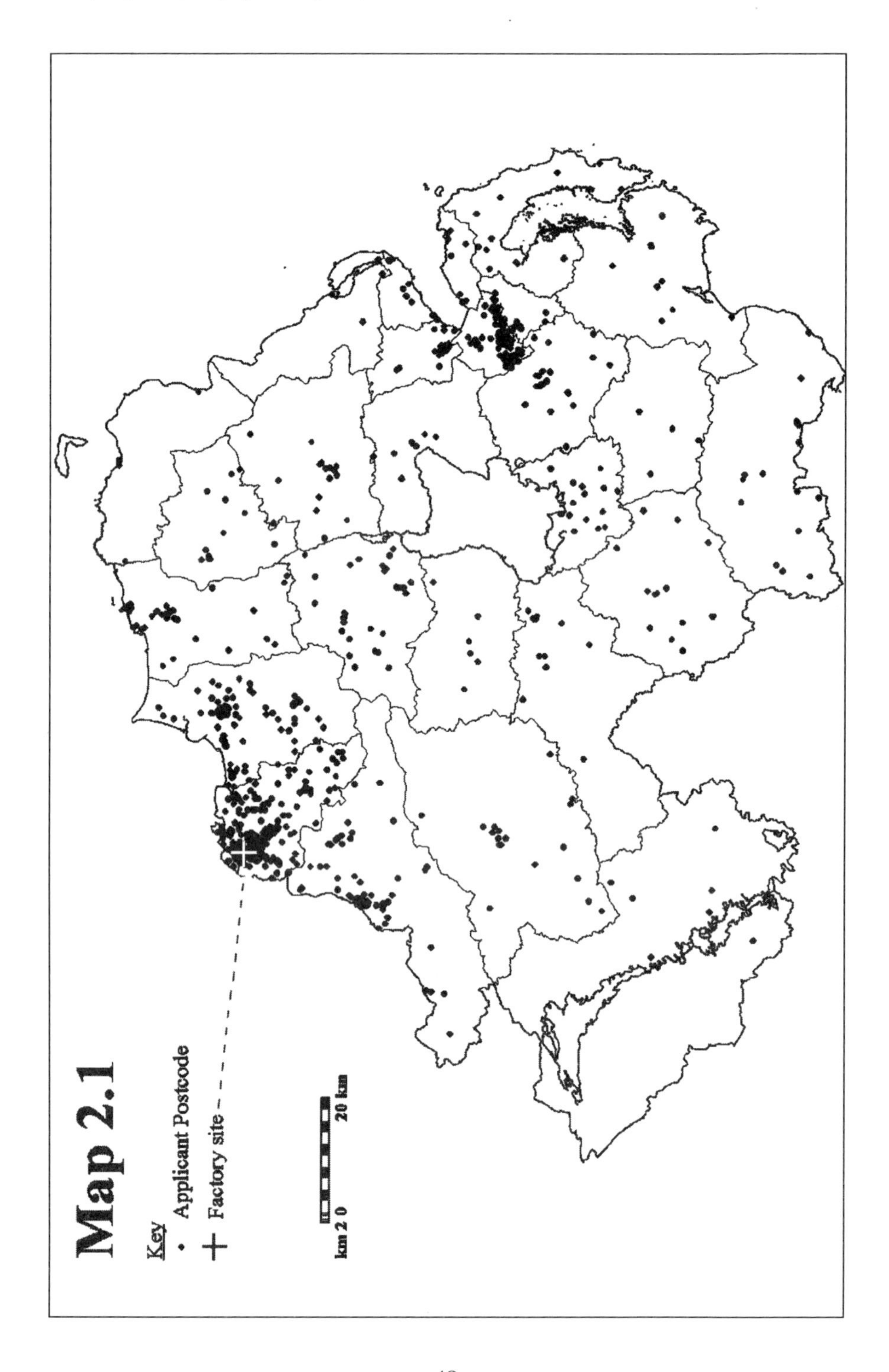
Map 2.1
Key
Applicant Postcode
Factory site
km 2 0
20 km

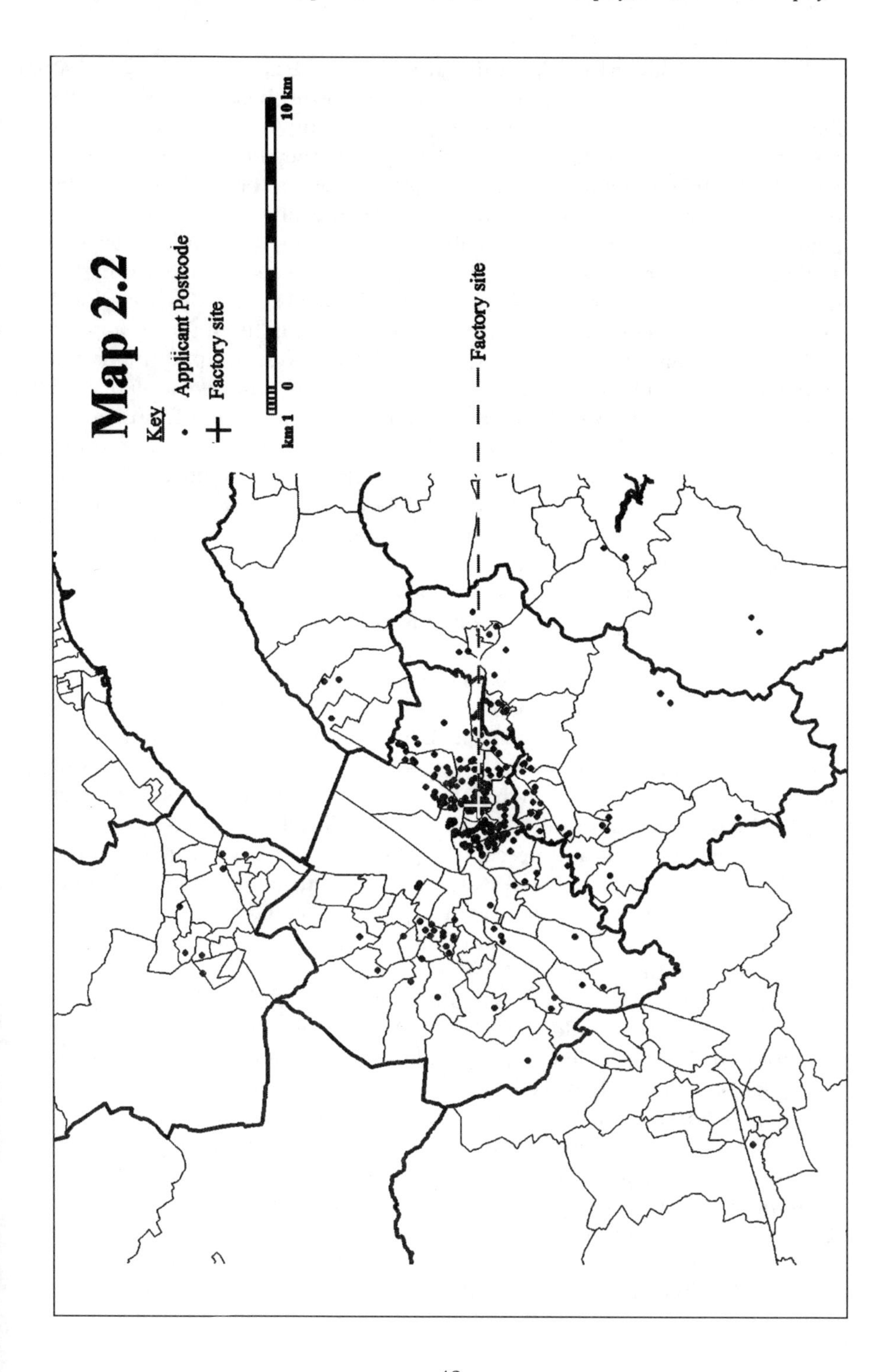
Map 2.2
Key
Applicant Postcode
Factory site
km 1
0
10 km
Factory site

The second issue arising from the inspection of Maps 2.1 and 2.2 is that targeting jobs at local unemployed communities is problematic. This can be illustrated with regard to the survey of the unemployed and inactive in Belfast and Derry and the polarised perceptions they held of jobs in their locality. On the one hand, labour markets were seen as being dominated by professional and skilled employment and, on the other, by part-time low-grade work. Map 2.1 shows the applicant pools for jobs that would be viewed as desirable in that they are relatively well paid, secure, relatively highly skilled and, in some cases, professional. These are the jobs that local unemployed people do not regard themselves as being fitted for because of their lack of qualifications and experience. Moreover, in applications for employment at this particular site, the local unemployed would face competition from all over Northern Ireland, and in any event from people outside Derry DCA. Map 2.2 shows applicant postcodes for jobs that would most likely be regarded as undesirable because they are part-time, low-skilled and mainly female. Because of their often poor conditions and wages, jobs of this type are often seen by the unemployed as uneconomic and too insecure to be worth taking. On the other hand, they have localised applicant pools, and jobs of this sort might, therefore, be assumed to have a greater likelihood of attracting local applicants and focusing on spatially-restricted pockets of unemployment.

This can cause a dilemma for policy makers, who might want to direct jobs to local pockets of unemployment. Some employers, such as the site shown in Map 2.2, could achieve a spatial match between applicant pools and spatial concentrations of unemployment. Therefore, by encouraging enterprises of this type to locate in areas of high unemployment, it might be possible to get the local community into work. However, these locally recruited jobs suffer from gender mismatch and perceptual problems. Retail jobs such as these are often perceived as being female, and in a strongly gendered labour market they do not attract the predominantly registered male unemployed into work. Moreover, they are also often seen as being poor payers and as having poor conditions.

On the other hand, desirable manufacturing jobs, of which the site in Map 2.1 is an example, could be more attractive to the male registered unemployed. However, they suffer problems of skills and spatial mismatch. The jobs require levels of skill and qualifications that local unemployed people may not possess. At the same time, they do not have local catchment areas. The local unemployed are in competition with other unemployed and people in other labour market positions on a much wider spatial scale. Bringing these jobs to an area is therefore no guarantee that they will benefit the locality. Indeed, if Map 2.1 is any indication, they will benefit Northern Ireland as a whole but perhaps have little impact at the local scale.

The preliminary analyses of applicant postcodes also raise other questions that await further analysis. Considering the distribution of applicant postcode locations, we are reminded of the responses from our survey of the unemployed in Belfast and Derry, when only a third of respondents said they had access to their own transport. The reliance on public transport and the restrictions arising from lack of transport are suggested at several sites, in our study particularly in semi-rural areas, where the distribution of applicant postcodes were clearly influenced by the positioning of major roads. To encourage people from areas of high unemployment to apply for jobs may thus mean a transport policy more closely geared to the labour market (see also Chapter Six, this volume). Another issue is the role of perceptions in shaping applicant behaviour. This goes beyond the ways in which certain jobs are seen and extends, instead, to the ways in which certain employers are seen. Even for employers in the same industrial sector, offering very similar wage rates, marked differences in the spatial extent of applicant pools were observed in this study. This probably reflects factors such as company culture and the perceptions that some employers are better than others. This shows some of the problems of attempting to generalise but also illustrates the need to analyse recruitment and applicant behaviour at the level of individual sites if we are to understand what the likely impacts of job creation will be on spatial concentrations of unemployment.

DISCUSSION

The data that have been presented suggest that there are substantial obstacles which prevent the unemployed from gaining work. These obstacles can be classed in two groups reflecting the way they operate. Firstly, there are barriers operated by employers which mean that the unemployed are not offered jobs. These include stigma effects which associate the unemployed with a lack of discipline and laziness and the preference of employers in the growth areas of retailing and other services for women and school-leavers. Some confidence can be attached to these factors since they were noted by several interviewees, both from companies and from government agencies. Secondly, there are barriers that lead to the unemployed to decline work once it is offered. Many of these are very much like those noted outside Northern Ireland, with low wages, insecurity and a lack of childcare provision cited as significant hindrances that caused over 30% of our sample of the unemployed to have turned down an offered job.

Operating at a different level to these barriers in the labour market are institutional and social problems. The unemployed perceived themselves as being mismatched with available vacancies in terms of their experience, qualifications, age and skills when asked to explain those factors which they felt had led to them being without work. At the high status end of the labour market the growth of professional employment has excluded many of the unemployed but at the other end the growth of female and part-time employment has created the 'wrong' type of vacancies for the registered (mainly male) unemployed (see also McLaughlin, 1991). This squeeze has left many of those surveyed extremely pessimistic about their chances of gaining work in the foreseeable future. The findings about age are particularly noteworthy. The average age of applicants to our case study firms was in the mid-20's, and Job Centre staff spoke in one case about middle-aged men who were unmotivated and simply pretending to seek work to meet benefit requirements. This suggests that there is a large segment of the population that has been excluded from work using the criterion of age.

These institutional and social mismatches are similar to those observed outside Northern Ireland (see for example Haughton *et al*, 1993). However, in Northern Ireland there is the additional factor of religion which also complicates job search behaviour and which is an extra barrier above those active elsewhere. Our findings suggest that there is a 'chill factor' which discourages workers from working in areas of the opposite religion. The influence of the 'chill factor' in preventing people from gaining employment is hard to estimate. However, at the least, sectarianism can be assumed not to do any good for employment prospects. No definite proof of this effect exists and it is difficult to quantify (though we may be able to examine it via further analysis of applicant patterns). Despite this, the 'chill factor' is likely to be important not least because of its wide currency as revealed by discussions with employers, Job Centre staff and the unemployed. Perceptions and anecdote are likely to have as much weight as quantifiable evidence not least because most people exist in social networks which amplify and transmit this sort of information, making it part of the decision making environment.

Attempts by policy makers to overcome all these barriers by advancing on a 'broad front' will probably be weakened by the over-thinning of effort. However, concentration on one or two areas might yield results and get the unemployed back to work. In our research we noted the positive part played by some kinds of government-sponsored training in facilitating one employer to recruit the unemployed. In the right environment, with growth in the workforce, training schemes can act as a useful stage in a longer process of screening which eventually led to permanent jobs in one company. One area of intervention might, therefore, be to encourage more of these relationships. We also noted the importance of attitudes toward the unemployed and towards work. There is evidence of a mismatch between employers and the unemployed in how they view each other. Employers with a realistic perception of unemployment (for example, as a state that many people now pass through) were much more prepared to give the unemployed an opportunity to work. In contrast, employers who had had negative experiences of the unemployed (or perhaps had less well-founded prejudices) were less prepared to give work to the unemployed. Measures to introduce the unemployed to employers might therefore be a useful step, together with an education package for the unemployed and employers. The alternative could be that questions about past employment history or present labour market status should be discouraged as being biased against the unemployed because of the stigma effect. A further way to overcome the stigma effect could also be to countenance 'doing the double'. Some employers recognised this as a way of demonstrating initiative that increased employability. Finally, efforts might be made to evaluate more carefully the impact of job creation on localities. It is insufficient to bring jobs to Belfast or Derry (or any other locality) and then to assume that they will be filled by the local unemployed. Our experience shows that this is rarely the case, with most companies having catchment areas that range beyond the immediate locality. One way to ensure that the local unemployed get at least some of the jobs is to encourage employers (perhaps by financial inducements or other forms of support) to employ locals. The other means is to consider the types of jobs being located in different areas. High-skill jobs are unlikely, for example, to do much for most local labour markets.

CONCLUSIONS

At a more theoretical level, the arguments discussed here suggest that conventional measures of the labour market impact of job creation are flawed. There is a problem with the use of registered unemployment as a measure of success in job creation given the nature of modern labour markets. There are now many other sorts of unemployment and means of classifying economic life than the rigid and immutable distinctions between employment and unemployment. These mirror the changed nature of work and the rise of flexible, female-dominated and part-time employment. The old model of registering when out of work and being subject to means-tested benefits presupposes that eventually full-time and well paid work will arise, which will be worthwhile taking in terms of the logic of the benefit system and its supporting institutions. However, in contemporary polarised labour markets these distinctions are blurred. At the lower end, the registered unemployed face competition with the hidden unemployed, and are seeking to fill jobs that are hardly economically viable. At the upper end of the labour market, professional jobs are also out of their reach. When the registered unemployed are only part of a larger pool of unemployed and changes in the labour market mean that one can no longer be sure how they see themselves, then it seems that registered unemployment loses its coherence as an analytical category. In its place, a measure of 'non-employment' which incorporates the economically inactive, might be more appropriate.

Similarly, attempts to measure the effects of labour market interventions spatially are also problematic. The term 'local labour market' is often used but lacks any empirical basis, as Haughton *et al* (1993) suggest. Many of the spatial definitions used, such as DCAs and TTWAs, do not seem to conform to the actual behaviour of applicants or to the perceptions of the unemployed. As arbitrary units they do not encompass the spatial and social reality of recruitment behaviour of either employers or the unemployed. Estimates of the spatial impact of job creation on unemployment reduction are scale and boundary dependent. Different boundaries will yield different estimates (see Openshaw, 1984). Since there are no *a priori* reasons for choosing one particular unit of measurement over another when analysing labour markets, analyses at either TTWA or DCA are likely to be flawed. The only way to overcome these problems to inform policy making is to look at the spatial location of applicants and appointees outside these restrictive terms. This means more thorough analysis of data of the type presented in Maps 2.1 and 2.2. By looking directly at applicants we can minimise the errors that arise from the choice of unit of measurement and so make more reliable estimates of labour market impacts of job creation.

ENDNOTES

1. The main interest of the chapter is the registered unemployed. However, it is difficult to understand the fortunes of this group without reference to other kinds of unemployed. Therefore, the discussion, unless otherwise stated, takes a broader view of the problem of unemployment.
2. Hereafter referred to simply as Derry.
3. The companies are not referred to by name or in any detail to preserve anonymity.
4. Our thanks to John Power of the Fair Employment Commission for advice offered on the techniques used.

REFERENCES

Borooah, V., McGregor, P. and McKee, P. (1995) 'Working Wives and Income Inequality in the UK', *Regional Studies,* 29(5): 477-487.

Daniel, W. (1990) *The Unemployed Flow,* London: Policy Studies Institute.

Dawes, L. (1993) *Long-Term Unemployment and Labour Market Flexibility,* University of Leicester: Centre for Labour Market Studies.

Green, A. and Owen, D. (1989) *Long-Term Unemployment: JUVOS Analysis,* Research Paper 72, London: Department of Employment.

Haughton, G., Johnson, S., Murphy, L. and Thomas, K. (1993) *Local Geographies of Unemployment,* Aldershot: Avebury.

McLaughlin, E. (1991) 'Work and Welfare Benefits: Social Security, Employment and Unemployment in the 1990s', *Journal of Social Policy,* 20(4):485-508.

Meager, N. and Metcalf, H. (1987) *Recruitment of the Long-Term Unemployed,* IMS Report 138, Brighton: Institute of Manpower Studies.

Metcalf, H. (1992) 'Hidden Unemployment and the Labour Market', in McLaughlin, E. (ed.) *Understanding Unemployment,* London: Routledge.

Murphy, A. and Armstrong, D. (1994) *A Picture of the Catholic and Protestant Male Unemployed,* Employment Equality Review Research Report 2, Belfast: CCRU.

Nickell, S. (1980) 'A Picture of Male Unemployment in Britain', *Economic Journal,* 19: 776-794.

Openshaw, S. (1984) *The Modifiable Area Unit Problem,* Norwich: Geobooks.

Pissarides, C. and Wadsworth, J. (1992) 'Unemployment Risks', in McLaughlin, E. (ed.) *Understanding Unemployment,* London: Routledge.

Ward, R. and Cross, D. (1991) 'Race, Employment and Economic Change', in Brown, P. and Scase, R. (eds.) *Poor Work: Disadvantage and the Division of Labour,* Milton Keynes: Open University Press.

Chapter Three

LONG-TERM UNEMPLOYMENT IN WEST BELFAST

Maura Sheehan and Mike Tomlinson[1]

INTRODUCTION

This chapter discusses the results of a postal questionnaire sent out to long-term unemployed people in West Belfast in December 1995. The survey was one part of a three-pronged research strategy designed to assess the likely relevance of the Community Work Programme (CWP), the latest in a long line of government responses to unemployment in Northern Ireland (see Chapter Four, this volume). In conjunction with interviews with employers and those involved in the CWP (also discussed in Chapter Four), the survey was designed to inform the debate on remedial policies towards long-term unemployment. The survey results also contribute to the continuing debate over the causes and significance of differences in unemployment by religion and gender which have been a central feature of the employment equity debate for at least two decades.

For the purposes of the survey, 'West Belfast' was defined as the section of West Belfast chosen for one of the pilot CWP schemes. This comprised the three District Electoral Areas of Court, Upper Falls and Lower Falls. The last two areas are almost exclusively Catholic while Court is Protestant.

The chapter begins with a discussion of the scale and nature of the long-term unemployment problem. It then examines policies towards unemployment and the growing emphasis on compelling the unemployed to participate in training and employment schemes. The survey results are then used to examine a number of 'motivational' propositions about the long-term unemployed (LTU). These include the idea that the LTU have little financial incentive to work, or that they are trapped in worklessness through apathy and other personal deficiencies, or ill-health. Another idea is that 'cultural factors' trap people in long-term unemployment and that fear of travelling and working in some areas has led to a build-up of large numbers of the LTU in places such as West Belfast.

THE PROBLEM OF UNEMPLOYMENT

Economic and social commentators of all shades of opinion are agreed that the task of stimulating economic regeneration and employment growth in Northern Ireland is a daunting one. The economy continues to be beleaguered by deep-seated structural problems, and the most cogent indicators of this economic weakness are high rates of unemployment and long-term unemployment.

Analysis of unemployment data for Northern Ireland reveals several important features. First, Northern Ireland's overall unemployment rate is persistently above the average for the 15 European Union (EU) member states and surpassed only by Spain, Finland and the Republic of Ireland. Within the United Kingdom (UK), no region's unemployment rate (based on the 'claimant count') is higher than that of Northern Ireland, which stood at 11.0% in March 1996 compared with the UK rate of 7.8%.

Secondly, Northern Ireland has by far the most serious problem of long-term unemployment (as defined by more than one year without work) in the UK. For example, in January 1995, 57% of unemployed claimants had been out of work for more than a year. Only the Greater London area came close to this (at 42%), while the Northern region of England, which has the second highest rate of unemployment within the UK, had 38% LTU. This is close to the overall UK figure of 39% (Convery, 1995). Moreover, 23% of unemployed claimants in Northern Ireland have been unemployed for over five years compared with less than 5% in the UK as a whole (NIEC, 1994). The only exception to these trends is unemployment amongst 16 and 17 year olds in Northern Ireland which is the lowest in the UK at a mere 4%. This arises from a very high rate of participation in training schemes and education (MacLagan and Convery, 1995).

The persistence of high rates of unemployment has led to growing concern that some unemployed people may become permanently excluded from employment. Duration of unemployment has an important influence on the probability of leaving unemployment - that is, the longer a person remains unemployed the less likely they are to find employment (White, 1991; 1994(a)). This may reflect a 'discouraged' worker effect (whereby a person stops searching for work as the duration of unemployment increases), the obsolescence of job skills, or that employers use the length of unemployment as a screening device when hiring - or some combination of all three. Whatever the reasons, it is clearly the case that in the 1990s the chances of leaving the unemployment count decline sharply as years of unemployment increase. More than two-thirds of unemployed claimants in Northern Ireland are estimated to leave the count within the first year of unemployment. Of people unemployed for two to three years, about a third leave the count, but less than 20% of those unemployed for more than four years do so. This pattern is consistent with the UK in recent years except that a lower percentage of the very LTU move off the count in Northern Ireland compared to the UK as a whole (where nearly a quarter of those unemployed for four years or more leave the register each year (NIEC, 1994; 1996). Leaving the claimant count is not of course necessarily the same thing as finding paid employment - claimants may retire, become long-term sick, go on a scheme or lose entitlement to benefit through a change in household circumstances.

The fourth important feature of unemployment in Northern Ireland is its social and geographical distribution. Unemployment rates vary significantly by geographical area, gender, class and religion. In terms of religion, Catholic men remain more than twice as likely to be unemployed as their Protestant counterparts (Smith and Chambers, 1991; Murphy and Armstrong, 1994). Geographically, the claimant-based unemployment rate varies from 8% in the Ballymena Travel to Work Area (TTWA) to 18% in Strabane TTWA (DED, 1995). At the even smaller level of local council wards, unemployment rates vary from 4% in the ward of Hillsborough to almost 50% in the West Belfast wards of Falls and Whiterock. Particular areas of Northern Ireland, such as West Belfast, Newtownabbey's Rathcoole estate, Derry's Bogside and many towns along the border, have become well-known for their chronically high levels of unemployment.

Despite its severity, long-term unemployment has not featured strongly in research and discussion on fair employment. In all the debate over whether, and to what degree, 'discrimination' and 'religion' explain differences in the unemployment rates of Catholics and Protestants (Smith and Chambers, 1991; Murphy and Armstrong, 1994; Gudgin and Breen, 1996), the long-term unemployment rate differential has scarcely been mentioned. Yet this difference is, and has been, strong, whereas the differences in short-term unemployment rates are much less marked. In the early to mid-1980s when unemployment in Northern Ireland was rising to rates exceeding 20%, 36% of unemployed Protestant women had been out of work more than a year compared with 49% of unemployed Catholic women. For men, the figures were 57% for Protestants and 69% for Catholics (Smith and Chambers, 1991:164). Combining Labour Force Survey data for the years 1985/6 and 1990/1, Armstrong (1994) suggests that the differences are even greater. He estimates that unemployed Catholics are 1.5 times as likely to be LTU (more than a year) and very LTU (in this case defined as more than four years) as unemployed Protestants. Once unemployed, therefore, Catholics are less likely to escape from long-term unemployment than Protestants.

Since the passing of the 1989 Fair Employment Act, there has been continuing argument over the significance of unemployment to the achievement of fair employment (Gallagher, 1991). Gudgin and Breen (1996:42) have argued specifically that differences in unemployment rates are not a valid indicator of employment equity. Their mathematical simulation of the labour force covers the period 1971 to 1991, a period which, for the most part, was prior to any possible effects of the 1989 Act. Differences in the duration of unemployment by religion are not discussed by these authors, who presumably regard such inequalities either as unimportant or intrinsically 'fair'.

There is a strong case to be made that unemployment is now a more significant indicator of labour market inequalities than it was 20 years ago when the first Fair Employment Act was introduced. Firstly, there is the issue of the size of the problem. In the mid-1970s, one in 18 of the workforce was unemployed. Rising unemployment throughout the 1980s and 1990s has meant that at any one time between a fifth and an eighth of the total workforce have been unemployed claimants and more than this experience a spell of unemployment in a given year. It would be wholly unreasonable to exclude this large segment of the workforce from monitoring and discussion of employment equity.

Secondly, there is clear evidence of a simultaneous growth in workless households and two income households over the last two decades - a polarisation between work-poor and work-rich households. When new jobs become available they are 'disproportionately taken by people in households where someone is already working... [In the 1990s] this effect is likely to be stronger than during the 1980s recovery as the differential in favour of members of work-rich households has substantially increased' (Gregg and Wadsworth, 1995:20). Essentially, the argument is that changes in the structure of the labour market, in particular the growth of part-time jobs, have made it more difficult than it used to be to move from unemployment into work, thus increasing the depth of the unemployment experience (McLaughlin, 1991). If this situation is not actively addressed, the effect is to 'freeze' substantial inequalities into the unemployed population.

Finally, the degree of unemployment inequality between Protestants and Catholics is not fully appreciated without taking account of differences between short- and long-term unemployment. Although the claimant-based unemployment rate for Northern Ireland has declined from over 17% in the mid-1980s to 11% in the mid-1990s, long-term unemployment has grown as a proportion of all unemployment. Since the 1989 Fair Employment Act, an increasing majority of the unemployed have been out of work for one year or more, notwithstanding the expansion of the Action for Community Employment scheme, which at any one time absorbs almost 10,000 long-term unemployed (not all from the claimant count). It makes sense to acknowledge this trend by calculating long-term (and short-term) unemployment rates, and the ratios of these rates, as a means of evaluating changes in inequalities. These calculations are difficult to do given the limitations of existing published sources such as the Labour Force Survey Religion Reports (PPRU, 1992; 1993; 1994) which show rounded percentage figures based on relatively small sample sizes. Nevertheless, the 1991 figures showed that the Catholic/Protestant short-term unemployment ratio was 1.66:1 and the long-term ratio was very considerably higher at 3.08:1.

The existing literature, therefore, has tended to ignore what happens to people once they become unemployed and the processes which shape whether they stay unemployed or not. With notable exceptions (Evason and Woods, 1995; Evason, 1985; McLaughlin *et al*, 1989; Trew and Kilpatrick, 1984), there is little understanding of the attitudes, behaviour and needs of the LTU in Northern Ireland. There is also a dearth of empirical evidence - though much speculation - about how political conflict affects the behaviour of the unemployed, especially in an area such as West Belfast. There is also limited information on how the LTU view the effectiveness of the government's labour market interventions in areas such as assistance with job search, special training and employment measures. The implementation of effective policies targeted at the LTU requires an understanding of these processes. Moreover, if the objective of such policies is to reduce unemployment differentials, then an understanding of how processes vary between religion and gender is essential. Equally, there is little research on employers' attitudes towards hiring the LTU or employers' assessments of the effectiveness of employment and training programmes, especially the operation of these programmes in areas of highest unemployment. It was for all of these reasons that the present research was carried out.

The findings presented in this chapter challenge many common assumptions made by policy makers and economists about the behaviour of the LTU. The research differs from past studies on fair employment and unemployment in Northern Ireland in that the analysis is based on primary data from both the LTU and employers in an area of very high long-term unemployment. It is therefore able to examine some of the processes behind the outcomes analysed by other researchers.

POLICIES TOWARDS LONG-TERM UNEMPLOYMENT

At the start of the 1980s, and again in the late 1980s and the early 1990s, unemployment in the UK rose to levels that were unprecedented since the 1930s. At the same time there was a distinct shift in economic and labour market policies towards tackling inflation, trade union power, labour market rigidity and the size and role of the public sector. Unemployment became a marginalised policy issue in Britain, if less so in Northern Ireland. This was not because there was little unemployment but because:

> unemployment has been redefined as a residual and individualised problem, for which the enterprising free-market Thatcher administration had no direct responsibility. There was, then, no crisis (McLaughlin, 1992:1).

The policy shift in the allocation of responsibility from government to individuals resulted in high rates of unemployment becoming tolerable politically, notwithstanding widespread concern with social disturbances and growing evidence of links between unemployment, ill-health and crime.

The Development of Compulsion

Consistent with Conservative governments' supply-side monetarist approach towards the economy as a whole, and central to this re-allocation of responsibility, has been a new focus on the supply side of the labour market. Policies and responses to unemployment have centred on two main issues: the skill levels of unemployed individuals and how to motivate the unemployed. In the early 1980s, the agenda was vigorously laid out as being a problem of high benefits (therefore absence of work incentives), lack of labour discipline and the growth of the informal, waged economy, including such practices as 'doing the double' (earning a wage while claiming benefits as unemployed) (see, for example, Minford, 1985). It was, and still is, frequently asserted that unemployment, especially long-term unemployment, is largely due to the characteristics, attitudes and behaviour of the unemployed themselves. In particular, it is argued that the unemployed lack skills ('human capital shortfall'), or they live in the wrong place and are unwilling to travel to work ('low mobility'), or they have priced themselves out of jobs and refuse to take certain kinds of jobs ('inflexible'), or they do not try hard enough to find work ('low search intensity'). The LTU in particular are said to have too many children and therefore no incentive to work. As noted by White (1991:130):

> Such beliefs help to justify the continuation of unemployment and inequitable treatment of individuals in long-term unemployment. Allies were found in the tabloid press, together with some sections of popular opinion, who are particularly impressed with the image of unemployed people as scroungers, dropouts, or incapable.

The arguments around 'motivational policies' have not, however, been clear-cut, nor have they been implemented unambiguously.

By the end of the 1980s, benefit entitlement of the unemployed, particularly the young unemployed, had been reduced both in value and accessibility. Older unemployed workers disappeared from the register. Others were encouraged to move from the status of unemployed to claim Invalidity Benefit, a trend which it is now intended to reverse through the introduction of Incapacity Benefit (which is more restrictive than Invalidity Benefit). This is predicted to increase the claimant count by as much as one quarter over the next few years, adding to the volume of sickness and disability amongst unemployed claimants (Tomlinson, 1995:3). In addition, the unemployed have been scrutinised more heavily than in the past regarding fraud, willingness to work and job search. Such measures will be further developed in the near future with the (delayed) implementation of the Jobseeker's Allowance (JSA) from October 1996. JSA will remove about 30,000 claimants from the unemployment count for the UK as a whole and will cause a quarter of a million to lose entitlement to Unemployment Benefit, of whom a third will not qualify for Income Support (Finn, 1995(a):8).

The JSA requires the unemployed to enter into a contract (the Jobseeker's Agreement) which specifies the measures that the unemployed person agrees to take in order to find work. Individuals who fail to demonstrate their continued availability and efforts to improve their chances of getting a job will be subject to the withdrawal of benefits. Claimants may be issued with a 'Jobseeker's Direction' requiring them to participate in any available training and employment schemes, and failure to comply can mean the withdrawal of benefits. This has intensified the debate over 'compulsion': the idea that benefits will only be paid on condition that the unemployed participate in training and employment schemes, which some critics have in any event cynically dismissed as an attempt to disguise the true level of unemployment (Donaldson, 1985).

On the one hand, there is the view that worklessness (or idleness) itself undermines the individual and, therefore, no-one should simply be allowed to languish on benefit. A condition of benefit, therefore, should be participation in one of the special measures. Known as 'workfare' in the United States, this level of compulsion already applies to 16 and 17 year olds in the UK and the Jobseeker's Act will give powers to impose benefit penalties on adults up to the full duration and amount of benefit. On the other hand, workfare, and other elements of compulsion within the benefit/training complex, may seriously damage motivation and generate or increase negative attitudes among the unemployed towards training providers and social security staff. Compulsion may lead to people taking up inappropriate training places, reinforce existing scepticism about the value of schemes among both the unemployed and employers, and can lead to wastage of resources through high drop out rates (Finn, 1995(b); Unemployment Unit, 1994(a)).

As the House of Commons Employment Committee points out (1996:xxiv):

> Although it may fall short of a formal Workfare programme, the Jobseekers' Act marks the culmination of a policy which has approached the problem of mass unemployment as essentially one whose cause is the lack of sufficient jobseeking skills amongst jobless individuals. [...] It seems unlikely that the Government can go much further down the path of emphasising individual activity as a means of tackling joblessness.

Similar schemes have been experimented with for many years in the United States. In the 1980s, the Republicans tried to get every state to introduce Community Work Experience Programmes (CWEP), regarded as the 'purest' form of workfare scheme. CWEPs are targeted on lone mothers with children (in receipt of AFDC - Aid to Families with Dependent Children) and they require participants to work for their benefit. The scheme has proved unpopular politically and is regarded as too expensive because working single parents obviously require childcare. Only around 15,000 people are on compulsory work schemes in the US at present (*ibid:* xvii). The closest any British schemes come to CWEP is the Project Work scheme, piloted (under section 29 of JSA) in Hull and Medway and Maidstone from April 1996. Anyone who refuses a placement (or fails to attend, leaves or is asked to leave) loses their benefits and the £10 premium.

Whilst unemployed people are increasingly compelled to participate in training schemes, participation of the unemployed in further and higher education has not been encouraged. There has been a long-standing debate about whether to change the '21 hour rule' - the Income Support regulation which allows no more than 21 hours part-time study without loss of benefit - to a 16 hour rule (Craven, 1995; Finn, 1995 (c)).

The necessity or desirability of compulsion can be evaluated from the survey of long-term unemployed people in West Belfast reported below. This provided evidence, amongst other things, on motivational factors behind job search behaviour and willingness to work, central issues in recent policies towards the unemployed. Before discussing responses to questions relating to these factors, the next section presents a brief profile of the long-term unemployed.

THE LONG-TERM UNEMPLOYED IN WEST BELFAST

The postal questionnaire was sent to a sample of unemployed claimants living in the pilot area for the West Belfast Community Work Programme. Further details of the sample are provided in the Annex at the end of this chapter. The final sample consisted of 314 useable returned questionnaires. Compared with the 1995 claimant count population of LTU in West Belfast, the sample was biased towards women (26%), who are underrepresented in the claimant count, and slightly overrepresented the very LTU (five years+) (50%) and Protestants (27%) (see Figure 3.1).

It is unlikely that any of these biases significantly alter the main findings of the research. The sample is broadly representative of the age structure of West Belfast LTU claimants. Unemployment in both the sample and claimant count population is concentrated in the age groups 25-34 and 35-44 years of age, which together account for 60% of those in the claimant count population and 63% of those in the sample.

Figure 3.1: West Belfast Long-Term Unemployed Survey

Population and Sample by Religion

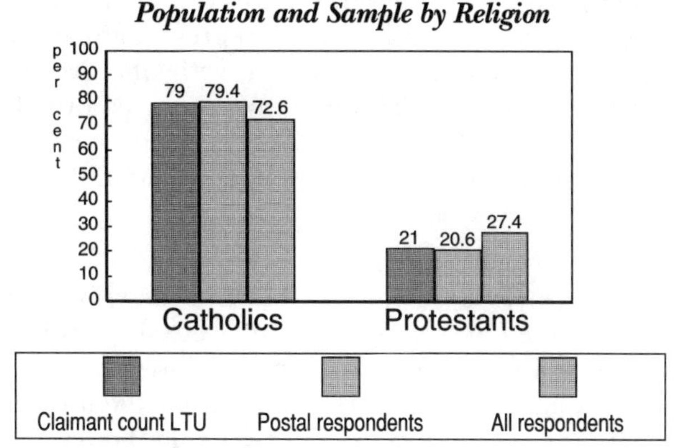

Households and Children

Table 3.1 shows the breakdown of the sample by the number of children in households. Just over half (56%) of the sample were living in households with children. Of these, 84% were in households with three or fewer children and the average number of children was 2.36 (Catholic average 2.4 and Protestant, 2.2). This compares to 2.39 for Northern Ireland as a whole according to the 1991 Census (NIEC, 1995(b)). Catholic households were more likely to contain four or more children but such households were a very small percentage of the total sample.

Table 3.1: Households and Children, West Belfast LTU Survey, 1995

Children	N	%
0	137	44.2
1	51	16.5
2	63	20.3
3	31	10.0
4	14	4.5
5	7	2.3
6	5	1.6
7	1	0.3
10	1	0.3
Total	310	100.0

Just over a third (36%) of respondents were single (34% of men and 44% of women), 35% were married or living with a partner (40% of men and 20% of women), 22% were separated (19% of men and 30% of women), 5%

divorced (6% of men and 5% of women) and 2% were widowed (2% of men and 1% of women). The very different proportions of men and women who were single suggests that the sample was overrepresentative of single women. This is further supported by comparison with the Northern Ireland population as a whole in which 28% of all women aged over 16 are single. The figure for men is 35% (NIEC, 1995(b)). The corresponding implication is that women with children may be underrepresented in the sample.

Economic Status

Nearly three-quarters (72%) of all respondents described themselves as seeking work, 14% were not seeking work, 4% were sick or disabled and 4% were waiting to start a job, scheme or course. Protestant men (10%) were more likely than Catholic men (5%) to describe themselves as 'sick or disabled' and this was not sensitive to age. Generally, however, Catholic and Protestant men gave very similar answers. The most significant differences between respondents were in terms of gender. Women were less likely to describe themselves as seeking work than men (64% to 81% respectively).

Unemployment Duration

Almost all of the results presented below are sensitive to the duration of unemployment. It is therefore useful to examine the distribution of unemployment durations by religion, gender and age.

Just over half the LTU had been unemployed for five years or more. Average age did not seem to be a significant factor in unemployment duration. Those aged 35 or more, however, were more likely to have been unemployed for more than five years than those under 35. The average duration for individuals who had been unemployed for five years or more was 13 years.

Figure 3.2 examines differences in the duration of unemployment by gender and religion. Protestant and Catholic women followed the same pattern, with about 40% of LTU falling in the five years or more category. Catholic and Protestant men, however, were markedly different. Only 7% of Catholic men LTU had been unemployed for between one and two years, compared to a fifth of Protestant men. At the other end of the spectrum, 62% of Catholic LTU men were five or more years unemployed compared to just over a third of Protestant men. The pattern of Catholic men having longer unemployment than Protestants and being less likely to be short-term unemployed is broadly consistent with findings elsewhere (Murphy and Armstrong, 1994).

Among households with children, the number of children in a household has only a slight effect on unemployment duration (Table 3.2). Respondents in households with four or more children were less likely than childless households (and other households with children) to have been unemployed for between two and four years and more likely to have been out of work between four and five years. However, there was almost no differencebetween those who had been unemployed for more than five years (50%) across household types.

Figure 3.2: West Belfast Long-Term Unemployed Survey

Duration of Unemployment: Religion/Sex

Table 3.2: Number of Children and Unemployment Duration, West Belfast LTU Survey, 1995

Unemployment duration Years	All %	No Children %	1-3 Children %	4+ Children %
1-2	14.3	11.8	15.9	14.3
2-3	10.5	12.5	9.0	7.1
3-4	12.4	13.2	11.7	7.1
4-5	12.7	14.0	11.7	21.4
5+	50.2	48.5	51.7	50.0

Education and Unemployment Duration

In general, higher educational qualifications are associated with lower rates and shorter durations of unemployment (Nickell, 1979; Gallagher *et al*, 1994). For Northern Ireland as a whole, approximately six-tenths of the LTU have no formal qualifications. This rises to seven-tenths for those unemployed for more than four years (Armstrong, 1994). In terms of religion, results from the 1991 Census indicate that amongst the economically active population there are relatively few differences in the proportions of Catholics and Protestants with a qualification of some sort. Catholic males, however, are overrepresented amongst those without qualifications (64% compared to 59% for Protestant males). According to the 1991 Census, Catholic unemployment rates for men and women are higher than those of Protestants for every level of qualification (Gallagher *et al*, 1994), including none.

Since the West Belfast survey was for the LTU only, comparisons to other studies can only be limited. It is possible, however, to examine the relationship between level of educational qualification, unemployment duration, age and religion. Three categories of educational attainment are distinguished: GCE 'A' level and the vocational equivalents (for example, BTEC (National)), and above; up to 'O' level and its equivalents; and no qualifications.

One-eighth of respondents (14% of Catholics and 9% of Protestants) had 'A' levels (or the vocational equivalent) and above, including 4% with degrees. Four out of ten of the LTU (41% of Catholics and 42% of Protestants) had up to 'O' levels and 46% (41% of Catholics and 49% of Protestants) had no formal qualifications. Although 46% of the LTU in West Belfast had no formal qualifications, this was substantially lower than the average for the Northern Ireland population of LTU (60%), suggesting that the West Belfast LTU are relatively better educated. In addition, West Belfast long-term unemployed Catholics were less likely to have no qualifications than LTU Protestants, the opposite trend to that in Northern Ireland as a whole. Men were more likely to have no formal qualifications than women (48% compared to 40%). Educational qualifications were also linked to age. For example, 29% of respondents aged 18-24 had no formal qualifications compared to 55% of those aged 45-54 and 72% of those aged 55 or more.

Figure 3.3: West Belfast Long-Term Unemployed Survey

Education and Duration of Unemployment

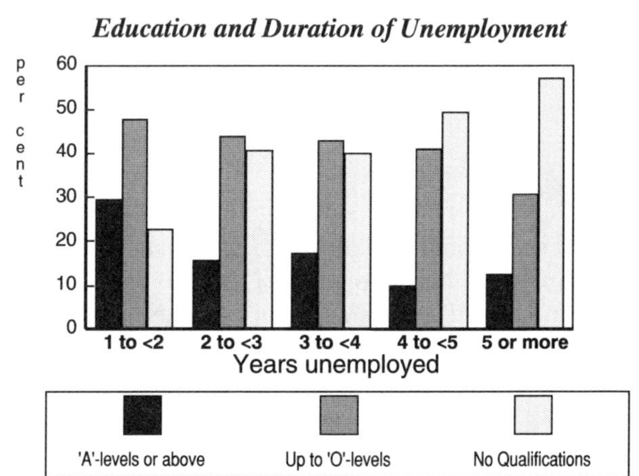

Figure 3.3 shows that unemployment duration was found to be associated with educational qualifications. For example, of those unemployed less than two years, 23% did not have any formal qualifications compared to 57% of those unemployed for 5 years or more. Nevertheless, a relatively high percentage (43%) of the very LTU in West Belfast had a formal qualification compared to the Northern Ireland population as a whole (30%), again suggesting that the West Belfast LTU are relatively well educated.

Mental and Physical Health

The impact of increasing levels of long-term unemployment, combined with relatively low out of work income, on physical and mental health is an important issue, though less well researched than other aspects of unemployment. Townsend and Davidson (1992) and Wilkinson (1994) highlight the sensitivity of health to socio-economic circumstances, and Wilkinson (1994:26) concludes that 'the most likely pathways [to ill-health] are through feelings of failure, insecurity, depression, anxiety, low self-esteem and the like'. Additional evidence of the effects of long-term unemployment specifically on mental health is provided by Fryer (1992:104): '...much of the psychological ill-health of unemployed people and their families is caused by income-related factors rather than by, or even as well as, the absence of employment itself'. Fryer, therefore, refutes the argument posited from the 1930s onwards by the Jahoda school that the principal adverse mental health effects of long-term unemployment are due to the absence of integrative and supportive social relationships provided by employment. Fryer's analysis implies that the depression, anxiety and passivity commonly associated with unemployment are largely the result of the restrictions imposed on unemployed people by the material context of unemployment, rather than being the cause of (continued) unemployment or the effect of the absence of employment (McLaughlin, 1994(a)). Similarly, studies carried out in Northern Ireland by Evason (1985) and Trew and Kilpatrick (1984) emphasised psychological deterioration and boredom, as well as the loss of physical health, consequent on long-term unemployment. Depression was common in both studies.

In the present study, people were asked a series of questions on mental and physical health and how unemployment had affected their health. Just over half reported that they did not suffer from any health problems. Eighty-seven percent of respondents described their overall state of health as 'good' (46%) or 'fair' (41%), with 13% answering 'not so good'. Catholic men were the most likely to describe their health as 'not so good' (16% compared to 3% of Protestant men). It is likely that this reflects the effects of long periods of unemployment on physical health, but it is a finding which appears to contradict the point reported earlier that Protestants were more likely than Catholics to describe their current economic status as 'sick or disabled'. This is explained by the fact that most Catholics whose health was 'not so good' still regarded themselves as seeking work. There was little difference in overall health amongst those unemployed less than five years (only 5% of individuals unemployed for five years or less reported that their health was 'not so good'). In contrast, 22% of individuals who had been unemployed for five years or more reported that their health was 'not so good', 50% reported that their health was 'fair', while only 28% described their health as 'good'.

People were also asked if their general health had changed since becoming unemployed. Over a third (37%) reported that their health had become 'worse', 59% 'the same' and 4% 'better'. Again the most significant effect was amongst those unemployed for five years or more, of whom 48% reported that their health had become worse.

Consistent with other studies, the most common form of health difficulty was depression (15%). Depression was most common amongst Protestant men. Protestant men also scored the lowest on a mental health index constructed from a series of questions about stress, depression, sleeping problems and consideration of suicide. Women, especially those with children, scored the highest on the index. These patterns follow the findings of other studies on the mental health effects of unemployment.

Evason (1985) found that Protestants were much more likely than Catholics to report loss of self-esteem and confidence as a result of unemployment. Howe (1990) suggests that this stems from the different position and experience of Catholics and Protestants in relation to the economy. This is likely to reflect the fact that in some areas of Northern Ireland, like West Belfast, people in the area, especially young people, had become used to unemployment in the sense that they never expected to have work (Rolston and Tomlinson, 1988). This difference in attitude to unemployment may also be the product of different political perceptions and responses and differences in social support structures.

Respondents Who Had Never Had a Job

An important characteristic of the sample, in terms of both current and future trends in long-term unemployment, was that 23% of all respondents had never had a job. Over half (55%) of these were Catholic men, 20% Catholic women, 18% Protestant men and 7% Protestant women. As expected the people who reported never having had a job tended to be gathered in the younger age bands. Eighty-seven percent of these respondents were aged 34 or less, which meant that 46% of this age group had never had a job.

Although respondents who had never had a real job tended to be grouped in the younger age bands, a high percentage had been unemployed for long durations. Six out of ten of the 'never worked' had been unemployed for five or more years (accounting for 27% of all five or more years unemployed). In terms of qualifications, 49% of the 'never worked' had qualifications up to 'O' level and 9% had qualifications of 'A' level or above. Seven out of ten (71%) of the 'never worked' had been on a government scheme and 85% regarded themselves as searching for work.

JOB SEARCH AND WILLINGNESS TO WORK

As noted earlier, during the early 1980s the view that labour market rigidities reside largely in the unemployed themselves became commonplace in the UK. In addition, there is a widespread notion that the informal economy is buoyant, especially in inner city areas such as West Belfast, and that the unemployed are readily able to supplement their benefits with substantial earnings from the informal economy. The findings presented below, however, challenge many of the common myths about the LTU and, in particular, many of the unsubstantiated assumptions about the LTU in West Belfast.

Search Behaviour

It is generally argued that the effort people devote to job search will be affected both by the perceived value of getting a job and the perceived likelihood of success. This implies that as the duration of unemployment increases, and the individual believes that the probability of success becomes low, search effort will reduce.

Over three-quarters (77%) of the LTU in the West Belfast survey were searching for work, and this rose among men to 82% of Catholic men and 83% of Protestant men. As expected, unemployment duration has a significant effect on job search, especially after five years or more of unemployment. For example, 87% of men unemployed less than two years were searching for work. This figure drops to 81% of those unemployed four to five years and was only 69% of those unemployed five years or more. The reasons people gave for not searching supports the 'discouraged worker' effect, the most common being 'looked but couldn't find work' (67%), 'no suitable jobs available', (23%), 'illness' (20%), and 'lack of qualifications' (13%).

Catholics had a higher search rate than Protestants for each unemployment duration (for example, 89% of Catholic men unemployed less than two years were searching for work compared to 85% of Protestant men). The largest difference in search activity emerges between Catholic and Protestant males who have been unemployed for more than five years - 73% of Catholic men compared to 64% of Protestant men. It appears, therefore, that the discouraged worker effect in West Belfast is particularly significant amongst Protestant men.

Women were less likely to be looking for work than men but Catholic women (64%) were more likely to be searching than Protestant women (57%). In contrast to the results for men, unemployment duration had little effect on women's likelihood to be searching for work. The main reason why women were not looking for work was caring responsibilities: 'responsibility for young children' (83%) and 'responsibility for other dependants' (11%).

The presence of children in a household had an effect such that unemployed people in childless households were more likely to be searching for work than others. But the number of children in a household had little effect. Approximately 85% of all the LTU with no children were searching for work compared to 72% of those with one to three children and 71% of those with four or more children. While 86% of men without children were searching for work, 84% of men with four or more children were searching for work. Both Catholic and Protestant women without children were more likely to be searching for work (73%) compared to mothers (63%).

Finally, only 4% of individuals (all men) answered that they were not searching for work because they felt that political beliefs or their religious background would prevent them from obtaining employment. It is difficult to interpret this result but it may be the answer chosen by ex-prisoners who, if the employers' attitudes reported in Chapter Four are taken into account, are more likely to be excluded from the labour market than the LTU as a whole. Alternatively, it may be that intimidation, discussed later in this chapter, produces some 'discouraged' workers. In any event, the number deterred from seeking work for these reasons is very small.

It is generally expected (though not necessarily correctly) that the more intensely someone looks for a job, the more likely he or she will be to find work. To gauge search intensity, people were asked about the type and number of search methods used, the number of jobs applied for and the number of interviews undertaken over the past year. They were presented with 12 possible search methods (Table 3.3) and more than three-quarters (79%) used more than one method (84% of men compared to 74% of women). People used an average of 4.8 methods. These results, like those on job search (though to a lesser extent), are sensitive to unemployment duration - the number of methods declined as unemployment duration increased. For example, those unemployed less than two years used an average of seven search methods, whereas those unemployed for five years or more used an average of three methods. Amongst those unemployed less than two years, Catholics on average used 7.4 and Protestants 7.1 search methods. Protestants unemployed between two to four years used slightly more job search methods than Catholics. There was no difference amongst those unemployed for five years or more.

Table 3.3: Job Search Methods and Religion, West Belfast LTU Survey, 1995

Search method	Catholics %	Protestants %	All %
Job/Club Market	63.8	61.5	62.1
Job Centres	7.2	58.9	53.1
Private Employment Agency	3.8	4.9	4.3
Looked at adverts on shop windows/notice boards	44.5	41.2	43.3
Looked at adverts in local newspapers/magazines	81.8	78.5	79.6
Looked at adverts in Northern Ireland wide newspapers/ magazines	80.5	79.9	80.2
Looked at adverts in national newspapers/magazines	17.3	11.2	14.9
Looked at adverts in trade/ professional journals	4.2	5.8	5.1
Looked at adverts on TV (teletext)	17.2	16.1	16.8
Approached employers	26.3	27.9	26.9
Asked family connections	37.2	40.1	39.2
Asked friends and neighbours	53.1	49.9	51.4
Other	2.1	2.3	2.3

These findings are broadly consistent with other studies (for example, the most common form of job search is looking at adverts and visiting Job Clubs), with one exception. Murphy and Armstrong (1994) found that 41% of the unemployed sample approached employers directly (39% of Catholics and 45% of Protestants). In contrast, only 27% of the West Belfast LTU contacted employers directly (26% of Catholics and 28% of Protestants). Since employer contact is considered to be a more intensive form of job search than other methods (Dawes, 1993; Hughes and McCormick, 1990), this is an important difference in the case of West Belfast. It is likely to reflect several factors: the relatively low numbers of employers in the West Belfast locality, past rejection by the limited number of employers and low turnover of jobs.

Another indicator of whether an individual is actively searching for work is the frequency of job applications to employers. Amongst the LTU who were searching for work, 86% had applied for a job in the past year (87% of Catholic men, 92% of Protestant men, 83% of Catholic women and 74% of Protestant women). The average number of jobs applied for by these individuals in the past year was 8.5 (9.1 for Catholic men, 10.6 for Protestant men, 5.2 for Catholic women and 3.1 for Protestant women). There was, however, significant variation in the number of jobs applied for and this was again linked to unemployment duration. Individuals who were unemployed for less than two years applied, on average, for 19.2 jobs in the past year. Approximately a fifth of these individuals had applied for more than 25 jobs in the past year. In contrast, individuals who had been unemployed for five years or more had applied for only 3.3 jobs on average. Approximately 36% of those who had applied for at least one job had an interview in the past year. Catholic men who applied for jobs were significantly less likely to have had an interview (33%) than Protestant men (46%).

Type of Work Considered

While the results presented above suggest that the vast majority of respondents were actively searching for work, the issue of the type of work which respondents search for is also important. It has often been argued that the LTU restrict their job search (are 'inflexible') because they are attached to a particular industry, occupation or trade, even when such employment opportunities are in decline. It has also been argued that the structure of social security benefits for the unemployed is inflexible, financially and administratively, preventing some of the unemployed, particularly 'bread-winners' with children and unwaged partners, taking up part-time jobs and temporary contracts (McLaughlin *et al*, 1989; McLaughlin, 1994(b); NIEC, 1995; Social Security Advisory Committee, 1994).

Figure 3.4: West Belfast Long-Term Unemployed Survey

Job Search and Willingness to Consider Any Job

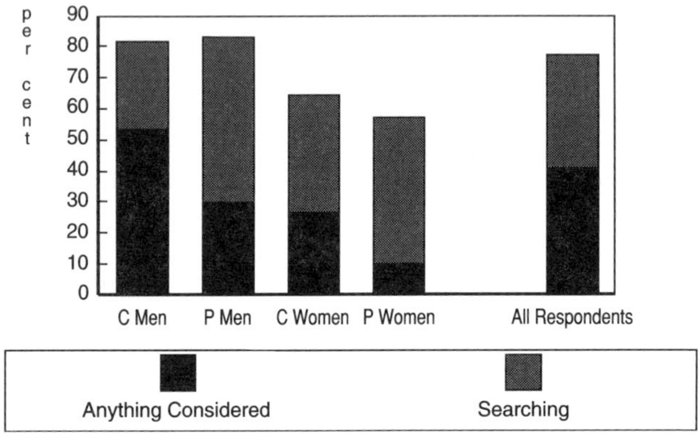

Dawes (1993:134) found that about half of LTU men (51%) and women (49%) were looking for any type of job. In this West Belfast study, 52% of the

LTU who were searching for work said that they would consider any job. Statistically, significant differences emerged between religion and gender, the latter in contrast to Dawes' findings, as shown in Figure 3.4. Nearly two-thirds (65%) of searching Catholic men would consider 'anything' compared to 35% of searching Protestant men, 40% of searching Catholic women and 17% of searching Protestant women. It is likely that the gender result reflects both the gender segregation of the labour market and constraints faced by women in terms of childcare, care of other dependants and their partner's employment status.

The difference between Catholic and Protestant men in their willingness to consider any type of work reflects, to some extent, different work histories as well as differences in socio-economic backgrounds. Briefly, in terms of work histories, Protestants had had more 'stable' jobs than Catholics. As a result, Catholics were more likely to have held more jobs and worked in more occupations and more industries than Protestants. Catholics were also more likely to say that they did not have a 'usual type of job'. These general patterns were much more pronounced amongst the LTU aged 35 or more. Amongst those in the age bands 18-24 and 24-34, while the general pattern was sustained, few of the differences in work history were statistically significant. Using age as a proxy for work history, of those aged 18-34, 69% of Catholic men would have considered 'anything' compared to 55% of Protestants, while amongst those aged 35 or over, 58% of Catholics would consider anything compared to just 28% of Protestants. This figure rose among those who had never had paid work to 61%, but again, statistically, significant differences existed by religion (66% of Catholics and 50% of Protestants).

Differences also emerged in willingness to consider part-time or full-time employment, which might be an indicator of flexibility and associated constraints of benefit entitlement. Four out of ten (41%) of all the LTU were prepared to consider either part- or full-time employment (compared to 14% part-time only and 45% full-time only). As expected, women were more likely to be looking for part-time work only compared to men (40% of women compared to 5% of men). There were religious effects: among women, 36% of Catholics were prepared to consider either part- or full-time work compared to 21% of Protestants. In contrast, 42% of Protestant women were considering only full-time employment compared to 22% of Catholics. Among men, 51% of Catholics were prepared to consider either part- or full-time employment compared to 26% of Protestants. In contrast, 71% of Protestant men were considering full-time employment only, compared to 44% of Catholics.

Such differences in flexibility are not as prevalent in relation to short-term or temporary jobs. Nearly two-thirds (64%) of all the LTU were prepared to consider a short-term or temporary job. Here, there was little religion or gender effect - 67% of Catholic men, 59% of Protestant men, 64% of Catholic women and 67% of Protestant women said that they would consider such jobs. The most common reasons given for considering temporary jobs were, first, financial, and second, the hope that they might lead to permanent work. The most common reasons for not considering temporary jobs were linked to the social security system: the need to re-apply for benefits, the amount of time it takes to receive benefits when first signing on and the loss of benefits.

Men with four or more children were the most likely to answer that they were willing to consider any type of work (72%), compared to 61% of men with no children and 52% of all respondents. Men with four or more children, however, were the least likely to consider a temporary or short-term job (59%), compared to 62% of men with no children and 64% of all respondents. The risk associated with a temporary job in terms of the social security system referred to above was the most important factor behind why these respondents would not consider temporary jobs. This is consistent with the arguments and findings of McLaughlin (1994(a); 1994(b); 1991).

Assistance With Job Search

As discussed earlier, the government has given priority to counselling and guidance services for the unemployed, such as Restart interviews and courses, Claimant Advisors and Job Clubs. There is a dearth of information, however, on the views of the LTU on the usefulness of such services. In this study, people were asked about the type of assistance they had received and their assessment of its effectiveness. About two-thirds (65%) had received assistance with job search. Men were much more likely to have received assistance than women (especially Catholic women, of whom 64% reported they had not received help). This finding does, however, reflect the inclusion of some women in our sample who are not required to register as unemployed as a condition of benefit and would not, therefore, be subject to regular interviews with Claimant Advisors.

According to the respondents, Job Clubs and Job Centres are the most useful forms of assistance (53% of respondents rated Job Clubs as 'very useful' or 'useful'; 46% rated Job Centres as 'very useful' or 'useful'). Careers Officers at T&EA offices and Claimant Advisors at Social Security Offices were rated as 'very useful/useful' by 44% and 34% of respondents respectively. Only 20% of respondents stated that the Restart Interview was 'very useful/useful'.

For all forms of job search assistance, Catholics (especially men), were much more likely to state that the assistance was 'not very useful' or 'useless'. These differences were statistically significant for all forms of assistance except Restart. It is not clear why Catholics and Protestants view assistance with job search so differently. Part of the difference is explained by longer unemployment duration. For both Catholics and Protestants the longer the unemployment duration, the less favourably job search assistance was rated. Even amongst Catholics and Protestants with the same unemployment duration, however, Catholics viewed the assistance less favourably. These findings need further investigation, possibly with regard to differences in the way the Lower Falls and Shankill Social Security Offices and other facilities are experienced and operate.

Further evidence of difference between Catholics and Protestants in their experience of the public employment service came from whether people had ever been notified about a job, or had ever been called for a job interview, by the Social Security Office, Careers Officer or Job Club. Clearly, the public employment service generally had little to offer in this regard, with 80% of the LTU never having been notified of a possible job. However, there were further important religious effects. Catholics were less likely than Protestants to have been notified about potential jobs - 82% of Catholic men, 63% of Protestant men, 90% of Catholic women and 76% of Protestant women had never been notified of potential jobs. There also appears to be a religious effect in terms of the source of job notifications: 4% of Catholic men, 15% of Protestant men, 2% of Catholic women and 14% of Protestant women had been notified by the Social Security Office. Similarly, 1% of Catholic men, 9% of Protestant men, 3% of Catholic women and 5% of Protestant women said they had been notified by a Careers Officer at the local T&EA office. Catholic men were only slightly less likely (13%) than Protestant men (12%) to have been notified about a job through a Job Club. These findings do suggest a need to review the degree of pro-activity of the public employment services in Catholic compared with Protestant areas, or those with Catholic and Protestant clienteles.

Nearly three-quarters (73%) of respondents had never been called for a job interview. Catholics (77% for Catholic men and 85% of Catholic women) and Protestant women (76%) were significantly less likely to have been called for a job interview than Protestant men. Approximately 18% of respondents reported that they had been called for a job interview via the Social Security Office (32% of Protestant men compared to 15% of Catholic men), 6% by a Job Club and 3% by a Careers Officer.

Job Search and Intimidation

It has often been argued that past intimidation or attack contributes to a 'chill factor' which influences job search and where people will search for work. Of those who had had a job in this study, 30% said they had experienced religious or political intimidation at work and most (85%) of these were men - 88% of whom were Catholics. Four out of ten (42%) of Catholic men (who had had a job) and 18% of Protestant men had been intimidated. The equivalent figure for Catholic women was 18% and for

Protestants, 14%. Half of the intimidation occurred before 1979, a third during the 1980s and 15% in the 1990s. Of those intimidated, 28% experienced multiple forms of intimidation. The most common form was 'words spoken' (74%), but over a third (35%) of the intimidated claimed that they had experienced physical violence. Nearly three out of ten (25%) of intimidated Catholic women reported physical violence but none of the intimidated Protestant women did so. Intimidated women were much more likely to report 'other forms of intimidation' compared to men (25% compared to 8%), suggesting a sexual harassment factor. Overall, nearly two-thirds (64%) said that intimidation was a factor in leaving a job (67% of Catholics and 50% of Protestants). A quarter of Catholic male participants in training and employment schemes reported intimidation compared to 9% of Protestant men.

Figure 3.5 illustrates that intimidation does indeed reduce the rate of job search. The effect was not statistically significant for religion or gender. Intimidation also had an effect on where individuals search for work - an effect which is statistically significant for men only. In Figure 3.5 the percentage of individuals searching for work is compared with those who have searched for work beyond the confines of West Belfast. The 'gap' between the two columns represents those who seemed to be looking for work in West Belfast only. This gap increased for all those intimidated and was largest for intimidated Catholic men (ICM), but it was also sizeable for intimidated Protestant men.

Figure 3.5: West Belfast Long-Term Unemployed Survey

Intimidation and Job Search

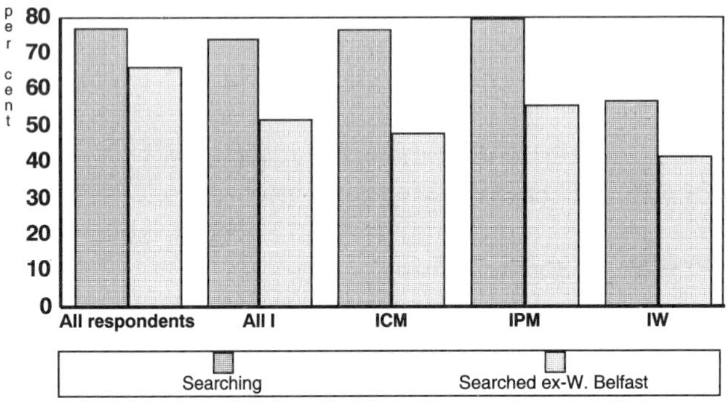

KEY: I=Intimidated; C/PM=Catholic/Protestant Men; W=Women

It is also possible to break down 'outside West (ex-W.) Belfast' into two areas - the 'rest of Belfast' and 'elsewhere in Northern Ireland' (that is, outside Belfast). Protestant men with experience of intimidation who are searching outside of West Belfast are much more likely than their Catholic equivalents to be searching elsewhere in Belfast. Conversely, Catholic men with experience of intimidation are more likely to search elsewhere in Northern Ireland, presumably in Catholic areas.

It appears that these patterns of search will change little in the future. Eight out of ten (82%) of Catholics and 65% of Protestants said that there were areas they would not work in before the ceasefires, and 90% of these Catholics would still not work in certain areas after the ceasefires, compared with 62% of Protestants. In other words, only 10% of Catholics had changed their view since the ceasefire, compared to 38% of Protestants. The majority of those who changed their views were women.

In terms of occupations, rather than areas, 71% of Catholics and 21% of Protestants said there were occupations they would not work in. The main excluded occupations were 'Police/Army/Prison Service' (92%), while 4% mentioned 'construction' and another 4% 'roads'. Reluctance to join the 'Police/Army/Prison Service' only reduced very slightly after the ceasefires (6% changed their view - all were Protestants).

Finally, people were asked about their willingness to leave Northern Ireland to look for work and whether they would leave if offered a job outside of Northern Ireland. Over a third (34%) would consider leaving Northern Ireland to look for work (36% of Catholics and 31% of Protestants) and 35% would consider leaving if offered work (36% of Catholics and 37% of Protestants). People who had worked outside of Northern Ireland in the past (26% of Catholics had worked outside of Northern Ireland in the past compared to 11% of Protestants) were more likely to consider leaving Northern Ireland in the future. Women were less likely than men to consider leaving Northern Ireland (40% of men compared to 13% of women) and all individuals with children were less likely to consider leaving Northern Ireland than people without children. This is related to the reasons why people would not consider leaving. Firstly this was because they did not want to leave their family and friends (61%), while another 18% were 'attached to their area', 12% expressed concern for their children's schooling and 9% expressed concern for elderly relatives who would be left behind. Interestingly, no-one identified expenses associated with moving, or difficulty in obtaining housing as important reasons for not considering leaving Northern Ireland.

WAGE FLEXIBILITY

The influence of the 'replacement ratio' (defined as the ratio of the income which an individual could get in work to the benefit income which an individual can get when out of work) on the probability of leaving unemployment, and hence on the duration of unemployment, has been the subject of a considerable amount of research by both economists and analysts of social policy. Economists have tended to regard replacement rates as a key motivational factor, arguing for a greater gap between wages and benefits, while social policy analysts have emphasised non-financial factors and security, rather than level of income (Stone, 1985; McLaughlin *et al*, 1989; McLaughlin 1991; 1994(a); 1994(b)).

In general, the majority of studies which use unemployment and benefit data from the mid-1980s onwards have found the effect of replacement rates on return to work probabilities to be quite small (for surveys of this literature see Blundell, 1994; Dawes, 1993; Dilnot, 1992). A recent British (Arulampalam and Stewart, 1995) study which used data from actual Social Security benefit records (instead of the usual method of imputing estimated benefit levels) found that the effect of the replacement ratio was significant only in the first three months of an unemployment spell and is therefore likely to be irrelevant for the LTU.

To date there has been only a limited analysis of replacement ratios and their influence on unemployment in Northern Ireland (Armstrong, 1994; NIEC, 1995(a)). The most thorough examination of theoretical replacement ratios for different household sizes has been carried out by the NIEC (1995(a)). The study was based on the assumption that out of work income creates an inherent employment disincentive and that the disincentive effect of out of work income is more significant in Northern Ireland for two main reasons. Firstly, average wages tend to be lower compared to the UK as a whole (while benefits are the same), and secondly, average family size is higher in Northern Ireland. Following the Social Security Advisory Committee Review (1994), the Council recommended various changes to in-work and out-of-work benefits which, amongst other things, would make part-time work more attractive to the unemployed. These included increasing 'earnings disregards' (the amount of earned income benefit recipients are allowed to keep before facing 100% withdrawal of benefit) and childcare costs allowances for both Income Support and Family Credit. The NIEC also proposed that where earnings disregards were not used, they could be 'rolled over' for when a person does find a job. The Council further recommended steps to smooth the transition from the position of unemployed benefit recipient to worker, by means of continuing some of the advantages of benefit receipt for a short time (receipt of so-called 'passported benefits,' such as free dental care) and the granting of lump sums to those finding work.

In arguing that the replacement rate issue is more serious in Northern Ireland than in the UK as a whole, the Council follows the assumption that, as economic actors, individuals are primarily motivated to derive 'utility' from the consumption of commodities and that in order to buy these commodities they have to obtain an income. Most individuals are assumed to undertake paid work to obtain income only as a means to this end: it is assumed there is no intrinsic utility derived from the activity of work itself. 'Rational' individuals (those who maximise individual utility functions), choosing how to allocate the scarce commodity, time, between two activities, work and 'leisure', are therefore assumed to supply labour hours up to the point where the wage rate equals the marginal rate of substitution between work and leisure (also assumed to be equal). Building on these assumptions, neo-classical economic theory argues that the welfare state has provided opportunities for individuals to 'opt out' of employment by making it financially viable for them to do so (that is, enabling them to derive utility by consuming goods and services through income provided by the welfare state).

As noted by Bryson (1994: 123):

> The idea that individuals, or households, simply calculate the level of paid work which maximises their financial returns and supply their labour accordingly, ignores the complexity of individuals' motivations in taking jobs. Yet the idea that financial motives predominate has proved difficult to dislodge.

Traditional research on replacement rates has ignored the non-financial importance of work. White (1991) provides an overview of some of the non-financial aspects of work. Firstly, a job fills a large part of the day, week and year with structured and productive activity which the majority of individuals find intrinsically interesting. Secondly, people's status or position in society depends largely upon their work and, thirdly, jobs provide social contact and recreation with fellow employees, customers, etc. In other words employment is important because it provides income, activity, social contact, and status all in one. Non-financial aspects of work are likely to alter significantly the size of an individual's 'reservation wage' rate (the minimum they will work for) and therefore replacement rates. Indeed, a growing body of literature challenges the idea of a benefit-induced disincentive to work, both empirically and theoretically, thus calling into question the usefulness of replacement ratios in explaining why people are unemployed (Atkinson *et al*, 1984; McLaughlin *et al*, 1989; Smith and McLaughlin, 1989; Dilnot, 1992; Dawes, 1993). In particular, there is evidence that a considerable number of employees work at rates of pay that are below or very close to their notional benefit levels (White, 1993; 1991).

In this study, people were asked to state the minimum amount they would work for (their 'reservation wage'). The overall mean reservation wage rate for all respondents was £121.37 a week (around £3.40 an hour), which was well below the weekly 'going wage' rate of the majority of employers interviewed in the West Belfast area (see Chapter Four). Overall, Catholics and women had lower mean reservation wage rates than Protestants and men respectively. As expected, the reservation wage varied according to the number of children in the household. For example, households with three children (10% of households in the sample) had a mean reservation wage rate of £155.56 compared to £107.41 for a single parent with one child (11% of households in the sample). The one exception to this pattern was single people with no children (33% of the households in the sample) who had a mean reservation wage rate of £117.67.

McLaughlin (1991) has argued that individuals fix their reservation wages by reference to their basic household commitments rather than benefits levels. In this study, most people (65%) said that the most important factor in deciding the minimum amount of money they would work for was 'the amount of money needed to meet financial commitments'. A fifth referred to 'the amount people should get for the type of job I'm looking for' but only 15% referred to their benefit levels as the benchmark. There was little variance in these responses by religion, gender or unemployment duration. The most significant difference occurred in households with three or more children (19% of households in the sample), where 35% referred to benefit levels. However, the majority (61%) of these respondents still referred to the amount needed to live on.

Dawes (1993:24) argued that if respondents set their reservation wage by reference to their household costs, 'then we would expect to see some correspondence between the previous levels of earnings and the reservation wage since household costs are likely to be determined predominantly by the past level of income'. The reservation wage rate of people who had worked in the past three years was compared to their previous level of earnings. Approximately 11% set their reservation wage at exactly the same level as their last earnings. Following Dawes, a regression analysis showed a statistically significant (r=.40) relationship between the most recent earnings and the reservation wage; and when this was confined to those who said that their most recent job was their normal type of work the relationship was stronger (r = .47). When confined further to include those whose most recent job was in Northern Ireland the relationship increased again (r = .52).

These results are generally consistent with other studies where individuals are actually asked about their reservation wage rate and the factors which influence this wage. The results imply that other factors, not just benefit levels, influence people's decisions about working. Consistent with the findings of McLaughlin *et al* (1989) and Dawes (1993), the results indicate that household commitments (the amount of money that people need to live on) remain the dominant influence on people's assessment of the earnings they require.

To calculate replacement rates the reservation wage rate was compared to what different types of families should receive in benefits, making assumptions about children's ages and housing costs. The replacement rate is simply calculated as follows: the replacement rate (RR) is equal to notional benefits divided by the stated reservation wage (with/without taking Family Credit into account) multiplied by 100. If the RR is more than 100%, people are saying they will work for less than their benefits. If the RR is less than 100%, people are pitching the minimum wage they will work for above their benefits.

Figure 3.6 shows that respondents with a number of dependants appear to be willing to work for wages below their notional benefit entitlement. Only single respondents with no children set their reservation wage substantially above benefit levels. People were also asked if they had taken Family Credit (the social security benefit for low-paid workers with children) into account when deciding the minimum they would work for. Nearly half (49%) said they had taken Family Credit into account (54% of women, 45% of men, 53% of Catholics and 46% of Protestants). In all cases, except for single parents with one child, the reservation wage rate was lower for those who had taken Family Credit into account than among those who had not.

Figure 3.6: West Belfast Long-Term Unemployed Survey

Replacement Rates: With/Without Family Credit

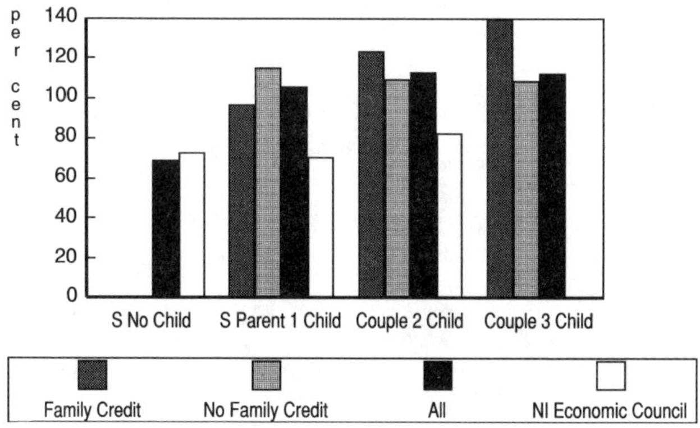

per cent
140
120
100
80
60
40
20
0
S No Child
S Parent 1 Child
Couple 2 Child
Couple 3 Child
Family Credit
No Family Credit
All
NI Economic Council

Figure 3.6 also includes a comparison with the theoretical RRs calculated by the NIEC for the respective households at their average stated reservation wage. The NIEC values show what the 'real' RRs are for households in work at their stated reservation wage, 'real' in so far as it is assumed that these households apply for and receive all the in-work benefits they are entitled too. That these values are substantially lower for the one and two child households in the West Belfast study suggests that people do not have a very precise or clear appreciation of whether they are better off working or claiming at particular wage rates because of the complexities of taxes and benefits.

Single people with no children had RRs of 69% and a mean reservation wage of £117.67. The average age of these respondents (28) was younger than the mean age of all respondents in the sample (36) and these respondents were less likely to have ever had paid work. Similar signs of apparent 'inflexibility' amongst young workers without dependants have been found in other studies (White, 1991). White suggests that these individuals may have had low previous wage rates (which often would have involved juvenile wage rates or training allowances) and were seeking pay increases when they looked for work. White also suggests that stated wage expectations often have little bearing on what people actually do: faced with a real job offer, people will often take wage 'cuts' (White, 1991; McLaughlin *et al*, 1989). This might be particularly the case with young people without dependants who can afford to adjust to real offers quickly.

From Figure 3.7 it can be seen that Catholic and Protestant men have different replacement rates. Except for single Catholic men with no children, the chart indicates that Catholic men were more likely than Protestant men to say they will work for less than their benefits (the 100% line in Figure 3.7). Catholic men were also more likely to take Family Credit into account when calculating their reservation wage. The difference in replacement rates between Catholic and Protestant men is likely to be influenced by higher previous earnings by Protestant men and therefore higher labour market expectations.

Figure 3.7: West Belfast Long-Term Unemployed Survey

Replacement Rates: Men/Religion

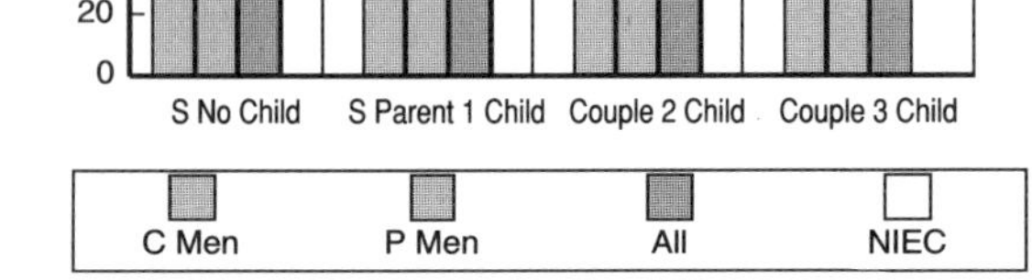

per cent
140
120
100
80
60
40
20
0
S No Child
S Parent 1 Child
Couple 2 Child
Couple 3 Child
C Men
P Men
All
NIEC

Claiming and Earning

Participation in the informal economy may reduce job search and detract from involvement in the formal economy in various ways. Research into the informal economy and 'doing the double' (working while claiming benefits as unemployed), however, suggests little or no impact on the financial and other incentives to take up paid work in the formal economy. Setting aside the problem of organised crime and 'racketeering' in West Belfast (see

Tomlinson, 1994:29-32), and not forgetting the considerable methodological difficulties of this type of work, studies carried out in Northern Ireland and elsewhere provide little support for the idea that there are rich pickings to be had from claiming benefits and earning cash on the side (Jenkins and Harding, 1988; Hakim, 1992; Leonard, 1994; Evason and Woods, 1995; Evason, 1994). Hakim argues that the linking of unemployment and the informal economy has important policy implications because it provides:

> the justification for policies which invest substantial resources in investigating possible benefit fraud ... [T]he introduction of stringent job seeking regulations for the unemployed, and the restriction of benefit levels, creates a climate of opinion in which unemployment is to be explained primarily by the attitudes and behaviour of the unemployed. [G]iven the weak evidence so far available on the size and rise of the black economy, policies addressing the issue must rest on an act of faith rather than solid fact (Hakim, 1992:145, 155).

Despite lack of evidence, the perception remains that the informal economy, especially in an area such as West Belfast, is buoyant and that the unemployed are able to readily supplement their unemployment benefit with substantial earnings. It was, therefore, important to try to obtain information on the extent to which the LTU in our sample engaged with the informal economy. The questionnaire pointed out that working and claiming is within the rules (up to a point) and asked a number of questions as to people's knowledge of the earnings rules. People were only then asked if they had managed to get any paid work in the past year and, if so, to name the amount earned.

The response rate to the question was perhaps surprisingly high. Ninety-eight percent (308 individuals) of those who completed a questionnaire answered this question. Nearly a quarter (23%) said they had worked in the informal economy in the past year (24% of Catholics and 21% of Protestants). Eight out of ten of these respondents were men and 20% were women. Those unemployed for five years or more were slightly less likely (19%) to have worked in the informal economy which may reflect poor health amongst the very LTU. Of those who had worked last year, 18% had previously worked in 'construction', 10% in 'metal work' and 8% in either 'shopkeeping' or 'catering'.

Figure 3.8 shows the percentage of Catholics and Protestants earning different amounts while unemployed. There appeared to be more scope for Protestants to earn £100 to £500 per annum than for Catholics, but strikingly similar proportions of Catholics and Protestants (about 78%) earned below the annual equivalent of the existing earnings disregard for lone parents and couples unemployed for two years on Income Support, namely £15 per week (£780 per annum). The £15 disregard remains at the same level as in 1988, but if it had been increased in line with the Retail Price Index (and benefit levels) it would be worth £21.50 (or £1118 per annum) by the first quarter of 1996 (Convery, 1996:21). Only a small proportion of those working and claiming (10%), reported earnings of more than £29 per week, while 6% had the equivalent of £39 per week or more. These were very small proportions of the total LTU - 2.3% and 1.4% respectively. It appears, therefore, that while around a quarter of the LTU received supplementary income from the informal economy, the amount of income is very small scale. It is likely that people get opportunities to earn money in the informal economy sporadically (the 'odd day's work') at quite low rates of pay.

Figure 3.8: West Belfast Long-Term Unemployed Survey

Claiming and Working: Earnings in Last Year

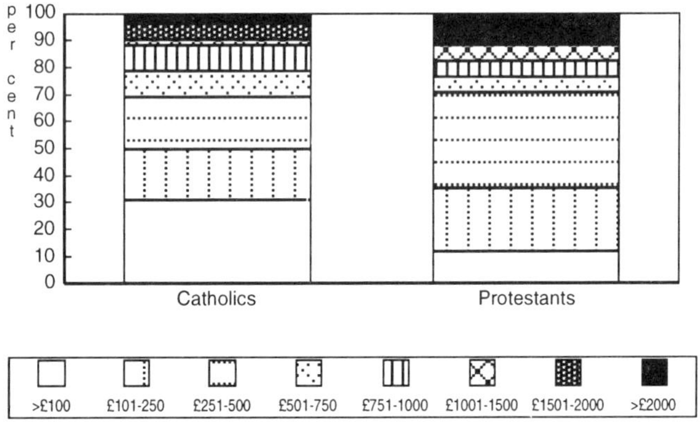

per cent
100
90
80
70
60
50
40
30
20
10
0
Catholics
Protestants

>£100 | £101-250 | £251-500 | £501-750 | £751-1000 | £1001-1500 | £1501-2000 | >£2000

While relatively few respondents in the sample worked in the informal economy, and fewer still were earning sizeable amounts of money, it is still important to assess the argument that participation in the informal economy reduces an individual's desire to secure work in the formal economy. Comparisons of search rates in fact showed that people who had worked in the informal economy had higher search rates (79%) than those who had not worked (76%). This effect was particularly significant for men.

Respondents were asked what the earnings disregard should be for people in their position, as well as how many hours they should be allowed to work without their benefit being affected. Over a quarter (27%) named £55 per week as a disregard and a further 40% gave amounts of £45 or below. About a half (48%) thought the disregard should be between £55 and £75, and nearly one half of respondents wanted to be able to work for 16-20 hours without affecting their benefits (another 25% specified 11-15 hrs or less). This implies a reservation wage of around £3.70 an hour, which is close to the mean reservation wage rate for all respondents of £3.40 an hour. There is, therefore, a very clear difference between what social security rules currently allow and what claimants themselves think would be appropriate.

CONCLUSIONS

This research project has sought to provide a better understanding of one of the most marginalised sections of the workforce in Northern Ireland. The survey of the LTU in West Belfast has demonstrated that while long-term unemployment is severe in scale and chronic in nature, the unemployed themselves remain remarkably labour market active. Catholic men were much more likely to be unemployed for five or more years than Protestant men and report more ill-health, but Protestant men suffered more depression. Just over a half of the people surveyed had been unemployed for five years or more, and for these people the average time unemployed was 13 years. Almost a quarter of all the LTU, and nearly a half of those aged 34 or less, had never had a job. Since the mid-1980s a growing majority of the unemployed in Northern Ireland as a whole have been out of work for more than a year. The polarisation of work and unemployment at the household level indicates that it is more difficult to escape from long-term unemployment than it was. These changes make unemployment a more significant indicator of labour market inequalities than it was in the past and gives support to the development of routine monitoring of long-term (and short-term) unemployment rates (by religion and gender) both at Northern Ireland and small area levels. If employees can be monitored at the level of the individual firm, then the unemployed and LTU can be monitored at a local level. Flows on and off the unemployment count also need to be better understood, and monitoring could be designed to assist this.

The survey's findings provide little comfort for those who seek to explain unemployment differences between social groupings, and unemployment *per se*, in terms of the characteristics and behaviour of the unemployed themselves. The LTU in West Belfast were searching and applying for jobs, were prepared to work for modest wages and were generally flexible in the type of work they will take. There is no evidence to support the view that the greater incidence of Catholic long-term unemployment is due to particular 'cultural' factors. On the contrary, Catholics in this study were in many respects more 'flexible', and less 'discouraged', unemployed workers than Protestants. These factors did not vary significantly by family size except that people with children wanted more security and were less likely to consider temporary, short-term jobs. Less than a quarter of people in the survey reported 'doing the double' in the past year and nearly 80% of these had earned less than the amount couples on Income Support for two years are allowed to earn without jeopardising their benefits. Protestants appeared to have better opportunities in the informal economy in terms of earnings. The

West Belfast LTU, in this study at least, were also significantly better educated than the LTU in Northern Ireland as a whole.

Substantial differences by gender and religion were recorded by the survey. Women were losing out on education, training and employment because of childcare and other caring commitments. They were much less active in job search than men for these reasons. Differences by religion tended to be highest in relation to men but both Catholic men and women were much more likely to consider taking any type of job than Protestant men and women. The higher labour market expectations of Protestants were also apparent in reservation wages. Such expectations and opportunities clearly relate to past and present structural differences between Catholics and Protestants in the overall labour market.

The survey found that twice the proportion of Protestants (men and women) than Catholics had been notified about a job by a Careers Officer, Social Security Office or Job Club. Although the numbers reporting job referrals were fairly low, there still appeared to be a religious effect of some importance which requires a response from the Social Security Agency and the T&EA.

The most important findings for fair employment policy concern the impact of intimidation and the experience of various forms of assistance with job search. Experience of intimidation was found to be widespread, with over 40% of Catholics who had had a job having experienced intimidation at some time. Intimidation is usually considered in terms of effects at the individual level. But just as informal networks and information are important in encouraging access to jobs, they can also work to discourage and deter. Experiences become part of the shared knowledge of communities about where it is, and is not, safe to work, and they shape collective perceptions of where it is possible to get jobs. The effects of intimidation, therefore, travel well beyond the individual. The survey showed that intimidation had a strong effect on where people were prepared to search for work. Both Protestant and Catholic intimidated men were much less likely to look for work outside of the West Belfast area. When they did, Catholics were far less likely than Protestants to be looking for work elsewhere in Belfast.

These spatial dimensions to job search lend added importance to considerations of job location (see Chapter Ten, this volume). In research conducted for SACHR's review of fair employment in the 1980s, Smith and Chambers (1991: 376) concluded that:

> concentrating resources in particular areas would not reduce inequality much: for example, the unemployment differential would not be much reduced by creating jobs in West Belfast.

Smith and Chambers also argued that the physical scale of Northern Ireland is very small, implying that jobs are readily accessible irrespective of location.

But this point is of limited relevance if large parts of the rest of Belfast are known as 'no go' employment areas by the LTU in West Belfast. Our findings on intimidation and job search suggest that the chances of the long-term unemployed in West Belfast being brought (back) into employment will only be substantially improved by locating work in the area and ensuring that new employment goes to the LTU. This needs to occur in addition to existing efforts to combat discrimination in recruitment and intimidation in the workplace. These conclusions are discussed in more detail in the next chapter.

ENDNOTES

1 The authors wish to thank Sharon Milner and Patrick Neeson who were employed as research assistants for this project and who responded to the time constraints with remarkable efficiency and enthusiasm. We are also grateful for the advice and support of Mary Trainor and Seamus McGuinness. The project could not have been carried out without the co-operation of DED Statistics Branch, DCI Newcastle, the SSA, the T&EA, CWA board members and CWA staff, the Falls Road DSSO, Falls and Shankill Road CABs and a number of West Belfast community groups - we are grateful to all of them.

ANNEX

The long-term unemployed postal sample was drawn from the claimant register of the unemployed in the relevant West Belfast wards at October 1995, but in order to stratify the sample, figures for July 1995 were used. Sixty-three percent of total unemployed claimants (7893) in West Belfast were LTU (in July 1995). The distribution of long-term unemployment in West Belfast at July 1995 was: 3528 Catholic men (71% of the total LTU); 894 Protestant men (18% of the total LTU); 398 Catholic women (8% of the total LTU); and 149 Protestant women (3% of the total LTU). Thus, Catholics comprised 79% of the total LTU and Protestants 21%. The claimant count is an inadequate measure of unemployment because of the underrepresentation of young people, married women, people with disabilities and 'discouraged workers' (Unemployment Unit, 1994(a); Royal Statistical Society, 1995). However, there was little alternative to the count in securing a large sample of the unemployed from a small area, especially in view of the time constraints. In the present study, additional methods were used to supplement the count-based sample (see below).

The sample was stratified by District Electoral Area (as a proxy for religion), sex and duration for men (one to less than five years, and five or more years). Questionnaires were posted to 30% of all LTU claimants in West

Belfast (selected at random from NUBS - the National Unemployment Benefit System). The claimant register at 12 October (1995) yielded a sample of 1410. Due to unforeseen difficulties with data protection issues, the posting was delayed by six weeks. Using procedures applied in previous studies on unemployment in the UK (for example, Dawes, 1993; White and Lakey, 1992), the plan was to ask the Social Security Agency to contact the sample with an introductory letter from the researchers. This letter would invite people to participate in the research, on a strictly confidential and anonymous basis, by filling in a survey which would be posted to them shortly by the researchers. The letter would ask them to object if they did not wish their name and address to be passed on to the researchers. Their 'negative consent' would be sought, that is to say they would be invited to write or phone the SSA if they did not wish their names to be passed on and to receive a questionnaire in the post. DCI Newcastle cleared this procedure with their own data protection staff but the final authority lay with the Department of Health and Social Services for NI.

The DHSS(NI) took the view that 'positive consent' was required from claimants, suggesting that a letter went out inviting potential respondents to contact the researchers to agree to participate. This procedure was rejected by the researchers on the grounds that very few people were likely to respond. Considerable delay resulted from this issue while the Data Protection Registrar at Wilmslow was asked for a ruling. The Registrar finally suggested that the SSA send out the questionnaire 'cold' as a mail shot with an explanatory covering letter on behalf of the researchers. While the researchers regarded this as rather more intrusive than the original plan, there was little choice but to follow the Registrar's suggestion.

This meant that questionnaires arrived just two weeks before Christmas. The questionnaire arrived without warning in a Social Security Agency envelope with no prior introductory letter. It was clear from feedback that many people were suspicious of the questionnaire and its assurances of confidentiality, and associated it with benefits' administration. As a result, only 98 questionnaires were obtained this way. The remaining questionnaires were obtained in a follow up exercise with the help of community groups, the Citizens' Advice Bureaux in the area and through face-to-face interviews. Many of these respondents had received a questionnaire in the post but had thrown it away. All respondents were assured that the answers given were completely confidential. No names or addresses were asked for and individual questionnaires were identified solely through a reference number.

REFERENCES

Armstrong, D. (1994) *Long-Term Unemployment in Northern Ireland: Characteristics and Causes*, Belfast: Northern Ireland Economic Research Centre.

Arulampalam, W. and Stewart, M. (1995) 'The Determinants of Individual Unemployment Durations in an Era of High Unemployment', *The Economic Journal,* 105(429): 321-332.

Atkinson, T., Gomulka, J. and Micklewright, J. (1984) 'Unemployment Benefit, Duration and Incentives in Britain: How Robust is the Evidence?', *Journal of Public Economics,* 23(3): 3-26.

Blundell, R. (1994) 'Work Incentives and Labour Supply in the UK', in Bryson, A. and McCay, S. (eds.) *Is it Worth Working? Factors Affecting Labour Supply,* London: Policy Studies Institute.

Bryson, A. (1994) 'Is it Worth Working?' in Bryson, A. and McCay, S. (eds.) *Is it Worth Working? Factors Affecting Labour Supply,* London: Policy Studies Institute.

Convery, P. (1996) 'Inflation Erodes Non-Indexed Allowances and Top-Up Payments' *Working Brief,* 74: 20-22.

Convery, P. (1995) 'Long-Term Unemployment Declines', *Working Brief,* 62: 62.

Craven, J. (1995) 'Student Grant Cutbacks Increase Hardship', *Economic Bulletin,* 3(2), Belfast: West Belfast Economic Forum.

Dawes, L. (1993) *Long-Term Unemployment and Labour Market Flexibility,* Leicester: Centre for Labour Market Studies.

Department of Economic Development (1995) *Unemployment Statistics* (claimant count), July and September.

Dilnot, A. (1992) 'Social Security and the Labour Market', in McLaughlin, E. (ed.) *Understanding Unemployment: New Perspectives on Active Labour Market Policies,* London: Routledge.

Donaldson, P. (1985) *A Question of Economics,* Harmondsworth: Penguin.

Evason, E. (1994) 'Deregulation and 'Doing the Double'', Minutes of Evidence taken before the Social Security Committee, HOC, Monday, 7 March.

Evason, E. (1985) *On the Edge: A Study of Poverty and Long-Term Unemployment in Northern Ireland,* London: Child Poverty Action Group.

Evason, E. and Woods, R. (1995) *Poverty, Charity and 'Doing the Double',* Aldershot: Avebury.

Finn, D. (1995(a)) 'The Jobseeker's Allowance', *Capital and Class,* 57: 7-11.

Finn, D. (1995(b)) 'Jobseeker's Allowance: The Case Against Compulsion', *Working Brief,* 62: 12-14.

Finn, D. (1995(c)) 'Jobseeker's Allowance and the 16 Hour Rule', *Working Brief,* 66: 8-15.

Fryer, D. (1992) 'Psychological or Material Deprivation: Why Does Unemployment Have Mental Health Consequences?', in McLaughlin, E. (ed.) *Understanding Unemployment: New Perspectives on Active Labour Market Policies*, London: Routledge.

Gallagher, A. (1991) 'Employment, Unemployment and Religion on Northern Ireland', *The Majority Minority Review*, 2, Coleraine: Centre for the Study of Conflict, University of Ulster.

Gallagher, A., Osborne, R. and Cormack, R. (1994) *Fair Shares? Employment, Unemployment and Economic Status*, Belfast: Fair Employment Commission.

Gregg, P. and Wadsworth, J. (1995) *More Work in Fewer Households?*, Discussion Paper No. 72, London: National Institute of Economic and Social Research.

Gudgin, G. and Breen, R. (1996) *Evaluation of the Ratio of Unemployment Rates as an Indicator of Fair Employment*, Belfast: Central Community Relations Unit.

Hakim, C. (1992) 'Unemployment, Marginal Work and the Black Economy', in McLaughlin, E. (ed.) *Understanding Unemployment: New Perspectives on Active Labour Market Policies*, London: Routledge.

House of Commons Employment Committee (1996) *The Right to Work/Workfare*, HC82, 1995-96, London: HMSO.

Howe, L. (1990) *Being Unemployed in Northern Ireland: An Ethnographic Study*, Cambridge: Cambridge University Press.

Hughes, G. and McCormick, B. (1990) 'Measuring Unemployment and Cyclical Participation in the British Labour Market', *Scandinavian Journal of Economics*, 92:247-292.

Jenkins, R. and Harding, P. (1988) *Informal Economic Activity in Northern Ireland: A Review of the Literature*, PPRU Occasional Paper, No. 15, Belfast: Department of Finance and Personnel.

Leonard, M. (1994) *Informal Economic Activity in Belfast*, Aldershot: Avebury

MacLagan, I. and Convery, P. (1995) 'School-Leavers: Change Slows, Unemployment Remains High', *Working Brief*, 66: 22-23.

McLaughlin, E. (1994(a)) 'Employment, Unemployment and Social Security', in Glyn, A. and Miliband, D. (eds.) *Paying for Inequality: The Economic Cost of Social Injustice*, London: Rivers Oram Press.

McLaughlin, E. (1994(b)) *Flexibility in Work and Benefits*, London: Institute for Public Policy Research.

McLaughlin, E. (1992) 'Towards Active Labour Market Policies: An Overview', in McLaughlin, E. (ed.) *Understanding Unemployment: New Perspectives on Active Labour Market Policies*, London: Routledge.

McLaughlin, E. (1991) 'Work and Welfare Benefits: social security, employment and unemployment in the 1990s', *Journal of Social Policy*, 20(4): 485-508.

McLaughlin, E., Millar J. and Cooke, K. (1989) *Work and Welfare Benefits*, Aldershot: Avebury.

Minford, P. (1985) *Unemployment, Cause and Cure*, 2nd edition, Oxford: Blackwell.

Murphy, A. and Armstrong, D. (1994) *A Picture of the Catholic and Protestant Unemployed*, Belfast: Central Community Relations Unit.

Nickell, S. (1979) 'Education and Lifetime Patterns of Unemployment', *Journal of Political Economy*, 87:117-32.

Northern Ireland Economic Council (1996) *The 1995 UK Budget: Background and Implications for Northern Ireland*, Report 118, Belfast: The Northern Ireland Economic Council.

Northern Ireland Economic Council (1995(a)) *Taxes, Benefits, Unemployment and Poverty Traps in Northern Ireland*, Report 117, Belfast: The Northern Ireland Economic Council.

Northern Ireland Economic Council (1995(b)) *Demographic Review Northern Ireland 1995*, Research Monograph 1, Belfast: The Northern Ireland Economic Council.

Northern Ireland Economic Council (1994) *Autumn Economic Review*, Report 113, Belfast: Northern Ireland Economic Council.

Policy Planning Research Unit, *Labour Force Survey Religion Report 1992*, Belfast: PPRU.

Policy Planning Research Unit, *Labour Force Survey Religion Report 1993*, Belfast: PPRU.

Policy Planning Research Unit, *Labour Force Survey Religion Report 1994*, Belfast: PPRU.

Rolston, B. and Tomlinson, M. (1988) *The Obair Report: Unemployment in West Belfast.* Belfast: Beyond the Pale Publications.

Royal Statistical Society (1995), 'The Measurement of Unemployment in the UK', *Journal of the Royal Statistical Society*, Series A, 158(3).

Smith, D. and Chambers, G. (1991) *Inequality in Northern Ireland*, Oxford: Clarendon Press.

Smith, L. and McLaughlin, E. (1989) *The Labour Market Flexibility of the Long-Term Unemployed*, Sheffield: The Employment Service.

Social Security Advisory Committee (1994) *In Work - Out of Work: the Role of Incentives and Disincentives in the Benefits System*, Review of Social Security, Paper 3, London: Social Security Advisory Committee.

Stone, D. (1985) *The Disabled State*, London: Macmillan.

Tomlinson, M. (1995) 'Unemployment Count Falls Again', *Economic Bulletin*, 3(2), Belfast: West Belfast Economic Forum.

Tomlinson, M. (1994) *25 Years On: The Costs of War and the Dividends of Peace*, Belfast: West Belfast Economic Forum.

Townsend, P. and Davidson, N. (1992) 'The Black Report', in Townsend, P. and Davidson, N. (eds.) *Inequality in Health*, London: Penguin.

Trew, L. and Kilpatrick, R. (1984) *The Daily Life of the Unemployed*, Belfast: Queen's University of Belfast.

Unemployment Unit (1996) 'Memorandum submitted by the Unemployment Unit,' in Employment Committee (1996) *The Right to Work/Workfare*, HC82, 1995-96: 12-27, London: HMSO.

Unemployment Unit (1994(a)) *Workfare in Britain*, London: Unemployment Unit.

Unemployment Unit (1994(b)) *Creative Counting*, London: Unemployment Unit.

White, M. (ed.) (1994(a)) *Unemployment and Public Policy in a Changing Labour Market*, London: Policy Studies Institute.

White, M. (1993) *Long-Term Unemployment and Labour Markets*, London: Policy Studies Institute.

White, M. (1991) *Against Unemployment*, London: Policy Studies Institute.

White, M. and Lakey, J. (1992) *The Restart Effect: evaluation of a labour market programme for unemployed people*, London: Policy Studies Institute.

Wilkinson, R. (1994) 'Health, Redistribution and Growth' in Glyn, A. and Miliband, D. (eds.) *Paying for Inequality: The Economic Cost of Social Injustice*, London: Rivers Oram Press.

Chapter Four

LONG-TERM UNEMPLOYMENT AND THE COMMUNITY WORK PROGRAMME

Maura Sheehan and Mike Tomlinson[1]

INTRODUCTION

For nearly two decades, government responses to unemployment have centred on the supply side of the labour market. Issues around motivating the unemployed and the skill levels of unemployed individuals have been the primary focus of policies. The findings from the survey of the long-term unemployed (LTU hereafter) in West Belfast presented in Chapter Three of this volume suggested that the majority of the LTU are neither lacking in job search nor rigid or inflexible in terms of their wage and occupational expectations. Opportunities to earn large sums of money in the informal economy were scarce and did not reduce individuals' interest in searching for work in the formal economy. These results clearly challenge the relevance of policies and programmes targeted at remotivating the unemployed.

This chapter turns to the other main component of government policy towards unemployment - training and employment schemes. Findings are presented on the extent of scheme participation and attitudes towards training schemes. Particular emphasis is given to the government's latest response to unemployment in Northern Ireland, the Community Work Programme (CWP), currently being piloted in Belfast, Strabane and Fermanagh.

The most neglected area of labour market policy, labour demand, is also examined. Findings from interviews with human resources/personnel managers of major employers in the West Belfast area are presented. The interviewees were asked detailed questions about their recruitment practices, their attitudes to, and experiences of, hiring the LTU, their assessment of the usefulness of the government's training and employment schemes and their attitudes towards different types of policy interventions such as national insurance 'tax holidays', a minimum wage and local labour clauses. The chapter concludes with a discussion of policy proposals targeted at reducing long-term unemployment.

RESEARCH METHODS

The research reported here involved three elements:

(i) a postal questionnaire of the LTU in the West Belfast CWP pilot area. Details on the characteristics of the sample and findings on issues of motivation and flexibility were reported in Chapter Three. Findings on experiences with, and attitudes towards, training and employment schemes and, in particular, attitudes towards the CWP are reported below. These results should obviously not be read as a statement of what all scheme participants think of training and other special employment measures because the sample only contains the LTU who, despite having been on a scheme, have not secured employment;

(ii) interviews with those involved in devising and implementing the CWP, including staff and board members of City West Action (the company delivering the programme on the ground), some participants and providers of CWP placements (organisations contracted by City West Action); and

(iii) interviews with human resource/personnel managers of 14 major employers in the West Belfast area. Focus was given to employers' recruitment procedures, attitudes and barriers to hiring the LTU and employers' assessment and views on the Training and Employment Agency's (T&EA) training and employment programmes. Employers were also asked about a number of policy proposals to provide incentives to employers for hiring the LTU.

TRAINING AND EMPLOYMENT SCHEMES AND THE COMMUNITY WORK PROGRAMME

Chapter Three, this volume, presented an overview of government policies towards the long-term unemployed. It was argued that alongside the withdrawal of the 'right to be unemployed', the second facet of government policy on unemployment in the 1980s and 1990s involved training, retraining and work experience programmes for the unemployed and young people. Following OECD classifications, these programmes can be placed into two broad categories: training measures and direct employment schemes. In Britain, training measures included the Youth Training Scheme, Employment Training and Employment Action which were amalgamated into the Training for Work Programme in 1993. Training schemes in Northern Ireland included Adults in Training, Youth Training Programme (YTP) and Job Training Programme (JTP) which were amalgamated into the Jobskills Programme in 1995. The direct employment schemes which provide employment primarily in the 'social sector' of the economy included the Community Programme in Britain, and Action for Community Employment (ACE) and Enterprise Ulster (EU) in Northern Ireland. While the nature of training and employment schemes was broadly similar in Northern Ireland and Britain, there has been a much higher concentration in Northern Ireland on direct employment schemes, especially the ACE scheme (Scott, 1993).

As a result of European Union social policies, such training and employment schemes are now subject to considerable debate over targets, outcomes, delivery and impact on equal opportunities. It has been argued, for example, that policies and provision on training and retraining have lagged behind need (White and Lakey, 1992; White, 1991; Jackman, 1992). In particular, the percentage of 'unskilled' and low-skilled workers receiving training is the lowest of all groups (McLaughlin, 1992). Since 'unskilled' and low-skilled workers are the most likely to be long term unemployed, present policy initiatives do not seem to target those most in need of training and retraining. Indeed, Green (1994:78) concludes that:

> contrary to the ideology that an education and training revolution has opened up wide avenues of opportunity for the acquisition of skills in Britain, [...] access to training remains very unequally distributed.

In addition, the evidence about the employment effects and the quality of skills obtained from various schemes in Britain indicate that the gains have been moderate (Marsden and Ryan, 1991; White, 1994).

Training and Work Experience Provisions in Northern Ireland

Training and employment schemes have been particularly important in Northern Ireland because of the very high rate of long-term unemployment. As of February 1996, there were around 12,500 young people on the Jobskills scheme, and a further 17,000 on other employment or training schemes under the auspices of the T&EA. Just over half of the latter are participating in the ACE scheme, which had, until recently, been the centrepiece of the government's response to long-term unemployment in Northern Ireland. Similar to the Community Programme long since axed in Britain (1988), the ACE scheme has become an important feature of community-based, voluntary sector activity in areas of high unemployment. About 1500 ACE workers are involved in over 20 ACE projects in West Belfast. On some schemes, they are supporting essential and innovative services, albeit 'on the cheap', including nursery schools, youth-parent support, women's centres and transport and other services for people with disabilities.

Little over a third of ACE participants move into 'employment, training or education' within three months of finishing the scheme. Some insight into why this figure is not higher can be found in a survey of employers which found that 40% of firms surveyed would not normally consider interviewing those who had been on the ACE scheme for any vacancy which arose (NISB/NIERC, 1994). Other government schemes (such as the YTP and the JTP) also fared badly. Even though these schemes were beneficial to employers, only one in five of those surveyed used the schemes. These findings were broadly consistent with the findings from employers in West Belfast reported later in this chapter.

A top level (unpublished) internal review of the ACE scheme was carried out in 1993, with a view to informing the development of alternative schemes such as CWP. According to T&EA officials, the review showed that the scheme was attractive to women 'returnees' to the labour market (about one fifth of participants) and young people, but not to male heads of households with children. The suggestion was that the latter were 'benefit-trapped' out of ACE - the scheme did not provide wages above their existing benefit levels. It is unclear whether the review of ACE examined the issue of in-work benefits. However, if people claim all the in-work benefits they are entitled to, no-one should be better off out of work since the alignment of means tests (for Income Support, Housing Benefit and Family Credit) under the 1986 Social Security Act (see NIEC, 1995; McLaughlin, 1994(a), 1994(b)).

Whatever the accuracy of the 1993 review of ACE, the CWP was devised with two principal objectives: to reach the 'missing' target group identified in the ACE review and to test a new mode of delivery. The CWP is unique in that participants can stay on the scheme for up to three years, a recognition of the fact that one-year schemes, such as ACE, can be de-motivating and re/entry to paid work can take a long time.

To participate in the CWP, individuals must be aged 25 to 60 years and have been unemployed continuously for 12 months or more, or aged 18-24 years and have been unemployed continuously for 12 months or more and have a high level qualification (for example, degree, HND), a recognised vocational qualification or have completed a T&EA training programme (for example, ACE, YTP, JTP).

All of the participant's benefits are safeguarded for the duration of the Programme and a basic premium, formally called a 'training allowance,' of £20 per week is paid. Additional allowances or 'training premiums' may also be paid depending on skill and the level of responsibility associated with the post, as shown in Table 4.1.

Table 4.1: Additional Allowances of CWP Participants, 1995/96

		Additional Allowance per week £	Total per week £	
(i)	skills allowance	5	25	
(ii)	supervisory allowance*	1	35	(includes £5 skills all.)
(iii)	managerial allowance*	30	55	(includes £5 skills all.)

*(ii) and (iii) are mutually exclusive.

The CWP is based on the assumption that there are motivational and skills problems amongst the LTU, and therefore represents a combination of the government's two primary active labour market policies. The design of the CWP also implies that the LTU need to acclimatise to work in a way that is risk-free in terms of benefit status. Although ostensibly the CWP is a work scheme (rather than a job), and participants retain their benefits as if unemployed, they are neither 'workers' nor 'unemployed'. According to the T&EA, participants' legal status is that of trainees. Indeed, the design of the scheme recognises that assistance with job search and training can be useful to the LTU. CWP participants are therefore offered a once-off bonus for participating on job search courses and can earn bonuses for obtaining NVQ qualifications (Level 2 or above).

The CWP has had a high political profile. It was given a clear political 'spin' when the Prime Minister chose to launch it at the special post-ceasefires International Investment Forum held in Belfast's Europa Hotel in December 1994. He announced that the DED was to begin implementing CWP by initially providing places for 1000 LTU in three areas: Strabane, Fermanagh and the largest (500 places), West Belfast. The Prime Minister stated that if the pilot was successful, the CWP might be extended to 20,000 places, more than double the size of ACE. The Programme was widely regarded as significant given the potential number of participants, and was unique because none of the existing employment and training measures provide placements of a three year duration, nor a range of benefit premiums differentiated by skill level.

The political profiles of both ACE and CWP remain high for two reasons. The sudden 25% cut in ACE funding announced in December 1995 (and vigorously campaigned against since) involves an estimated loss of 380 ACE jobs in West Belfast (O'Broin, 1996). Secondly, given the initial linking of CWP to post-ceasefires investment, the end of the IRA ceasefire has already cast doubts over CWP. In February 1996, the Economy Minister warned that cuts of up to 50% could be made to CWP in order to finance any required increases in security expenditure (Irish News, 1996).

Despite government statements to the contrary, in the minds of some scheme providers, there is a policy relationship between the 'down-sizing' of ACE and the new CWP. Unlike ACE, however, the CWP allows for the closer integration of Social Security-based work search and discipline measures with work skills. It is this closer integration of the two types (and sites) of labour market policies which was heralded by the Jobseeker's Act.

Given the potential number of CWP placements and its unique delivery mechanism, it is important to investigate the relevance of the CWP as a response to long-term unemployment in any review of employment equality.

EXPERIENCE OF EMPLOYMENT AND TRAINING SCHEMES

This section reports on the extent of scheme participation and attitudes towards schemes amongst the LTU in West Belfast, since these are likely to influence views about a CWP-type scheme. Four in ten people reported they had been on a training or employment scheme (42% of Catholic and Protestant men; 32% of Catholic women; and 52% of Protestant women). Thus, Catholic women were the least likely to have experienced a scheme (68% had never been on a scheme) while Protestant women were the most likely to have been on a scheme. Just over half (52%) of individuals had been on more than one scheme. These were mostly younger respondents who had been through YTP and then proceeded onto ACE or the Job Training Programme (now replaced by the Jobskills scheme). Interestingly, given the target group of the CWP, it was found that nearly two-thirds (64%) of men with four or more children had been on a scheme prior to the CWP (although the number of these respondents is small - 14). These individuals were most likely to have been on Adults in Training and Enterprise Ulster schemes.

The main reasons why people had taken up a place on a training or employment scheme were: 'to improve chances of getting a job' (65%), 'interested in the skills involved' (23%) and 'could make more money on the programme than on benefits alone' (22%). The latter answer was most common amongst young single respondents. These responses imply that when first going on a scheme people genuinely believed that it would increase their chances of getting work and help them to acquire new skills.

Three-quarters of those who had been on schemes completed them. Catholic men had the highest completion rate (80%) and Protestant men the lowest (66%). Interesting religious and gender differences emerged in the reasons why a minority had left a scheme before completion. Half of Protestant men who had left a scheme did so to take up a job, compared to only 7% of Catholic men, 25% of Catholic women and no Protestant women. An examination of work histories suggests that the jobs which people left a scheme for were of a very short duration (some lasted just a couple of weeks) and most averaged between four to six months. The most common reasons for Catholic and Protestant women leaving a scheme were 'childcare' and 'other personal or family reasons'. Both Catholic and Protestant men also answered that they left schemes because of childcare problems although this was to a much lesser extent than women. The most common reasons for Catholic men leaving a scheme were that 'wages/allowances were too low' or for 'transport problems'.

People's evaluation of how useful the scheme had been to them did not match their aspirations on entering the scheme. Nearly half (47%) felt that the scheme had 'no effect' on their chances of employment, 4% that it had 'decreased chances of employment' and 11% that they 'did not know'. Only

15% felt that the scheme 'greatly increased chances of employment' and 23% that it 'slightly increased chances of employment'. Catholic men were most likely to respond that the scheme had 'no effect' (51%) or had 'decreased chances of employment' (7%). Protestant men were most likely to respond that the scheme had 'greatly' (27%) or 'slightly' (23%) increased their chances of employment.

People were asked what they thought of the pay or training allowances which they received for participating on schemes. Only 3% felt that the pay or allowances were 'too high', 28% felt that they were 'about right'; but the majority of respondents (69%) felt that the pay or allowances were too low (73% of Catholic men and 59% of Protestant men).

Thus, there has been a relatively high rate of participation on training and employment schemes amongst the LTU in West Belfast but participants' evaluation of the effect of schemes on employment prospects was not very favourable. There also appears to be a high degree of resistance to further schemes amongst all respondents. When people were asked what they thought should be done to reduce unemployment in their area, nearly a third (30%) said 'no more schemes' and over a half (55%) said 'more real jobs.'

Attitudes Towards a Benefits-Plus Scheme

Since the CWP involves 'benefits-plus' rather than a wage, people were asked about the attractiveness of a scheme on which they worked full-time, kept all their present benefits and got at least £20 a week on top. Nearly half (45%) reported that they would be interested in such a scheme (Figure 4.1). Women (53%) were more likely to be interested in such a scheme than men (43%). Catholic men were least likely to be attracted to such a scheme (only 39%). Turning to the attractiveness of the CWP to its target group, 43% of men with one to three children were interested in such a scheme and this dropped only slightly to 41% of men with four or more children. Both men and women with no children were more likely to be interested in a CWP-type scheme.

People were also asked, if offered a place on a benefits-plus scheme, what the 'plus' would need to be for them to seriously consider going on the scheme. The average premium specified was £54 (Figure 4.2). Women specified lower average premiums (£49.06) than men (£57.12), consistent with the finding (reported in Chapter Three, this volume) that women have lower average reservation wage rates than men. Again, Catholic men showed the greatest resistance to the scheme by specifying the highest premium (£60). These premiums are substantially higher than those available under the current CWP.

Figure 4.1: West Belfast Long-Term Unemployed Survey

Interested in Benefit-Plus Scheme

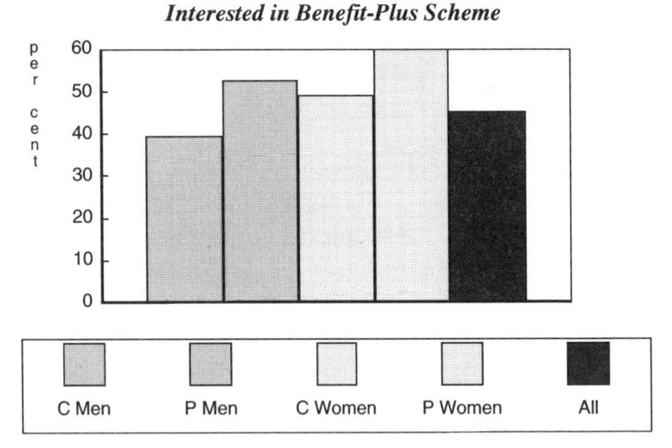

Figure 4.2: West Belfast Long-Term Unemployed Survey

Benefit-Plus Scheme: Level of Weekly Addition

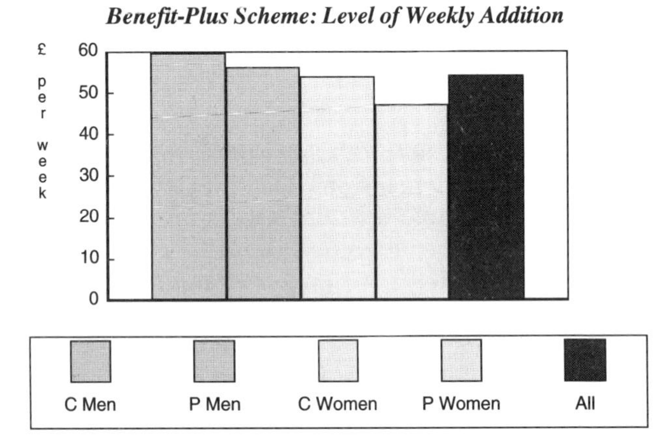

WEST BELFAST EMPLOYERS

Given the influence exerted on the labour market by employers through various employment practices and, in particular, the recruitment process, it was important that the research included a survey of employers. As noted by Maguire (1992:80), employers:

> effectively act as gatekeepers to the labour market. They are able to structure the entry to work and to constrain movement within the labour market by virtue of their control over the recruitment process.

Employers' attitudes and behaviour towards the long-term unemployed and their views on training and employment schemes have received considerably less attention than those of the LTU, yet '..the importance of employers' role in the labour market means that unemployment is also a problem of employers' attitudes and behaviour' (*ibid*). Maguire argued that, in the absence of measures to influence employers' attitudes and behaviour, governmental policy of supply-side intervention is 'not only misguided but neglectful'.

In terms of employer attitudes to, and hence the recruitment prospects of, the LTU, findings from previous research are not encouraging (see Dawes, 1993; Maguire, 1992; Meager and Metcalf, 1987). Maguire (1992:100) found that there has been little movement in employers' traditional ideas of suitability and suggested that, 'if employers' attitudes and stereotyping are key factors which work to the disadvantage of certain groups of jobseekers, then some means of effecting a change in employer behaviour needs to be sought'. Dawes (1993:12) concluded that:

> recruitment practices of employers appear to present major difficulties for the LTU because recruiters are highly risk averse in their approach to potential employees. They put a premium on characteristics which are difficult for the long-term unemployed to exhibit.

It is useful to consider briefly the reasons why the LTU may not be recruited. Risks attached to recruitment from the employer's point of view arise from a lack of information about the applicant's true productivity. The employer tries to gain as much information about the applicant as possible before deciding whether to hire the person. The main sources of information come from the applicant's Curriculum Vitae and information revealed during a job interview. Information is also obtained through formal and informal (word of mouth) references from past employers. 'Unemployment' is itself a piece of information and research has found that it weighs heavily in an employer's hiring decisions (Crowley-Bainton, 1987; White, 1991). It has been found that employers believe that being long-term unemployed is negatively correlated with applicants' likely performance or general suitability for the job. In particular, employers often believe that the LTU lack motivation, a good 'work ethic' or lack the ability to do the job through either lack of practice or lack of ability (Meager and Metcalf, 1987). The LTU may therefore not be recruited by virtue of being long-term unemployed.

In addition, studies of employers' recruitment preferences have found that the more objective characteristics which were regarded as important included a steady work history, experience in a similar job and references from past employers, all of which pose difficulties for the LTU. Other characteristics were far more subjective and involved assessing the 'attitude' of the applicant. These 'attitudinal' characteristics required applicants to display self-confidence, active enthusiasm but not desperation, a smart appearance and domestic stability. Again, all of these may be difficult for the LTU to display.

Survey of Employers in West Belfast

If there has been limited research generally on employers' attitudes and behaviour towards the LTU, there has been none in Northern Ireland. Given the constraints of this study, research was limited to employers in the West Belfast area. The research concentrated on the larger employers in the area. Of the 14 employers surveyed, six were locally-owned, five were multinationals, two were GB-owned and one was publicly-owned. Four companies were in the service sector and the remaining in manufacturing. Approximately two-thirds of the companies employed between 30 and 150 people and the remaining one-third employed over 150 people. Confidentiality prevents a more detailed description of the employers involved. Two methods were used in the study of employers. Once an employer agreed to participate, a questionnaire which asked for basic data on employment and recruitment levels (number and type of current employees, expected recruitment, etc.) and personnel policies was sent and each employer was subsequently interviewed about more qualitative and sensitive issues. Only one employer declined to participate in the study.

Recruitment Practices

All employers studied appeared to have highly professional recruitment procedures and were very knowledgeable and interested in fair employment issues, and only one employer complained about additional paper work generated by the legislation. Recruitment procedures had changed in all of the firms in response to the 1989 Fair Employment Act.

There were very similar methods of recruitment across firms and across employee categories (for example, managerial, technical, semi-skilled, etc.). All employers reported that they placed advertisements in newspapers for each category of employee (though not for every employee) recruited. Private employment agencies and backfiles were used only for managerial /professional workers and for some clerical office staff/sales personnel. Job Clubs and T&EA pre-employment programmes (discussed below) were used to recruit semi- and unskilled manual workers and some skilled manual workers. None of the employers reported that they used word of mouth, personal contacts or unsolicited applications.

When asked about the drawbacks of various recruitment methods, several employers commented that while newspaper advertisements assured a very high number of applications several dozen of these would be 'token' applications - that is, applications whose sole intent was to demonstrate that the person was 'actively seeking work'. Employers complained that it was often difficult and very time consuming to 'spot' these applications. Such applications also contributed to the problem of people not turning up to interviews. Employers were concerned that the Jobseeker's Act would exacerbate this situation.

In the recruitment of skilled, semi-skilled and 'unskilled' manual workers (as discussed below, almost all of the LTU who were recruited were in these categories), employers identified as very important, 'experience' and a 'stable employment record'. They identified as important, 'personal characteristics/qualities', 'skills', 'references', 'qualifications' and a 'history of previous unemployment'. None of the employers identified 'age', 'gender' or 'personal recommendations' as important in the recruitment decision. The importance of the applicant conveying motivation and the 'right attitude' during an interview was emphasised. Several employers commented that the unemployed, especially the LTU, 'don't really have a lot to talk about' during interviews and that it was often 'difficult to keep a conversation flowing'.

Given the high number of ex-prisoners in West Belfast, employers were asked about their attitude towards the hiring of ex-prisoners and, in particular, those charged with politically motivated offences. Responses varied considerably. Approximately half of the employers said that they would definitely not hire ex-prisoners. A few of these employers noted that the firm had been adversely affected by the political conflict (for example, lorries hijacked or employees shot at). Others said that their employees would not want to work with ex-prisoners who might create tension and conflict on the shop floor. One employer currently employing ex-prisoners reported no problems. The remaining employers said it would 'depend what the person did and how long ago he did it'. These employers also commented that ex-prisoners probably would not have sufficient work experience. Several employers were unsure what the fair employment implications were of not hiring someone because they were an ex-prisoner and said they needed guidance on the issue from the Fair Employment Commission.

Attitudes to the Long-Term Unemployed

Nine of the employers had recently recruited long-term unemployed people. The responses varied considerably by sector and industry and the age of the firm. These firms included all of the employers in the service sector and most of the 'newer' firms, including three of the five multinationals. The types of jobs for which the LTU were recruited were sales, skilled manual and semi- and unskilled manual. In the manufacturing sector, a high percentage of the LTU were recruited for temporary jobs. Two employers responded that they 'didn't know' if they had hired any LTU recently. These results suggest that despite the barriers which exist for the LTU (reported below), they had access to at least some of the vacancies in more than half of the surveyed firms.

All of the employers said that the length of time an individual had been unemployed affected their attitude towards hiring the person. The explanations fell into two broad categories: 'motivational' and 'ability'. Many employers felt that a lengthy period of unemployment indicated a lack of motivation and, as a result, said they were 'suspicious' of someone who had been unemployed for a long time. A common comment was, 'what have they been up to all that time?'. Interestingly, these suspicions were lessened if the applicant revealed that they had worked in the informal economy which employers regarded as demonstrating 'motivation' and 'initiative'. Other employers said that long-term unemployment indicated that the applicant must have some undesirable characteristic which they had not discovered but other employers had. This view was summed up by one employer who commented:

> If someone has been unemployed for, say, less than six months, that is OK, it may be just bad luck. But if he has been unemployed for a year or more, there must be something wrong with him. He must not be up to doing the work. No one else has taken him, right? There must be something wrong.

Six of the nine employers who had recently recruited long-term unemployed people said that there was 'really no difference' between the LTU and other workers in terms of work performance. They commented that there were often 'settling in' problems, related primarily to timekeeping, amongst most new workers and, in general, the LTU were no different from other new workers in this respect. Three of these employers considered the LTU recruits, especially men with children, to be their best and most loyal workers because they were 'very grateful to have a job'.

The three employers who found differences in performance between the LTU and other workers identified poor timekeeping (especially amongst shift workers) and high rates of absenteeism as the most significant problems. Two of these employers operated a warning system where workers were given three warnings about poor performance before being sacked. In most cases the warnings resolved these problems. One employer commented:

> Maybe they just didn't know what was expected of them if they hadn't worked for a long time and that is why the warnings work for most.

Increasing the Recruitment of the LTU

Employers were asked what might encourage them to recruit more LTU. The most important factor identified was a 'growth in the volume of sales'. Approximately half of employers said an improvement in the job applications, skills, presentation, motivation and attitudes of the LTU would encourage them to recruit more LTU. This response appears to reflect common stereotypes of the LTU rather than their actual characteristics, because most employers contradicted themselves in a subsequent question when they said that there was little difference between the LTU and other applicants in terms of the quality of applications, skills and presentation.

Other factors identified as important were 'evidence that unemployed applicants had recently received some training or work experience through a government-sponsored scheme' and 'changes in the organisation of work in the business (that is, greater emphasis on temporary or casual employment)'. Few employers felt that a shift towards more jobs requiring low skills would increase recruitment of the LTU. Three out of four employers said that a greater willingness on the part of the LTU to work for lower wages (that is a reduction in reservation wage rate) would not encourage them to recruit more LTU. Only one employer said that a reduction in National Insurance contributions for companies that recruit people who have been unemployed for two years or more (as proposed in the Jobseeker's Act) would encourage the company to take on such people. Interestingly, a high proportion of employers were concerned about the fair employment implications of the policy. Only one employer (service sector) was opposed to the introduction of a national (or European) minimum wage set at around £4.00 per hour. All of the other employers stated that it would have 'little or no effect' because they already paid wage rates above or around that rate. Most of the employers surveyed, therefore, paid wage rates above the mean hourly reservation wage rate of £3.40 of the LTU in our sample (see Chapter Three).

Employers were asked whether they could fulfil conditions such as having to hire a certain percentage of their workforce (for example, 10%) either from the local labour market and/or from the long-term unemployed, if these were introduced in public grants (for example, from the IDB and T&EA). All of the employers studied said that they probably could, not least because the majority already exceeded such a local labour condition, and several thought that they also exceeded such a long-term unemployed requirement. Their attitudes towards such conditions varied, however. Employers were again concerned with the fair employment implications of the conditions. Several employers noted that grants were already conditional upon fulfilling many requirements and that a few more conditions 'wouldn't make a difference'. Interestingly, American-owned companies noted that these types of conditions were quite common and probably more rigorous in the US. For example, companies which receive government contracts in the US are often required to purchase a proportion of their inputs from firms owned by ethnic minorities or 'community' businesses.

Employers were asked to assess the help which the government provides for the LTU in terms of job search skills and training and employment schemes, and whether enough is being done to help the LTU. Many said more help should be given to the LTU with filling in applications and CVs and improving their motivation. However, when asked if there were marked differences in the quality of CVs and job applications between the LTU and others, most said this was not the case. The majority, however, reported that the LTU often lacked confidence in interviews. Several suggested that job search courses should encourage the LTU to highlight skills that they have acquired outside the workplace (for example, family budgeting, childminding, car repair, etc.) and other activities (for example, voluntary work) that they have been involved in while unemployed. It was felt this would help the LTU to have more complete application forms and would be particularly important for women returnees who often underestimated the skills which they had.

In general, employers did not believe that training and employment schemes were helpful either in terms of increasing participants' chances of being hired or in improving skills. Indeed, a few employers said that they would not consider hiring anyone who had been on either the Job Training Programme or the Youth Training Programme. Participation on these schemes was taken as a 'negative' signal about the applicant by these employers. Many employers felt that the quality and relevance of the skills acquired were minimal. One important exception cited by employers was a customised training service run by the T&EA which is available to multinationals. Employers noted that since the skills learned on the programme were customised, they were directly relevant and of a high quality. In addition, several employers said that it gave them the opportunity to hire unemployed people with confidence. This is because participants on the schemes (referred to as 'pre-employment' programmes) are unemployed. Participants who complete such a pre-employment programme are guaranteed an interview with the firm. It appears, therefore, that this employer-linked training benefits both the firm and the unemployed (see also Chapter Two, this volume, for a similar finding).

PROSPECTS FOR THE CWP

There has been a relatively high rate of participation in training and employment schemes amongst the LTU in West Belfast. Forty-one percent of respondents said they had been on a training or employment scheme. Over half (52%) of these had been on more than one scheme. In general, people did not believe that participating on a scheme increased their chances of employment greatly. Over 70% of respondents felt that the training allowance which they received for participating on schemes was too low.

There also appeared to be a high degree of 'scheme-resistance' amongst respondents. Catholic men, who had the highest rate of participation on previous schemes, were the most 'scheme-weary' and would find a CWP-type scheme less attractive compared to other respondents. The premium needed to attract them on to the scheme was higher than that suggested by Protestant men. Further evidence for such scheme-resistance was found in responses to an open-ended question which asked people what they felt should be done to reduce unemployment in their area. The most common answers were 'more real jobs' (55%) and 'no more schemes' (30%). The two responses were often given together.

Medium to large employers in the West Belfast area were found to have professional recruitment procedures. The employers were genuinely interested in issues of fair employment, including the fair employment implications of various labour market policies. But their attitudes to the LTU were often contradictory. The LTU tended to be dismissed in stereotypical fashion, yet personnel managers were broadly sympathetic to the plight of the unemployed. One of the most important findings was that no employer objected to being required to recruit the unemployed as a condition of government assistance.

The findings on training and employment schemes do not augur well for the CWP. In general, the LTU do not want more schemes, they want proper jobs. Furthermore, the CWP is operating in the context of ACE cuts, a high political profile linked to the 'peace process' and an increase in compulsion heralded by the Jobseeker's Act. Some potential participants have been deterred from going on the scheme by the prospect of changes in the way they receive their benefit (or 'training allowance'). On both the Falls and Shankill there were rumours (verified in two cases) that some CWP participants had had their benefit entitlement and continuity questioned. This suggests a lack of pre-planning and co-ordination between the T&EA and the Social Security Agency.

Some of those involved with the CWP (City West Action Board members, providers and participants) complained about the lack of consideration given to childcare issues for participants. The scheme seems to assume that because men with children are the target, childcare provision is unnecessary. Although women were much more likely to cite lack of childcare as a reason for not participating in education and training, childcare was also an issue for many of the men in the sample. The lack of thought given to childcare in the CWP is also surprising in the context of a broad acknowledgement in the social policy community that families can only escape unemployment (and poverty) through adequate, subsidised childcare which allows as many adults as possible within a household to have (some degree of) paid work. If the scheme does prove to have difficulties attracting participants, these may be resolved by the greater level of compulsion heralded by the Jobseeker's Allowance. This would be a poor solution, however, since all the evidence to date shows that compulsory schemes are wasteful, demotivating and demoralising, so much so that, even in the United States, they are limited in scope.

The alternative is to find ways of improving the CWP, as well as exploring other policy avenues. The CWP is based on a very traditional approach to work and workers. In particular, it is based on the assumptions that 'work' requires a 35 hour working week, is carried out by one individual and is done primarily by men whose partners stay at home and look after the children. These assumptions do not reflect existing labour market realities or innovative approaches to work, and the supports on which labour market participation rests need to be considered. One obvious change is to create part-time CWP posts. Innovative approaches to work, such as job-sharing and flexi-time, could also be considered under the CWP. These more flexible approaches would make the scheme much more attractive because of the considerations discussed above of childcare, the informal sector and the stress and ill-health felt by individuals who have been out of work for long periods of time (see also Chapter Three). The very long-term unemployed might be more attracted to a scheme which allows them to increase the hours worked (i.e. to transfer from part-time to three-quarter or full-time) over time.

The size of the premiums is also worth consideration. Increasing the average weekly premium to £60 a week has significant cost implications, even if a quarter of places were offered part-time and continued to pay a premium of £25 a week. Indeed, it would more than double the annual costs of premiums. It can be argued, however, that these additional costs should not rule out completely adjustments being made to the scheme. If the scheme is to be expanded, greater flexibility by the government in terms of financing the CWP will almost certainly be required. In particular, it seems unreasonable that the 'savings' on benefits from the social security budget cannot be transferred to the Northern Ireland public expenditure block (whether to the T&EA specifically or not). Looked at another way, if the cost of participants' benefits was to be paid out of the social security budget (as it is not at the moment), the cost to the T&EA of running the CWP would be reduced by £2.8 million in 1996/97. This saving exceeds the additional £1.4 million required to increase the size of the average CWP premium. An increase in the size of the average premium, combined with the availability of some part-time posts, should increase the attractiveness of the CWP and make its expansion affordable.

The fair employment implications of the distribution of CWP places, especially if the Programme were to be expanded, require careful consideration. If the 500 pilot places are distributed as planned, this will cause a fall in the Protestant share of the LTU in West Belfast from 21.0% to 19.6%. Although this is a slight effect, if the scheme were to be enlarged to the size of current West Belfast ACE provision (and distributed as now), the Protestant share of the LTU in West Belfast would fall from 21.0% to 15.7%

and the Catholic share of the LTU would increase from 79% to 84.3%. Such equity issues could be tackled by means of the adoption by the T&EA (and/or the CWA Board) of a policy on what it is hoped to achieve in terms of participation. This might include, for instance, allocating a certain number of places for individuals with disabilities and deciding what is a desirable gender balance. Arguably, the T&EA/Partnership Board/Provider structure makes it more difficult to achieve any desired representation, though even small providers could still be asked to contribute to the targets in particular ways.

While there are ways in which the CWP could be made more attractive and 'user friendly,' it is, however, yet another supply-side intervention by government which fails to incorporate the 'missing ingredient' required in successful labour market policies - labour demand. An alternative, therefore, is to consider whether policies which affect labour demand offer more hope to the LTU. Demand-side labour market policy intervention is well-established in Northern Ireland and is making a come-back in EU countries, with a particular focus on the unemployed. Throughout Europe, interest is turning away from employee-based subsidies such as Family Credit and towards employer subsidies tied to recruitment of the unemployed coupled with minimum wages policies. For example, the Task Force on Long-Term Unemployment in the Irish Republic recently recommended higher rates of subsidy to companies recruiting the LTU, as well as setting aside a proportion of public sector jobs for graduates from training and employment schemes (Office of the Tánaiste, 1995).

Subsidies to employers, often geared to attracting inward investment, take two main forms: tax allowances and grants, and often there is a 'regional' structure to such assistance, as in Northern Ireland (see also Chapter Ten, this volume). Grant-making bodies, such as the Industrial Development Board (IDB), are aware of the need to locate new jobs in areas of high unemployment, and not only provide higher grant-aid for such areas, but have developed policy goals under Targeting Social Need. The IDB, for instance, aims to attract 75% of new investment to parts of Northern Ireland 'in or adjacent to' areas of social need. This somewhat loose concept enabled IDB to achieve that figure long ago in the late 1980s (see also Chapter Seven, this volume). The LTU survey evidence (Chapter Three, this volume) strongly supports the desirability of locating jobs in areas of high unemployment.

Creating new jobs within or close to areas of high unemployment, however, does not necessarily mean that the unemployed, and especially the LTU, will benefit, as the employer interviews show (see also Chapter Two, this volume). Some companies deliberately target the unemployed and have collaborated successfully with the T&EA through customised pre-employment training schemes. But the general picture is that most new jobs go to job changers, and to take one person from the unemployment count three or more jobs need to be created - assuming jobs continue to be created as they are now and in the absence of other policies to influence recruitment. Because of this, it is popular to advocate that the state guarantees some sort of work scheme as a last resort - much like ACE or CWP. The drawbacks of this approach should be evident from the research presented here. As Britton (1996:38) argues, 'any scheme which is confined to the long-term unemployed runs the risk of perpetuating their isolation from the rest of society'.

A different strategy is to involve employers much more actively in a policy to reduce unemployment and the numbers of LTU. The main policy instrument might be to tie the receipt of grant-aid, and government contracts of all kinds and for all employers, to the recruitment of a set quota of the LTU - 15%, 20% or even higher might be justified depending on the circumstances and the occupations involved. Significantly, no employer in this study voiced strong objections to such a policy. A policy of this sort would, of course, run counter to many of the everyday assumptions of personnel officers about the necessity of 'experience' (though see McCrudden, 1996, for a critique of such assumptions) - a requirement which could be regarded as a form of indirect discrimination against the LTU and certainly against those who have never had a job.

CONCLUSIONS

To conclude, there is a need for a fresh approach to long-term unemployment and employment equity which takes account of real labour market changes and processes, and which involves employers sharing more of the responsibility for actively targeting the unemployed. In advocating such a policy, the general social desirability of reducing long-term unemployment *per se* can be matched to the specific fair employment objective of dealing with unemployment differentials. To tackle long-term unemployment with the urgency it deserves, individual employers *in areas of high unemployment* need to be encouraged by government and its agencies to be less preoccupied with the finer points of a 'balanced workforce' and more supported in their efforts to recruit the unemployed. As argued in Chapter Three, such a strategy needs to be complemented by action *outside areas of high unemployment* to deal with all forms of workplace intimidation and other discriminatory practices.

ENDNOTES

1. The authors wish to thank Sharon Milner, Patrick Neeson, Mary Trainor and Seamus McGuinness for research assistance. We are also grateful to DED Statistics Branch, DCI Newcastle, the SSA, the T&EA, CWA board

members and CWA staff, the Falls Road SSO, Falls and Shankill Road CABs and all the community groups which helped with the survey. Finally, our thanks go to all the employers who showed an interest in the project and agreed to be interviewed.

REFERENCES

Britton, A. (1996) *The Goal of Full Employment*, London: National Institute of Economic and Social Research.

Crowley-Bainton, T. (1987) 'Unemployed Jobseekers - an underrated talent?', *Personnel Management*, August.

Dawes, L. (1993) *Long-Term Unemployment and Labour Market Flexibility*, Leicester: Centre for Labour Market Studies, University of Leicester.

Green, F. (1994) 'Training: Inequality and Inefficiency', in Glyn, A. and Miliband, D. (eds.) *Paying for Inequality: The Economic Cost of Social Injustice*, London: Rivers Oram Press.

Irish News, 26 February 1996, Belfast.

Jackman, R. (1992) 'An Economy of Unemployment?', in McLaughlin, E. (ed.) *Understanding Unemployment: New Perspectives on Active Labour Market Policies*, London: Routledge.

Maguire, M. (1992) 'The Role of Employers in the Labour Market,' in McLaughlin, E. (ed.) *Understanding Unemployment: New Perspectives on Active Labour Market Policies*, London: Routledge

Marsden, D. and Ryan, P. (1991) 'Initial Training, Labour Market Structure and Public Policy: Intermediate Skills in British and German Industry,' in Ryan, P. (ed.) *International Comparisons of Vocational Education and Training for Intermediate Skills*, London: Falmer Press.

McCrudden, C. (1996) 'The Merit Principle and Fair Employment in Northern Ireland', in Magill, D. and Rose, S. (eds.) *Fair Employment Law in Northern Ireland: debates and issues*, Belfast: SACHR.

McLaughlin, E. (1994(a)) 'Employment, Unemployment and Social Security', in Glyn, A. and Miliband, D. (eds.) *Paying for Inequality: The Economic Cost of Social Injustice*, London: Routledge.

McLaughlin, E. (1994(b)) *Flexibility in Work and Benefits*, London: Institute for Public Policy Research.

McLaughlin, E. (1992) 'Towards Active Labour Market Policies: An Overview', in McLaughlin, E. (ed.) *Understanding Unemployment: New Perspectives on Active Labour Market Policies*, London: Routledge.

Meager, N. and Metcalf, H. (1987) *Recruitment of the Long-Term Unemployed*, Brighton: Institute of Manpower Studies

NIEC (1995) *Taxes, Benefits, Unemployment and Poverty Traps in Northern Ireland,* Report 117, Belfast Northern Ireland Economic Council.

NISB/NIERC (1994) *An Evaluation of Government Training Programmes in Northern Ireland,* Belfast: Northern Ireland Economic Research Centre.

O'Broin, E. (1996) 'ACE Cuts: West Belfast to Lose 380 Jobs', *Economic Bulletin,* 3(4), Belfast: West Belfast Economic Forum.

Office of the Tánaiste (1995) *Report of the Task Force on Long-Term Unemployment,* Dublin: Central Stationery Office.

Scott, R. (1993) 'Long-Term Unemployment and Policy Response in Northern Ireland,' in Gudgin, G. and O'Shea, G. (eds.) *Unemployment Forever? The Northern Ireland Economy in Recession and Beyond,* Belfast: NIERC.

White, M. (ed.) (1994) *Unemployment and Public Policy in a Changing Labour Market,* London: Policy Studies Institute.

White, M. (1991) *Against Unemployment,* London: Policy Studies Institute.

White, M. and Lakey, J. (1992) *The Restart Effect: Evaluation of a Labour Market Programme for Unemployed People,* London: Policy Studies Institute.

Chapter Five

EMPLOYMENT EQUALITY, EDUCATIONAL AND TRAINING POLICY

Leslie Caul

INTRODUCTION

Despite the efforts of government to encourage investment and to promote equal opportunity and fair employment through anti-discrimination legislation, some groups, including unqualified school-leavers, 18-25 year olds, adults with literacy or numeracy problems and those moving in and out of low-skill employment, appear to have been largely bypassed by any improvements which may have occurred. In Northern Ireland within such labour market trends religious differentials remain (see Whyte, 1990; Cormack and Osborne, 1991; Murphy and Armstrong, 1993). Most research (for example, Compton, 1991; Smith and Chambers, 1991) has tended to concentrate on the adult labour market, and particularly, the male unemployment differentials between Catholics and Protestants which have persisted for a considerable period of time. However, the focus has tended not to be on the means by which these inequalities have been reproduced - for instance, the relationship between religion, schooling and early careers. Despite a lack of quantitative evidence, it is likely that the experience of young people in the transition from school to adult life is important in determining the later life chances of Catholics and Protestants.

Recent research in other regions in the British Isles (for example, Breen, 1991; Narendranathan and Elias, 1993) suggest that the transition from school to adult working life has a strong influence on later life histories. In Northern Ireland, Armstrong (1994) has analysed the characteristics, attitudes and experiences of young people on the Youth Training Programme. This showed how religion, qualifications, the type of school attended and social class affected entrants to the programme. It is, therefore, reasonable to suggest that the career experiences of Northern Ireland's young people are of major importance in the re-creation of structural differences in the experience of employment and unemployment. It has been estimated that between 7% and 25% of inequality is due to an inadequate level of skill (Freeman and Katz, 1994). In Britain, for example, Nickell and Bell (1994) argue that the decline in real demand for unskilled workers contributed up to 20% of the increase in unemployment between the 1960s and 1980s. Given the persistence of inequality in educational performance between Catholics and Protestants in Northern Ireland, and differences in the proportions of young Catholics and Protestants in employment and in training, consideration needs to be given to the extent to which these influence inequalities.

This chapter traces the relationship between vocational training and employment inequality in Northern Ireland. Inequalities have been created through the reconstruction of manufacturing and its location in specific localities that reflect imbalances between the two communities. It is on this unequal basis that vocational training has been built. It is not surprising, therefore, that inequalities exist in Catholic and Protestant participation in vocational education and training. The chapter analyses these inequalities and provides a number of explanations of differentials in employment between Catholics and Protestants. A concluding section analyses the weaknesses in vocational education and training and makes a number of comparisons with the vocational educational systems of some of the United Kingdom's industrial competitors.

THE HISTORICAL RELATIONSHIP BETWEEN TRAINING AND EMPLOYMENT INEQUALITY IN NORTHERN IRELAND

Britain's distinctive heritage in vocational education and training is synonymous with craft apprenticeship. In Northern Ireland, the perceived importance of craft apprenticeships in the Belfast Iron Trades and in the large manufacturing industries located around Belfast, have, from the conception of the Northern Ireland state, played a significant part in discrimination in the workplace through the important hold over access exercised by Protestant craft associations. Historically, Catholics were incorporated into the labour market in Northern Ireland as ex-agricultural workers and regarded as semi-skilled workers (Jenkins, 1990). This process was dependent upon their systematic and organised exclusion from skilled work by a closed alliance of organised Protestant labour and, indeed, by employers in the industrial heartlands (Caul, 1988).

After the 1930s, government support for training was located in those large industries in the Belfast conurbation. This meant that, until the collapse of Belfast-based manufacturing in the 1960s, most training was targeted at Protestant apprentices, and skilled trades grew up which were exclusively Protestant in composition. Similar training did not exist in those trades which employed Catholic workers, for example, the building industry or catering. This process was to some extent offset by the introduction of the

Industrial Training Boards in the 1960s, when the demand for apprenticeship training declined while simultaneously becoming more exclusive.

During the 1960s and 1970s, Caul (1988) identified a number of phases in the organisation of manufacturing in the unionist heartland of South East Antrim. As factory-based employment provided by unionist industrialists restructured to become employment in multinational companies, production and recruitment was controlled and managed informally by a number of organisations, including, in the 1970s, a number of paramilitary groups. Patterns of recruitment in training and to skilled positions were set up which combined, within the sectarian geography of Northern Ireland, with violent intimidation during times of tension to ensure a virtual monopoly of skilled work by Protestants (Caul, 1988). This pattern ensured that Protestants were more likely to obtain employment and apprenticeships than Catholics, who were more likely to, at best, be offered places on government training schemes (see also Cormack and Osborne, 1983; Murray and Darby, 1983). High levels of long-term unemployment among Catholics and their concentration in certain kinds of employment rendered them disproportionately less likely to have access to the important informal dimensions of skill acquisition.

THE ORGANISATION OF VOCATIONAL EDUCATION AND TRAINING IN NORTHERN IRELAND

The failure of the voluntary efforts of employers, allied with Britain's worsening economic performance, meant that the role of the state in training provision increased from the mid-1960s. As a result, understanding the location of young people in the post-school sector has been further complicated by vigorous interventions in the transition of young people moving from school to adult working life through the provision of a series of training programmes. Following a number of training schemes piloted throughout the 1970s, a Youth Training Programme (YTP) was introduced in Northern Ireland in September 1982. This means that, for some time now, as Shuttleworth (1994) has argued, young people in Northern Ireland have not been confronted with a simple choice of leaving school and either going to work or unemployment. For a few (6% Catholic males and 13% Protestant males), the path from school to work still exists at age 16, but for the majority, transition from school is marked by spells of training (sometimes delayed until the ages of 17 and 18) and the completion of post-compulsory education. In Northern Ireland, the issue has become one of whether provision and access is equitable to both Protestant and Catholic young people approaching the end of compulsory schooling. It is now generally agreed that Catholics are more likely than Protestants to be YTP trainees. More than 25% of trainees (Armstrong, 1994) were Catholic compared to

20% Protestant. Shuttleworth (1994) showed that 28% of 17 year old Catholic males and 17% of 17 year old Protestant males were in training, while 15% of Catholic females and 12% of Protestant females of the same age were similarly placed.

YTP was an ambitious and extensive project which aimed to lay the foundation for a skilled, flexible workforce, while also helping 16 and 17 year olds to make the transition from school to adult working life. It represented the combination of a series of attempts to cater for the needs of young people in Northern Ireland. The programme was provided by partnerships organised among community workshops, employers (including Industrial Training Boards), colleges of further education and government training centres. It offered full-time training to those 16 and 17 year olds not yet in employment, additional training to young people and increased vocational preparation for those who remained in full-time education.

There have been several evaluations of YTP since the initiation of the programme. Studies of 16 year old school-leavers who joined the Northern Ireland YTP programme revealed serious weaknesses in their preparation for life in terms of basic communication, general knowledge and personal and social life skills (Whyte, 1990). In addition, Whyte argued many young people had left school with strong negative feelings about education. It was also suggested that the educational element in YTP was not adequately structured or organised to meet the challenge presented to it, although individuals undoubtedly did what they could within the brief assigned to them. Dissatisfaction may also be seen as underlying the numerous proposals for improvement suggested by participants at every level of the programme. Whyte concluded that evaluations of the YTP programme have shown that the educational system in Northern Ireland urgently needed to make changes in the knowledge and skills it provided for young people.

Progressive changes to the YTP scheme under the present Conservative administration led to a movement away from the strategic role occupied by the further education sector towards an emerging role for the private sector in youth training. As Northern Ireland moved to a scenario relatively similar to that evident in England, a Jobskills programme was introduced in 1995. Jobskills aims to provide young people and adults with training opportunities and practical skills identified by employers which will equip them to compete in the labour market for employment through the completion and achievement of training qualifications in the form of NVQs (National Vocational Qualifications). These practically-oriented qualifications are based on standards set in consultation with employers and are designed to provide the means of developing a skilled, competent workforce. Training is available in a broad spectrum of occupational skills, including construction, civil engineering and the hotel and catering industries. The government hope that by 1997, 80% of young people will achieve at least NVQ level 2 or its equivalent (National Training Target). In contrast, under YTP, a mere 14% reached NVQ level 2 or its equivalent. Whether Jobskills will achieve a better outcome is not, of course, yet known. It differs from YTP in its commitment to the attainment of National Training Targets for education and training through the universal use of NVQs. Recognised Training Organisations (RTOs), normally government training centres, colleges of further education, businesses whose core service is the provision of training and individual employers, deliver the programmes. To attain RTO status, an organisation must meet rigorous criteria set by the Training and Employment Agency (T&EA).

CATHOLIC AND PROTESTANT PARTICIPATION IN VOCATIONAL EDUCATION AND TRAINING

The extent of inequality by religion among young people in terms of participation in education, training, employment and unemployment is of considerable importance. A narrow perspective which seeks to analyse rates of employment only in the youngest age groups will fail to assess the impact of changes in participation in vocational education and training. Since the 1970s, Catholics have consistently had a higher proportion in training than Protestants, particularly at the age of 17. For 16 and 17 year olds (1990-91), the proportion of unemployed Catholics was about the same as that of Protestants. In relation to those older than 17 years, Catholic rates of unemployment increased faster than Protestant rates until they were about twice as high. Table 5.1 provides a recalculation of Shuttleworth's (1994) data on young people in training and employment. It shows Catholic overrepresentation in training, education and economic inactivity, as well as a considerable underrepresentation in employment.

Table 5.1: 17 Year Olds in Training, Education and Employment (1990-91)

Denomination	Employment %	Training %	Unemployment %	Education %	Economic Inactivity %
Catholic	24.3	21.6	7.6	41.7	4.9
Protestant	32.4	14.8	8.9	40.8	3.1

Source: Shuttleworth (1994)

Catholic overrepresentation in training and education reduced, however, after age 18, when Catholics became much more likely than Protestants to be economically inactive and unemployed. Shuttleworth's analysis also showed important gender differences.

Differences in participation rates were especially marked between

Catholic and Protestant males. Catholic males aged 16 to 18 had higher rates of participation in government training and post-compulsory education than Protestants but lower rates of employment. For males over 18, the religious differential in unemployment rapidly increased, so that Catholic males at age 24 had an unemployment rate about twice as high as Protestants. For females, Catholics under 18 years tended to have lower participation rates in post-compulsory education than Protestants. Simultaneously, females over 20 years generally had higher rates of economic activity if they were Catholic rather than Protestant. With regard to young people, a more complex explanation than that offered in relation to structural unemployment among adults is required. For instance, a 'scheme effect' which ceases at the age of 18 can be seen to be an important factor. The relative numbers of Protestants and Catholics aged 16-18 years in the labour market is about the same but fewer Catholics are in employment. The number of young people in training at 16 years doubles in their 17th year, while the number in employment increases by a factor of 2.5. While the employment profile remains relatively constant for males, it gradually rises for females from 1123 (2%) females in employment at 16 years to 6858 (13%) in employment at 20 years. For males, the unemployment rate levels off at 18 years at 20%, while it rises gradually for females to around 18%.

Shuttleworth (1994) argued that the influence of religion is sufficiently strong and consistent to allow considerable confidence in assessing its influence. Catholics, everything else being equal, have a greater chance of remaining in education than Protestants. Once Catholics leave school they have, other factors being equal, a greater chance of being in training. Figure 5.1 shows estimated participation in education, training and employment in Northern Ireland. The table has been calculated using school fifth form enrolments over the three years 1991, 1992 and 1993, thereby giving an index for the period 1992-94. Although a slightly higher proportion of Catholics remained in education, the total number of pupils was still less than the number of Protestants in full-time schooling; while the number of Catholics in employment was consistently less than the number of Protestants. Figure 5.1 illustrates how consistent the proportions of young people remaining in full-time schooling and those entering training and employment have been since 1992.

The Secondary Education Leavers' Survey (1990-91) showed that of the young people leaving school at fifth form or lower sixth level, 30% of male Protestants entered employment, while 17.7% of male Catholics did likewise; 19.8% of female Protestants entered employment, with 17.4% of Catholics doing likewise. In the post-compulsory school sector, 35.3% of Protestant males and 50% of Catholic males entered training. Comparable percentages for females were 34% Protestants and 27.4% Catholics. In terms of entry to further education, 27.2% were Protestant males as compared with 27.9%

Catholic males, and 40.5% of Protestant females and 50% of Catholic females entered further education. If all school-leavers are considered, then 21.4% of Protestant males and 34.2% of Catholic males entered the youth training markets. The figures for gender were 21% and 16.6% respectively. The evidence reviewed here does not support a human capital thesis, as more Catholic youth enter training, while consistently less are likely to obtain employment.

Figure 5.1: Index for Training, Education and Employment for Northern Ireland, 1992-1994.

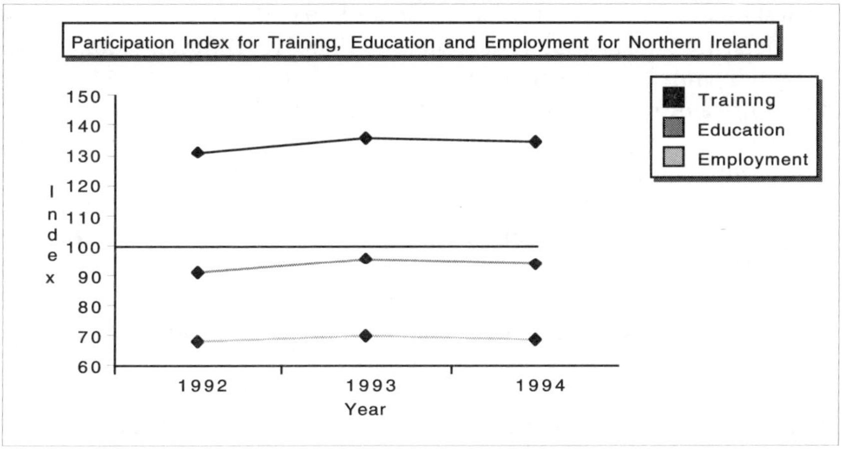

Participation Index for Training, Education and Employment for Northern Ireland

Training
Education
Employment

150
140
130
120
110
100
90
80
70
60

Index

1992
1993
1994

Year

Note: An index of 100 represents equal participation while an index of more than 100 reflects greater Catholic participation and of less than 100 lesser Catholic participation.

Source: DENI Fifth Form Enrolment Figures 1992-94.

There are more Catholics than Protestants in the YTP/Jobskills programme, while fewer Catholics are enrolled in education or employed. The percentage of Catholics remaining in education is slightly higher than the proportion of Protestants, but the number of Protestants in education is higher than that of Catholics. Within Northern Ireland's four Training Regions the number of 16 year olds leaving school with no qualifications decreased over the period 1991-1993 in all regions (from 8% to 6%) and in both communities. The North East Region was something of an exception, where performance declined in 1991/92 but improved in 1992/93. In the Western Region and in Belfast, the number of Catholics leaving school with no qualifications was consistently greater than that of Protestants, while in the South East region the number of Catholics and Protestants leaving school with no qualifications was approximately equal. In regions with an improved performance, Catholic rates of improvement between 1991 and 1994 were greater than for Protestants. However, the Western Region had the lowest percentage of unqualified Protestant school-leavers and the highest percentage of Catholic young people leaving school with no qualifications. It is significant that the two regions (Western and Belfast) which have the greatest proportion of unqualified Catholic school-leavers, also have the largest participation rates of Catholic young people in training.

Explaining Employment Differentials Between Catholics and Protestants

Shuttleworth (1994) argued that Catholics behave differently than Protestants as soon as they leave school, based on evidence from the Northern Ireland Labour Force Survey (1990-91). Differentiation between Catholics and Protestants in recent years has operated largely through different rates of take up of education and training, rather than through differences in employment and unemployment, as had been the case in the past. A number of hypotheses with very different policy implications can be put forward to explain these differentials in education and training.

The first is that young Catholics, because of a history of high communal unemployment and because they live in areas of high unemployment, are 'discouraged workers' (Raffe and Willms, 1989). This view suggests that young people delay entry to the labour market through continuing in education because they expect to have a high chance of becoming unemployed. However, an alternative view is that Catholics are seeking to accumulate human capital so as to compete in what they expect to be a difficult labour market. The tradition of craft apprenticeships in manufacturing industry in Northern Ireland referred to earlier may have embedded a prejudicial position with regards to unionist labour and nationalist labour. This may indeed be one of the historical causes of the differential uptake of employment and training.

Shuttleworth (1994) suggests, however, a further explanation, which is supported by Teague (1993), and is derived from the social construction of labour markets. Labour markets, Teague suggested, were not always open in areas where there were large employers; rather, extended internal markets may operate to reinforce and embed a company in its locality. Social ties created between the company and the local community mean that vacancies are often filled by informal means. Large companies in Northern Ireland have often been accused of using such informal methods for recruiting labour and this approach has been the focus of much of the fair employment legislation in the recent past. Shuttleworth's work showed that of approximately 300 young respondents who were in employment, almost 40% reported that they had found jobs through friends of the family, providing evidence of informal networking among the employed.

In the case of school-leavers who have obtained jobs in the labour market, the value of the qualifications they possess must also be explored. There are two explanations for the value of qualifications - the human capital and the screening hypothesis. In the human capital thesis, Becker (1975) drew a direct link between education and personal economic success, arguing that education influences individual productivity and hence employability. Differential labour market performance, whether between qualified and unqualified staff, or between Catholics and Protestants, then, simply results from personal human endowment. The second, the screening hypothesis (Gray, 1983), suggested a break in this link and argued that employers use qualifications as a means of ranking potential workers. The clearest distinction between this and the human capital argument is that the screening approach treats qualifications as a proxy for other factors. Qualifications are not important in themselves, but rather are seen as general measures of ability and personal attributes. Most skills are learned 'on the job' and qualifications at school have little intrinsic relevance. Raffe (1988) argued that employers do not look for specific subject choices but for indications of examination success and, therefore, general employability. Hence, Shuttleworth (1994) argued that qualifications have socially defined value and can be used to locate young people to different segments of the labour market or different careers (see also Bates and Riseborough, 1993). Less qualified youth, it can be argued, have poorer self images and less career-orientation than more qualified school-leavers and that translates into poor labour market performance. In an area such as Northern Ireland where there has been considerable differentiation in performance, with more Catholic children leaving school with no and lower qualifications than Protestant children, qualifications could perform as a discriminating factor. However, the evidence on this point is mixed. McWhirter (1989) suggested that for school-leavers, qualifications do not appear to be important in determining whether Catholic or Protestant young people get jobs. On the other hand, Miller *et al* (1993) concluded that subject choice explains a large part of the earning and employment differential between Catholics and Protestants. Miller *et al* argued it is likely that the effect of qualifications varied both by type of job and by social class. Nevertheless, there is no evidence to link subject choice, examination passes and employability, as would be hypothesised by a human capital theorist. Thus, the role of qualifications and subject choice remain unclear. In addition, the Secondary Education Leavers' Survey (1990-91) showed that the type of employment being obtained by young people is now largely unskilled work in construction and retailing, in which the possession of qualifications, or particular subject choices, would be thought to be of relatively little consequence. In addition, other variables such as local unemployment rates have been found to be significant in explaining personal economic success once individual examination attainment and social background have been taken into account (Garner and Raudenbusch, 1991; Bagnall, 1992). If subject choice does not appear to explain inter-religious differences and behaviour, and if contemporary education policies lead to parity between maintained and controlled schools, then it could be expected that religious differentials in the labour market should diminish in the long term. The identification of a large proportion of young people leaving school with no qualifications, in contrast to the high academic performance of a small number of grammar school educated pupils, focused growing attention on school performance during the 1980s. It became evident that many children educated in a largely neighbourhood-oriented and academically successful primary school sector rapidly became under-achievers by the age of 16 (Caul, 1992). As Caul (1993) demonstrated, government has, since 1989, been involved in a reconstruction of educational provision which has been the most far-reaching since the 1947 Education Act. The introduction of the Northern Ireland Curriculum addressed the perceived narrowness of the existing primary school curriculum and the under-achievement evident among a large number of 16 year olds. The compulsory introduction of science in all schools and relegation of vocational subjects including Craft, Design and Technology and Business Studies at 11-16 years (Key Stages 3 and 4) suggested a renewed emphasis on achievement of the basic skills normally associated with the compulsory school curriculum, and is likely to impact on religious differences in subject 'choice'. There are, therefore, grounds for re-evaluation of the subject choice line of research. On the other hand, the failure to introduce the Technical and Vocational Education Initiative (TVEI) weakened the movement towards the introduction of vocationalism into the secondary school. This is important in a school system where there were historically differences in curriculum between Catholic and Protestant schools (McEwen, 1990). The dual opportunity of introducing a technical and vocationally-orientated curriculum and of increasing the number of pupils staying on in full-time education after compulsory leaving age was lost. This initiative could have had considerable impact on the maintained school sector where there were a shortage of science and technical facilities. The DENI, however, introduced a parallel initiative, the Certificate of Pre-Vocational Education (CPVE), which was designed to increase the importance of pre-vocational elements within the secondary school sector: The CPVE has so far remained marginal within the secondary school sector.

THE DISTRIBUTION OF TRAINING PLACES

In a region so heavily fractured by sectarian geography and with such low levels of youth employment, the location and availability of training places is of considerable importance. In 1995, of the 30,878 contract training places in the YTP/Jobskills programme, just over half were occupied (56%). Of the available places, over a half are in the Western Region and in Belfast. The largest proportion of unoccupied places is in the Belfast Region, as Figure 5.2 shows. Those regions with large Catholic populations have pools of available training places, and where the number of training places in individual regions is large, the relative proportions of occupied and unoccupied places are similar. In the North Eastern Region, where the proportion of training places is smaller than in other regions, there is a relatively small proportion of unoccupied training places (25%).

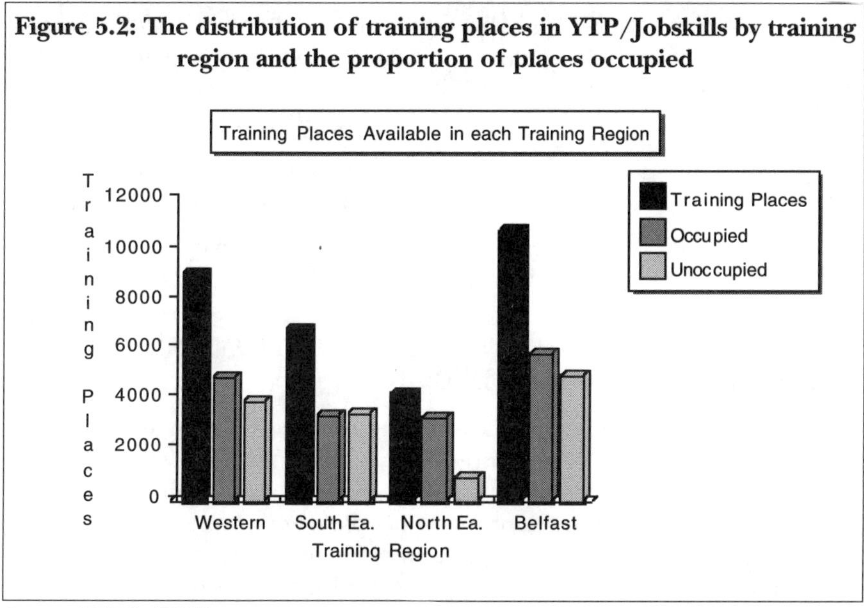

Figure 5.2: The distribution of training places in YTP/Jobskills by training region and the proportion of places occupied

Source: T&EA (1995).

The data above includes training places with all Recognised Training Organisations in Northern Ireland, including further education colleges, training agencies and private employers. Table 5.2 provides an analysis of the relative proportions of places offered in 1995 by the various kinds of providers, using information provided by the T&EA. Overall, two-thirds of places are provided by training agencies (usually in community workshops), nearly a quarter (23%) in further education and less than 1 in 10 in employer-based schemes. Both the areas with urban concentrations - Western and Belfast - have disproportionately high numbers of places which are employer-based. The South East and North East Regions have high numbers of places in further education, and Belfast, but not the Western Region, has disproportionately few places in further education. The Belfast and the North East areas also have disproportionately high numbers of agency/ workshop places.

Table 5.2: Training Place Provision by RTO Type and Training Region (1995)

	Further Education		Agency (Workshop)		Employer Based	
	N	%	N	%	N	%
Western	2001	(28.1)	5659	(27.2)	1419	(47.4)
South East	2040	(28.7)	4446	(21.4)	297	(9.9)
North East	1218	(17.1)	2970	(14.3)	56	(1.9)
Belfast	1856	(26.1)	7696	(37.1)	1220	(40.8)
Total	7115	(100)	20,771	(100)	2992	(100)

Source: T&EA

Community workshops tend to have the highest proportion of trainees with no GCSE passes and it is significant that the proportion of such schemes is high in Belfast, where there are larger than average proportions of unqualified school-leavers and where the majority of trainees are Catholic.

THE WEAKNESS OF VOCATIONAL EDUCATION AND TRAINING IN NORTHERN IRELAND

The last decade in vocational education and training has seen a multitude of schemes designed to reform and restructure policy in Northern Ireland. Its political importance has risen significantly as it has been progressively recognised that the movement of young people from school to adult working life is no longer a simple question of employment/unemployment. Vocational education and training has become a more complex issue involving a set of rigorous interventions from a powerful state sector. The inherent weaknesses in vocational education are not unique to Northern Ireland, but are likely to have been exacerbated by an education system that has remained set firmly in a strongly academic framework, with the continued dominance of selective schools working often at the expense of a non-selective sector (Caul, 1992). In addition, the priority afforded to vocationalism in Northern Ireland has to be understood in the context of political instability and increasing youth unemployment, which it was feared provided potential recruits to paramilitary organisations.

The many measures adopted by government have promoted greater state control of the management and organisation of education. Within this movement towards greater centralisation was a series of attempts to promote a new concern about vocationalism and training. Centralised state management introduced a YTP located in further education colleges at the expense of a number of pre-vocational courses for 15 year olds. This approach gradually gave way to a scheme of recognised training agencies with an emphasis on employer-led schemes. The Jobskills programme presently being introduced is intended to lead youth training into the millennium. The introduction of managerialism throughout the crafting of a series of new approaches to vocationalism into government practice resulted in the increased use of measurements of performance of public bodies, which was demonstrated in testing at age 8,11,14 and 16 years in schools and in the National Vocational Qualifications beyond formal schooling.

The latest available data show that the proportion of young people with five GCSEs at grade C or above has increased in Northern Ireland from 44% in 1991/92 to 50% in 1993/94, while the proportion with no qualifications has fallen from 8% (1991/92) to 4.7% (1993/94). In terms of the National Training Targets, an estimated 64%-68% of young people achieve the NVQ 2 or five GCSEs at grade C or above in Northern Ireland (1993). Around 35% of 17 year olds in Northern Ireland enter training, and in order that 80% of those young people achieve NVQ level 2 or equivalent, requires that 38% of those young people who do not have five GCSEs complete NVQ level 2. The majority of such young people are in training places. Evidence from the Western Region of the T&EA (estimates of performance in NVQs provided by the Western Region, T&EA) would suggest that this is a feasible target for many young people in training, although little official data is presently available with which to assess completion rates.

It is often suggested that 'more training' is required for young people in Northern Ireland, but this may reflect a concern for more training of a particular genre or some disquiet with regard to the quality of training presently available. There is considerable evidence to suggest that there is a sufficiency of training places in Northern Ireland. In 1995/96, 46% of contracted places were unoccupied. Although there may be local pressure for some places among the popular occupational groups, both an abundance of places and a range of skill levels is available. Clearly, the system rests heavily on training providers, and the movement towards an employer supply model in contemporary training relies on training agencies to identify training places in specific localities. Thus, the move to an employer-driven system of local training reflects the duality between individual employers providing training and local agencies identifying firms where work experience is available. The question of quality remains unsolved. Given that around 5% of both Catholic and Protestant young people leave school with no qualifications and are likely to enter training, the view that youth training certifies low achievement might be sustained.

Another factor that constrains Northern Ireland's vocational educational performance is the relatively small size of Northern Ireland's post-compulsory school age education system (Keep and Mayhew, 1990). Shuttleworth (1994) has reported that the proportion of young people remaining in school past the age of 16 in Northern Ireland is 50%. This 50% does not include young people who attend colleges of further education: their inclusion would increase participation rates in post-compulsory education. Recent figures published by the Times Education Supplement show a relative figure of 60% in England and Wales. The problem for Northern Ireland is reliance on the talents of an extremely well-educated minority. This is reflected in an educational ethos dominated by elitist grammar schools. Educational achievements that have been practical, technical and vocational have been traditionally undervalued.

Contemporary vocational training has become bi-modal, as large scale manufacturing industry has reformed yet again in Northern Ireland with the introduction of an information technological base to meet the needs of new Asian companies and the newer specialist exclusive trades practised in small manufacturing units. It is particularly important, given Northern Ireland's poor record of employment, to compare its system of vocational education and training with that of other countries beyond the United Kingdom. It has been argued for over 150 years that many of our industrial competitors have better systems of vocational education and training. The German and Scandinavian systems, for example, succeed in attracting high levels of participation of 16-18 year olds and in providing high quality vocational training. However, the systems work because of close co-operation between employer organisations and trade unions. This infrastructure is weaker in Northern Ireland, although there is growing pressure from government on employers to maintain training standards. The German system is highly geared to employer control, and a similar system in Northern Ireland could lead to the short-term needs of employers being met at the expense of the long-term needs of the trainees and the local economy. Very few Northern Ireland firms are in a position to commit themselves to a three to four year training programme. A re-introduction of three to four year apprenticeships could also exclude trainees from higher education.

Historically, the structure of education in Northern Ireland does not lend support to developing a common education for all 16 to 19 year olds. The availability of a common post-16 institution has been at the corner-stone of much conscious reform among the United Kingdom's industrial competitors. Many foreign competitors, including Germany, Sweden and Japan, provide at least four years of vocational training pre-18. This can be done if schools provide pre-18 years vocational training to be followed by short, highly structured apprenticeships. The link between the pre- and post-18 years training is less clear, but vocational schools would clearly have a part to play in the post-18 training since firms would require assistance in the provision of high quality training. Clearly, pre-18 courses should be linked to post-18 apprenticeships and certification available at 18 years that would permit an equality of access to higher education for all students, irrespective of whether they came from a vocational or an academic route. Such pipe dreams are at odds with the realities of an education system that is driven by a powerful academic emphasis and set of interests from existing providers.

CONCLUSIONS

The economy in Northern Ireland has, and is, suffering from a multitude of shocks to which education and training can only offer a partial response. De-industrialisation, reconstruction and relocation of manufacturing, de-unionisation, low cost competition and the value of the pound probably explain 80% of unemployment and inequality (Freeman and Katz, 1994). Stronger trade unions, redistributive taxation and an active industrial policy, along with education and training policies, may be part of a balanced approach to increasing demand and investment levels. Such an approach in Northern Ireland must, however, also include targeting the inequalities which exist among Catholic and Protestant youth in terms of participation in training and employment. Caul (1996) shows that levels of staying on in education have tended to level off at 16 years among both Catholics and Protestants, but that more Catholics are in training and less in employment at 17 years. A 'scheme effect' ensures low levels of Catholic unemployment until 19 years, when a large proportion of Catholic youth finds itself 'on the dole'. Male unemployment doubles between 16 and 19 years while 50% more Protestants than Catholics are in employment at 17 years. It is not possible to put the blame for Catholic unemployment onto Catholic unwillingness to 'invest' in human capital since more Catholics avail themselves of the training system at 16-18 years. However, the training system in Northern Ireland rests heavily on further education colleges and on workshop provision, and very little on opportunities in employer-led schemes. While practical placements are an integral part of training, there is evidence of difficulty with movement from NVQ 2 to NVQ 3, and of the availability of permanent employment possibilities in some community workshop provision. Thus, Catholic youth may find their opportunities for work limited even before consideration is given to the potentially sectarian nature of the location of available employment.

The provision of vocational education and training reveals a number of paradoxes. Firstly, growing globalism of capital has been matched by a localism in training. Localism is especially poignant in a society which is so tightly structured by its sectarian geography. Secondly, the implementation of national policy in training has been devolved to individual employers and to community workshop provision. Again, the sectarian divisions evident in Northern Ireland may lessen the impact of the local market forces in shaping local responses to training needs as some groups become isolated from certain skill provisions. In this context, inequality will prevail. Thirdly, the demand for a skilled and competent work force has led to the introduction of an atomised approach to skill training delivered in individual units. This may in itself remove some broad issues from training agendas. Fourthly, the identification and definition of what constitutes a skilled labour force has been left to local interpretation based on local need. In an area so heavily fractured, this must limit, to some extent, the availability of some opportunities for some young people. Fifthly, new fundamentalism has in itself led to the re-traditionalisation of training and the rebirth of orthodoxy with the re-invention of the new apprenticeship. Each of these paradoxes are especially powerful in the context of the historic weakness of the Northern Ireland economy and the vacuum in training found among some local employers.

This is the lesson of Northern Europe. Local co-ordination is necessary to link employers with educational institutions, while at regional and national level employer involvement is necessary in the development of modules, courses, curriculum and in staff training. The experience of developing high quality training in Sweden and in Germany suggests the importance of the incorporation of the trade unions within the local and regional framework.

A higher degree of co-ordination in decision-making about vocational training policy is therefore required if optimal results are to be achieved. Such co-ordination is a large and complex task and involves many layers in government. There is a tension between the need for national co-ordination and the need to avail of the relative benefits of the market, even if those are not all that viable in an economy as weak as Northern Ireland. The answer to the problems of improved co-ordination lies in a sensitive analysis of both the public and private sectors and their many institutions. In this, vocational education and training is a particularly difficult element in a cost benefit analysis. Not only is vocational education important for the local economy, it is also important for the kind of society in which we live. If our schools produce young people with low levels of attainment, this does not only have implications for the quality of the labour force, it also means that the individuals will become marginalised and live out their lives at the edges of society.

REFERENCES

Armstrong, D.M. (1994) *Young People on the Youth Training Programme: an analysis of their characteristics, attitudes and experiences*, Belfast: Northern Ireland Economic Council.

Bagnall, G. (1992) *Deprivation and Leaving School*, Edinburgh: Centre for Education Studies.

Bates, I. and Riseborough, G. (1993) *Youth and Inequality*, Buckingham: Open University Press.

Becker, G.S. (1975) *Human Capital*, 2nd edition, New York: Columbia University Press.

Breen, R. (1991) *Education, Employment and Training in the Youth Labour Market*, ESRI Paper 15, Dublin.

Caul, L. (1996) *A Review of Selected Aspects pf Education and Training Policy in Northern Ireland,* unpublished report, Belfast: SACHR.

Caul, L. (1993) 'School Performance in Northern Ireland' in *The 18th Annual Report of the Standing Advisory Commission on Human Rights*, London: HMSO.

Caul, L. (1992) 'School Effectiveness: policy, practice and research', in *The 17th Annual Report of the Standing Advisory Commission on Human Rights*, London: HMSO.

Caul, L. (1988) 'State Management and Urban Development: a case study of Newtownabbey 1958-1983', unpublished PhD, Belfast: Queen's University of Belfast.

Compton, P. (1991) 'Employment differentials in Northern Ireland and job discrimination: a critique', in Roche, P. and Barton, B. *The Northern Ireland Question: Myth and Reality*, Aldershot: Avebury.

Cormack, R. and Osborne, R. (1993) 'Higher Education in Northern Ireland', in Osborne, R., Cormack, R. and Gallagher, A. *After the Reforms: Education and Policy in Northern Ireland*, Aldershot: Avebury.

Cormack, R. and Osborne, R. (1991) *Discrimination and Public Policy in Northern Ireland,* Oxford: Clarendon Press.

Cormack, R. and Osborne, R. (1983) *Religion, Education and Employment: Aspects of Equal Opportunity in Northern Ireland,* Belfast: Appletree Press.

Freeman, R. and Katz, L. (1994) *Working Under Different Rules*, New York: Russell Sage.

Garner, C. and Raudenbusch, S. (1991) 'Neighbourhood effects on educational attainment: a multi-level analysis', *Sociology of Education*, 64(4): 251-262.

Gray, J. (1983) *Reconstructions of Secondary Education: Theory, Myth and Practice Since the War*, London: Routledge.

Jenkins, R. (1990) 'Discrimination and Equality in Employment: Ethnicity and Race in the United Kingdom', in Esland, G. (ed.) *Education, Training and Employment*, Wokingham: Addison-Wesley Publishing Company.

Keep, E. and Mayhew, K. (1990) 'The assessment: education, training and economic performance', in Esland, G. (ed.) *Education, Training and Employment*, Wokingham: Addison-Wesley Publishing Company.

McEwen, A. (1990) 'Segregation and integration in Northern Ireland's education system', in Caul, L. (ed.) *Schools Under Scrutiny*, London: Macmillan.

McWhirter, L. (1989) 'Longitudinal evidence on the teenage years', in Harbison, J. (ed.) *Growing Up in Northern Ireland*, Belfast: Stranmillis College.

Miller, R., Osborne, R., Cormack, R. and Curry, C. (1993) 'Higher education and labour market entry: the differing experiences of Northern Irish Protestants and Catholics', in Osborne, R., Cormack, R. and Gallagher, A. (eds.) (1993) *After the Reforms: Education and Policy in Northern Ireland*, Aldershot: Avebury.

Moore, R. (1990) 'Education, Employment and Recruitment', in Esland, G. (ed.) *Education, Training and Employment*, Wokingham: Addison-Wesley Publishing Company.

Murphy, A. and Armstrong, D. (1993) 'The Incidence and Duration of Male Unemployment in Northern Ireland', in Gudgin, G. and O'Shea, G. (eds.) *Unemployment Forever? The Northern Ireland Economy in Recession and Beyond*, Belfast: Northern Ireland Economic Research Centre.

Murray, R. and Darby, J. (1983) 'The Londonderry and Strabane study: out and down in Derry and Strabane' in Cormack, R.J. and Osborne, R.D. (eds.) *Religion, Education and Employment*, Belfast: Appletree Press.

Narendranathan, W. and Elias, P. (1993) 'Influences of past history on the incidence of youth unemployment: empirical findings for the UK', *Oxford Bulletin of Economics and Statistics*, 55(2): 161-186.

Nickell, S. and Bell, B. (1994) 'Unemployment and Skill Inequality, 1960-80', *Oxford Review of Economic Policy*, 11(1).

Raffe, D. (1988) 'The story so far: research on education, training and the labour market from the Scottish surveys', in Raffe, D. (ed.) *Education and the Youth Labour Market*, Brighton: The Falmer Press.

Raffe, D. and Willms, D. (1989) 'Schooling the discouraged worker: local labour market effects on educational participation', *Sociology*, 23 (4): 559-581.

Shuttleworth, I. (1994) *An Analysis of Community Differences in the Pilot Northern Ireland Secondary Education Leavers' Survey*, Studies in Employment Equality Research Report No. 3, Belfast: CCRU.

Smith, D. and Chambers, G. (1991) *Inequality in Northern Ireland*, Oxford: Clarendon Press.

Teague, P. (1993) 'Discrimination and fair employment in Northern Ireland', in Teague, P. (ed.) *The Economy of Northern Ireland: Perspectives for Structural Change*, London: Lawrence and Wishart.

Whyte, J. (1990) 'YTP - Some lessons for education?', in Caul, L. (ed.) *Schools Under Scrutiny*, London: Macmillan.

Willatt, N. (1982) 'Germany's industrious apprentices', *Management Today*, March.

Chapter Six

THE IMPLEMENTATION OF THE POLICY APPRAISAL AND FAIR TREATMENT GUIDELINES IN NORTHERN IRELAND

Robert Osborne, Anthony Gallagher, Robert Cormack
with Sally Shortall

INTRODUCTION

One of the dominant themes of public policy in Northern Ireland in the past quarter of a century has been the introduction of various measures designed to ensure fairness in the political process and in access to housing, jobs and public services (Cormack and Osborne, 1991). In the more recent past, there have also been attempts made by government to improve community relations and, within the spending of government departments, the targeting of public resources towards those most in need through Targeting Social Need (TSN) (Osborne, 1996; Knox and Hughes, 1994).

While these efforts together constitute major reforms, they did not include the policy process itself. Throughout most of Northern Ireland's existence the political administration was not trusted by a substantial proportion of the Catholic minority (Phoenix, 1994; Buckland, 1979). The lack of trust was most obviously concentrated on the political part of the administration but significant mistrust of the civil service also existed. The Northern Ireland Civil Service (NICS) in the days before 1972 extolled its commitment to high standards of probity and fairness, and some former senior civil servants have suggested that they were the unwilling partners in decisions that were controversial (Oliver, 1978). However, the unrepresentative nature of the civil service's employment profile together with the documented examples of religious discrimination reinforced the sense of distance and isolation (FEA, 1983). Since 1972 much has changed. Most notably, the profile of the NICS has altered substantially, although there are still few Catholics at the most senior levels (Harbison and Hodges, 1991; Equal Opportunities Unit, 1994).

Under Direct Rule from London, successive governments have committed themselves to ensuring fairness in public policy decisions and the delivery of services. For many in the nationalist community, however, particularly those who feel themselves totally excluded from the wider society - socially, economically and politically - the suspicions about the fairness in the administration of policy remain. The scale of the changes which have taken place in the past 20 years remain largely invisible to them because they have yet to be the beneficiaries. It is in this context that the Policy Appraisal and Fair Treatment (PAFT) initiative must be viewed. The PAFT guidelines have the potential to provide a clear mechanism for ensuring that public policy is adjusted for equity. A successful implementation of PAFT, alongside TSN, should, over time, provide evidence of demonstrable change in policy making and the targeting of resources. Of course, on the other hand, a weak PAFT initiative, because of the gap that will be apparent between the policy's rhetoric and performance, is likely to end up feeding and confirming long-standing suspicions. The successful implementation of the PAFT guidelines has much to offer both communities. PAFT provides reassurance that any differential impact on that community will be as carefully scrutinised and considered as any other. Finally, by extending beyond the traditional religious divide to other groups of people, there is a sense of inclusion offered to those who perceive their interests to have been neglected.

This chapter summarises our investigation into the implementation of the PAFT guidelines in Northern Ireland. The chapter has three main sections. In the first section, we outline the methodology used for the assessment of the initiative in the Northern Ireland departments and associated Non-Departmental Public Bodies (NDPBs). In the second section, we present and evaluate the evidence concerning the implementation of the guidelines including the summaries of a number of case studies. In the final section, we draw our conclusions and outline our recommendations.

METHODOLOGY

The research on which this chapter is based was conducted between September 1995 and February 1996. The early part of the period was spent acquiring basic documentation and familiarisation with the key issues - an essential process before the sequence of interviews commenced. The main method used in the collection of information was semi-structured interviews with relevant personnel in departments, agencies and NDPBs. Initial interviews occasionally required further meetings and all interviews identified data and document requirements. In addition to these meetings, departments were requested to provide a list of three areas of policy or programme development or evaluation. From this list, the research team selected a case study for each department. In allowing departments to nominate their own pool of prospective case studies, the research team acknowledges that it was providing an opportunity for departments to offer those examples which might show the implementation of PAFT to best advantage. This was a deliberate action as it would enable our research to be representative of the best situation across the civil service. In this way, the research is not vulnerable to the suggestion that 'good' examples had been omitted thereby giving an unduly negative picture.

The list of departments, case studies and associated NDPBs and other agencies which were part of the investigation are shown in the Annex at the end of this chapter. In addition, interviews were also conducted with the Department for Education and Employment in London and contact was made with Unison. A number of other bodies and individuals were also consulted informally during the research.

THE ORIGINS OF THE PAFT GUIDELINES

The Standing Advisory Commission on Human Rights (SACHR), in its major investigation of the fair employment issue in the period leading to the 1989 reforms, emphasised that fair employment policy had to be complemented by actions taken by government in relation to all policies which could influence the securing of greater equality (SACHR, 1987). In SACHR's second fair employment report, the Commission argued that there was a need for government and other public bodies to accept the desirability of implementing procedures for monitoring the impact of legislation and of administrative decisions, or policies, on equality of treatment and opportunity across the community (SACHR, 1990). Many other bodies (including the statutory equality agencies and the trade unions) argued that it was crucial that government actions across a range of policy areas worked towards securing greater fair employment rather than frustrating its achievement.

The forerunner of what are now known as the PAFT guidelines were the 'equality proofing' guidelines which originated as a UK-wide initiative concerned with securing greater gender equality. Specifically, they came from a Ministerial Group on Women's Issues and under their terms all Whitehall departments were encouraged to develop, under general guidance, departmental-specific guidelines. The guidelines covered sex and race in Britain. The Northern Ireland Office (NIO) was treated as a single department, and the NIO, through the Central Secretariat (the senior co-ordinating unit in the Northern Ireland Civil Service), issued the 'tailored' guidelines for Northern Ireland in early 1990. The Northern Ireland guidelines covered religion and gender and specific attention was drawn to the relevant legislation including international commitments (for example, International Labour Organisation commitments).

The Central Secretariat in the 'proofing' guidelines argued that 'Northern Ireland departments, as an integral part of policy making and operational planning should adopt a positive and proactive approach to equality of opportunity' (Central Secretariat, 1990:1). These guidelines, however, advocated 'proofing' that was closely tied to legal requirements. Even where attention was drawn to the possibility of indirect discrimination it was in the context of legal definitions rather than the more general idea of 'differential impact'. These guidelines suggest that 'it is up to departments to weigh [the equal opportunity dimension] against other policy considerations' (Central Secretariat, 1990:6).

These limitations were extensively criticised by the equality agencies and the trade unions. The criticism concentrated on additional areas where both direct and indirect discrimination could take place, notably race, disability and age. Other criticisms related to the inadequately positive tone of the document and the absence of significant emphasis on affirmative action available to redress inequalities. Following these criticisms the then Minister, Richard Needham, undertook to review the policy. The review was conducted by the Central Community Relations Unit (CCRU).

Extensive consultations (at least in contrast with circumstances in Britain - see below) were embarked on by the CCRU, not only with government departments but also with the statutory equality agencies - SACHR, the Fair Employment Commission (FEC) and the Equal Opportunities Commission (EOC), as well as Disability Action and the trade unions. The revised guidelines were given endorsement by the Secretary of State and were issued as Central Secretariat Circular 5/93 on 22 December 1993, and came into effect in January 1994.

It is important to recognise that the revised PAFT guidelines remain a UK-wide initiative. However, the experiences in Northern Ireland compared with the rest of the UK vary quite significantly. In moving from 'proofing' to PAFT in Britain there was no external consultation; the revised guidelines were an 'in-house' exercise. When, in interview, the Department for Education and Employment was asked for copies of the addition, the gender origins of the 'proofing' initiative would seem to predominate over some of the other categories in implementation. The suggestion was also made that the main issue for the implementation of the guidelines is the need to get the guidelines into the 'mainstream' of policy making. On this last point there is some similarity in circumstances in Britain and Northern Ireland.

There can be little doubt that considerably more co-ordinated activity is being undertaken in Northern Ireland in relation to PAFT than is currently the case in Britain. It remains to be seen if a change of government would have any impact on the priority given to the PAFT guidelines in Britain.

PURPOSE AND STATUS OF THE PAFT (NI) GUIDELINES

The aims of the guidelines are to ensure that in practice issues of equality and equity are fully integrated into:

> policy making and action in all spheres and at all levels of Government activity, whether in regulatory and administrative functions or in the delivery of services to the public. The guidelines identify a number of areas where there is potential for discrimination or unequal treatment to occur and outline steps which those responsible for the development of policy and the delivery of services should take to ensure that, in drawing up new policies or reviewing existing policies, they do not unjustifiably or unnecessarily discriminate against specified sections of the community (CCRU, 1995).

The categories of the population are groups distinguishable by religion or political opinion, gender, age, ethnic group, disability, marital status and sexual orientation.

The guidelines cover the activities of government departments and all 'Next Step Agencies' and other relevant NDPBs. We found no serious challenge to the categories covered by the guidelines, although the Department of Finance and Personnel (DFP) expressed some criticism both of the external consultation process which had led to the redrafted guidelines and of the number of groups included.

The Status of the Guidelines

The core issue about the PAFT guidelines stems from their status. There are two broad understandings about the status of the guidelines. These can be categorised as the 'strong' and the 'weak' views. The strong view sees the guidelines as providing a substantial commitment by government to ensuring that policy making and service delivery decisions in Northern Ireland do not directly or indirectly discriminate against the identified groups of people. There is a belief that government has accepted the argument advanced by SACHR and other equality agencies and lobbyists that fair employment policy had to be complemented by a commitment by government to equity in all aspects of policy making. The increase in the categories, argued for by the advocate groups, seemed to be an enhancement of this central commitment and a move towards greater inclusion. In this view, the PAFT guidelines set an overarching equity framework for policy making in Northern Ireland.

The weak view is more limited in that the guidelines are seen as a way of emphasising the government's 'strong and long-standing commitment to equity issues'. However, equity issues, while of great importance, have to take their place alongside other policy imperatives. These other policy concerns stem from the fact that Northern Ireland is not an autonomous political entity. As a result of the constitutional relationship with the rest of the UK, policy in Northern Ireland ranges from areas where there are no differences with the rest of the UK, such as social security, through to areas where there is considerable discretion. Under Direct Rule, the extent to which there is discretion for policy departures in Northern Ireland depends, to a significant extent, on the disposition of NIO Ministers and the views of the Treasury and DFP. In this view, there may well be examples of UK-wide policy imperatives which will necessarily override a consideration arising from the PAFT guidelines.

By and large, the first view is, or perhaps was, held by groups outside government while the latter view is more commonly held within government. Baldwin (1995), in his pioneering study of 'rules' in government, has drawn attention to the ambiguous status, political and legal, of all guidelines or rules which do not have the status of legislation (primary or secondary). He has suggested that as a result of justificatory expectations, claims of such rules 'should not be pitched at levels that are unrealistically high' (Baldwin, 1995:121). However, he further suggests that since such rules are often justified in the contribution they can make to effective government, 'they must be rules with the appropriate dimensions and they must be rules that can be applied effectively on the ground' (Baldwin, 1995:121). The contrasting views of the PAFT guidelines and the strictures of Baldwin are well illustrated in the case of Compulsory Competitive Tendering (CCT).

CCT and the PAFT guidelines

Concerned to increase the efficiency of public services, Conservative governments have sought to separate core functions of public bodies from 'peripheral activities'. The latter are put out to tender and, given success in the tendering process, are likely to be undertaken more cheaply by the private sector. The policy received its first major application in Northern Ireland with market testing through competitive tendering of health and education ancillary services. Considerable disquiet has been expressed about this process, particularly in relation to the terms and conditions for those workers who work for the new contractors. A recent EOC Report in Britain argued that CCT in local government has had a differential impact on men and women in manual occupations (EOC(GB), 1995), and the EOC in Northern Ireland has reached the same conclusion in relation to health and education services (EOC (NI), 1996).

Of particular interest in Northern Ireland is that the introduction of CCT in the health services prompted the largest trade union concerned, Unison, to legally challenge the policy. While a part of Unison's case rested on the need for the Health and Social Services Trust concerned to take account of the new evidence from the EOC in Britain, the union also argued that the Trust had 'failed to have regard and give effect to' the PAFT guidelines. Mr Justice Kerr dismissed Unison's case in relation to PAFT because the DHSS had failed to send the guidelines to Health Trusts and therefore the Trust in question could not be expected to take them into account. The judge, however, offered some observations on the guidelines. He suggested that 'there was not a little force' in the submissions made on the significance of the PAFT guidelines by Unison's lawyers to the issues. He went on to suggest that the argument of the Trust's lawyer that the guidelines 'were not a blueprint but more in the nature of a series of strategic objectives' was not attractive. He specifically suggested that:

> if PAFT applied to deliberations and decisions by Trusts, one would expect to see evidence that there had been specific consideration by the Trust of its precise provisions rather than a general dismissal of them as being incapable of practical fulfilment (unreported judgement, Mr Justice Kerr, p12).

After the court's ruling, the DHSS issued the PAFT guidelines to Trusts. In the accompanying letter, the Chief Executive of the NHS Management Executive indicated that the PAFT initiative:

> does not supersede market testing but complements it. In conducting a market test, HPSS organisations should take into account PAFT considerations and, if necessary, set them against the savings which would flow from accepting economically the most advantageous tender. It is clearly important that if it is decided that financial savings, and any other beneficial factors are such that they outweigh the PAFT considerations, then such a decision, and the basis for it, should be fully documented (Letter from the NHS Management Executive, 6 July 1995).

The new position was confirmed by the Minister responsible for Health Services in a debate in the House of Commons on 18 July 1995.

During the research it became apparent that, as a result of the sending out of the letter and the actions taken by Unison with respect to other Trusts, CCT in 1995 and 1996 had become a fraught process in the Health and Personal Social Services. The same issues surrounding CCT have also arisen with the Education and Library Boards (ELBs). However, the position of the DENI is more straightforward. It has written to the ELBs advising them that, under the terms of the 1993 Education and Library Boards Order, ELBs can only take commercial considerations into account alongside legal obligations under the Fair Employment Act. The PAFT guidelines cannot be taken into account. As a result, there is considerable confusion over the significance of the guidelines in the ELBs because of the contrast in relation to the role given to the PAFT guidelines in CCT in health.

In relation to health and education, then, it would appear that CCT is a more important public policy than PAFT. In relation to Health and Personal Social Services, although the DHSS circulated the guidelines to Trusts in 1995, it has made clear that they must be considered alongside financial and other criteria: they are not to be given priority. In education, there does not seem to have been any suggestion that a clash between the existing legislation and the PAFT guidelines requires that the legislation, which predated the guidelines, should be reconsidered.

In summary, in Health and Personal Social Services the guidelines should be 'taken into account' but in education they should not. Such a contradiction requires urgent clarification as there is a resultant confusion about the status of the guidelines. Baldwin's advice outlined above seems directly applicable.

The Status of the Guidelines in NICS Departments

The ambiguous status of the guidelines is reinforced by the positions adopted within the Northern Ireland departments. A somewhat sceptical position is taken by the Department of Finance and Personnel, which expressed reservations during the drafting of the guidelines. Thus, while the Department states that it welcomes the guidelines as 'a further endorsement of the principles of equality and equity,' there remain reservations. In the DFP's view, heightened expectations of 'equity of treatment' for everyone are unrealistic because such equity cannot be achieved and delivered within a short period of time and the 'complexities and cost of effective monitoring seem to have been underestimated'. Moreover, the Department affirms that 'the early experience of PAFT confirmed these concerns' so that within months:

> some outside organisations had expectations of: radically new systems and structures introduced in departments as a response to PAFT; substantial numbers of appraisals completed on existing policies and services; and new monitoring frameworks created (DFP Statement to the Research Team, February 1996).

Moreover, PAFT was seen as a potential lever against some national government policies which had been accepted by Ministers as applying equally and appropriately to Northern Ireland, presumably an indirect reference to the CCT issue. In expressing these concerns, the DFP has flagged an important constraint, not on the principles of equity and fairness, but in the practical application of the guidelines. The DFP believes that expectations of the guidelines in the real context of government in Northern Ireland are far too high.

The 'real context' of government in Northern Ireland, runs the DFP argument, stems from Northern Ireland's position in the UK. The long period of devolved government which ended in 1972 has given aspects of policy making in Northern Ireland a distinctive character (Birrell and Murie, 1980; Buckland, 1979). Some observers have suggested that the distinctive nature of the policies themselves is being eroded through a gradual extension of UK-wide measures (Birrell, 1990). Nevertheless, there are areas where Northern Ireland departments have policy discretion. In particular, in interview, it was officials in the Department of the Environment (DoE) and Department of Economic Development (DED) who suggested that these departments had scope for policy innovation. The DFP, because of its role in the public expenditure process, undoubtedly reflects a conservatism towards any activity that requires additional funding. The squeeze on public expenditure emanating from London has, according to the DFP, constrained the exercise of policy discretion by departments.

In the first PAFT report (CCRU, 1995), it is suggested that some departments have virtually no policy discretion. The Social Security part of the DHSS (and the Agency) were depicted as an example of this, together with the DANI. However, there are considerable differences between the approaches of the two departments. In Social Security, following the parallel introduction of social security legislation in Northern Ireland to that in Britain in the 1940s, a policy of parity prevails. Benefits and their regulations are determined on a UK basis with no regional variations. However, it has become a practice in the DHSS to monitor all policies closely with a view to 'getting the Northern Ireland view' into any emerging policy as early and as forcefully as possible. It is recognised that, as Northern Ireland only represents a small part of the UK population, it can be difficult for the DHSS to secure a change of policy, but the Department tries to identify opportunities where it may be possible to fine tune the detail of a policy to take account of the local situation. The process of trying to put a Northern Ireland perspective on the agenda is assisted by the independent Social Security Advisory Committee (SSAC), which has a Northern Ireland representative. The SSAC was described by the DHSS as a 'PAFT parliament', as its concerns cover the implications of policy changes in social security in terms of the groups identified by PAFT. The advent of the PAFT guidelines has augmented rather than altered this approach by departmental officials. The new category added to the list by PAFT is religion, and officials now consider in responding to developments whether there is a differential impact by religion. This additional element has, however, only very recently been incorporated. A small ongoing example was given in relation to the funeral grant. Different burial practices take place in Northern Ireland compared to the rest of the UK and the Department, as part of the national review, is seeking to establish the extent to which the various church practices in Northern Ireland might increase funeral costs.

In contrast with this relatively proactive approach, the position of the DANI is one where the PAFT guidelines have yet to alter traditional patterns of activity. The DANI regards itself as having relatively little policy discretion - largely responsible for implementing policies that originate from London or Brussels (but in interview, it was suggested that 44% of the Department's expenditure was not determined by these external agencies). As a result of this view, the Department, despite pressure from the DFP, does not undertake policy evaluation although it is responsible for feeding information into national or EC evaluation exercises. Currently, no data are collected in relation to the delivery of agricultural policy in terms of religion. The DANI perceives difficulty in relating the 'social' concerns of PAFT to the 'business' of agriculture, both within the Department and the agricultural community at large. Nevertheless, the most 'social' arm of the DANI, the Rural Development Council (RDC), at the time of this study, did not recall receiving the guidelines. Since such large amounts of public money are channelled through the DANI, it is striking that the Department is unable to say how these resources impact on the two communities in Northern Ireland. It may well be that the capacity of the DANI to substantially influence policies set elsewhere is limited. Nevertheless, being armed with the appropriate information could identify and strengthen locally-based arguments that could be made when major policies are being evaluated in Britain. The position taken by the DANI (and the RDC) does, in effect, reduce the status of the PAFT guidelines.

A concern about the status of the guidelines and their implementation led the Permanent Secretaries of the Northern Ireland Departments to consider how the implementation of the guidelines could be more focused. The concern was stimulated by the Unison action and possibly also by the commissioning of this research. In September 1995, it was agreed that the following would be undertaken: the addition of specific PAFT annexes to submissions to Ministers on new policies; legislation etc. which will set out transparently the process of PAFT assessment; greater CCRU involvement in departmental five-yearly reviews of major policy areas; and further approaches to NDPBs to ensure commitment to PAFT principles.

Such recommitment to PAFT by the NICS at the most senior levels is significant. However, such reaffirmation will require effective action on implementation.

IMPLEMENTATION

The Role of the CCRU

The CCRU has the central responsibility for the implementation of the PAFT guidelines. It circulates the guidelines to departments, monitors how departments' policies are being put into practice and promotes and co-ordinates action where appropriate (CCRU, 1995). The CCRU is described as having 'a key challenge role in respect of equality and equity issues in departments' programmes and oversight of the implementation of PAFT' but it is also important that 'departments take full responsibility for assessing the implications of their own policies in relation to PAFT' (CCRU, 1995:6-7). In interview, it was stressed that the success of PAFT could only come about if the guidelines became absorbed 'in the bloodstream of the department,' because the CCRU:

> has no power to insist, in the context of PAFT or otherwise, that a particular policy be recommended to Ministers, nor that a particular course of action be adopted or enjoined upon a non-departmental public body. Indeed, it would be wholly inappropriate for the normal process of decision making and accountability to be distorted in that way' (CCRU, 1995:.7).

Thus, while the CCRU has both a challenge role and a responsibility for co-ordination, it does not have the power or authority to insist on a particular policy or form of action - ultimate responsibility lies with each department.

In order to effect its co-ordination of the implementation of PAFT by departments, the CCRU established a Lead Officers' group. The Lead Officers' group comprises a representative from each department, usually at Grade 5 (Assistant Secretary) or Grade 7 (Principal). The group was created as a forum for discussion between the Lead Officers, allowing experience to be pooled and common approaches developed. Topics discussed at initial meetings included monitoring and training requirements and the format of annual reports. The performance of the group is outlined below. Commenting on the experience of the first year of implementation of PAFT, the CCRU suggested that 'the PAFT guidance has taken root in the culture of Northern Ireland administration', although 'the process may take some time to come to fruition' (CCRU, 1995:25).

The implementation of the PAFT guidelines by the CCRU has rested on the idea that after initial awareness training, the primary responsibility lies with the departments. The comment made on several occasions by the CCRU was that the PAFT guidelines would only succeed 'if they enter the bloodstream of departments'. The Lead Officer group was designed to assist in this process, as is spelled out in the first annual PAFT report (CCRU, 1995).

The model for implementation of the PAFT guidelines adopted by the CCRU seems to be very similar to that used initially by the DFP in relation to the dissemination of the Treasury guidelines concerning the undertaking of policy evaluation towards the end of the 1980s. When the Treasury sought, under the Financial Management Initiative (FMI), to establish the evaluation of policies on a regular basis, the DFP passed on these guidelines to the Northern Ireland departments with the view that departments themselves would be best placed to implement them. However, the Northern Ireland Audit Office's (NIAO) 1992 investigation of policy evaluation in the NICS departments found only a patchy performance. Major deficiencies were found in some of the evaluations scrutinised by the NIAO, and this led to the recommendation that:

> While accepting that departments were aware that policy evaluation should become a normal and expected part of management, NIAO believes that development of formal comprehensive procedures would have established a fuller appreciation of the need for and benefits of policy evaluation (NIAO, 1993:8).

The DFP subsequently issued detailed guidelines on policy evaluation to the Northern Ireland Departments and has enhanced its role in assisting policy evaluations completed by departments (DFP interview with research team).

The CCRU has adopted a similar approach to that used by the DFP in its initial phase of implementing the policy evaluation guidelines - the approach that the NIAO had found to have largely failed. There is significant merit in the CCRU's belief that the guidelines will only become fully operational if they are fully incorporated into a department's activities and are 'owned' by departments. However, the existing method used to encourage this process is not, as yet, achieving this objective because (as with the NIAO investigation of the implementation of policy evaluation guidelines) it has resulted in a 'patchy' performance thus far. This judgement is based on the detailed interviews with departments, the evaluation of case studies, the scrutiny of statements of future intentions and the NDPBs examined.

The role of the CCRU in the implementation of the guidelines requires clarification and rethinking. In interview, the DOE suggested that there was disappointment that the CCRU was not exerting its challenge role more decisively. The Department suggested that, although it was impossible for the CCRU to monitor all policies in the Northern Ireland Departments, it could be more proactive at senior levels within departments. Although the ways in which this could be done were not spelled out by the DoE, a regular cycle of meetings between the CCRU and the most senior officers in departments could offer the CCRU the opportunity to probe commitments made and to assist with major decisions with PAFT implications. It is clear however, that, while the DoE would welcome such a development, other departments would be more resistant. The DFP, for example, tends not to see the guidelines as a new initiative but 'as giving a new emphasis and impetus to the principles of equity and equality which have conditioned new and existing policies and services for years' (DFP statement to the research team) and would probably regard such an enhanced role for the CCRU as unnecessary. Nevertheless, if the guidelines are to play the role we understand government as a whole wishes, as is suggested by the Permanent Secretaries in their September 1995 meeting, then a more proactive role by the CCRU would seem to be required.

Lead Officers' Group

The role described for the Lead Officers' group by the CCRU in the first annual report is not taking place. The group has met very infrequently and has not been a mechanism for the identification of good practice. It has identified some training needs but these have not resulted in any particular training initiative. In interview, Lead Officers suggested that the training initiative 'lies with the CCRU' but there was uncertainty as to when or what would be forthcoming. Similarly, some Lead Officers felt that the CCRU needed to provide full support in addressing and understanding the conceptual and technical issues associated with PAFT; at least one Lead Officer indicated that he was in need of specific advice and support in interpreting the guidelines to his department. The Lead Officers' group is a valid idea, as there is a need for the types of activity outlined by the CCRU for the group to be undertaken.

CCRU - Status and Size

A legitimate question to be asked relates to the status of the CCRU and the resources available to it. The CCRU was created as part of the government's commitment to achieving better community relations in Northern Ireland. It is located within the Central Secretariat, which is a discrete command within the DFP. Central Secretariat is headed at Under- Secretary level and provides a support service to the Head of the NICS and to Ministers. The CCRU provides policy advice to the Secretary of State on all community relations issues. The total annual budget, including EU resources for community relations programmes organised by the CCRU, DENI and DFP, in 1994/95 was £10 million. There are six main community relations programmes under the overall budget: a district council programme; the Community Relations Council; the activities of various reconciliation bodies; a cultural traditions programme; a research programme; and a capital programme to provide community facilities for both communities. The major policy initiatives designed to improve community relations include Targeting Social Need, race relations, the support of the Irish language and PAFT.

The CCRU's responsibilities, therefore, are substantial and include some of the most sensitive policy issues in Northern Ireland. In terms of the CCRU's location within the civil service, it is difficult to suggest an alternative. A location within the Central Secretariat ensures that it is at the heart of co-ordination and that it has ready access to both the top administrative and political levels of authority. Nevertheless, it was suggested by the CCRU that its status is such that it cannot require departments to take action but can only advise and encourage. The CCRU, despite the sensitivity and significance of its programmes, is small, with only 16 staff including support services. Judging whether this is adequate from the perspective of the implementation and potential of PAFT is difficult. Such a judgement rests significantly on the role which the CCRU should play in relation to PAFT alongside its other responsibilities. Having said that, an examination of whether the CCRU's internal resources are appropriately distributed between its community relations responsibilities and its equity responsibilities (PAFT, TSN, etc) would be useful. There may be scope for some re-allocation from the former to the latter, as much of the earlier responsibilities associated with community relations have been devolved to the Community Relations Council. It may be, however, that, notwithstanding this review of internal resources and changes in internal resources, additional resources may be required. The fact that the issues associated with PAFT and TSN are often complex, operate at a high conceptual level and are of a highly political nature, needs to be taken into account in any review of resources.

Lead Officers in Departments

The role of the Lead Officers group has been discussed above and we turn now to the role of Lead Officers within departments. There were significant variations in the location of individual Lead Officers in their respective departments. Some Lead Officers were located in areas outside the main policy branches and divisions, for example, the Lead Officers in the NIO and DANI. Other Lead Officers played a co-ordination role across the range of a department's activities without being located in the policy areas of any of them, e.g. the DHSS Lead Officer. In other departments, the Lead Officer was located in a key position for the evaluation of existing policies and for the development of new policies, for example, the Lead Officers in the DENI and DoE. If Lead Officers are to successfully embed PAFT in policy making then it is surely preferable for Lead Officers to be located within the senior management structure of the department concerned. In addition, in large departments with separate areas of activity, such as the DHSS, it may be necessary to appoint more than one Lead Officer. It follows that Lead Officers should be appointed at a grade commensurate with this location.

A final point with regard to the role of Lead Officers relates to their responsibilities towards NDPBs. Although Lead Officers had ensured that the PAFT guidelines had been sent to the NDPBs associated with their department, there was a perception in some NDPBs that some departments did not regard it as appropriate for Lead Officers to provide any guidance on interpretation or to provide training to NDPBs on PAFT. However, a new initiative, as shown by the earlier experience of the introduction of policy evaluation, needs specific action to ensure its dissemination within the full range of NDPBs and other agencies.

Monitoring and Data Requirements

A new initiative such as PAFT has at its core the implicit assumption that data from appropriate statistical monitoring will form the basis of an appraisal or review. Judgements about differential impact on the PAFT categories of a new policy or changes in service delivery will be more robust if they are based on statistical comparisons. In the collection of data there are generally three approaches. First, developing mechanisms which incorporate a direct measure of the variable in question, such as asking for religious identity. Secondly, using techniques which provide a surrogate or proxy measure. These could include using school attended or geographical area to provide a religious categorisation. The third approach is essentially to do nothing. All three approaches were evident in the NICS in this research.

The availability of data desegregated by religion and gender has increased dramatically in the past few years. The introduction of religious monitoring under the fair employment legislation has demonstrated its acceptability to the general public. Routine continuous surveys, such as the Continuous Household Survey and the population census, record high levels of response to questions concerning religion. Most departments have mechanisms for monitoring religion and gender. Some of these are derived from data based on asking a direct question or are based on surrogate measures. Examples of surrogate measures include the schools-based data used by the DENI (although this is supplemented by the monitoring done by each school) and the religious monitoring undertaken by the Equal Opportunities Unit of the DFP. Other departments are just beginning the process of religious monitoring. The NIO, for example, has commissioned external consultants to advise on monitoring in the criminal justice system. Other departments have yet to fully address the data requirements that may be necessary in order to conduct a PAFT appraisal in many service delivery areas. The DANI, for example, has not established a source of religious monitoring to measure any impact the Department's activities may have on the two communities in Northern Ireland. Consideration has been given in the past to adding a religion question to regular surveys of farms but this idea has been dropped because of concerns about its acceptability, even though religious monitoring is generally accepted in Northern Ireland. The DANI's reluctance to monitor may also be a result of its perception that it is mainly implementing policies which originate from elsewhere (see above). While most departments have begun to consider the issues associated with monitoring in relation to gender and religion, there is, as yet, little evidence of significant consideration being given to any of the other categories covered by the guidelines. With new legislation scheduled for implementation with respect to disability and the promise of race relations legislation, there is a substantial case for the NICS, through the CCRU, to work with departments to consider new data requirements. The kinds of data required for monitoring are strongly determined by the nature of the model for practical implementation of the guidelines and it is to this matter that the chapter now turns.

Implementation: the 'Sensitivity' and 'Checklist' Approaches

The ways in which the guidelines could be implemented in departments was the subject of considerable discussion within departments at the time of the research. In some instances, the unresolved discussion had led to relatively little action being taken.

Two main models of implementation were under discussion. The first, the sensitivity model, suggested that rather than relying on large scale monitoring with potentially huge and costly requirements for new sources of data as the basis for undertaking PAFT reviews, a senior officer could be entrusted with monitoring proposals, evaluations and changes to policies and subjecting them to subjective scrutiny, using the individual's sensitivity to the issues to identify PAFT implications. In some ways this is the model used by the CCRU when it makes an input into a major policy initiative or is asked to advise on a particular policy issue. In these instances, data will be used if they are available; otherwise, detailed knowledge of the issues will be used.

The second model for implementation was variously described as a 'checklist' or 'scientific' model. This approach is driven by the analysis of data, with decisions taken in the context of a PAFT assessment largely dictated by the analysis of data, which in turn is determined by the assumptions built into the data model. In this sense, the 'checklist' approach becomes more of a mechanistic exercise. The worked example of a PAFT appraisal provided by the DoE comes closest to this mechanistic approach. In this example, the DoE outlined a case study based on the closure of a number of benefit offices. The identified PAFT implications were weighed against financial savings and the latter factor was deemed to outweigh others.

These two models are idealised versions of the debate. In reality each approach will also involve aspects of the other. In practice, those departments which are conducting PAFT appraisals (the DoE, DENI, DHSS, DED and NIO) reveal differences in emphasis. The DFP sets its face most resolutely against the 'checklist' approach. It is not the DFP's intention to apply the PAFT guidelines in a mechanistic fashion, although there may be occasions where it is straightforward, for example, in relation to new legislative proposals, PAFT brings fresh impetus to an already impartial administration of policies and practices which are already developed and applied as far as possible in consultation and discussion with appropriate bodies and interested parties (DFP statement to the researchers, February, 1996).

Within the DENI there is also sympathy for the sensitivity model. However, this is based on a ready source of data on schools in terms of religion and gender (but less useful for further and higher education). The DoE's case study, as previously identified, was substantially based on a 'checklist' approach with a tendency towards mechanistic drawing of conclusions. The DED, although well sensitised to some of the issues through its responsibilities for the equality laws, had not, at the time of the research, resolved its own dilemma of whether the 'checklist' or 'sensitivity' model was more appropriate.

The variations between departments in terms of the sensitivity/checklist issue is a reflection of the different approaches taken to the guidelines as a whole, as well as reflecting difficulties in identifying the best way forward. Although a 'checklist' approach is presently the minority model, it represents an important foundation for enabling PAFT reviews to be undertaken. A 'checklist' approach should involve two elements: the framework of questions that need to be asked and the types of information, qualitative and quantitative, that will need to be accessed. On the other hand, such an approach does not necessarily imply that comprehensive sources of data for all the PAFT categories have to be developed. Each department will need to carefully assess data that is available generally and from within the department and then to assess the need for further sources of information. In some instances, existing 'surrogate' information may be adequate. In assessing its needs, a department should be able to use CCRU advice and assistance. There are good grounds for an incremental approach to enlarging the data available to departments.

Nor does a checklist approach necessarily imply that PAFT reviews can be reduced to a largely mechanistic process. Rather, the checklist part of an appraisal should provide a substantial part of the information available to the senior officers of a department on which a judgement will be reached on whether there is a PAFT implication or not and the weighting to be given to it against other concerns. It is important that judgement and discretion can be exercised, notwithstanding the statistical conclusions.

Examples of the application of PAFT are given towards the end of this chapter. They illustrate some of the variations in practice that exist between the departments.

Policy Evaluation

Earlier in this chapter, we drew attention to the development of policy evaluation in Northern Ireland departments. It was noted that the NIAO had found, some years later, a patchy implementation. As a result, the DFP prepared detailed guidelines for policy evaluation in departments, which were subsequently amended to include a reference to PAFT. In addition, the DFP has now adopted a more interventionist approach with departments - agreeing programmes of policy evaluations on a five year cycle and establishing quality assurance mechanisms for assessing completed evaluations.

Most, but not all, departments are now engaged in policy evaluation (the exceptions being the NIO and DANI). These departments indicated that they were proposing to incorporate PAFT reviews into their evaluations of policy as the evaluation guidelines suggest. However, although the policy evaluation guidelines incorporate a reference to PAFT, unlike the rest of the evaluation guidelines, which give detailed suggestions on procedures, there is no equivalent detailed guidance for the undertaking of a PAFT review. More detailed guidance on the undertaking of PAFT reviews needs to be prepared by the CCRU for inclusion in the policy evaluation guidelines. This guidance would take the form of a discussion of general issues, together with a number of worked examples of good practice.

Non-Departmental Public Bodies (NDPBs)

Under Direct Rule there has been a marked growth in NDPBs in Northern Ireland. They are responsible for an increasing range of activities and their budgets reflect additional responsibilities. Studies have sought to assess the extent to which these bodies are publicly accountable in various ways for their actions and activities. The most comprehensive study argued that, in common with parallel developments in Britain, public accountability tended to be limited and was not consistent (Democratic Audit, 1994). Wide variations exist in the relationships between these bodies and government departments. Within this there are two important issues from a PAFT perspective. The first concerns the membership of these bodies. The research conducted in Northern Ireland has pointed to the closed nature of the way people are chosen and the poor representation of women on these bodies. The NIO has recently commissioned research into this whole issue, and practices and procedures in several European countries are being examined to assist with the identification of better procedures and practices.

The second issue is the extent to which the NDPBs have implemented the guidelines. Our research, which by its nature could only examine a small number of examples, found a patchy picture. In relation to the ELBs, as discussed earlier, there was still some confusion over the status of the guidelines in relation to CCT, but in general, little priority was being given to their implementation. This came at least in part from the perceived lack of pressure from the DENI. With respect to Laganside (the public corporation set up to redevelop the waterfront area in the centre of Belfast), the guidelines had been accepted. It was suggested that the new corporate plan would incorporate specific targets which would be PAFT-related. On the other hand, the Rural Development Council could not recall receiving the guidelines, although its Chief Executive recognised their importance when they were described. The Industrial Development Board (IDB) tends to concentrate more on TSN, since the agency does not itself match people to jobs. It was pointed out that advance factory and office units are planned for people with disabilities. The Training and Employment Agency (T&EA) has developed an equality unit where PAFT and TSN matters are dealt with. Thus far, their main concentration has been on the creation of monitoring systems relating to TSN. Within LEDU, although the guidelines had been received, there was frustration that there had been little back-up advice from the DED or CCRU. It was suggested that, while TSN had been given a significant boost from the DED, this had not happened for PAFT. The agency was consulting with the T&EA to develop religious monitoring. Within this small group of bodies there is enough evidence that a very uneven picture prevails. There can be no doubt that the CCRU should be seeking much clearer evidence from departments that the NDPBs are fully implementing the guidelines and that departments are providing appropriate advice and support. One important way in which the NDPBs could be given clear guidance on the importance of implementing the guidelines is through the five-yearly evaluation process under which each NDPB is evaluated by the associated department under Treasury guidelines. At the end of the evaluation, new aims and objectives are formulated for the body in question which will form the basis for the next review. The PAFT guidelines could be incorporated in the new aims and objectives established for each body at the end of its evaluation. Of the NDPBs we examined, only one, Laganside, had been reviewed recently. The review did not incorporate an appraisal of how far PAFT had been implemented and neither were the PAFT guidelines formally incorporated into the new aims and objectives.

Reporting and Accountability

In general, as the strictures of the Scott Report make clear, the UK policy process is characterised by intensive secrecy. The non-availability to the public of the PAFT guidelines in Britain contrasts poorly with the open policy practised in Northern Ireland. The decision to publish an annual report on PAFT in Northern Ireland is a further welcome commitment to openness. In a further commitment to openness, the NICS should consider making PAFT appraisals, particularly with respect to major policy issues, publicly available. In the event of a local Assembly, it may be that PAFT reviews will be routinely considered by committees and thereby become publicly available. There is an important issue about whether PAFT reviews should become available to an NDPB when a PAFT review conducted by the department concerning the body's area of competence has reached a conclusion - should the body have a right to see that review? In normal circumstances, the PAFT review should be available.

The decision by SACHR to fund this research into the implementation of PAFT has provided the first opportunity for external audit of the initiative. The question of future accountability needs consideration. Within the existing political framework, accountability lies through Parliament. The Northern Ireland Affairs Select Committee has already begun a programme of work under its current chair, Clive Soley, MP. Although it has tended to avoid controversial issues thus far, it would be appropriate for that

Committee to add a review of equity issues, which would include PAFT, to its schedule. In addition to Parliament, the implementation of PAFT also falls into the remit of the Anglo-Irish Agreement as a measure concerned with human rights issues in the broadest sense. SACHR is well placed to repeat its research in the near future. Finally, it is likely that the courts will play a part in the process of defining PAFT if Unison or another body seeks to challenge government policy once again.

Summary of the Case Studies

In this section we briefly summarise five of the case studies undertaken during the research.

(a) Relocation of the Department of Education (NI)

The Department of Environment (NI) is the department responsible for the location of government offices and it offered the relocation of DENI as a case study. Research conducted for SACHR in the early 1990s (SACHR, 1991, 1992) amongst other issues identified the relative lack of confidence in the Catholic education system in the DENI. This lack of confidence stemmed from the low representation of Catholics in the employment profile, which, in turn, partially resulted from its location in predominantly Protestant North Down. In addition, the Department's location was not perceived as 'neutral' between the two communities.

The NICS had considered relocation in the aftermath of this research but it was rejected on cost grounds. The issue emerged again in 1995, when it became apparent that the existing building required considerable maintenance expenditure. The appraisal of the options in 1995 identified either a relocation of the Department to central Belfast or upgrading the existing premises. In the appraisal of these options, a PAFT review was conducted. Surprisingly, however, rather than conducting the PAFT review itself, the DoE sub-contracted it to the DENI. This was a highly problematic action as the Department was unlikely to be a disinterested party, and secondly, this was a clear example of the necessity for the involvement of the CCRU since the whole issue of relocation was based on community relations and equity issues. The PAFT review, after identifying its employment profile as the main issue, sought to argue that overall relocation would have little impact as the Department's employees were disproportionately in senior positions and hence more mobile. Moreover, turnover in lower staff levels was such that any change would be very slow. The evidence, however, could have been used to argue for the opposite case. Thus, relocation could ensure the Department was located in a neutral position for both communities; the removal of 450 jobs would have had some impact on the host area, but as an area of relatively low unemployment this would be limited, whereas 450 jobs in central Belfast would, over time, open up these opportunities to the disadvantaged areas of both communities; and, gradually, the Department's employment profile would better reflect the two communities, especially amongst the lower grades where the DENI has the lowest representation of Catholics in all NICS departments. These data were not presented in the PAFT review.

(b) The EU Structural Funds

In accordance with the Structural Fund Regulations, member states were required to submit proposals for the use of European funding over the six year period, 1994-1999. The Northern Ireland programme was agreed with the European Commission in July 1994. Although the drafting of the plan largely took place before the publication of the PAFT guidelines, the exercise was undertaken long after the 'equality proofing' guidelines had been launched and while the PAFT initiative was being drafted. The importance of PAFT to the process is indicated by the CCRU (1995). The drafting of the plan, co-ordinated by the DFP, involved extensive consultation with community and voluntary bodies as well as statutory bodies. Amongst the latter, the Fair Employment Commission and the Equal Opportunities Commission gave detailed suggestions. The FEC suggested that in the general quest for greater employment equality, those business organisations in receipt of EU monies should be required to demonstrate 'fair participation'. This advice was rejected by the DFP as being 'unenforceable'. The existing form of contract compliance under the fair employment legislation was deemed adequate. The EOC welcomed the general commitment to equity and equality issues but made detailed recommendations about how these commitments could be given detailed representation in specific programmes. However, none of these were specifically accepted in the final plan.

It is striking that the specific suggestions of the FEC and particularly the EOC, which could have given direct expression to the general commitments to equity and equality failed to be adopted. This failure questions the extent to which the follow through from general support for equity issues, including PAFT, is more than symbolic in the programme.

(c) Domestic Energy Efficiency Scheme

This scheme was launched, with a parallel scheme in Britain, by the DED in January 1995. The scheme is designed to save energy and improve comfort levels in the homes of those in receipt of one of five state benefits and those aged 60 or over. The annual budget is approximately £2.5 million. The scheme is operated on behalf of the Department by a non-profit making private body based in Dungannon. It uses sub-contractors, recruited under open competition, to undertake installation. The DED sought to introduce PAFT concerns in the scheme and did so in three ways:

(i) a PAFT appraisal of the policy identified that Catholics were more likely to benefit from the policy than Protestants as Catholics are more dependent on state benefits and that the scheme was not available to the under 60s. Both of these differential impacts on groups were deemed appropriate because of the purpose of the scheme;
(ii) specific contractual obligations were laid on the firm and its sub-contractors not to discriminate on the grounds of religion or sex; and
(iii) the setting up of mechanisms to monitor the implementation of the scheme by religion.

This is a small example of good practice with respect to PAFT and is capable of acting as a template for examples within other departments.

(d) The Safer Towns Scheme.

This scheme is run by the NIO and tries to implement a variety of crime prevention schemes. The scheme is administered for the NIO by Extern. Following an evaluation, it was decided that one of the areas which received funding should be dropped. It then appeared that funding was available for the selection of two further areas to join the existing two towns. The NIO sought advice on selection from Extern and from the CCRU. The CCRU, in particular, pointed out that there was no town in the scheme with a Catholic working class area and that this should form part of the consideration of the new selection. Extern provided advice on the incidence of recorded crime in particular towns. The combination of these analyses produced a ranked list. However, several of these towns/areas were eliminated after advice from the police and/or the existence of other agencies. Two towns were then selected which included one with a large Catholic working class representation. It is unlikely that this town would have been selected without the introduction of PAFT concerns. Subsequently, the operation of the scheme in the town with a substantial Catholic population ran into difficulties because of the reported hostility of Sinn Fein, whose members were reported to be threatening shopkeepers who sought to participate.

(e) Transport to School

In December 1995, the DENI announced a review of existing arrangements for transport to school because, under the system of open enrolment, the costs of providing transport had risen from £323m in 1990 to £335m in 1995. It was felt that this increase had constrained the resources available on classroom and other expenditure. Under the proposed new arrangements it was envisaged that assistance should be restricted to pupils and students who had not been able to find places in a suitable school or college within statutory walking distance.

The DENI confirmed that the proposals were subject to a PAFT preliminary analysis which focused on four distinctive issues. Firstly, as parents would be entitled to express a preference for schools based on denominational or non-denominational grounds, or for integrated or Irish-medium schools, the proposals were seen not to have adverse impact on the grounds of religion or political opinion. Secondly, the definition of a suitable school did not differentiate between single-sex and co-educational schooling. On the grounds that the impact on boys and girls was identical, there was seen to be no adverse impact on the grounds of gender. Thirdly, a slightly higher proportion of pupils in Catholic-managed schools stay beyond the compulsory age. In addition, a slightly higher proportion of leavers from Catholic schools go to further education colleges, in comparison with leavers from other schools. On both grounds, the proposals would have an adverse impact on pupils in Catholic schools, but the DENI judgement was that the extent of the impact was so slight as not to constitute a problem. In the light of the available evidence this appears to be a reasonable judgement. Finally, the proposals contained no implications for pupils with special education needs.

The PAFT preliminary analysis illustrates the ways in which data routinely collected by the DENI as part of its normal operations make the process of PAFT appraisal more straightforward. In the case study, all of the data necessary to arrive at judgements were readily available through existing systems.

A further point raised by this case study is more general in character. The decision not to include any difference between single-sex and co-educational schooling in the definition of suitable schooling clearly has no adverse PAFT impact on boys or girls in that it treats both groups equally. However, under certain circumstances it has been recognised that, to achieve equity between diverse groups, it is sometimes necessary to treat groups differently, particularly when the need for affirmative action measures has been identified. On this issue there is a continuing debate on the comparative impact of school type on the attainment level of girls, while it is known also that some ethnic minority communities prefer single-sex schools for girls for religious and cultural reasons. It is not claimed that these factors necessarily apply in this instance, but rather that, in more general terms, adverse impact need not be avoided by treatment as equals.

CONCLUSIONS

To some in the civil service, the PAFT initiative is yet another scheme emanating from the centre which is 'urgent' and of 'vital importance'. The

PAFT guidelines represent yet another new idea which requires new activity. There is no doubt that the civil service could be described as suffering from 'initiative fatigue'. There have been a series of fundamental changes to the organisation and structure of the civil service in the past decade. These, together with the incorporation of private sector management techniques, have provided huge changes for individuals to cope with in a relatively short period.

The particular importance of the PAFT initiative in Northern Ireland was spelled out in the introduction to the chapter. The traditional absence of trust in the policy process amongst the nationalist community has been added to with increasing Protestant alienation. In this context, the mixed picture found in the early implementation of PAFT is unfortunate. A PAFT initiative which is only partly adopted is likely to be particularly damaging politically. The message sent out by the guidelines - a commitment to equity in policy making - will be perceived as more of a gesture than a fully incorporated dimension to policy. That priority has not yet been given to the PAFT guidelines may be a reflection of the consequences of 25 years of Direct Rule. Civil servants may have become increasingly integrated in policy terms to the UK-wide policy agenda. Without a local legislature, striking its own priorities in areas of policy discretion and providing for local accountability, many civil servants have little direct contact with the political parties that would be represented in a local assembly. In this way, some civil servants may have become somewhat removed from the local agenda.

There are major issues to be resolved concerning the status government wishes to accord to the guidelines. As Baldwin (1995) has noted, the position and status of the PAFT guidelines, as 'soft laws', are often ambiguous. Accountability to Parliament may be lacking as a result of inadequate time and the grounds for judicial definition tend to be limited. The CCT example shows the current confusion that exists on the status of the guidelines. If it is accepted that there are a range of competing policy priorities, derived at least in part from the constitutional position of Northern Ireland in the UK, then how will PAFT considerations be judged in relation to these other priorities?

There are also major questions to be resolved in the implementation of the guidelines. The role of the CCRU is central to this issue. It is clear that urgent consideration needs to be given to how the CCRU exercises its challenge role with departments. The allocation of resources and their deployment within the CCRU are also worthy of reconsideration. Major questions remain concerning the operation of the Lead Officers group and the location and status of Lead Officers in departments. Similarly, the competing sensitivity/checklist models for implementation should be resolved with a model which reflects both approaches. Data requirements also need further specification. Finally, much further work remains to be done to ensure NDPBs implement the guidelines.

A final point to note is that the conduct of the research deviated from the classical approach often described in textbooks. In these descriptions, the researcher is depicted as independent of the topic being investigated and measuring through tested objective techniques the relevant phenomenon - an approach known as positivist. During the research, it became apparent that the exercise was taking on some of the characteristics of unintended action research. Action research is undertaken in order to promote a particular outcome. In this instance, it became clear that the commissioning of the research and its conduct was resulting in officials giving significantly more thought to implementation. In this case the result was, we believe, entirely beneficial.

ANNEX

The departments interviewed were:
Department of Agriculture for Northern Ireland (DANI)
Department of Education for Northern Ireland (DENI)
Department of Health and Social Services (DHSS)
Department of Economic Development (DED)
Department of the Environment (DoE)
Department of Finance and Personnel (DFP)
Northern Ireland Office (NIO)
Department for Education and Employment (London)

In addition, several interviews were undertaken with the Central Community Relations Unit (CCRU).

The NDPBs examined were:

Training and Employment Agency (T&EA)
Local Enterprise Development Unit (LEDU)
Industrial Development Board (IDB)
Laganside Corporation
South Eastern Education and Library Board (SEELB)
North Eastern Education and Library Board (NEELB)
Rural Development Council (RDC)

REFERENCES

Baldwin, R. (1995) *Rules and Government*, Oxford: Clarendon Press.

Birrell, D. (1990) 'The Westminster Parliament and Northern Ireland Business', *Parliamentary Affairs*, 43,4: 435-447.

Birrell, D. and Murie, A. (1980) *Policy and Government in Northern Ireland*, Dublin: Gill and Macmillan.

Buckland, P. (1979) *The Factory of Grievances: Devolved Government in Northern Ireland 1921-1939*, Dublin: Gill and Macmillan.

CCRU (1995) *Policy Appraisal and Fair Treatment: Annual Report 1994*, Belfast: CCRU.

Central Secretariat (1993) 'Policy Appraisal and Fair Treatment Guidelines', Mimeo, Belfast.

Central Secretariat (1990) 'Equal Opportunity Proofing, Circular 1/90', Mimeo, Belfast.

Cormack, R.J. and Osborne, R.D. (eds.) (1991) *Discrimination and Public Policy in Northern Ireland,* Oxford: Clarendon Press.

Democratic Audit (1994) *Extra-governmental Organisations in the UK and their Accountability,* London: Charter 88 Trust.

EOC(GB) (1995) *The Gender Impact of Compulsory Competitive Tendering in Local Government,* Manchester: EOC(GB).

EOC(NI) (1996) *Report on the Formal Investigation into Competitive Tendering in the Health and Education Services in Northern Ireland,* Belfast: EOC(NI).

Equal Opportunities Unit (NICS) (1994) *Equal Opportunities in the Northern Ireland Civil Service: Fifth Report,* Belfast: Equal Opportunities Unit.

Fair Employment Agency (1983) *Report of an Investigation into the Non-Industrial Northern Ireland Civil Service,* Belfast: FEA.

Harbison, J. and Hodges, W. (1991) 'Equal Opportunities in the Northern Ireland Civil Service', in Cormack, R.J. and Osborne, R.D. (eds.) *Discrimination and Public Policy in Northern Ireland,* Oxford: Clarendon Press.

Kerr, J. (1995) Unreported judgement by Mr Justice Kerr in the matter of the Application of Unison for Judicial Review, June 6 1995.

Knox, C. and Hughes, J. (1994) 'Equality and Equity: an Emerging Government Policy in Northern Ireland', *New Community,* 20, 2: 207-225.

Northern Ireland Audit Office (1993) *Policy Evaluation in Government Departments in Northern Ireland,* London: HMSO.

Oliver, J. (1978) *Working at Stormont,* Dublin: IPA.

Osborne, R.D. (1996) 'Policy Dilemmas in Belfast', *Journal of Social Policy,* 25,2:181-199.

Phoenix, E. (1994) *Northern Nationalism, Nationalist Politics and the Catholic Minority in Northern Ireland, 1890-1940,* Belfast: Blackstaff.

SACHR (1992) *The 17th Annual Report of the Standing Advisory Commission on Human Rights,* London: HMSO.

SACHR (1991) *The 16th Annual Report of the Standing Advisory Commission on Human Rights,* London: HMSO.

SACHR (1990) *Religious and Political Discrimination and Equality of Opportunity in Northern Ireland,* Second Report, London: HMSO.

SACHR (1987) *Religious and Political Discrimination and Equality of Opportunity in Northern Ireland - Report on Fair Employment,* London: HMSO.

Chapter Seven

TARGETING SOCIAL NEED

Pádraic Quirk and Eithne McLaughlin

INTRODUCTION

After the enactment of the 1989 Fair Employment Act, government in Northern Ireland introduced complementary non-legislative measures aimed at securing greater equality of opportunity and equity. One such measure was Targeting Social Need (TSN), announced by the then Secretary of State, Peter Brooke, in February 1991 and described as a 'public expenditure priority'. As it was intended to improve social and economic conditions by targeting resources on Northern Ireland's most disadvantaged areas and people, TSN has attracted considerable political attention since its inception. This chapter will examine the origins of TSN, the political rationale behind it, and its implementation to date. First, we examine the background to the introduction of TSN, before outlining the problematic status of a number of elements of the policy. The chapter then summarises the results of research carried out into the implementation of TSN between 1991-1995 within Northern Ireland government departments.

PROMOTING EQUALITY: AN OVERVIEW

Following the proroguing of the Northern Ireland Parliament (Stormont) in 1972, the British government introduced a series of reforms in an attempt to eradicate the discriminatory practises associated with unionist hegemony between 1920 and 1972 (see SACHR, 1987: 9-11). However, the continued high levels of unemployment among Catholics, and its contribution to divisions and tensions in Northern Ireland, made the issues of employment and unemployment the central focus of the equality debate from the mid-1970s onwards. The Fair Employment (NI) Act of 1976 and its enforcement body, the Fair Employment Agency (FEA), reflected this focus. It has been argued that this approach failed to take account of key socio-economic differentials which had built up over time between the two communities in Northern Ireland. The nationalist community explained these in terms of the historical legacy of pervasive discrimination within the state of Northern Ireland (Farrell, 1976) rather than 'irrational' individual acts of discrimination by some employers. Greater evidence from the Census of Population and other work by academics (for example, Cormack and Osborne, 1991; Smith and Chambers, 1991) began to challenge the 'isolationist' approach - that is, an approach predicated on legislative action rather than broader equality measures - and to confirm the extent of these differentials. As a result, towards the end of the 1980s, pressure from a number of significant national and international players was mounting on government to look beyond the confines of this approach.

Pressures for Reform

Internally, a key centre for debate was within the Northern Ireland Civil Service (NICS), as historically, there was strong evidence of discrimination in public employment throughout the period of Stormont (Whyte, 1983). Furthermore, in 1983, the Fair Employment Agency (FEA), conducted a review of the employment practices and work profiles within the NICS (FEA, 1983) which exposed the underrepresentation of Catholics, especially in senior positions. In an attempt to 'put its own house in order', the NICS began to develop a series of equal opportunities measures, including workforce monitoring. In addition, the Central Community Relations Unit (CCRU) was established in 1987. The unit, which reports directly to the Secretary of State, is tasked with formulating, reviewing and challenging policy throughout the Government system with the aim of improving community relations and addressing equality and equity issues (see also Chapter Six, this volume).

Forces outside the civil service were also bringing pressure to bear on the government. In September 1987, the Standing Advisory Commission on Human Rights' review of fair employment policy made detailed recommendations for both legislators and policy makers (SACHR, 1987). It has been argued that this report shifted the terms of the debate from concentrating on the eradication of prejudiced discrimination, to reducing unjustified structural inequality in the labour market, whether caused by discrimination or not (McCrudden, 1991: 2) and that it was 'a scathing indictment of almost every facet of the 1976 Act' (Sheehan, 1995). Additional international pressures from Irish-America, through the MacBride Campaign (see Magill and Rose, 1996), and from the government of the Republic of Ireland, though the Anglo-Irish Secretariat, have also been identified as major external catalysts for change. Internationally, the government's previous employment equality efforts (the Fair Employment Act 1976) had been seen to fail and its 'self preservation as the dispassionate arbiter of the inequalities and divisions within the province was undeniably tarnished' (Wilford, 1991: 37).

The result of this pressure was the Fair Employment (NI) Act 1989, described as 'arguably ... not only the most stringent anti-discrimination legislation in the UK but also in Europe' (Osborne, 1996:185). Sheehan, however, has argued that the introduction of the 1989 Act was not 'a benevolent proactive measure it was a reactive, damage limitation response to national and international pressure (Sheehan, 1995:74). However the 1989 Act itself is regarded, it was accompanied by a wider approach to equality involving an incremental series of significant non-legal measures, for example, in the sphere of educational policy (Knox and Hughes, 1993) and local government (Knox and Quirk, 1994). In addition, Targeting Social Need (TSN), announced in 1991, was an extra tool aimed at changing the policy making process. Furthermore, in 1994 TSN was complemented by PAFT, previously known as 'equality proofing', and discussed in Chapter Six of this volume.

THE INTRODUCTION OF TARGETING SOCIAL NEED

Announcing that Targeting Social Need (TSN) was to become the Government's third public expenditure priority, Peter Brooke, the then Secretary of State for Northern Ireland, stated:

> I must stress that we recognise that there are problems of disadvantage and need within both sides of the community. We have to examine carefully the impact of existing major policies and programmes. I intend to pursue the scope for targeting these policies and programmes even more sharply on areas and people in greatest need. To achieve this I have now decided that Targeting Social Need will be the third public expenditure priority in addition to the existing priorities of law and order and strengthening the economy ... We are seeking to address deep rooted problems. Solutions must, therefore, involve a long-term commitment in order to ensure that real and lasting changes are achieved. This will not be a quick nor an easy process. But it does make sense that, if we genuinely wish to address the issue of social need that we have identified and achieve a reduction in community differentials, we must target our resources in the way I have outlined (Peter Brooke, CCRU Equality Review Conference, February 1991).

Embedded within Brooke's definition of TSN were a number of elements which have since formed the framework within which TSN is debated - community differentials and the politics of need; targeting on areas and people in greatest need; TSN as a public expenditure priority; TSN as a policy paradox within UK policy; and the impact of TSN on policies and programmes.

Community Differentials and the Politics of Need

TSN stemmed from a realisation within the NICS that 'on all major and social and economic indicators, Catholics are worse off than Protestants' (DED, 1992, internal memo). As a result, the CCRU had suggested that the initiative be called the 'Community Differentials' programme. However, as Osborne (1996) notes, there was an opposing school of thought within NICS which argued that socio-economic need existed in both communities and that any attempt to promote TSN in terms of directly reducing community differentials would both fail to address equivalent needs in some Protestant areas and increase what was to become known as 'Protestant alienation'. Brooke's speech, and ministerial statements thereafter, imply the triumph of the latter argument (Osborne, 1996), although the aim of reducing community differentials was also retained as a key objective. To a considerable extent, then, government discussion and implementation of TSN since 1991 has attempted to occupy a middle, and arguably ambivalent, road between these two approaches. At times this ambivalence has resulted in a failure to act as later sections of this chapter show.

Targeting on Areas and People in Greatest Need

The attempt to both reduce religious differentials, while simultaneously assuaging fears that (growing) levels of disadvantage in Protestant communities were being ignored, has been carried forward by the development of a spatially conceived programme. This approach is facilitated by the high degree of residential segregation in Northern Ireland: for example, 90% of residents in 35 out of the 51 electoral wards in Belfast are of the same religion. However, to achieve this approach, objective indicators of need at a relatively small spatial level are required. Such indicators were not available in 1991 when the TSN policy was announced nor for the first three years after its announcement.

To redress this, the Policy Planning and Research Unit (PPRU), in 1993 and 1994, commissioned and published a study on relative deprivation in Northern Ireland (Robson *et al*, 1994). Drawing on the 1991 Census, Robson *et al* produced a matrix of deprivation at three spatial levels: District Council (DC), Electoral Ward (EW) and Enumeration District (ED) (see also Chapter Nine, this volume). The ED level analysis provides information on deprivation at a level of no more than 400 houses. The matrix, measuring the degree, intensity and extent of deprivation, has become important to the identification of need in Northern Ireland. Some government departments, particularly the Department of Economic Development (DED), and agencies were quick to adopt it in their TSN efforts. Two important TSN programmes, Making Belfast Work and the Londonderry Initiative (see later section on these special area initiatives), have recently used the model in defining their operational areas. 'Robson' (as it will be referred to hereafter) does not go unchallenged. The West Belfast Economic Forum (WBEF), an independent research and lobbying group, has challenged the theoretical underpinning of the indicators used, suggesting that the statistical methods minimise the effects of extreme values because they give all variables equal weighting. The WBEF argue that this has led to an underestimation of the extent of Catholic deprivation (cited in the Committee on the Administration of Justice submission to SACHR in 1995).

TSN as a Public Expenditure Priority

There have been notable difficulties in ascertaining how the planning, and actual allocations, of public money are affected or influenced by each of the three public expenditure priorities operating between 1991 and 1994, particularly those of 'strengthening the economy' and 'targeting social need' (NIEC, 1994:57). Apart from these problems, considerable debate has revolved around the weighting of the TSN priority relative to those of 'law and order' and 'strengthening the economy'. Following the IRA and Combined Loyalist Military Command ceasefires of 1994, the Secretary of State for Northern Ireland in the 1995 public expenditure announcement stated that the 'top priority' of government between 1996/97 -1998/99 would be 'promoting and sustaining economic growth' unless violence resumed in which case the 'law and order' priority would again come to the fore. It is significant that, even in the post-cease-fire climate, TSN has not been accorded an explicit ranking but rather described as 'continuing to be an important public expenditure priority' (Northern Ireland Information Service, 1995).

A further problem is the relationship between the 'strengthening the economy' and the TSN priorities. Teague and Wilson (1995) have argued that 'there is still a fundamental difficulty in how it [TSN] is implicitly perceived as qualifying, modifying or indeed contradicting the higher goal of strengthening the economy'. Such a 'contradiction' has been a focus of attention within the Department of Economic Development (see discussion below). Teague and Wilson argued that the 'strengthening the economy' priority is narrowly and wrongly focused on an economic orthodoxy which gives pride of place to the 'firm' without acknowledging wider social relationships:

> Let us recognise also that the separation between the second and third government priorities of 'strengthening the economy' and 'targeting social need' is intellectually, as well as morally, indefensible. In that context, the system of government priorities should be scrapped. (Teague and Wilson, 1995: 90).

TSN as a Policy Paradox

However TSN or other public expenditure priorities are defined, the general characteristics of the policy-making process are important in their implementation. Connolly (1992) identified two interrelated trends in the operation of the policy process within Northern Ireland. First, there has been a convergence of Northern Ireland policy with that of the UK. Second, although principles of parity and convergence have been increasingly applied, there remains 'a dominance of Northern Ireland Departments and the Northern Ireland Civil Service in policy making within Northern Ireland'(Connolly, 1992:11). Both of these characteristics are relevant to TSN in so far as they identify its limits and potential.

Northern Ireland departments have argued that TSN is limited by the principle of parity - for example, parity between the social security functions of the Department of Health and Social Services (NI) and the Department of Social Security (GB) - and this is contrasted with the 'scope for policy innovation' which the Department of the Environment (NI) and DED are argued to have (see, for example, Chapter Six, this volume). The scope for action that at least some departments have derives from the fact that policy is, more often than not, co-ordinated at official rather than ministerial level (Connolly, 1992:11). As public expenditure in Northern Ireland is allocated from the UK Treasury in the form of a block grant, Ministers and senior civil servants in Northern Ireland departments have a considerable degree of flexibility in distributing resources, and thus considerable potential to target resources. This explains why Ministers have argued that TSN, through financial planning and shifts in public expenditure patterns, is capable of 'skewing resources to the areas most in need'. On the basis of this logic, TSN should be discernible in a review of public expenditure over time.

The Impact of TSN on Policies and Programmes

Although, as discussed above, the Secretary of State in 1991 indicated that TSN was a long-term commitment which would not be 'quick nor easy', no time frame for implementing and assessing the impact of TSN was given at that stage. TSN implied that government departments would have to introduce monitoring systems capable of assessing the impact of programmes and provisions on community differentials over time, but NICVA (1994) argued that no evidence of even elementary progress towards establishing such processes could be found for 1991, 1992 and most of 1993:

> The TSN policy is potentially the most significant policy initiative in the area of social need, deprivation and disadvantage ever taken by Government ... However, it has yet to take root in all Departments or to make real impact where it is most needed ... Unless Government establishes new ways of progressing the policy and of challenging Departments to

> implement it with vigour and enthusiasm it may unfortunately remain a nice idea existing in the margins of Government and the minds of a few committed individuals (NICVA, 1994: 6).

The results presented in the rest of this chapter lend validity to NICVA's critique, whilst documenting some advances in particular areas.

RESEARCHING THE IMPLEMENTATION OF TSN 1991-1995

The first part of this chapter has summarised the policy context within which TSN emerged and the key themes underlining its implementation. In the rest of the chapter, we review information gathered on the implementation of TSN in research carried out in the winter of 1995 and the spring of 1996. The purpose of the research exercise was twofold: to determine the adequacy of the implementation, operation and impact of TSN since its introduction in 1991 and to compare this across government departments. All the Northern Ireland departments were included in the research, as were the Northern Ireland Office (NIO) and the cross-departmental CCRU.

The research used a structured questionnaire with a number of open-ended questions on training, planning, definitions of need, departmental baselines and monitoring. The scope and content of the questionnaire was developed from analysis of government statements in relation to TSN and public expenditure estimates between 1991 and 1995. Government departments were, therefore, asked to respond to Ministerial statements on the operation of TSN. In addition to general information under the five topics above, each department was asked questions about patterns and trends within their expenditure over the period 1991-1995. The open-ended nature of most questions offered departments the flexibility to reflect the diversity of their individual responsibilities. Some specific examples of public expenditure changes were also selected as 'test cases' in each department for examination in terms of whether TSN had influenced these specific programmes or areas of expenditure. Each department was asked to provide documentary evidence in support of their explanations of how they had defined and implemented TSN (for example, planning documents and internal memoranda on TSN).

Questionnaires were received by all Northern Ireland departments, the NIO and the CCRU in late December 1995 with a deadline of six weeks set for response. This time period was intended to be long enough for collation of existing information and documentation but not long enough for departments to begin their own research or evaluation into how they had implemented TSN (since the latter would mean that they did not in fact 'know' how they had done so). No government department met this deadline and responses were received in mid-February 1996 from the DED and the Department of Agriculture for Northern Ireland (DANI), mid-

March from the DHSS and the DoE and the beginning of April from the CCRU and the Department of Finance and Personnel (DFP). Two government departments, the Department of Education for Northern Ireland (DENI) and the Northern Ireland Office (NIO), failed to respond to the questionnaire despite numerous telephone reminders and letters to each of the Permanent Secretaries in May 1996.[1] Departments were also given the opportunity to meet with the researchers, if they wished, to explain their response in more detail and one department - the DED - elected to do so.

We begin the reporting of research results with the two bodies which play central roles in the process of implementation of TSN and the public expenditure survey process - the DFP and the CCRU. Subsequent sections report on each of the four departments which responded to the research and we also provide some analysis of issues in relation to education, although without the benefit of a response from the DENI.

IMPLEMENTATION OF TSN BY THE DEPARTMENT OF FINANCE AND PERSONNEL

Examination of the DFP's definition, and explanation of the impact, of TSN raised a number of key issues - a lack of accountability surrounding what this public expenditure priority has meant, the obscurity of the balancing of conflicting and overlapping priorities, and the conservatism of current governmental approaches to public expenditure - which were also reflected in spending departments' submissions. The DFP confirmed that TSN was, indeed, ranked last in the public expenditure priorities during the period 1991-1995, although bids 'with strong TSN implications could be met before bids which contributed to the other two priorities'. The DFP stressed that public expenditure priorities are not 'synonymous or coterminous with public expenditure programmes' but rather act 'as a general guide to resource allocation at the margins and not as a prescriptive formulae'. Factors other than TSN which 'come into play in a complex matrix of considerations' include 'legal and contractual obligations, parity in policy and service delivery, Ministerial commitments and Value for Money judgements' in public expenditure planning and provision.

As a result, the DFP argued that the implementation of TSN could not be assessed through evidence of the movement or skewing of departmental baselines. Such an argument, taken together with the fact that TSN 'bids' by departments were assessed in terms of an undefined quality, would mean that TSN would never be capable of objective assessment. While it is obvious that assessment is bound to be difficult, because priorities (whether public expenditure or otherwise) may overlap and even contradict one another, the DFP's approach raises, rather than answers, important questions about how 'public expenditure priorities' can be monitored by those inside or outside government. The absence of strategic planning documents for public expenditure priorities, and the general failure of the DFP to publish any information on TSN since 1991, underline this problem of a substantial lack of accountability surrounding TSN (and indeed the other two priorities). The result is that it is almost impossible to stipulate what may be attributed to TSN in the 1991-1995 period.

Despite this vagueness, the DFP nevertheless argued that public expenditure priorities have been, and are, important on three counts. First, the priorities determine the way in which each government department shapes and manages their programmes, even though, the DFP argued, this 'is not quantifiable' (or by implication measurable). Further, they are used by the DFP as a means of interprioritising additions to, and reductions in, baselines during each survey period, though as noted above this process is predicated upon undefinable notions of the 'quality' of bids. And finally, the priorities are used by the Policy Co-ordinating Committee of Permanent Secretaries (PCC) in assessing the survey recommendations of the DFP before they go to Ministers. Neither the DFP nor other departments have been able to provide more than a few examples of these processes resulting in change in public expenditure patterns.

Osborne *et al* in relation to the implementation of PAFT (see Chapter Six) describe a conservatism in the DFP approach stemming from their role in the public expenditure process. This same conservatism was evident in the DFP approach to TSN, which the department placed firmly in the context of declining public expenditure where Ministers 'are routinely required to make difficult choices in determining PE Survey allocations'. Indeed, the DFP argued that the priority of TSN has been manifest more through the protection of TSN-relevant baselines than through expansion. Such 'protection' may result in TSN-relevant baselines becoming a larger proportion of total spending over time. The examples given by the DFP of this process were the 'two main social programmes, Health and Personal Social Services and Education' which have increased from 52% to 53.6% of the managed block (that is, excluding payments on social security) between 1991/92 and 1995/96. Nevertheless, the department did not claim that the introduction of TSN in 1991 has been followed by major changes in public expenditure. Rather, the department argued that public expenditure has always been 'about' need of some kind and that this in itself makes change difficult:

> the great bulk of Northern Ireland Public Expenditure is, to a greater or lesser extent, targeted at some form of social need. Indeed, targeting of social need is the single most important influence over resource allocation within the Northern Ireland Block. This largely explains the fact that the proponents of TSN outside government appear to have some difficulty in identifying which programmes should be re-targeted or cut to free

resources for TSN relevant expenditure (DFP TSN Submission to SACHR).

The notion that government addresses need through almost all public expenditure is, however, fundamentally different from the type of targeting implied when TSN was introduced. Then, the central issue was the level of public expenditure which would be directed at disadvantaged areas or individuals *over and above* what would normally be expected. The DFP was unable to provide any examples of such 'over and above' expenditure because, as outlined above, 'it is not possible to quantify the amount of resource redistribution that has arisen due to TSN because of the classification difficulties [of TSN] and because resource allocations are influenced by a number of factors'. This suggests not merely conservatism within the DFP, but a complacency which will inevitably add to the growing gulf between public expectations of TSN and civil service views. The issue of TSN is central to wider political considerations of governing a divided society, and within that, the transparency of policy is a critical issue of governance. The DFP's approach to TSN provided little evidence to suggest an appreciation of this within the Department.

THE ROLE OF THE CENTRAL COMMUNITY RELATIONS UNIT IN TSN

The CCRU's primary function is to provide policy guidance to the Secretary of State on community relations and equity issues and to 'challenge' departments on these issues. As with the implementation of PAFT discussed in Chapter Six, the CCRU submission on TSN suggested that the nature and extent of this 'challenge' role was problematic. We consider this first in relation to training provided by the CCRU to departments on TSN, since that is an indicator of the Unit's advisory and guidance role.

The 'Guidance' Role

Prior to, and immediately after, the public announcement of TSN in 1991, the CCRU organised a series of briefing seminars to introduce departments to the initiative. Such briefings appear to have been short, one-off events (for example, the 'detailed session' given to the DED by the CCRU in 1991 was scheduled to last for two hours), despite the fact that TSN involves issues that 'are often complex, operate at a high conceptual level and are of a highly political nature' (see Chapter Six). The CCRU continued to organise similar seminars on an 'ad hoc basis' with other government agencies including the RUC and the Army in 1993. Turning to training on implementation matters, the CCRU's submission noted that the responsibility for training staff below Grade 5 (senior management) level rests with each government department. However, no training appears to have been provided by the CCRU for above

Grade 5 staff or by government departments for below Grade 5 staff on the operation of TSN between 1991 and 1995 beyond the introductory briefings referred to above or the inclusion of TSN as a small item within more general departmental induction sessions.

The 'Challenging' Role: Monitoring

The CCRU's 'challenging' role can be examined in relation to two main areas of activity: first, encouraging departments to obtain the information necessary to effectively target social need and, second, encouraging departments to formulate TSN bids in the public expenditure survey process. In relation to the first of these, the CCRU submitted three reports on the informational and monitoring requirements of TSN which had been presented to the inter-departmental Social Steering Group (SSG). In the 1993 report, the CCRU set out an ambitious specification of the informational requirements of TSN:

> In order to implement the initiative effectively (and in order to be seen to do so) it is essential that the government knows the precise extent to which its whole range of policies has a differential impact upon the two main communities ... it is necessary to have information which will detect an improvement or deterioration in areas where there are recognised differentials, for example, employment, unemployment, housing, education, skills and income levels. Secondly, ongoing monitoring of policy areas where there appears to be no current differential is also a requirement, if newly developing differentials are to be identified quickly ... Thirdly, it is important to have a range of detailed monitoring information so that policies can be designed and implemented in ways which reduce existing known differentials. Fourthly, monitoring systems are essential so that when new policies are implemented differential effects can be detected. In this context it is important to recognise that differentials can arise as unintended consequences of policies which, on the surface, appear to be fair (CCRU, Report to the SSG, 1993: 2-3).

Pointing out that surveys such as the Continuous Household Survey (CHS) and Labour Force Survey (LFS) are 'too macro' to deliver good quality monitoring information and subject to sampling errors, the CCRU argued that monitoring needed to become part of routine activity and that 'this should be presented as a requirement for Departments rather than the present ad hoc arrangements' (CCRU, Report to the SSG,1993:6). The 1994 report showed disappointingly little progress on any of the detailed suggestions for new or reformed information-gathering by departments made by the CCRU in 1993. The 1995 report did not attempt to compare departmental activity in 1995 to what the CCRU had outlined as necessary for effective implementation of TSN in 1993, even though either no development had occurred or options contrary to those recommended by the CCRU had since been adopted by departments.

The 'Challenging' Role: encouragement of bids

In terms of 'encouraging departments to bring forward TSN bids,' confusion appears to have arisen between the roles of the DFP and the CCRU. In the 1994 PAFT Annual Report (CCRU, 1995), the DFP was ascribed this role, yet in response to this research, the DFP assigned this role to the CCRU. Meanwhile, the CCRU described itself as 'assisting', rather than encouraging, departments in making bids, and assisting the DFP in the prioritisation of departmental bids. It would appear, then, that neither the CCRU nor the DFP have taken, or been given, the responsibility for encouraging departments to bring forward TSN bids. The lack of clarity and ambiguity surrounding the roles of the DFP and the CCRU in relation to encouraging departments to bring forward TSN bids clearly needs to be addressed.

In summary, the 'challenging' role of the CCRU in respect of TSN appears to be confined to advice and reports to the interdepartmental Social Steering Group (SSG) and correspondence with Ministers. Both place the CCRU on the margins of a TSN planning process which in itself is unclear and unsystematic, if not non-existent. Further, the evidence in relation to TSN supports Osborne *et al*'s conclusions about the general weakness of the CCRU's 'challenging role' (Chapter Six).

Increasing the pace of change

Given the 'challenging' role of the CCRU within government in relation to equality and equity issues, the CCRU was asked to comment on the appropriateness of setting goals and timetables for TSN, on the grounds that these might constitute 'affirmative action' measures by government, parallel to those which employers are encouraged to adopt under fair employment legislation. The CCRU regarded the setting of goals and timetables for the reduction of community differentials by departments as problematic on two grounds: first, because the ability of departments to impact directly on these differentials through their programmes varies considerably; and secondly, because some important areas are 'outwith' government. The example the CCRU chose was that of long-term unemployment:

> For other socio-economic differentials, notably male long term-unemployment, more complex mechanisms are at work. Since many of these are outwith the control of the Secretary of State for Northern Ireland in particular, and the Government at large, the value of such targets, other than for declaratory and aspirational purposes, is dubious (CCRU TSN submission to SACHR).

Given that in 1991, prior to the launch of TSN, it was agreed within the NICS that the priorities for TSN were enhancement of employment and employability, many outside government will find this approach to long-term unemployment disturbing. We turn now, however, to the issue of variable abilities across departments to address differentials through TSN, or indeed to implement TSN at all, as exemplified in the DANI response.

IMPLEMENTATION OF TSN IN THE DEPARTMENT OF AGRICULTURE FOR NORTHERN IRELAND

As with approaches to PAFT (see Chapter Six), the parity issue framed both the DANI, and the Social Security part of the DHSS (discussed further below), responses to TSN. In addition, the DANI approach illustrates how some departments redefined 'Targeting Social Need' as simply 'meeting need', (consistent with the DFP's approach discussed above), thereby justifying little change in their provision since, they argued, much of their activities 'met need' prior to 1991.

Parity

The DANI argued that it has limited ability to incorporate TSN because it is primarily an 'agent' delivering national and European Union policies. Nearly half, 44% (£133 million), of the DANI's budget is not, however, connected with the pursuit of European or national policies, although two-thirds of this are consumed in departmental running costs, leaving £ 44 million to be spent on 'purely local policies.' The latter include activities such as urban and rural drainage, agricultural education and research and development work and, significantly, the department's activity under European Union Structural Funds and Community Initiatives.

The force of the argument that the DANI's approach to TSN (and PAFT) is limited by its 'agent' role is challenged by the fact that the only provision identified by the DANI as 'TSN' (apart from rural development) falls within the 56% of the department's budget 'determined' by national and European Union policies. This provision (also cited by the DANI as evidence of its PAFT approach) - the Hill Farmers payments scheme (HCLA) - compensates Hill Farmers for 'the permanent social and other handicaps faced and ... help[s] maintain the population in those areas'. The DANI pointed out that these payments 'are one example of a means by which we have always sought to target social need' (that is, they pre-date TSN). Annual expenditure on payments to hill farmers between 1991/92 and 1995/96 averaged £16.1 million but the payment trend has been downwards since 1993/94, even though 65% of HLCA payments are subsequently reimbursed through the European Agricultural Guidance and Guarantee Fund. This example therefore provides evidence against which to assess the success of what the DFP called the 'protection' of TSN relevant baselines.

Targeting Social Need or meeting need?

The DANI's use of the HLCA example highlights a common argument used throughout all of the spending departments' submissions - that the introduction of TSN created an 'artificial' time line. Government departments obviously did meet (some) needs prior to 1991. However, it could be argued that if TSN is to 'mean' anything, departments must recognise two significant differences between TSN and the general function whereby government addresses need. First, as discussed in the DFP section above, unless the level of public expenditure directed at particularly disadvantaged areas or individuals is *over and above* what would normally be expected, TSN cannot be regarded as achieved. Second, TSN was intended to be, more or less directly, 'about' reduction of socio-economic differentials between the two main communities in Northern Ireland. For these two reasons, this research focused not on the adequacy with which government addressed need through mainstream departmental programmes but how these programmes were enhanced or changed as a result of TSN. Departments were asked to illustrate examples of increased efforts in the targeting of resources within the particular confines of TSN as conceived and defined by Government Ministers in or since 1991. The DANI failed to provide any examples of skewing of baselines post-1991 apart from the addition of rural development as a small programme of activity (see below).

The DANI mainstream programmes and provision have, therefore, been untouched by TSN and TSN has been pursued by the department through a small new area of activity - rural development. This accounts for 6.5% of the DANI's expenditure, and depends heavily (75%) on European Union funding. The programme is clearly marginal, and separate from, the department's overall activities.

Monitoring

The weakness of the department's incorporation of TSN into its activities is related to the department's lack of monitoring by religion. This, and the result that the Department is unable to assess policy outcomes in terms of community differentials, contrasts with key Ministerial statements. The 1993 CCRU report to the SSG identified several potential areas for priority action and one of these was that 'the system of grant support and aid to the farming community should be monitored to determine its fairness and its impact upon the two main sides of the community' (1993 CCRU Report to SSG, Annex: 2). The 1994 CCRU report noted that the DANI had strongly opposed options for introducing the gathering of information on religious affiliation and implied that only 'a Ministerial steer' would produce action.

Such a steer has, presumably, not been forthcoming since in their response to this research, the DANI argued that, given the difficulties of altering the focus of agricultural policies (that is, parity), religious monitoring would be of limited benefit.

It is not necessarily the case, however, that the level of policy flexibility available to departments should be the determinant of knowledge of actual or potential differential impacts of policies. It could legitimately be argued that such concerns do not 'excuse' a department from the responsibility of assessing activity with regard to its beneficiaries, particularly those in most need. From this point of view, departments should be able to estimate the effects of policies in terms of TSN, whether they are driven by forces outside Northern Ireland or not.

IMPLEMENTATION OF TSN IN THE DEPARTMENT OF THE ENVIRONMENT (NI)

While the DANI may be constrained by UK and EU policy, this is not the case for the DoE (NI) whose extensive policy, executive and regulatory responsibilities stem primarily from the removal of powers from local government in Northern Ireland and the unique arrangements for governance associated with Direct Rule. Whether such greater scope has resulted in a different approach to TSN by the DoE is the first question we address, a question given greater weight by the considerable spending power of the department (which in 1996/97 is estimated at £1200 million) (The work of the DoE's Urban Affairs Division is reviewed later in the 'Special Area Initiatives' section of this chapter).

The department did not incorporate TSN within its corporate planning process until 1996 and consequently none of its executive agencies or divisions have planned for TSN. This non-committal approach was reflected in the narrow definition with which the DoE views its role in TSN. For example, the DoE did not place TSN within any framework of reducing community differentials. In general, the department's approach to TSN has been, at best, minimalist and, at worst, narrow and contradictory. The department argued that certain areas of their activity (such as urban regeneration, housing and public transport) focus directly on aspects of social need, and by reporting these areas of work as TSN, the problem of departments arguing that the general function of government in addressing need is the same as TSN is again highlighted. Thus, while narrowly defining the applicability of TSN to DoE functions in general, the department defined social need very widely with regard to the transport function.

In this way, it argued that the provision of concessionary fares to pensioners and young people under 16, and financial assistance provided to disabled people, was 'TSN', and the division concerned argued that there was no need to monitor provision by religious affiliation as concessionary fares were a universal benefit which applied equally to both sections of the community. Clearly, the purpose of TSN in reducing community differentials has not taken root in this area of the DoE.

The department acknowledged that other activities, such as the provision of road and transport infrastructure and planning decisions, 'may have TSN implications' and the department further acknowledged that planning service decisions have an important bearing on 'access to employment, housing and social facilities in areas of social need'. However, the department did not analyse their activities in these areas in terms of TSN. This is unfortunate given that road and transport infrastructure and planning service functions are probably most central to public expectations of TSN in relation to the DoE. Nationalist politicians and equality lobbyists regard TSN, through its skewing of resources, as the vehicle for undoing past discriminatory practises associated with, for example, road planning in Northern Ireland. Nationalists argue that there remain major infrastructural differences between the road system west of the Bann, which has a largely Catholic population, and that east of the Bann, which is predominately Protestant. Road infrastructure is argued to have direct TSN relevance because improved roads create more favourable conditions for potential investors and hence improve employment prospects.

In the light of this, current public expenditure estimates of long-term capital road projects in Northern Ireland do little to address such concerns. These estimates, at 1996/97 prices, provide for 84% of road projects east of the Bann. Whatever the merits of this example, it serves to underline the increasing gap which exists between the public perception of TSN and its practical application in government. This gap results from a failure by government to set the parameters of the TSN debate within its own administration and to communicate that to the wider community. In terms of the road infrastructure example, the 1993 CCRU report to the SSG argued that 'all departments should consider monitoring those capital and other programmes and projects which have a potential for employment generation in order to measure the effects on community differentials' (1993 CCRU Report to the SSG, Annex: 2). The CCRU report to SSG in 1994 argued that expenditure on water service and roads were available and analysed at the level of the District Council area, and therefore could be examined relative to need (1993 CCRU Report to the SSG, Annex:3). Although the 1995 CCRU report stated that 'TSN has been built into all Policy Evaluations and Policy Appraisals which are undertaken by [DoE] divisions', which presumably includes road infrastructure and spending, the department did not produce evidence of this.

IMPLEMENTATION OF TSN IN THE DEPARTMENT OF HEALTH AND SOCIAL SERVICES

This Northern Ireland department has two divisions - Health and Personal Social Services (HPSS) on the one hand and Social Security on the other. The nature of the Department's response differed between each division. We turn first to health and personal social services, where some, though uneven, activity has occurred, before turning to social security, where the issues of parity and the juxtaposition of the general meeting of need with TSN have assumed great importance.

The Health and Personal Social Services

Within the HPSS, TSN has generated considerable discussion, and some activity. Progress in the area, however, is indicative of the length of time that can elapse between a Ministerial announcement of an initiative and its translation into actions with demonstrable effects. In the case of the HPSS specifically, it could be argued that the coincidence of the introduction of the purchaser/provider split in the early 1990s, which quite fortuitously placed the sector in a prime position to change historic patterns of resource allocation, should have permitted earlier implementation of TSN than has been the case.

In 1992, the DHSS adopted the Targeting of Health and Social Need (THSN) into its Regional Strategy (1992-97). Despite this, a departmental-led THSN working group was not established until May 1994. Until this date, Area Health and Social Services Boards were left to carry responsibility for THSN without guidance, support and information from the department. The THSN Working Group has since carried out reviews of literature on 'variations' (or inequalities) in health and social well-being, commissioned additional research, and visited each of the four Area Boards in December 1994/January 1995 to discuss their THSN work, including their population needs assessment and internal resource allocation procedures. The principal outcome of the group's work has been the inclusion of guidance on how to progress THSN in the Draft Regional Strategy for 1997-2002, something which was wholly lacking from the 1992-1997 Regional Strategy. However, had such guidance been included then, it might have been possible for the development of the purchaser role during the first half of this period (and through that the capacity to assess needs for health and social care) to be explicitly tied into the development of THSN.

In terms of increased skewing of resources to those most in need - which we have argued to be the hallmark of TSN - the allocation of resources by the department to the Area Boards is currently under review by a Capitation Formula Review Group. This Group is charged with creating a formula which is methodologically sensitive to THSN. Resource allocations within Board areas to Trusts or other providers have continued to be primarily determined by historic patterns, rather than through the use of funding formulae based on assessments of needs. Only the EHSSB was reported by the department to use such formulae and only the EHSSB committed itself, in its Area Strategic Plan for 1992-1997, to a general redirection of resources in response to THSN and then only in relation to new resources. The 1997-2002 Draft Regional Strategy will require all Boards and other purchasers to establish formal links between their population needs assessment and the consequent allocation and use of resources and, by 2002, to demonstrate shifts in resources to improve equity and efficiency of resource distributions relative to health and care needs. The implication is that there may not be any substantial shifts in public expenditure allocations within at least three of the four Board areas as a result of THSN until 2002.

Social Security Policy and Provision

As previously noted, the Social Security side of the DHSS has distanced itself from implementation of TSN on the grounds that parity considerations leave no room for Northern Ireland-specific initiatives. The strength of this argument has, however, been lessened by the introduction of pilot social security schemes in England and Wales (see, for example, Chapter Three, this volume) which mean that it is no longer true that every citizen of the UK receives the same treatment under social security law and regulations. The Department's second argument against the relevance of TSN for social security is that all social security payments target social need. Again, this is an instance of a division or department re-defining TSN so that it is no longer about targeting 'on areas in need' (that is, the spatial element, and indirectly community differentials). It is also another example of a department redefining TSN as being 'about' the general function of public expenditure in meeting need. It is the absence of the 'spatial element' to which we first turn.

It was socio-economic indicators such as the lower household incomes of Catholics compared with Protestants, and the higher (almost double) proportion of Catholic households dependent on social security, which formed the statistical evidence on which TSN was introduced. However, in their response to this research, the Social Security Agency (SSA) and the department argued that these differentials were irrelevant to the operation of social security provision, largely because of the dictates of parity, but also because the SSA 'treats all claimants equally'. However, it is important to distinguish between social security provision and social security policy. Whilst the latter may be constrained by parity (though see discussion above), the former involves issues such as the take-up of benefits by different kinds of claimants, the behaviour of staff, and so on, all of which fall within the remit of local social security provision.

This is why the 1993 CCRU report to the SSG argued that take-up of benefits was a TSN issue and that 'information on eligibility for Social Security Benefits is necessary in order to calculate take-up rates. Differential take-up is a possible TSN issue and information on the eligibility and receipt of benefits should, therefore, be available by religion' (1993 CCRU Report to the SSG, Annex:1). In 1994, the CCRU noted that the SSA did see TSN monitoring as relevant to issues of eligibility and take-up, and together with the DHSS, were 'investigating the possibility of monitoring the effectiveness of SSA's take-up promotion activities by sampling existing claimants on their entitlement with a religious identifier' though the plans were 'not yet ... finalised nor cleared with the Minister' (CCRU Report to the SSG, 1994: 2).

However, in their response to this research, neither the DHSS nor the Social Security Agency indicated that they regarded these kinds of issues as relevant to TSN. There was also no indication that research has been undertaken, or is planned, on the relative success rates of claims for specific benefits or the relative take-up of entitlements to benefits in each community, despite indications in the CCRU report to SSG in 1995 that this was under active consideration. Neither did the department or the agency discuss the funding provided to the independent advice sector for social security take-up work in areas of disadvantage under Making Belfast Work and Londonderry Initiatives, which suggests that there is some, but partial recognition of the spatial dimension to TSN in social security provision.

The absence of routine monitoring information on religion, or of special research focusing on community, differences in their experiences of social security, was used by the department to justify its inability to undertake assessments of potential or actual differential impacts on the Catholic and Protestant communities stemming from social security policy changes: 'as no information is collected on the religious affiliation of social security benefit claimants or recipients, the differential effects of benefit changes, expenditure, etc. cannot be assessed.' Thus, there have been no assessments of differential community impacts anticipated from the forthcoming change from Unemployment Benefit to Jobseekers Allowance (October 1996) or actual differential impacts from the April 1995 change from Invalidity to, the more restrictive, Incapacity Benefit. The latter may have had differential impacts, because the rate of increase of Catholic working-age male economic inactivity in recent years has been higher than that among Protestants (see Chapter One, this volume). The inability to make such assessments does not sit well with the department's claims, both in relation to PAFT and TSN, that it attempts to introduce local considerations into the early stages of UK social security policy formulation. How it is able to do so if it is unable to identify the differential effects of potential changes remains obscure. In addition, as with the DANI, it could be argued that it is a responsibility of a Northern Ireland department to know, and document, the impact of UK policies on the Northern Ireland population (and indeed preferably to make that information available to those involved in public and political debate).

SOCIAL NEED AND THE DEPARTMENT OF EDUCATION FOR NORTHERN IRELAND

The Secretary of State and the Education Minister have considerable power to decide how much of the education budget should be allocated to recognise the effects of social deprivation on educational attainment. This is through:

(a) the formulae used to allocate funds directly to voluntary grammar and integrated schools;
(b) the amounts distributed to each Education and Library Board (ELBs) and the extent to which these are affected by social need criteria;
(c) regulations governing how ELBs delegate funds to schools, and the balance between allocation on a per capita basis only and weightings for social needs;
(d) allocations to projects such as Making Belfast Work and the Londonderry Initiative;
(e) general policy decisions such as whether the selection system should be maintained.

The DENI's non-participation in the main research exercise (noted earlier) prevents a full analysis of all of these mechanisms, particularly the first two which are of great relevance to TSN. The DFP argued that the allocation by the DENI to ELBs (£889m in 1995/96) is a TSN-relevant baseline, because the expenditure is skewed to Boards and schools where needs are greatest. However, neither the DFP nor the DENI have provided evidence on this point. In what follows we concentrate on the mechanisms for skewing resources to compensate for social disadvantage operated by the Education and Library Boards (ELBs)[2].

Recent research has shown that there are considerable disparities in the levels of social disadvantage, as measured by entitlement to Free School Meals, by religion and school type in Northern Ireland (Magill, 1996). The most privileged sector is that of Protestant Voluntary Grammar schools, where less than 3% of pupils are entitled to FSM, compared with the worst-off sector - maintained (Catholic) secondary schools - where entitlement is 46%. Within all grammar schools in Northern Ireland, the average proportion of pupils entitled to FSM is 9%, and Catholic grammar schools pupils are four times more likely to come from low-income households than their counterparts in Protestant schools. Pupils from maintained (Catholic) secondary schools are 1.75 times more likely to be entitled to FSM than pupils in controlled secondary schools (mainly Protestant). The absolute difference between the two is almost 20 percentage points. Whilst some of the unequal distribution of FSM by religion is explained by structural factors, such as the higher incidence of unemployment in predominantly Catholic areas, after allowing for this, children at controlled schools are still less likely to be eligible for FSM.

Given the size of such disparities, it is important to examine if funds are allocated in a way that reflects social need. Funding to schools in Northern Ireland is distributed either directly through the DENI in the case of voluntary grammar schools and grant maintained schools or through the five ELBs in the case of schools in the controlled and maintained sectors. The total sum is known as the General Schools Budget (GSB) and in 1995/96 this was almost £775 million. Approximately 21% of the GSB is retained by the DENI and the ELBs to cover central services and the remaining 79% is delegated to schools through the Aggregated Schools Budget (ASB) under the local management of schools system (LMS). The DENI requires Boards to allocate at least 75% of the ASB on an unweighted per capita basis. Thus a maximum of 25% of the ASB can be allocated according to a range of factors such as the size of premises, the need to protect the curriculum of small schools, special educational needs or social deprivation. In 1995/96, all Boards allocated more than 75% on an unweighted basis - ranging from 79% in the Western and North Eastern Boards to 85% in the South Eastern Board (average of 81% across the four ELBs). In terms of distributing the remaining funds, the ELBs and the DENI (with regard to voluntary grammar and integrated schools) have adopted two approaches which have different TSN implications. The DENI and three ELBs (North East, South East and Southern) allocate funding earmarked for social deprivation according to the number of pupils entitled to FSM. The Belfast and Western ELBs, in contrast, have attempted to concentrate resources (see Table 7.1) by imposing a FSM threshold, below which schools with a FSM index of less than 20% (BELB) or 9% (WELB) receive no additional funding for social disadvantage. The difference in mechanisms used produces anomalies with some of the most privileged schools in the United Kingdom receiving funding for social disadvantage through the DENI route. For example, Methodist College, where less than 1.5% of the enrolment is eligible for free meals, receives £10,276 of funding for social need. In other words, voluntary grammar schools funded by the DENI, and other grammars funded by other ELBs which do not operate a threshold mechanism, receive more than controlled grammar schools funded by the BELB which have equal or greater levels of deprivation. Grosvenor Grammar School in Belfast, for example, which has 93 FSM students, received no social disadvantage funding, while St Michael's in Lurgan (SEELB) received £25,975 because of their 91 FSM students.

Table 7.1: Formulae for allocating social deprivation funds, Secondary Sector, Northern Ireland, 1995/6

Area or Sector	Threshold	Amount per pupil once threshold reached £
Belfast	20%	360
West	9%	275
North East	1 pupil	220
South East	1 pupil	224
South	1 pupil	235
Voluntary Grammar	1 pupil	285
Integrated	1 pupil	253

Source: Magill, 1996, Table 10

Although the use of a threshold allows for a higher amount of resources to be concentrated on social deprivation once the threshold is crossed, if the BELB threshold was applied throughout Northern Ireland, 27 schools and 8% of FSM eligible pupils would be excluded from such funding (see Table 7.2). On the other hand, the amount per eligible pupil would more than double from £220 to £470 which would bring an ever increasing benefit to schools further down the FSM league in Table 7.2.

Table 7.2: Eligibility for FSM in secondary schools, Northern Ireland, 1995/6

FSM Range	N of schools	N of Pupils	N on FSM	%	Distribution of FSM
<20%	27	16,583	2470	15	8
20-30%	30	15,020	3751	25	12
30-40%	48	26,076	9115	35	28
40-50%	27	15,075	6797	45	21
50-60%	14	8775	4787	55	15
60%+	15	7888	5288	67	16
Total	161	89,417	32,208	36	100

Source: Magill, 1996, Table 11

The effect of the concentration of resources through use of a threshold is to shift resources from Protestant to Catholic schools because of the disproportionate levels of deprivation within the latter population. Whether a threshold should be used, and what it should be, is an issue which needs to be reviewed by government. Even more urgently, government needs to address the anomalies caused by use of thresholds in some areas and sectors and not in others.

IMPLEMENTATION OF TSN IN THE DEPARTMENT OF ECONOMIC DEVELOPMENT

As the question of employment and employability is central to TSN, the DED and its Non-Departmental Public Bodies (NDPBs) are by definition central players, either through direct job promotion and creation (IDB and LEDU) or through the T&EA's role in skills training. In the 1995 public expenditure announcement, the Secretary of State for Northern Ireland announced an additional allocation to industry, trade and employment of £40 million, or 10% on previous estimates, and emphasised that one of the key ways of targeting social need was through job creation (*Belfast Telegraph,* 12 December 1995). For all these reasons, it is disappointing that TSN did not take root in the DED until well into 1994. Although considerable TSN planning has been carried out since, the intentions and actions of the department and its agencies in relation to TSN appear low key and unambitious. We turn first, though, to the department's general approach to TSN.

As with other departments, the DED emphasised the extent to which pre-1991 programmes targeted social need. This claim of 'tsn before TSN' not only diminishes the political raison d'être on which TSN was based, but also places additional pressure on departments to show improved outcomes (since this argument means they have had a longer time period in which to do so). In practice, the converse has occurred - that is, the view that DED programmes were already targeted on social need appears to have prompted the initial non-response to TSN (between 1991 and 1994) in terms of strategic planning and programme changes. However, the DED's active role in TSN implementation post-1994 provides a useful insight into the problems of conceptualising TSN within a government department.

The stimulus for publicly advancing TSN stemmed from the department's commitment to publish its five year review - *Growing Competitively* - in 1995. In preparation for this, the DED commissioned consultants to undertake a review of, and provide recommendations on, the effectiveness of the department's implementation of TSN. As a result, 1994 represents a watershed for the DED in terms of transparency and explicitness the planning process and the politics of TSN. The department has adopted a declaration of intent 'to carry out its responsibilities in a way which effectively targets those people and areas in the greatest need, with the effect of reducing community differentials'. The nature of the declaration is unusual in that TSN is specifically and publicly stated to be concerned with reducing community differentials, whereas in the other main spending departments, particularly the DoE and the DHSS, TSN has been, to the extent that it has been adopted at all, 'religion-blind'.

On the ground, the first cause of concern within the DED and its agencies related to whether agencies should plan and monitor TSN with regard to both 'equality of outcomes' and 'equality of access'. The latter was regarded as unproblematic but differences of opinion occurred on the issue of 'equality of outcomes', with agencies arguing that these involved factors outside of an agency's remit and were, therefore, 'outwith' their control. An example given by DED representatives was the dependence of training outcomes on the educational attainment of trainees prior to age 16, the responsibility of the DENI. The DED was, however, also aware that too little emphasis on 'outcomes' could be interpreted as 'lessening the DED's resolve on TSN in general' and some outcome-type measures have been retained.

The DED's second area of concern in implementing TSN relates to potential conflict with the concept of competitiveness and its ideological basis in minimal market intervention. For example, the IDB view competitiveness in terms of profitable business without recourse to public support. TSN, on the other hand, implies a considerable degree of government intervention. Thus there were concerns over complexities in interpretation and implementation which the two objectives presented for staff on the ground, notwithstanding that departmental and government objectives were often multi-dimensional (for example, a parallel was made by the DED between reconciling 'competitiveness' on the one hand and health and safety requirements on the other). At the broader level, the competing nature of the public expenditure priorities of 'strengthening the economy' and TSN were of concern to the Department:

> In seeking to achieve these [public expenditure] objectives, the department must make choices. It has to find the right balance between sometimes competing programme expenditure possibilities and take into account the need to maximise value for money. (DED TSN Submission to SACHR).

Like the DFP, the DED noted that public expenditure for economic development has declined, although spending in recognition of regional needs has been maintained at higher levels in Northern Ireland than the rest of the UK, and that in such a context, TSN may have to be achieved 'as much by skewing programmes towards TSN areas as by new programmes'. Even if accepting these points, it is disturbing that the department and its agencies were unable to provide assessments of potential or actual differential impacts which may have occurred as a result of shifting and/or decreasing public expenditure patterns between 1991 and 1995. The non-availability of monitoring information by religion was cited as the primary reason for such deficiencies and there remains a level of hesitancy to monitor by religion within the DED, except for T&EA programmes which have been monitored by religious affiliation since 1993. Of particular concern is the failure of the IDB and LEDU to monitor by religion although it is anticipated that LEDU will introduce monitoring by religion for some programmes. As the CCRU itself argued in 1993 (see above), the lack of religious monitoring clearly has implications for the ability of government to measure the achievement of TSN's long term aim - the reduction of community differentials.

DED Action Plans For TSN Post-1994

By 1995, the DED had published TSN 'action plans' for its key NDPBs. Baselines have been established for each agency using monitoring information from 1994, focused on the amount of spending in designated TSN against non-TSN geographical areas relative to both the population in each and the degree of need for each agency's services measured by 'equality of outcome' measures such as the number of jobs assisted in each area or the level of qualifications achieved by participants. Since the identification of TSN areas (using modifications of the Robson model) involved a ward-level analysis, it is unfortunate, from the point of view of transparency, that future reporting by the IDB and the T&EA will be on a District Council basis (LEDU's position is unclear).

The approach taken by the DED in the development of action plans is important for a number of reasons. Firstly, it suggests that TSN is measurable, contrary to the arguments of some other departments and particularly the DFP. Second, the Robson model has been customised to suit departmental and agency responsibilities. Third, the plans make explicit that TSN is concerned with expenditure patterns within and between TSN and non-TSN areas and therefore there should be evidence of the skewing of resources in the future. Although there are criticisms which can be levied against each of the agencies' action plans, the conceptual basis of the plans can be regarded as a model which could be extended across Northern Ireland departments. It would also be preferable if such plans were part of a wider public process involving consultation with interested groups outside government.

There is insufficient space here to detail the DED action plans but one general criticism which could be levied is that they are neither as ambitious nor as detailed as might have been expected. For example, during the 1980s there was concern that the IDB strategy of targeting deprived areas through location in adjacent areas was too 'loose' in terms of getting jobs to people in deprived areas. This remains a problem in the 1995-1998 action plan, where one of the declared targets is that 75% of inward investment projects should locate 'in or adjacent to' TSN areas. TSN areas are defined as ten District Council areas which in turn have ten further District Council areas 'adjacent' to them, resulting in a coverage, by this target, of 20 out of the 26 Northern Ireland District Council areas. This may not be a problem in some areas (or in respect of some occupations) where there is full mobility between a TSN area and an 'adjacent' area but it could pose major problems for other TSN areas and/or some social groups where such mobility cannot be assumed or is known not to exist (see Shuttleworth *et al*, Chapter Two). That is, where strong 'chill-factors' exist, location of jobs in an 'adjacent' area will not address unemployment and inequality of opportunity for residents of TSN areas. Sheehan and Tomlinson in Chapter Three of this volume demonstrate a very strong chill factor operating in West Belfast. Although this would not necessarily be replicated in all TSN areas, it is true for some, and to this extent, the IDB TSN strategy for 1995-8 is too 'blunt'. Much more specific targets could have been set for particular areas (particularly as regards first time visits of potential investors) in order to acknowledge such differentials in mobility.

Further criticisms of the DED's post-1994 TSN approach have arisen from the decision at the end of 1995 to cut the ACE programme budget by 25%. In Northern Ireland as a whole this will involve the loss of 2300 ACE jobs and 200 core posts. In West Belfast, it will mean 380 lost places and 'the subsequent loss of earnings will amount to approximately £1,879,103, the drop in training allowance will amount to £64,640 and the loss of overheads, £213,217' (O'Broin, 1996: 10). At meetings of representatives of ACE projects in West Belfast early in 1996, participants argued that:

> the Agency [T&EA] is contravening government's own stated policy of TSN by introducing cuts across the board without giving particular consideration to the impact of the cuts in those areas suffering the worst levels of deprivation. In their letter offering groups the option of making the cuts themselves, they advise groups to pay particular attention to TSN requirements when deciding which posts should go. This is crass hypocrisy as they themselves have totally ignored TSN in the manner in which the cutbacks are being made.' (quoted in O'Broin, 1996: 10).

Subsequently, government offered a £2 million package of 'transitional help' to those groups most affected by the cuts. However, O'Broin notes that this is likely to reduce the effects of the cuts by, at most, 2% (O'Broin, 1996: 10).

TSN AND SPECIAL AREA INITIATIVES

Given the lack of progress documented above in implementing TSN within mainstream departmental provision, programmes such as Making Belfast Work (MBW), the Londonderry Initiative (LI) and the Rural Development Programme have to be regarded as the principal face of TSN. Significantly, both MBW and the LI predate TSN and while all three initiatives are clearly targeted on areas of multiple deprivation, in practice, the TSN impact of these programmes has been minimal both in terms of outputs and their effectiveness in changing the spending priorities of departments and agencies.

Government departments and their respective agencies prepare applications for additional funding through MBW and the Community Action Programme (CAP) of the LI annually. The budgets for both initiatives are 'ring fenced' and the sponsoring department remains the accounting officer for the life of the projects. For example, the £3 million allocated to MBW for the Raising Schools Standards Initiative is in effect accounted for through the DENI's budget. Almost £170 million had been spent on MBW up to the end of the 1995/96 financial year, while spend on the LI to 1994/95 was approximately £17 million. Figure 7.1 shows the percentage of the additional expenditure allocated to departments and agencies through MBW between 1988 and 1995. As Figure 7.1 shows, almost 50% of expenditure on MBW has been through the DoE (NI) and the DENI.

Figure 7.1: MBW Expenditure by Department 1988-1995

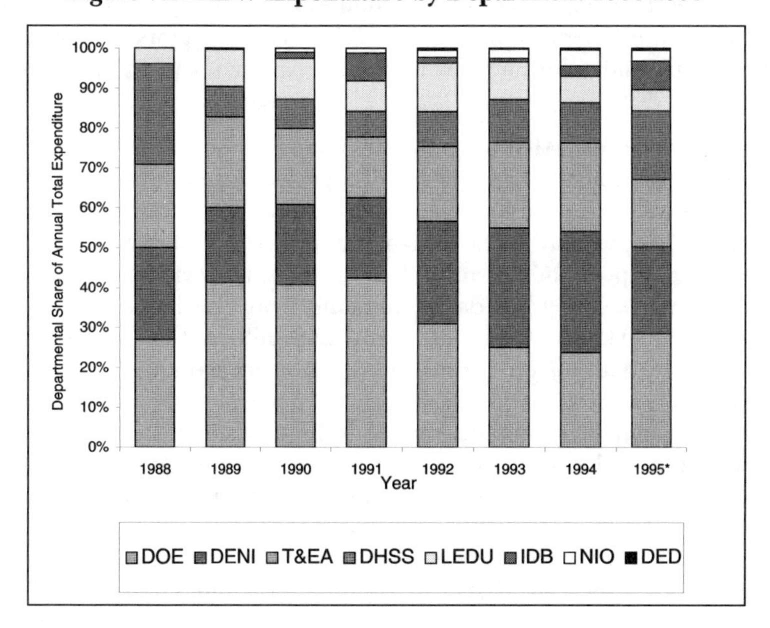

In relation to the public expenditure profile of MBW, Birrell and Wilson (1993) have estimated public expenditure in Belfast to be around £1000 million per annum. In 1995/96, almost £25 million was allocated to MBW, representing only 2.5% of total public expenditure in Belfast. Furthermore, Gaffikin and Morrisery (1990:140-149) argue that money spent on MBW has to be assessed in the context of the series of 'public disinvestments', particularly as a result of changes in the social security system, which have withdrawn income from the area. As regards the latter, they estimate that public disinvestment was about the same size as the amount spent by MBW in its first year (Gaffikin and Morrisery, 1990:145).

Another area of concern relates to the ability of area based programmes to influence wider policy directions. This is particularly pertinent in cases where projects funded through such programmes are viewed as successful either by the beneficiaries of the project or by the community at large. In a recent evaluation of the CAP, the evaluators found that the selection of projects was not driven by any independent strategy for TSN or 'strengthening the economy' (SE) and decisions to mainstream projects were 'mediated by the Agents' own perception of the need for modifying or reforming mainstream programmes' (Cebulla, 1995). Cebulla concluded that:

> the programme was not used [by government departments] as a strategic tool, nor was it perceived to be a central mechanism for redressing the social imbalance that existed in Londonderry. This may prove to be out of step with Governmental thinking if the latter decides to grant greater status to targeting and reforming mainstream programmes to assist targeting (Cebulla, 1995: 88).

The evidence of MBW's ability to shape policy and its success in mainstreaming projects (the transfer of a project into a department's main budget) has also been limited. Clearly, these two factors represent the most significant 'TSN potential' of area-based programmes, given the limited budgets of such programmes in their own right. The evidence in respect of mainstreaming is somewhat dated, deriving from the last review of MBW (1988/89-1992/93). At April 1992, only £2.8 million (4% of MBW's total expenditure) had been transferred to departmental mainstream programmes. As regards the shaping of departmental policy, there is evidence that some departments have actively constrained the ability of MBW to significantly influence change. For example, while MBW stipulates to departments that projects will not receive funding beyond a three year period (thus placing the onus on the sponsoring department to mainstream successful projects and free MBW resources for new projects), 20 of the 37 projects in the 1995/96 MBW programme with the DENI had received funding for more than three years. The result of this, in expenditure terms, is that 59.5% of the DENI/MBW budget relates to projects which began to receive funding prior to 1992/93 and nine projects (38% of the total DENI budget) have been funded by MBW since 1990/91. To rectify this position, and in order to free up its resources, MBW had to withdraw funding from a number of projects (such as Homework Centres) in an attempt to pressurise the DENI to mainstream the services.

Thus although area-based programmes have been given a high TSN profile, in public expenditure terms their impact is negligible, and recent research has shown that such programmes are not viewed by departments as significant players in the shaping of future policy. The problem is the extent to which these programmes may provide a screen or diversion away from the central issue in TSN - the extent to which TSN has been, and will be, applied as Ministerial announcements originally stated. The same issues, of course, arise with regard to European Union funding, to which the CCRU and the DFP, as well as spending departments, have laid claim as evidence of their implementation and progression of TSN.

SUMMARY AND CONCLUSIONS

Since its introduction TSN has attracted considerable political attention among both party and non-party political organisations and this is increasing (see Gillespie, Chapter One, this volume, and Wilford and Gillespie, forthcoming). However, the research reported here suggests there may be a growing gulf between public expectations and civil service views of the potential of TSN and its practical application by government. This gap results from a failure of government to set the parameters of the TSN debate within its own administration. This failure is exacerbated by the fact that, whether government wish it to be so or not, TSN is central to wider political considerations of governing a divided society, and as such transparency is a critical issue. The research reported here suggests that appreciation of this within departments is minimal, and this is especially problematic in relation to the most important department in terms of public expenditure - the DFP.

Initially, Ministers presented TSN as capable of skewing resources to those people and areas most in need through financial planning and shifts in expenditure patterns. This implies that TSN should be discernible in changes in public expenditure over time, which is facilitated by the allocation of public expenditure to Northern Ireland from the UK Treasury in a single block grant, leaving Ministers and senior civil servants some degree of flexibility in distributing resources within Northern Ireland, between departments and between programmes within departments. The DFP, however, has disputed this view of TSN and argued in the course of this research that TSN cannot be assessed through evidence of the movement of skewing of departmental expenditures.

The DFP's approach, however, calls into question the entire role and value of public expenditure priorities. There is considerable obscurity surrounding what a 'public expenditure priority' is, how it may be or is translated into action, and how overlapping and conflicting priorities are balanced. This is reflected in the absence of strategic planning documents for public expenditure priorities and a general failure to publish information on TSN. If a 'public expenditure priority' is neither to be evident in public expenditure change over time, nor to be obvious in terms of its input into the planning process, then the point of having such priorities (beyond 'public relations), is seriously undermined.

While the meaning of a 'public expenditure priority' seems to have been redefined away from the explicit and implicit statements surrounding the introduction of TSN, so too has the meaning of 'Targeting Social Need' specifically. Analysis of Ministerial statements on TSN suggests that it was meant to be distinct from the general function of government addressing need through public expenditure, and that the issue was the level of public expenditure directed at particularly disadvantaged areas or social groups over and above what would normally be expected. However, some departments, including the DFP, have argued that the general function of meeting need is the same as Targeting Social Need, and one department (the DHSS) has redefined TSN as Targeting Health and Social Need. This may reflect the influence of individual civil servants' acceptance or rejection of the 'ultimate' objective of TSN as it was originally set out by Ministers - the reduction of social and economic community differentials.

Civil Service implementation of TSN since 1991 has officially attempted to occupy an ambivalent road between, on the one hand, targeting community differentials and on the other, targeting all need, irrespective of community. Despite the fact that the NICS, and the CCRU in particular, are well aware that a 'religion-blind' approach to public policy in the past was not effective in reducing community differentials, most departments have adopted such an approach to TSN and/or have compressed the more direct alternative approach into special area programmes. The variability in the interpretation of TSN, between and within departments, is the result of the way government has allowed departments to set the parameters of TSN. Within departments this has meant that the nature of implementation is dependent on the views and influence of individual civil servants. It was inevitable that such an approach would lead to ambiguity, inaction, delay and inconsistency of outcomes.

From the outset TSN required political leadership at Ministerial level. Such leadership and direction does not appear to have been forthcoming from Ministers and this has fed through into the lack of advice, guidance and training offered by either the CCRU or the DFP to spending departments. Furthermore, the CCRU has been on the margins of a TSN planning process which is unclear and unsystematic. Given that our findings reflect in many ways those of Osborne *et al* on PAFT, the usefulness and/or effectiveness of units whose sole function is to encourage departments 'at a distance' is called into question. The weakness of such units is underlined by the failure of the DENI and the NIO to even respond to this research.

The blurring of the distinction between meeting need through general public expenditure and TSN and the claim of 'tsn before TSN' diminish the political raison d'être on which TSN was based. The DED is unusual in having adopted a declaration of intent which is specifically concerned with community differentials. In the other spending departments included in this research (the DANI, the DoE and the DHSS), TSN has been 'religion-blind'. The DED is also unusual in having drawn up action plans, which though open to criticism for being unambitious, nevertheless constitute a way forward in the implementation of TSN. For example, the DED plans are premised on the measurability of TSN, despite the DFP's argument to the contrary and the CCRU's dismissal of the setting of goals and timetables for change. The action plans are also premised on the assumption that TSN is concerned with expenditure patterns within and between TSN and non-TSN areas.

Whilst the argument that parity of provision with Great Britain has some force in terms of the limits it sets on the amount of change which can be achieved in given time periods, it is not the case that departments with 'more' policy flexibility are more likely to have implemented TSN. The DoE's failure to have acted on TSN issues around road infrastructure and the planning service is a case in point, and a particularly important example given that enhancement of employment and employability was set out initially as a key target of TSN. There is also no evidence that the extent of policy flexibility available to departments determines their knowledge of the actual or potential differential impacts of policies. In addition, we have argued that departments should be able to estimate the effects of policies in terms of TSN whether they are driven by forces outside Northern Ireland or not. Furthermore, such information should be publicly available to inform debate. In the case of the DHSS, the department's claims to bring a Northern Ireland perspective to bear in the early stages of UK policy formulation are undermined by their inability to identify the differential impacts of potential (and actual recent) policy changes. This inability was the result of the failure by the DHSS to either monitor or research the impact of their provision.

Given the low level of implementation of TSN in mainstream departmental activities, special area programmes (such as MBW, the LI and the RDP) have become the main public face of TSN. The TSN impact of these programmes is severely constrained by their small size relative to all public expenditure and they have been ineffective in changing the spending priorities of departments and agencies. These programmes and EU funding (all rather than 25% of it) are claimed by spending departments and the DFP and the CCRU as 'TSN' (particularly in the 1994-1999 period). Whilst such programmes and expenditure are welcome, they may provide a screen or diversion away from the central issue of TSN which is the extent to which TSN has, and will, live up to the initial Ministerial announcements made for it.

To summarise, the research reported here found little evidence that TSN, as it was initially framed politically, has had a substantial influence on the spending and decision-making of departments. This is not surprising, given the reluctance of most departments to monitor or research expenditure, programmes and policies in terms of their impacts on the Catholic and Protestant communities in Northern Ireland. TSN has not been, in our view, a public expenditure priority - rather it is a principle awaiting definition, operationalisation and implementation.

ENDNOTES

1. Although the DENI did not participate in the main research exercise (that is, did not reply to our questionnaire), we were able to analyse some information already in the public domain on the TSN approach of Education and Library Boards.
2. We are indebted to Paul Magill for collation and analysis of the information in this section on schools budgets and Free School Meals entitlements.

REFERENCES

Birell, D. and Wilson, C. (1993) 'Making Belfast Work: An evaluation of an Urban Strategy' *Administration*, 41: 40-56.

CCRU (1995) *Policy Appraisal and Fair Treatment: Annual Report (1994)*, Belfast: CCRU.

Cebulla, A. (1995) *Urban Policy in Londonderry: An evaluation of the Department of the Environment's Urban Regeneration Initiatives*, Central Statistics and Research Branch, Belfast: DoE.

Connolly, M. (1992) 'Learning from Northern Ireland: An acceptable model for regional and local government?' *Ulster Papers in Public Policy and Management*, 16, Belfast: University of Ulster.

Cormack, R.J. and Osborne, R.D. (eds.) (1991) *Discrimination in Public Policy in Northern Ireland*, Oxford: Oxford University Press.

Fair Employment Agency (1983) *Report of an Investigation by the FEA into the non-industrial NICS*, Belfast: FEA.

Farrell, M. (1976) *Northern Ireland: The Orange State*, London: Pluto Press.

Gaffikin, F. and Morrisery, M. (1990) *Northern Ireland: The Thatcher Years*, London: Zed Books Ltd.

Knox, C. and Hughes, J. (1993) 'Equality and Equity: an Emerging Government Policy in Northern Ireland,' *Ulster Papers in Public Policy and Management* 22, Belfast: University of Ulster.

Knox, C. and Quirk, P. (1994) *Responsibility Sharing in Northern Ireland Local Government*, Department of Public Administration and Legal Studies, Belfast: University of Ulster.

Magill, D. and Rose, S. (eds.) (1996) *Fair Employment Law in Northern Ireland: debates and issues*, Belfast: SACHR.

Magill, P. (1996) 'Briefing Paper on Social Deprivation in Schools in Northern Ireland,' prepared for the Standing Advisory Commission on Human Rights, Belfast.

McCrudden, J.C. (ed.) (1991) *Fair Employment Handbook,* London: Eclipse.

NICVA (1994) *The Implementation of Targeting Social Need,* Belfast: NICVA.

NIEC(1994) *April Economic Assessment,* Report 108, Belfast: NIEC.

Northern Ireland Information Service (1995) *Public Expenditure Announcement by Sir Patrick Mayhew 1996-97 to 1998-99,* Belfast: NIIS.

O'Broin, E. (1996) 'ACE Cuts: West Belfast to Lose 380 Jobs', *Economic Bulletin,* 3 (4), Belfast: The West Belfast Economic Forum.

Osborne, R.D. (1996) 'Policy Dilemmas in Belfast' *Journal of Social Policy,* 25 (2):181-199.

Quirk, P. and McLaughlin, E. (1996) A Report on the Implementation of TSN by NI Government Departments, report to the Standing Advisory Commission on Human Rights, Belfast.

Robson, B., Bradford, M. and Deas, I. (1994) *Relative Deprivation in Northern Ireland,* Centre for Policy Studies, Manchester University, Belfast: PPRU.

SACHR (1987) *Report on Fair Employment, Religion and Political Discrimination and Equality of Opportunity in Northern Ireland,* Cm 237, London: HMSO.

Sheehan, M. (1995) 'Fair Employment: An Issue for the Peace Process', *Race and Class,* 37: 71-82.

Smith, D.J. and Chambers, G. (1991) *Inequality in Northern Ireland,* Oxford: Clarendon Press.

Teague, P. and Wilson, R. (1995) 'Towards an inclusive society' in *Social Exclusion, Social Inclusion,* Democratic Dialogue, Report Number 2, Belfast: Democratic Dialogue.

Whyte, J. (1983) 'How much discrimination was there under the Unionist Regime 1921-68?' in Gallagher T. and O'Connell J. (eds.), *Contemporary Irish Studies,* Manchester: Manchester University Press.

Wilford, R. (1991) 'Inverting consociationalism? Policy, pluralism and the post modern' in Hadfield, B. (ed.) *Northern Ireland Politics and Constitution,* Buckingham: Open University.

Wilford, R. and Gillespie, G. (1996) 'Change and Continuity in the Views of Northern Ireland Political Parties and Non-Party Political Organisations on Unemployment Equality Issues and Fair Employment Legislation' in McVey, J. and Hutson, N. (eds.) in *Public Views and Experiences of Fair Employment and Equality Issues in Northern Ireland,* Belfast: SACHR.

Chapter Eight

THE IMPACT OF PUBLIC SECTOR JOB LOSSES ON EMPLOYMENT EQUALITY

Tony Dignan and Anthony Murphy

INTRODUCTION

The focus of this chapter is the effect of recent trends in public sector employment on the community balance in employment in Northern Ireland, that is, on the distribution of jobs among Catholics and Protestant communities. In the period from 1989 to 1995, the total number employed in the public sector declined by over 11,000. Much of the change resulted from privatisation of public sector corporations. Excluding public corporations, there has been a fall of almost 3000 in the number of public sector employees. This chapter is concerned with two empirical issues: first whether public sector employment losses affected Catholics and Protestants equally, and second, what have been the effects of changes in the provision of public services on the community differential in employment.

In relation to the first issue, it is not possible to answer the question directly since the available data do not allow for a full accounting of the components of employment change by religion.[1] Instead, the research focuses on the trend in the Catholic share of monitored public sector employment. The second empirical issue, the change in the provision of public services, is important because public sector job losses have arisen not only because of staffing reductions (for example, through early retirement as has been the case in the Northern Ireland Civil Service), but also because privatisation of public corporations has transfered a substantial number of jobs from the public to the private sector. Other initiatives, notably Compulsory Competitive Tendering (CCT), can also result in the transfer of public sector posts to the private sector (see EOC(NI),1996). Finally, initiatives such as the internal market in the health services and the switch to the purchase-provider system (see NIEC, 1994) may not necessarily result in job losses or transfers from the public sector. However, they may involve changes to the structure and pattern of services which in turn affect the geographical distribution of employment opportunities and thereby influence the community differential in employment. Data limitations mean that it is not possible to directly measure the effects of changes in the structure and provision of services on the community differential. In the absence of direct measurements, this issue is addressed by examining the extent to which the provision of public services has 'shifted' to the private sector as well as geographical patterns in the changes in public sector employment.

The employment equality context of this study results from the substantial gap between the Catholic share of the labour force[2] and the Catholic share of employment. According to the 1994 Labour Force Survey results, the Catholic proportion of the economically active population was 39.6%. By contrast, the Catholic share of employment was 37.6%, a 2.1 percentage points gap. The employment gap was larger in the case of men, 3.1 percentage points compared to 0.6 percentage points for women. Second, over the period 1990-1994, Fair Employment Commission (FEC) monitoring returns show that the increase in the Catholic share of public sector employment was 2.0 percentage points[3], or 1.3 percentage points if Northern Ireland Electricity, privatised in 1993, is excluded. This was less than the 2.7 percentage point increase in the Catholic share of employment in the covered private sector. This is a cause for concern in at least two respects. First, the employment gap in the public sector is as large as in the private sector. In the case of the public sector, this is entirely due to the size of the male employment gap. From an arithmetic point of view, the major 'cause' of this is the underrepresentation of Catholics in security-related occupations, though it can be argued that underrepresentation in security should be offset by overrepresentation elswhere in the public sector. In that regard, it should be noted that if security-related occupations are excluded, the Catholic share of male public sector employment in 1995 was 40.8%, a 4.2 percentage points increase on the 1990 share.

Additionally, public sector employment comprises a large proportion of total employment in Northern Ireland. In 1995, public sector employment (including publicly-owned corporations) accounted for 30% of total civil employment and over one-third of employees in employment. Given the public sector's large share of the workforce in employment, policy decisions which affect public sector employment levels may have implications for the Catholic share of total employment, and particularly the speed of convergence on the Catholic share of the workforce. This is because it is easier to close an employment gap in circumstances of employment growth. When employment growth is absent or negative, convergence can only be achieved through such mechanisms as differential rates of turnover and replacement recruitment. This is a problem in the public sector where turnover is low.

Outline of Chapter

This chapter begins by examining some of the main factors affecting public sector employment levels since 1989 by providing an overview on trends in public sector employment, by department and service area. FEC monitoring returns are then used to document the changes in the Catholic share of employment across the various components of the public sector over the period 1990 to 1995. This analysis is extended by means of a modelling exercise designed to evaluate the effect of the historical change in public sector employment on the community balance. The next section extends the modelling approach by presenting alternative scenarios for the future. The final two empirical sections examine the implications of shifts in the public sector share in various industries as well as geographical aspects of public sector employment growth.

FACTORS AFFECTING PUBLIC SECTOR EMPLOYMENT

The Trend in Government Expenditure

From 1989/90 to 1991/92 government expenditure, net of social security payments, declined by 2.9% per annum (see Dignan and Murphy, 1996, for a more detailed examination). The falling trend was reversed in recent years, and from 1991/92 to 1993/94 expenditure rose at a per annum rate of 3%. Expenditure was estimated to have risen by 2.5% in 1994/95. There have been even sharper contrasts within government departments. Overall, expenditure on services provided for 'consumption' by the public has tended to rise, with spending on health and social services and education rising by 3% and 1% respectively since 1989. Conversely, both transport and housing expenditure have fallen continuously since 1989, while spending on environment services has also declined sharply.

Future Prospects For Expenditure

Expenditure plans for future years, as published in March 1995, project a marked slowdown in total spending (Figure 8.1). According to the 1995 estimates, government expenditure, net of social security payments, are planned to decline by almost 1% per annum in the period to 1998. Across the departments, the 1995 estimates project continued reductions in some areas, and much reduced rates of growth in health and education. For example, health and social services spending is projected to fall to about 1% per annum. If carried through, these spending cuts are likely to bear particularly hard on non-departmental employment in health and social services and education. Substantial falls are planned in pay-related line items, to be accompanied by a 3% per annum cut in civil service job numbers. The planned reductions will be implemented through non-replacement of vacated posts ('wastage') and redundancies. About 1000 redundancies are projected for the civil service over the next few years.

While planned expenditure is useful as an indicator of how government may wish to see spending evolve over the near future, the planning assumptions shown in Figure 8.1 should not be taken as definitive. For a variety of reasons, government cannot precisely predict the rate at which spending may grow or decline. Government estimates of planned expenditure have often tended to understate the actual out-turn.

Figure 8.1: Government Expenditure Excluding Social Security

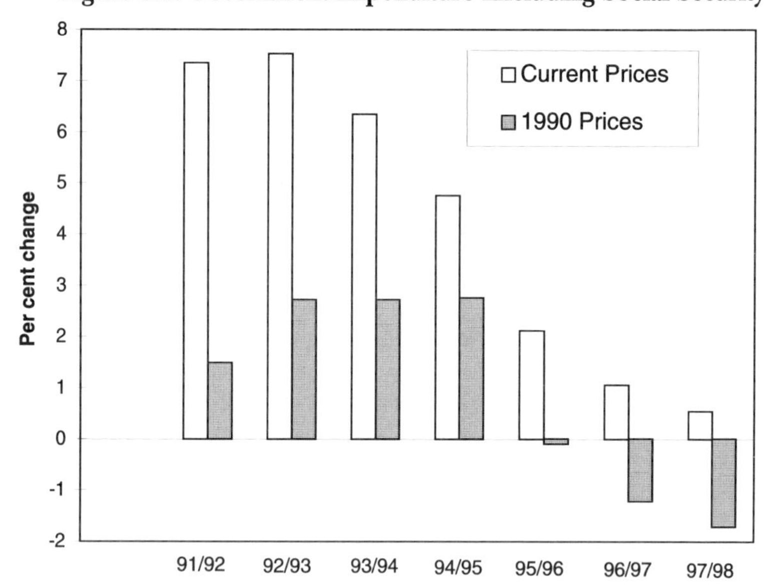

Prior Options

While the level of government expenditure is obviously among the more important determinants of public sector employment levels, it is not the only factor. A number of changes in government policy towards the public sector have weakened the link between government spending and the level of employment within the public sector, particularly by providing for private sector provision of publicly funded services. The 1991 White Paper, *Competing for Quality*, sets out the range of options which government departments must now consider in reviewing ways of carrying out their activities (CIPFA, 1995). In addition to internal restructuring, the prior options to be considered include abolition, privatisation, contracting out and market testing. A prior options review has the potential to result in job losses in a variety of ways. For example, market testing programmes covering UK central government and agencies through 1994 resulted in a 50% reduction in posts reviewed, a loss of about 27,000 jobs (CIPFA, 1995). There is also evidence to suggest job losses typically ensue in the wake of a contracting out process (Escott and Whitfield, 1995). Experience in the UK shows that public sector corporations typically shed labour subsequent to privatisation (Haskel and Szymanski, 1993).

The Reforms in Northern Ireland

All of the foregoing influences on public sector employment are now present in Northern Ireland, and CIPFA (1995) and EOC (NI) (1996) have reviewed developments to date. Market testing and competitive tendering were introduced in 1988 in areas such as health, education and the civil service, with local government following in 1991/92. Comprehensive data do not exist on the employment impacts of these policy initiatives, although it is apparent that many of the reforms have made fewer inroads in Northern Ireland than in Great Britain. Particularly with regard to contracting out, the bulk of services subject to CCT or Voluntary Competitive Tendering (VCT) have gone to 'in-house' suppliers. A (1996) Study by the EOC (NI) found that, in the health services, any 20% of contracts subject to CCT were awarded to private suppliers, while none were awarded to outside bodies in the case of education services. As in Great Britain, job losses have ensued in the wake of a number of market testing exercises. The job losses from CCT in local government in Northern Ireland were estimated at 55 in total (Knox and Young, 1994, cited in CIPFA, 1995) while EOC (NI) (1996) research studied 20 contracts in health and education and identified 310 job losses. Both of these studies illustrate that CCT can result in job losses without services being contracted out.

While privatisation has, to date, been fairly well contained in Northern Ireland, this may not be the case in future years. Market testing is being extended to white collar positions in a range of activities, including local government. For example, typing in the civil service, covering about 1000 people, is scheduled to be reviewed. The trend in government expenditure, as described above, is also likely to portend further reviews.

THE TREND IN PUBLIC SECTOR EMPLOYMENT

This section describes recent developments in employment levels in the public sector. It is not possible to precisely identify the separate influence of each of the set of policy developments described above. Instead, the analysis proceeds on the basis of departmental and service area distinctions (Table 8.1). Northern Ireland Central Government (NICG), which includes the administrative arm of government as well as security-related occupations, accounts for about one-quarter of total public sector employment. The majority of jobs in the public sector, 61%, are in bodies under the aegis of NICG plus the NHS Trusts and other Non-Departmental Public Bodies (NDPBs)[4]. In addition to the Health Trusts, NDPBs comprise almost entirely the various Health and Social Services Boards and the Education and Library Boards. Both UK central government as well as local government account for relatively small proportions of total public sector employment, less than 5% each in 1995. Finally, there are the Public Corporations. These span a variety of activities, including transport and public utilities.

Table 8.1: Employment Change in the Public Sector, 1989-1995

	All		**Male**		**Female**	
	Change	**% per annum**	**Change**	**% per annum**	**Change**	**% per annum**
NI Central Government	256	0.1	-1454	-0.7	1710	1.9
NI Depts	-714	-0.4	-1554	-1.6	840	1.3
Fire, Prisons & Security	970	0.7	100	0.1	870	3.8
Bodies under aegis NICG (incl NHS Trusts)	-1978	-0.3	-813	-0.5	-1165	-0.2
DHSS plus NHS Trusts	-5818	-1.6	-544	-0.8	-5274	-1.7
Education and Library Boards	3092	1.0	-305	-0.3	3397	1.5
Other Bodies	748	4.3	36	0.4	712	9.4
UK Central Govt	-102	-0.3	-195	-0.9	93	0.5
Local Govt	-1054	-1.8	-1232	-3.1	178	0.9
Total (excl Public Corporations)	-2878	-0.3	-3694	-0.9	816	0.1
Public Corporations	-8480	-8.4	-7293	-9.1	-1187	-5.8
Total	-11358	0.9	-10987	-2.2	-371	-0.1

Source: DED

Over the period 1989-1995 total public sector employment declined by 11,358 (Table 8.1). Excluding public sector corporations, but including employment in NHS Trusts, the trend in public sector employment has been steadily, albeit slowly, downwards (Figure 8.2). From 1989 to 1995, total employment declined by 2878, although there was considerable variation by category of employment around the average rate of change of -0.3% per annum (Figure 8.3). Employment in the NICG was broadly stable over the period with the modest increase of 256 registered by this sector comprising of two contrasting trends (Figure 8.3).

Figure 8.2: Employment in the Public Sector

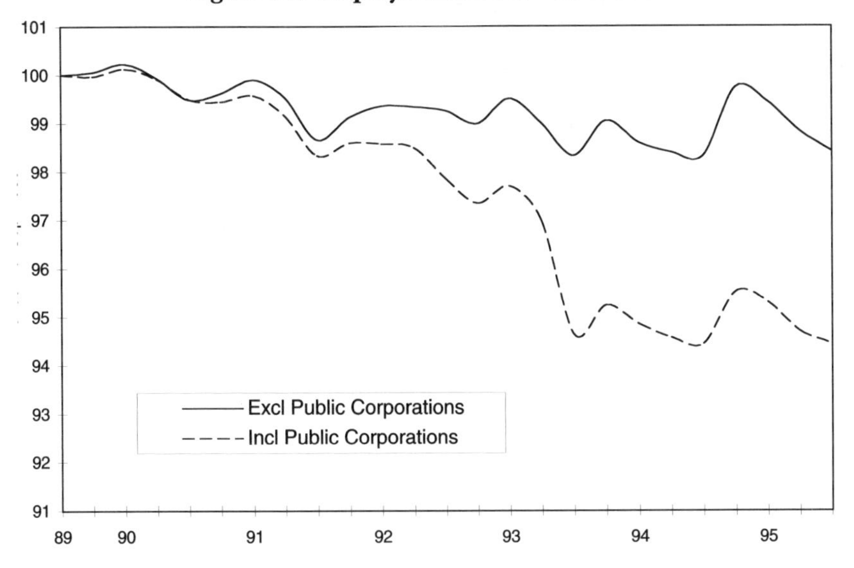

The Northern Ireland Departments, which comprise the civil service, suffered an employment loss of 714. But, the pattern over time has been uneven. Up to the beginning of 1993, civil service employment increased steadily at a rate of 1.4% per annum, yet it has been declining sharply ever since at 3% per annum and the trend looks set to continue downwards. Security-related employment, the other major component of NI Central Government, increased steadily at a rate of 0.7% per annum. The broad sectoral pattern in the public sector, then, has been one of growth in some areas coupled with decline in areas such as the civil service and health and social security.

The largest absolute decline occurred in the health and social services sector, which accounts for 30% of total public sector employment. From 1989-1995, non-departmental employment in Health and Social Services Boards plus the Trusts fell by almost 6000 (Table 8.1). By contrast, employment in Education and Library Boards increased by over 3000 (Figure 8.4).

Figure 8.3: Public Sector Employment Category

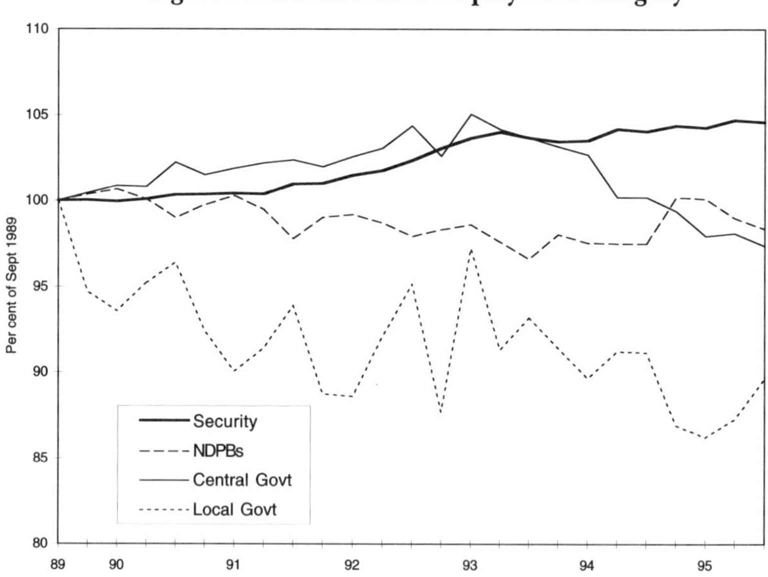

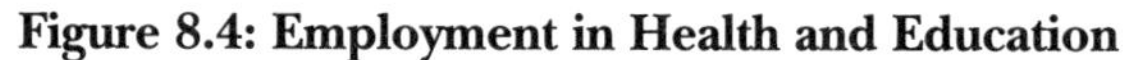

Figure 8.4: Employment in Health and Education

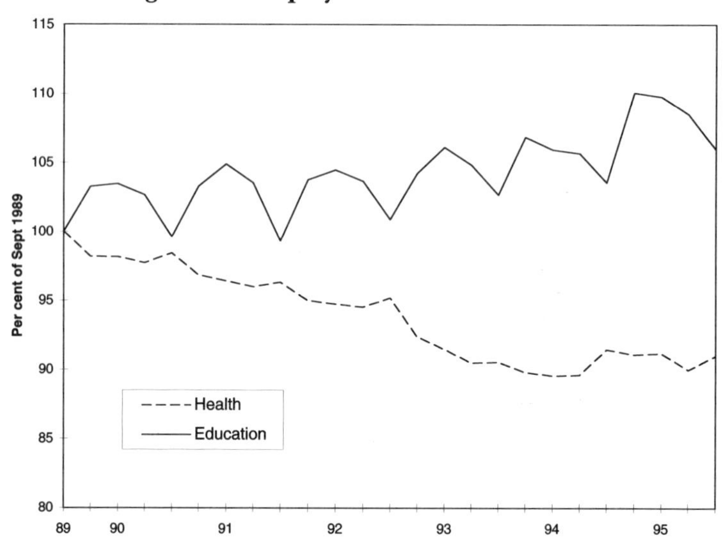

Gender

As well as these general trends, there were also marked variations by gender (Table 8.1). Excluding Public Corporations, male employment in the public sector declined by almost 3700 from 1989 to 1995, an average annual rate of about 1%. Female employment remained close to its 1989 level, rising by just over 800. Excepting the civil service, the decline in male employment was fairly evenly dispersed over the various components. This was not the case in regard to female employment where losses were concentrated in the health and social services sector.

Industrial composition

Public sector shares of employment by industry are only available from the Census of Employment. Conducted every two years, the most recent results are for 1993. Overall, the public sector share of total employees declined from 38.5% to 35.8% (Table 8.2). The largest reductions in the public sector share were in construction, energy and water supply and health services.[5]

Table 8.2: Employment Composition by Industry

	Public Sector Share		Employment Change 1989-1993		Catholic Share 1991
	1989	1993	Public Sector	Total	
			(Per cent)		
Production	6.6	4.8	30.2	4.4	31.8
Construction	12.2	5.2	62.9	13.9	46.9
Distribution	0.9	0.8	4.5	13.3	33.8
Trans & Comms	42.0	42.4	3.8	4.6	37.4
Fin'l & Bus Services	12.3	10.7	1.2	13.9	32.5
Public Admin & Defence	99.5	99.9	4.0	3.5	27.0
Sanitary Services	29.5	21.3	1.6	41.1	31.5
Education	89.5	87.5	1.8	4.1	43.4
Research & Development	86.0	82.3	21.7	18.2	25.0
Health Services	87.4	71.6	6.7	13.8	43.0
Other Public Services	56.5	50.8	8.7	1.3	40.0
Recreation/Cultural Services	52.8	49.3	10.2	18.0	38.8
Personal Services	14.9	10.3	36.7	8.2	40.9
Total	38.5	35.8	-3.1	4.2	35.6

Sources: DED; Census of Population, 1991.

Decreases in the construction sector were due to the Housing Executive's (NIHE) decision to cut its direct construction labour force from 750 to 100. About 45% of those losing their jobs were Catholics. The NIHE job cuts were real job losses, though there was some compensation from the subsequent issuing of maintenance contracts for NIHE dwellings. The health services industry, however, registered a sharp increase in employment, almost 14%.

Table 8.2 also shows the Catholic share in each industry, extracted from the 1991 Census of Population. Apart from construction, the Catholic share is highest in the public service industries, notably in education (43.4%) and health (43%). If it was the case that employment changes in the public sector were distributed *pro rata* on employment shares in each industry, then the Catholic share of public sector jobs lost from 1989-93 would have been over 43%, well above the 36% Catholic share of the workforce in employment as of 1991. In other words, relative to their share of the workforce, Catholics stood to lose a disproportionate share of the jobs lost to the public sector.

THE COMMUNITY BALANCE IN THE PUBLIC SECTOR: RECENT TRENDS

Information on the religious composition of the public sector workforce is published annually by the Fair Employment Commission (FEC). For a variety of reasons, these data are not well suited to tracking changes in employment levels. This is primarily because a number of categories of employment are not covered by the requirement to make monitoring returns. For example, the FEC data suggest a decline of 0.75% per annum in female employment in the public sector, whereas the DED data (which includes part-time workers) estimate a very much smaller decline of 0.1% per annum. This emphasises the need to exercise caution in using the FEC data to measure the absolute level of employment change. However, given that the monitoring returns cover about 70% of total employment, they will give a reliable indication of trends in the religious composition of the workforce, that is, in the distribution of employment between the two communities.

Recent trends

From 1990 to 1994, the Catholic share of the Northern Ireland workforce in employment increased from 34.9% to 37.6%, a rise of 2.7 percentage points (Table 8.3). Excluding Northern Ireland Electricity, the Catholic share of the public sector rose from 36% in 1990 to 37.3% in 1995, a rise of just 1.3 percentage points. There was, however, considerable variation around this average within the public sector. Excluding security-related occupations, the Catholic share rose by 3.2 percentage points, with the increase exceeding two percentage points in health, education and the District Councils. Excluding Police Authority for Northern Ireland (PANI) secondees, the increase in the civil service was less at 1.4 percentage points.

Similar patterns were found when the monitoring returns are analysed by gender. The share of Catholic males in total public sector employment (excluding NIE) rose by just 1.1 percentage points. However, when security-related occupations are excluded, the increase was much larger, over four percentage points. Amongst women, the Catholic share rose by just over two percentage points when security-related occupations are excluded.

Table 8.3: The Catholic Share of Monitored Employment

	Males			Females			All		
	1990	1995	Diff	1990	1995	Diff	1990	1995	Diff
	%		pps	%		pps	%		pps
Total Employment	32.0	35.0	3.0	38.5	40.7	2.2	34.9	37.6	2.7
Private Sector	33.0	36.5	3.5	36.8	39.7	2.9	34.6	37.9	3.3
Public Sector	30.4	32.3	1.9	40.4	42.1	1.7	35.3	37.3	2.0
Excl NIE	31.2	32.3	1.1	40.7	42.1	1.4	36.0	37.3	1.3
Excl Security-Related Occupations	36.6	40.8	4.2	41.8	43.9	2.1	39.4	42.6	3.2
Health	43.2	47.2	4.0	43.6	45.0	1.4	43.5	45.5	2.0
Education & Library Boards	40.8	44.2	3.4	41.1	43.5	2.4	41.0	43.7	2.7
District Councils	34.1	36.3	2.2	32.9	36.0	3.1	33.8	36.2	2.4
Civil Service	n/a	33.4	n/a	n/a	40.6	n/a	n/a	36.5	n/a
Excl PANI secondees	33.0	34.3	1.3	42.7	44.2	1.5	37.9	39.3	1.4
Excl Security-Related Occupations	29.7	29.8	0.1	32.6	33.0	0.4	30.3	30.6	0.3
Security-Related Occupations	7.0	7.3	0.3	9.6	9.9	0.3	7.4	7.7	0.3

Source: FEC Monitoring Returns

Notes: The 1995 Catholic shares for males and females combined were estimated for the Civil Service excl PANI secondees and the public sector excl NIE. NI workforce in employment and private sector returns were not available for 1995 at the time of going to print.

The pattern of change by occupation is also available from the FEC. These data again show a wide spread of increases in Catholic shares. The Catholic share of male employment increased in all but one of the nine occupational groups to which covered employees are allocated in the FEC monitoring returns. A similar pattern held amongst women.

Summary

The relatively slower, by comparison with the private sector, increase in the Catholic share of total public sector employment (excluding NIE) appears to have been, at least partly, due to a compositional effect arising from the fact that the Catholic share of security-related employment is not only at a very low level but has also not been growing to any significant degree. The next section examines the issue of whether or not the actual increase in the Catholic share was substantially less than would have been observed if there had been no decreases in public sector employment.

THE COMMUNITY BALANCE IN THE PUBLIC SECTOR: A SIMULATION MODEL

The effect of employment decline on the Catholic share in the public sector was evaluated by constructing a simulation model to explore alternative scenarios concerning employment growth rates. The model takes account of the components of change in the public sector workforce in employment and incorporates empirically-based variations between Catholics and Protestants in a number of key parameters, including separation and hiring rates. For each community, the model treats men and women separately. This reflects differences between males and females in a range of key parameters, including turnover rates, employment growth, distribution among the various components of the public sector and initial 1990 shares of public sector employment.

Structure of the Model

By definition, the change in employment in any individual component of the public sector (for example, males in the non security-related civil service) equals the difference between engagements or hires and job separations (quits, redundancies and retirement). Therefore, engagements equal the sum of separations and changes in employment. Job separations are determined by turnover rates and these are treated as given or exogenous. The number of Catholic job separations is the product of the Catholic turnover rate and the number of Catholics in employment one year ago. A similar calculation is performed for Protestants. The change in employment is also treated as exogenous.

The remaining issue is the sharing out of job vacancies between Catholic and Protestant applicants. In the simulation model, the Catholic share of applicants is assumed to equal the Catholic share of the labour force, adjusted to take account of the average age of recruits. This is the proportionality assumption. The model also takes account of Catholics' revealed preference for non security-related public sector jobs, reflected in the high share of Catholic applicants and appointees for such jobs. Finally, it is assumed that success rates, or the probability of an applicant filling a vacancy, is not affected by religion. This is the fair employment assumption.

The model thus depends crucially on assumptions made about differences between Catholics and Protestants in rates of labour turnover, the propensity to apply for public sector jobs and relative rates of success in obtaining appointments to vacancies. Whether or not the assumptions used are valid is essentially an empirical question. Values for the parameters used in the model were obtained from Labour Force Survey (LFS) results as well as FEC statistics on applicants and appointees by religion.

Turnover Rates

In the model, the turnover rate for Protestant men is assumed to be almost 1% higher than for Catholic men, reflecting their older age profile in the public sector. The turnover rates used are based on an analysis of Labour Force Survey (LFS) results for 1986, 1987, 1990 and 1991. These data show that Catholic males are generally less likely to have been in continuous service for five or more years. Whereas 77.5% of Protestant males had been in continuous service in the public sector for five or more years, the figure for Catholics was 72.2%. Catholic male jobs are thus, on average, less 'at risk' due to factors such as retirement. The LFS data also show that turnover rates in the public sector are very low. Only 5% of full-time males had less than one year's continuous service compared with 12% in the economy as a whole. The corresponding figures for full-time females are 10.5% in the public sector and 14.5% overall.

The Catholic Share of Applicants

Under the proportionality and fair employment assumptions, the share of Catholics in hires is assumed to equal the share of Catholics in the labour force.[6] The younger age structure of potential Catholic recruits means that the age-adjusted Catholic share of applicants is about 44%, slightly higher than the unadjusted Catholic share of the economically active. This means that Catholics are likely to be 'overrepresented' in the applicant pool. The proportionality assumption is consistent with FEC applicant and appointee data and the actual change in the share of Catholics in monitored public sector non-security employment over the period 1990 to 1994 (see Table 8.4; also Dignan and Murphy, 1996).

Table 8.4: Success Rates[1] by Religion in the Public Sector[2]

	Catholic	Protestant	Z-score[3]
Males	%	%	
1991	7.6	8.1	-2.4*
1992	7.7	7.9	-0.6
1993	7.1	7.3	-1.2
1994	6.5	6.2	1.4
Females	%	%	
1991	12.3	12.2	0.3
1992	13.6	14.5	-3.5*
1993	14.2	14.1	0.5
1994	10.0	10.9	-3.8*

Source: FEC

Notes: 1 The success rate is the ratio of appointees to applicants, expressed as a percentage.

2 Excluding security-related occupations. NIE, privatised in 1993, is also excluded.

3 Loosely speaking, Z scores of 2 or more in absolute value (denoted by an asterisk) indicate significant differences between the success rates of Catholics and Protestants, ie differences which are unlikely to be random.

The Employment Gap

In combination, the assumptions of higher turnover for Protestant males and the proportionality and fair employment assumptions mean that, for any given rate of net employment change, the Catholic share should rise. Of course, it cannot rise indefinitely and for that reason, the model also takes account of the employment gap, the difference between the adjusted share of Catholics in the labour force and their share in employment. In the model, the share of Catholics rises whenever there is a positive employment gap, that is, the Catholic share of employment is less than the Catholic share of the labour force. The speed at which this gap closes depends first and foremost on the size of the employment gap and secondly on the rate of labour turnover combined with the rate of employment growth/decline. The smaller the employment gap, the lower the rate of labour turnover and the higher the rate of employment decline, the more restricted is the potential for change.

The Catholic Share 1990-1994: Simulation Results

The model described above was simulated for the historical period 1990-1994 in order to construct a counterfactual path for the Catholic share under the assumption of no employment decline. That is, how would the Catholic share have evolved over the period from 1990 to 1994 if the only factors affecting the Catholic share were turnover variations by religion and proportionality in applications and appointments? The simulation results, shown in Table 8.5, suggest that, in the absence of employment decline in the public sector, the Catholic share for men would have risen by an additional 0.2 percentage points. The difference between the simulated and actual 1994 shares for women was negligible. This contrast between males and females is largely due to the fact that, in the base year 1990, there was less of a gap between the share of Catholics in female public sector employment and the proportion of Catholics in the female workforce.

Table 8.5: The Catholic Share in the Monitored Public Sector[1] Simulated Historical Trend with no Employment Decline

	Males %	Females %
1990	36.6	41.8
1994 - simulated	40.5	43.9
1994 - actual	40.3	43.9
1994 - actual minus simulated	-0.2	0.0

Note: 1 Excluding security related occupations.

The key conclusion to be drawn from the foregoing analysis is that employment reductions in the public sector have resulted in a marginally smaller increase (about 0.2 percentage points) in the Catholic share of male public sector employment. No discernible effect is apparent in the case of the Catholic share of female employment.

THE COMMUNITY BALANCE IN THE PUBLIC SECTOR: ALTERNATIVE SCENARIOS FOR THE FUTURE

This section employs the simulation model described above to evaluate the potential impact of alternative scenarios for the future evolution of public sector employment. The simulations are based on the 1994 FEC monitoring returns and cover the six year period 1994 to 2000. The simulation results are not forecasts, rather, they indicate the potential for change in the religious composition of employment, conditional on the assumptions adopted regarding likely rates of employment growth, rates of labour turnover and employment practices. The assumptions regarding labour turnover and fair employment have been discussed above. The major change for the simulations of alternative future scenarios is that, in the case of security-related jobs, the share of Catholic applicants is assumed to rise to half the Catholic share of other public sector jobs, that is, 22%.

Continuing employment decline scenario

The baseline scenario assumes a continuation of past trends in the FEC monitored public sector workforce, that is, male employment falls by 1.1% per annum while female employment declines by 0.75% per annum. Security-related employment is assumed unchanged until 1997, after which it declines in line with the average.[7] The results of the baseline scenario, projecting 'continuing employment decline', are set out in Table 8.6. The simulated share of Catholic males rises by 2.7 percentage points over the period to 2000. The rise in the share of Catholics in security-related employment is about double this, due to the very large employment gap in the base year combined with the assumption described above on the increase in the propensity of Catholics to apply for security-related jobs. The small simulated rise of 0.3 percentage points for females is almost completely due to the simulated rise in the share of Catholic females in security-related employment. Since there is effectively no employment gap for Catholic females in non security-related employment to start out with, their share in employment only rises marginally (this is not evident in Table 8.6 because of rounding).

Table 8.6: The Catholic Share in the Monitored Public Sector - Alternative Employment Decline Scenarios

	Males			Females		
	Total %	**Security** %	**Other** %	**Total** %	**Security** %	**Other** %
(a) Continuing employment decline scenario						
1994	32.1	7.2	40.3	42.1	10.1	43.9
2000	34.8	12.5	42.6	42.4	16.6	43.9
% change 1994-2000	+2.7	+5.3	+2.3	+0.3	+5.5	+0.1
(b) No employment decline scenario						
1994	32.1	7.2	40.3	42.1	10.1	43.9
2000	35.3	12.8	42.7	42.5	15.8	43.9
% change 1994-2000	+3.2	+5.6	+2.4	+0.4	+5.7	+0.1

Note: Base-year 1994 values correspond to actual shares from FEC data. Remaining year values are obtained by simulation.

No Employment Decline Scenario

Table 8.6 also presents the results of an alternative 'no employment decline scenario'. The simulated share of Catholic males now rises by 3.2 percentage points overall and by 2.4 percentage points in non security-related employment. There is, therefore, only a 0.5 percentage point difference in the overall results for Catholic males between the two scenarios (3.2 pps - 2.7 pps = 0.5 pps). With no employment decline, the simulated share of Catholic females now rises by 0.4 percentage points in total, compared to 0.3 percentage points when employment continues to decline. These results suggest that public sector job losses are likely to have little effect on the Catholic share in the female public sector workforce.

Accelerated Employment Decline Scenario

A number of other simulations were conducted to evaluate the effects of an acceleration in the rate of employment decline in the public sector workforce (Table 8.7). Employment declines of 3.5% per annum were assumed separately for each major category of the monitored public sector workforce as well as all categories taken together. The effect of accelerating employment decline in each individual category alone has a relatively limited impact on the Catholic share relative to the baseline scenario of continuing employment decline (Table 8.7). The effect is much larger when all categories together are subjected to a 3.5% per annum decline. Compared to the baseline, the simulated Catholic share is 0.8 percentage points lower for males and 0.2 percentage points lower for females. Compared to the 'no employment decline' scenario, the simulated Catholic share is 1.3 percentage points lower for males and 0.3 percentage points lower for females. Again, the difference between the results for males and females reflects the influence of differences in the size of the employment gap.

Table 8.7: The Catholic Share in the Monitored Public Sector - Accelerated Employment Decline Scenario

	Male			Female		
	Year 2000 Share	Difference From Scenario:		Year 2000 Share	Percentage Points Difference from Scenario:	
		(a)	(b)		(a)	(b)
3.5 pa decline in:	%	pps	pps	%	pps	pps
Civil Service (excl. security)	34.6	(-0.2)[1]	(-0.7)[2]	42.4	(0.0)	(-0.1)
Education and Library Boards	34.7	(-0.1)	(-0.6)	42.4	(0.0)	(-0.2)
Health Boards and Trusts	34.6	(-0.2)	(-0.7)	42.3	(-0.1)	(-0.2)
Rest (excl. Security)	34.4	(-0.4)	(-0.9)	42.4	(0.0)	(-0.1)
Total (all of the above)	34.0	(-0.8)	(-1.3)	42.2	(-0.2)	(-0.3)

Note: Scenario (a) is the base scenario of continuing employment decline. Scenario (b) is the no employment decline simulation. See Table 8.6 above.

Accelerated Reduction in Security-Related Employment

In light of the 1994 ceasefires, it was considered judicious to evaluate the potential impact of a more marked reduction in security-related employment. Though the ending of the IRA ceasefire in early 1996 has made this less likely, it is still a worthwhile scenario to review given the evolving nature of the political situation. The fall in security force employment was projected by assuming stable employment levels up to 1997 followed by reductions of the order of 10% per annum up to 2000. These assumptions result in a rise in the Catholic share of male employment to 35.7% by 2000 with the female share increasing to 42.7%. Compared to the baseline scenario (continued employment decline), these assumptions raise the Catholic share of male employment by 0.9 percentage points in 2000. The comparable figure for females is +0.3 percentage points.

Conclusions

The foregoing analyses suggest two broad conclusions. First, the Catholic share of public sector employment is likely to continue to rise. Second, in the case of males, the faster the rate of employment decline in the public sector, the slower will be the rate of convergence of the Catholic share of public sector employment on the Catholic share of the workforce. If employment is unchanged, the Catholic share rises by 3.2 percentage points over the six year period from 1994-2000. On average, for every one additional percentage point decline in public sector employment growth, the predicted increase in the Catholic share is reduced by about 0.37 percentage points over the six year period, or 0.06 percentage points per annum. This is because, as employment decline accelerates, the Catholic advantage of lower turnover becomes less important.

These conclusions relate to the Catholic share of public sector employment. For the historical period 1990-1994, the relatively minor impact of public sector job losses on the Catholic share in the public sector means that the direct effect of public sector job losses on the Catholic share of total employment, public and private, is likely to also have been quite small for males and absent for females. More specifically, the slower growth of 0.2 percentage points in the Catholic share of male employment estimated for the period 1990 to 1994 translates into approximately a 0.07 percentage point effect on the Catholic share of total covered or monitored male employment.[8]

EMPLOYMENT GROWTH IN THE PRIVATE PROVISION OF PUBLIC SERVICES

Public sector jobs can be transferred to the private sector in a number of ways, including privatisation of public corporations and contracting out.

Additionally, government may divert resources away from public sector bodies, for example, under the 'Care in the Community' programme. There are no comprehensive data which document such 'transfers' between 1989 and 1995. The approach adopted here is to compare private sector growth with public sector growth on an industry by industry basis, in order to document the shift in employment from the private sector to the public sector.

The 'Public Sector Shift'

As used here, the 'public sector shift' is simply the difference between the public sector share in some base year in a particular industry compared to the public sector share in a later year. A finding of a shift out of the public sector, or a reduction in the public sector share in a given industry, does not necessarily correspond to the identification of a 'transfer' of the type discussed in relation to the prior options policy framework. Nor does the quantification of a shift necessarily mean that the resulting increase in private provision is actually publicly financed. The rationale for evaluating the extent to which the public sector's share has shifted in various industries is that, especially in relation to public services such as health, government expenditure has not always moved in tandem with the trend in public sector employment.

For reasons of data availability, it is only possible to document the public sector shift for the period 1989 to 1993. Using Census of Employment data, the change in total and public employment in a range of industries was calculated for the period from 1989-1993 (Table 8.8). These data were then used to estimate the shift out of the public sector. For each four digit industry on the 1980 SIC, the public sector shift was approximated by first calculating the public sector share of total employment in the industry in 1989 and then multiplying the 1993 total employment level by the 1989 public sector share. This gives an estimate of the number of public sector jobs in each industry which would have been observed if the public sector's share had remained constant rather than falling. Subtracting out the actual 1993 employment level by industry gives an indication of the extent to which the public sector has 'withdrawn' from active provision of the services or goods provided by the industry. Of course, some industries are entirely comprised of public sector employees, notably public administration and health. Shifts from this industry simply cannot be identified. The shift statistic is nonetheless of interest in the case of other industries where the public sector share was very high in 1989, notably health. The calculations suggest a shift of the order of 15,000 jobs (Table 8.8). For the reasons given above, this should be viewed as indicative of the extent to which there has been compensatory growth outside the public sector. It is not a definitive measure. By comparison, the total number of jobs lost to the public sector from 1989 to 1993 through privatisation and other mechanisms was 11,000.

Table 8.8: Employment Change by Industry and the Public Sector Shift

	Employment Change: All Employees 1989-1993 %	Employment Change: All Employees 1989-1995 %	Employment Change: Public Sector 1989-1993 %	Public Sector Shift 1989-1993 '000s
Production	-4.4	-5.0	-30.2	1.3
Construction	-13.9	-6.1	-62.9	1.3
Distribution	13.3	17.7	4.5	0.1
Trans & Comms	-4.6	-2.6	-3.8	0.2
Fin'l & Bus Services	13.9	16.1	-1.2	0.5
Public Admin & Defence	3.5	0.7	4.0	-0.3
Sanitary Services	41.1	34.2	1.6	0.1
Education	4.1	14.2	1.8	1.2
Research & Development	-18.2	10.0	-21.7	0.0
Health Services	13.8	15.3	-6.7	8.4
Other Public Services	1.3	8.7	-8.7	1.5
Recreation/Cultural Services	18.0	19.0	10.2	0.4
Personal Services	-8.2	-9.3	-36.7	0.1
All Industries	4.2	6.9	-3.1	15.0

Source: DED.
Note: 1995 figures refer to March.

The size of the shift is most pronounced in health, where total employment rose quite significantly (+13.8%) from 1989-1993 while public sector employment declined by 7%. This was a major factor in the overall reduction in public sector employment from 1989 to 1993. Over the same period, however, public sector expenditure on health rose at about 3% per annum in volume terms. These considerations suggest a shift of activity from the public to the private sector which, on the calculations in Table 8.8, yielded 8400 jobs to the private sector in health.

Private Services in Division 9

There is no direct evidence available on the trend in the religious composition of employment at the detailed industry level shown in Table 8.8. The FEC monitoring returns give information on private sector employment in Division 9 of the 1980 SIC (Table 8.9). This is the industry division, where public sector employment accounts for 73% of total employment and in which is concentrated the vast bulk of activities which may be subjected to market testing. There are two points of interest. First, for both males and females, the Catholic share of private sector activity in Division 9 increased over the period 1990 to 1994, but by less than the increase for the private sector as a whole, particularly in the case of males. Second, for both males and females, the Catholic share of private sector activity in Division 9 was relatively high in 1990, close to parity in the case of males. More specifically, there was no employment gap in the base period. The scope for an increase in the Catholic share was thus much less than in other industries, especially for males. It is this factor, rather than an adverse pattern of shifts, which is the most likely explanation for the relatively slow increases in the Catholic shares of male and female employment in Division 9.

Table 8.9: The Catholic Share in Monitored Private Sector Concerns

	Male			Female		
	1990 %	1994 %	Change pps	1990 %	1994 %	Change pps
Division 9	46.0	47.4	+1.4	41.5	42.8	+1.3
All Industries	33.0	36.5	+3.5	36.8	39.7	+2.9

Source: FEC.

THE GEOGRAPHY OF CHANGE IN PUBLIC SECTOR EMPLOYMENT

The introduction to this chapter noted that both contracting out and the purchaser/provider split could potentially lead to geographical shifts in public sector employment. Given the high degree of residential segregation by religion in Northern Ireland, such shifts can potentially have adverse impacts on the community balance, even if no net loss of jobs is involved. A second reason for concern with the geography of employment change in the public sector is that some public services, notably hospitals, are typically highly concentrated in particular locations. This can make local communities highly vulnerable to changes in the geography of service provision as well as expenditure levels (see, for example, Centre for Public Services, 1993). The Royal Group and its relation to the local community in the Lower Falls area of Belfast is a case in point. There, the health sector accounted for 31% of total employment in 1993 (see Dignan and Murphy, 1996).

The Geography of the Public Sector

The approach taken here in examining the impact of geographical variations in public sector employment changes has been to cross-classify employment growth rates in the important public service sectors with geographic areas categorised by religion. The geographic unit used in the analysis is the District Electoral Area (DEA). Comprised of contiguous wards, the DEA is small enough to pick up shifts in the geographic distribution of employment which would not be apparent from an analysis of District Councils and large enough to mitigate at least some of the statistical and other pit-falls that occur in the use of ward-level employment data. For the purposes of the analysis, each DEA was categorised into one of four groups based on the percentage of the DEA's working age population which is Catholic. The classifications are shown in Table 8.10 along with the relative importance of the public sector and selected components in each of the different types of area. Overall, areas with a majority Catholic population rely more on the public sector as a source of employment than do areas with a majority Protestant population. This is particularly the case with respect to health and education services. By contrast, civil service employees account for a larger share of total employment in majority Protestant areas. Security-related employment is comparatively evenly spread.

Table 8.10:
The Public Sector Share of Employees in Employment[1] by Type of Area

	Per cent Catholic:				All
	Less than 25%	25%-49%	50%-74%	75% and over	Areas
Civil Service	8.4	3.1	5.9	2.9	5.8
Security	3.7	3.6	3.2	2.8	3.5
Health	4.7	7.7	9.3	11.4	7.3
Education	7.0	10.3	10.7	13.7	9.5
Division 9	30.7	32.3	36.7	36.7	33.1
All Public Sector	34.5	36.8	41.5	39.6	37.2

Source: DED
Notes: 1 Excluding agriculture, which is enumerated separately from the Census of Employment.
The percentage of total NI employees (excluding agriculture) accounted for by each area is:

41.7	24.5	19.9	13.8	100.0

The Geography of Employment Change

Table 8.11 shows growth rates by sector for the period 1989 to 1993. It should be noted that this type of analysis is far from satisfactory in a number of respects. A high (low) rate of employment change in a predominantly Catholic area does not necessarily imply that the jobs gained (lost) were all won (lost) by Catholics, or even won (lost) in proportion to their share of the working age population, and similarly for majority Protestant areas. Nor can it necessarily be inferred that all of the employment growth (decline) falls on local residents. Commuting patterns can have a large impact, depending on the types of jobs being gained or lost, such as whether they are part-time or full-time. Notwithstanding these caveats, the results provide some insight into whether or not there was a differential geographic impact from the changes in the level and composition of public sector employment which occurred over the period 1989 to 1993.[9]

Table 8.11: Employment Change, 1989 -1993, by District Electoral Areas, Categorised by Religion

	Per cent Catholic:				All
	Less than 25%	**25%-49%**	**50%-74%**	**75% and over**	**DEAs**
Number of DEAs	**35**	**30**	**19**	**14**	**98**
Total Employment	4.2	3.9	5.5	6.1	4.6
Public Sector	-1.1	-8.4	-1.1	-2.1	-3.1
Division 9 - All	7.2	2.6	10.2	7.4	6.8
Division 9 - Public	-0.5	-5.1	3.6	-1.2	-0.9
Civil Service	-0.7	-4.7	34.8	-9.0	3.5
Local Government	-3.2	15.1	130.9	-17.5	13.8
Security-Related	-1.0	3.4	4.4	2.4	1.4
Education	3.7	2.0	1.0	12.9	4.1
Health - All	18.3	22.0	0.3	15.9	13.8
Health - Public	-10.2	1.4	-15.1	3.5	-6.1
Rest of Division 9 - All	13.5	-8.0	18.0	2.1	6.7
Rest of Division 9 - Public	8.4	-24.3	17.1	-28.6	-6.4

Source: DED

As regards total employment changes, there was little difference by type of area. On average, the greater the proportion of Catholics in a DEA, the faster was the rate of employment growth. Public sector employment declines tended to be larger in DEAs with an underrepresentation of Catholics, though the loss from predominantly Protestant areas (less than 25% Catholic) was slightly less than the loss from predominantly Catholic areas. A similar pattern held for Division 9, that is, Catholic areas tended to register larger percentage rates of increase in total employment in Division 9. The geographical pattern was, however, more mixed as regards the public sector component. Health employment is of particular interest, due to the magnitude of the shift from public to private employment as well as the sector's tendency to concentrate in specific locations. Employment growth in the health industry tended to be fastest in predominantly Protestant areas. Contrary to the Northern Ireland trend, areas with a 50%-74% Catholic population registered virtually no increase in employment. By contrast, public sector employment in health rose by 3.5% in areas where the Catholic population comprised 75% or more of total population. There was also an increase in areas which contained 25%-49% Catholics. In other areas, employment declines were quite large. The results suggest that, overall, where particular categories of DEAs may have tended to lose out in respect of one particular component of the public sector, they tended to gain from some other component. Areas of concern can certainly be identified but the overall pattern of change was reasonably balanced.

Health and Education

The geography of change in the public sector can also be examined from FEC data on the trend in the Catholic share of employment in Health and Social Services Boards and Education and Library Boards, the two major public sector activities which are organised on a regional basis (see Dignan and Murphy, 1996, for more detailed analysis). These are rather large spatial units and cannot be used to probe for the effects of smaller scale geographical shifts as is the case with DEAs. The FEC data for health and education show widely spread increases in Catholic shares across the regions, even in areas where the Catholic share of jobs in 1990 was in excess of 60%. The only decrease in the Catholic share, -0.3 percentage points, occurred in male employment in the Western Education and Library Board. In that region, the Catholic share of male employment was over 62% in 1990. The reduction is more likely to signal the absence of an employment gap than an adverse impact from public sector job losses. Again, these data suggest that both communities suffered from public sector job losses.

CONCLUSIONS

The key issue addressed in this chapter was the extent to which recent trends in public sector employment have had an adverse impact on efforts to create more favourable conditions for equality of employment opportunity in Northern Ireland. For practical purposes, this was taken to refer to the speed with which the Catholic share of employment is converging on the Catholic share of the labour force. The key empirical issue addressed in this study has therefore been whether or not public sector employment trends have affected Protestants and Catholics equally.

Excluding corporations, public sector employment has been declining since 1989 at a rate of about 0.3% per annum, resulting in a loss of about 3000 jobs. There have been substantial variations around the overall average.

Employment in education has increased while health and social services and the civil service (excluding security-related occupations) have registered sharp falls. Analysis of expenditure patterns suggests that the factors underlying falling employment levels in health and social services are somewhat different to those affecting the civil service. In the case of the latter, downward pressures on expenditure have been accompanied by planned reductions in payrolls, a situation likely to persist and perhaps even accelerate. By contrast, in the health sector, departmental expenditure has been growing, at about 3% per annum. Public sector employment in health and social services has been under pressure from the introduction of market testing, a process which can potentially result in transfers of employment from the public to the private sector via privatisation as well as straightforward reductions due to the pressures of the tendering process. By contrast, employment in the health industry has been expanding, in that the private component of health service provision has been increasing in relative importance. Given the trend in government spending on health and social services, it is likely that public sector employment levels present an incomplete picture of the overall level of public sector activity. There has, in other words, been some compensatory shift from the public sector to the private sector.

These are the key facts underlying the empirical analysis of the impact on the community differentials. With respect to the public sector *per se*, it is possible to document the change in the religious composition of monitored employment. The FEC data show clearly that, from 1990 to 1995, the Catholic share of public sector employment rose consistently across all elements of the public sector, though only slightly in security-related occupations. A model for the Catholic share was used to simulate a counterfactual path for the Catholic share of the public sector. The model controls for differences by gender and religion in influences such as employment turnover, the propensity to apply for public sector employment and success rates. The main finding was that the actual increase in the Catholic male share was marginally slower than would have been observed if there had been no employment decline in the public sector. The conclusion drawn is that, for all practical purposes, public sector job losses to date have been equally shared among Catholics and Protestants.

As regards trends outside the public sector, the study constructed a measure of the public sector shift for the period 1989 to 1993. This identified the health sector as the main contributor to shifts from the public sector in the provision of public services. FEC data on the religious composition of private sector concerns in the relevant industrial sector did not suggest an adverse impact on the Catholic share. The conclusion in that regard was not definitive due to data deficiencies.

The research also documented the geographical pattern of change in public sector employment, with areas classified according to their religious composition. While there was a mixed pattern of change depending on the particular industry studied, public sector employment declines were greatest in areas where Catholics comprised 25%-49% of the working age population. Again, the study concludes that public sector job losses have not adversely affected the community balance.

As to the future, a number of points can be made. Government expenditure plans suggest growing pressures on public sector budgets. The rates of growth in both education and health and social services are planned to fall to about 1% per annum. Particularly in the case of the latter, this would put employment levels under some pressure, both in the public sector and in the private sector. Such plans do need to be discounted to a certain degree since their implementation, particularly in demand-driven services, is not wholly within the control of government and because such plans will almost certainly be resisted by those affected.

A range of alternative employment growth scenarios were analysed with respect to their potential impact on the future evolution of the Catholic share in the public sector. These suggest that, if employment decline is accelerated, then this will tend to slow down the speed of convergence of the Catholic share of public sector employment on its share of the labour force. Under all of the scenarios examined, however, the Catholic share continues to increase. The rising Catholic share assumes continued proportionality in applications from the Catholic community combined with fair employment practices and lower turnover among Catholics (reflecting their younger age profile in the public sector). The key issue for the future, therefore, is the speed of convergence of the Catholic share of public sector employment on its share in the labour force. If monitored public sector employment continues to fall by 1% per annum, the Catholic share is estimated to increase by 2.7 percentage points between 1994 and 2000. This compares with a simulated 3.2 percentage point rise if public sector employment remains stable. A range of different scenarios, constructed around alternative paths for employment levels in the public sector, suggest that for the period 1994 to 2000 each 1% per cent per annum decline in public sector employment results in a reduction in the Catholic share of about 0.05 percentage points per annum. While the Catholic share is likely to continue to increase for other reasons, as described above, this indicates the size of the trade-off between the rate of decline in public sector employment and the speed with which the Catholic share of public sector employment converges on the Catholic share of the workforce.

As regards the impact on the Catholic share in total employment, a key issue is the path of public sector expenditure. This is because there may be compensating effects due to transfers and shifts from the public sector, for example, due to contracting out. The size of the compensatory effect will depend on the magnitude of changes in public sector expenditure, particularly in employment-intensive areas such as health and social services. If carried forward, the planned expenditure levels published in March 1995 would leave little scope for compensatory shifts and transfers. The whole economy effect of a particular rate of decline in public sector employment (which is the most likely outcome, though the precise rate of decline is open to question) will depend on the difference between the direct effect of job losses in the public sector and compensatory shifts. Overall, the research for this chapter suggests that, over the historical period at least, there has not been a significant differential impact by community affiliation.

Whether or not the public sector should be used as a vehicle for promoting a more rapid growth in the Catholic share is an issue for policy which is not addressed in this chapter. The research has shown, however, that the Catholic share of employment in the public sector is not independent of the rate of growth of public sector employment. There are a number of reasons for this, including the higher turnover of Protestants due to their older age profile in the public sector, the younger age profile of Catholics in the applicant pool and the size of the Catholic employment gap. Though not substantial, there is a trade-off between the rate of employment growth in the public sector and the increase in the Catholic share.

ENDNOTES

1. A little over 70% of total private sector employees in employment are monitored by the FEC. The FEC has been monitoring private sector concerns with 26 or more employees since 1990. Concerns with between 11 and 25 employees have been monitored since 1992. A number of categories of employment are not monitored, including those on government training schemes, those who work less than 16 hours per week, school teachers and those working in firms with 10 or fewer employees (FEC, 1996). Particularly for women, part-time employment has been increasing steadily in recent years, both in absolute terms and as a percentage of the total workforce in employment (see Dignan, 1995).
2. The labour force comprises employees in employment plus the self-employed and the unemployed plus those on government-sponsored employment training schemes.
3. Throughout this chapter, the measure of the Catholic share is computed by excluding 'non-determined' employees. This is the so-called 'square brackets' share which is typically used in monitoring reports such as the FEC publications. In 1995, the non-determined proportion of all public sector employees was 6.3%. There was no variation by gender.

4. See Dignan and Murphy (1996) for a more detailed analysis of public sector employment.
5. It should be noted that the shift in the public sector share in the health sector was not a function of the introduction of trusts in 1993 since these are still counted as part of the public sector, albeit as public sector corporations rather than NDPBs.
6. It might be argued that the model should also take account of the kind of 'structural factors' documented by Murphy and Armstrong (1994) in their analysis of male unemployment in Northern Ireland. Murphy and Armstrong modelled the unemployment rate and found that the Catholic-Protestant differential in unemployment could be 'decomposed' into a structural component and a residual component. The residual component, accounting for about 50% of the unemployment differential, reflects the effect of religion on the probability of a Catholic being unemployed. The structural component is due to factors such as socio-economic background, education and occupation. Murphy and Armstrong's findings have subsequently been used by Gudgin and Breen (1996) to argue that the probability of an 'average' Catholic obtaining a job is less than that of an 'average' Protestant. Notwithstanding the fact that Murphy (1996) contests the accuracy of the measure of disadvantage used in the Gudgin-Breen model, their argument is not relevant to the present study. There are a number of reasons for this. First, the Gudgin-Breen argument relates to the Northern Ireland economy as a whole whereas the simulation model used in this study is focused on one sector of the economy. More importantly, the empirical success rates data shown in Table 8.9 suggest that Catholic applicants do at least as well as Protestant applicants in the public sector, on average.
7. To date, security force employment has remained static, notwithstanding the ceasefires and reduced security needs. The adjustment to the reduced level of security needs has thus far been made via reduced overtime work, that is, hours have been cut, not jobs.
8. That is, 0.2 multiplies by 0.33, the public sector's share of total employees in employment in 1995.
9. Date for 1995 at the DEA level is not yet available.

REFERENCES

Centre for Public Services (1993) *Social and Economic Audit: Down Lisburn Trust, Northern Ireland,* Belfast: UNISON Northern Ireland.

Centre for Public Services (1993) *Social and Economic Audit: Royal Hospitals Trust, Belfast,* Belfast: UNISON Northern Ireland.

Chartered Institute of Public Finance and Accountancy (CIPFA) (1995) *Achieving Value for Money Through Competition Within the Public Services in Northern Ireland: The Context Statement,* Publication No. 1, Belfast: CIPFA.

Department of Finance and Personnel/HM Treasury (1995) *Northern Ireland: Expenditure Plans and Priorities: The Government's Expenditure Plans 1995-95 to 1997-98,* London: HMSO.

Dignan, T. (1995) *Demographic Change and Labour Availability,* Belfast: EOC (NI).

Dignan, T. and Murphy, A. (1996) *The Impact of Public Sector Job Losses on Employment Equality,* Unpublished report, Belfast: SACHR.

EOC (NI) (1996) *Report on Formal Investigation into Competitive Tendering in Health and Education Services in Northern Ireland,* Belfast: EOC (NI).

Escott, K. and Whitfield, D. (1995) *The Gender Impact of CCT in Local Government,* EOC (GB), Research Discussion Series No. 12, Manchester: EOC(GB).

Fair Employment Commission (1996) *A Profile of the Northern Ireland Workforce: Summary of the 1994 Monitoring Returns,* Monitoring Report No. 6, Belfast: FEC.

Gudgin, G. and Breen, R. (1996) *Evaluation of the Ratio of Unemployment Rates as an Indicator of Fair Employment,* Belfast: CCRU.

Haskel, J. and Szymanski, S. (1993) 'Privatisation, Liberalisation, Wages and Employment: Theory and Evidence for the UK', *Economica,* 60: 161-182.

HM Treasury (1991) *Competing for Quality,* CM 1730, London: HMSO.

Murphy, A. (1966) 'Comment' in Gudgin, G. and Breen, R. *Evaluation of the Ratio of Unemployment Rates as an Indicator of Fair Employment,* Belfast: CCRU.

Murphy, A. and Armstrong, D. (1995) *A Picture of the Catholic and Protestant Male Unemployed,* Belfast: CCRU.

Northern Ireland Economic Council (1994) *The Reform of Health and Social Care in Northern Ireland: An Introduction to the Economic Issues,* Report No. 110, Belfast: NIEC.

Chapter Nine

LOCAL COUNCILS' ECONOMIC DEVELOPMENT ACTIVITIES

Ronnie Scott and Kathleen Hoye

INTRODUCTION

Prior to 1973, there were 72 local government authorities in Northern Ireland. Belfast and Londonderry were two all-purpose county boroughs, with the remainder structured on a two-tier system of 15 counties or boroughs and 55 urban and rural district councils. The counties were responsible for education and libraries, welfare and roads and planning. The lower tier's responsibilities included housing and water and sewage. Unionists controlled most councils, and inequalities of service provision between the two communities, particularly in housing, precipitated the reform of the local government system in 1972.

Following this re-organisation the number of authorities was significantly reduced, from 72 to 26, and their executive functions largely constrained to what has been described as 'bins, births and burials'. In practice, however, district councils have a slightly wider remit including responsibilities for leisure and tourism (specifically the provision and management of recreational, social, community and cultural facilities and the provision and management of tourism), which have a direct relationship to local economic development issues. Leisure and recreation accounted for 28% of councils' expenditure in 1994/95, while tourism accounted for 5.2%. With the introduction of Direct Rule in 1972, local councils represent the only democratically elected local bodies.

The Local Government Act of 1972 (Section 107) gave district councils the ability 'to make contributions towards the expenses of any voluntary body which carries on activities within the district council for the purpose of developing trade, industry or commerce'. Discretionary power was also given to councils (Section 115 of the Local Government Act, 1972) to 'make any payment for any purpose which in its opinion is in the interests of the council, of its district or of its inhabitants'. The total payments made under this Section were limited to 3p in the pound on the rateable value of the district.

Councils could therefore undertake economic development activities under Section 115 or make payments to voluntary bodies engaged in such activities under Section 107 of the Local Government Act. The use of these powers has been limited and sporadic. In a survey of 16 councils, John (1993) found that 12 councils had used Section 115 powers for a variety of minor incidental uses in 1990/91 and 1991/92. Expenditure on economic development through this mechanism in 1992/92 was estimated at £20,000 (16% of Section 115 spending and 0.01% of total council expenditure). In 1994/95, spending under Section 115 totaled £0.2 million (0.1% of total spending). Councils identified the major constraints on the use of Section 115 for economic development as the limited amounts of money available to councils and a lack of clarification of the legality of using the power for this purpose. Nine of the 16 councils surveyed recommended that a specific economic development power should be given to district councils (John, 1993).

Nevertheless, district councils did gradually become more involved in economic development activities. Two major initiatives which began in the late 1980s were particularly important in establishing a more central role for local councils. The Local Economic Development Unit (LEDU), the International Fund for Ireland (IFI) and the European Union (EU) jointly funded the establishment of Local Enterprise Agency (LEA) premises in each district council area. The LEAs were perhaps the first major collaborative effort in local economic development engaged in by the councils. The second major initiative was the Tourism Operational Programme 1989-93. Under this programme, the district councils were able to seek funding for major public sector tourist projects. This gave the councils additional experience in negotiating and implementing core economic projects with government and the EU. However, much of the developments pre-1993 were project-based and few district councils had the capacity or experience for planning and financing strategic plans.

Subsequently, the Local Government (Miscellaneous Provisions) Order 1992 gave councils the power to 'make payments for promoting the economic development of its district subject to an annual limit of 2p in the pound on the rateable value of the district'. The financial limit on council spending was raised from 2p to 5p in the pound of rateable value of the district in April 1995. In 1994/95, £3 million (1.2%) of district council expenditure was incurred under economic development. Guidance issued by the Department of the Environment (NI) in October 1992 made it clear that 'the Department would not sanction any proposals that conflict with the aims and objectives of the statutory agencies working in this area'. Examples of activities councils might usefully undertake were largely restricted to developing strategies for local economic regeneration, trade development, support for Local Enterprise Agencies, and support in various areas of the Industrial Development Board (IDB), the Local Economic Development Unit (LEDU) and the Training and Employment Agency (T&EA). These recent changes to the local government legislation and the introduction of a Local Economic Development Measure under the Single Programme Document for Northern Ireland Structural Funds (1994 to 1999) have allowed district councils the first real opportunity to become involved in strategic planning and delivery of economic programmes at local level. The funds available from the Local Economic Development Measure are limited, but the strategies become more significant if they are seen as a base for applications for other EU and central government programmes. In particular, it is envisaged that funding for the EU Peace and Reconciliation Programme will be four times the level allocated to the Local Economic Development Measure. Moreover, if councils demonstrate a competence for delivering economic development programmes there is scope for devolving more powers and responsibilities in theses areas, provided there is broad political support for such developments.

Against the background of the growing importance of the role of district councils in local economic development, this chapter examines the socio-economic and labour market context at council level, councils' potential spend on local economic development, the allocation of funds under the EU Local Economic Development Measure, council's economic development strategies and planned expenditure on the strategies. The research involves four key elements:

(a) documentary research of the evolution of councils' powers in respect of local economic development and analysis of councils' potential expenditure on local economic development;
(b) a desk-based review and analysis of all councils' economic development strategies and action plans;
(c) in-depth semi-structured interviews with five councils - Ballymena, Belfast, Derry, Fermanagh and Magherafelt; and
(d) interviews with representatives of the voluntary and community sector in Northern Ireland.

A particular emphasis of the analysis is to review recent local economic development issues with reference to Targeting Social Need and equality of employment issues. However, the explicit aim of the EU Measure is 'to encourage local economic development through a locally-based, district council-led strategic approach, complementing the activities of government departments and agencies'. The following analysis should not, therefore, be interpreted as a full assessment of the Measure, but rather an examination of some aspects of its likely impact.

DEFINING LOCAL ECONOMIC DEVELOPMENT

It is important to define what local economic development is before proceeding to discuss the model adopted in Northern Ireland. The

Directorate General for Regional Policies, Commission of the European Communities, has defined Local Economic Development as:

> Economic development policy applied to a consistent, generally infra-regional, territory which is led by local actors. Through integrated action on socio-economic factors and structures this policy aims to develop the range of local resources with the purpose of creating or the maintaining of stable business employment (European Commission, 1994).

Furthermore, the Commission has endorsed the value of local economic development by asserting that:

> Local development now makes up part of the strategic approach in regional policy - along with environmental and structural actions. It is the necessary complement to most interventions and it gives back more than it takes. Although the financial means available for LEDU are modest it has, nevertheless, become inconceivable to launch large-scale ('hardware') actions without ensuring their success through 'soft' measures that directly involve the local people most affected (European Commission, 1994).

Within the EU, Northern Ireland has been granted Objective I status; our GDP per head is less than 75% of the EU average, and as such, Northern Ireland is eligible for the highest levels of EU Structural Funds assistance. The EU is promoting LED as an integral part of regional development strategies in its lagging regions. To date, however, the extent to which LED priorities for Objective I regions of the EU are put into practice remains inadequate because local communities are not sufficiently involved or appropriately trained. A systematic approach to local development is clearly needed, as is the creation of networks of local participants. In the United Kingdom context, Hambleton and Taylor (1993) assert that national government needs a stronger endorsement of local economic development initiatives to realise their full potential, and to allow areas like Northern Ireland to benefit from lessons learned in other countries:

> In the UK, central government support has been tantamount to an abandonment of local economies, with local strategies tying local authorities into programmes aimed at exposing their economies to the full impact of wider international market forces, with the consequences that many localities have seen a weakening of their economic bases. National politics have to engage for policy transfer to be effective (Hambleton and Taylor, 1993).

The introduction of the EU Local Economic Development Measure in Northern Ireland was designed to create a partnership approach to local economic development in Northern Ireland with the partnerships being led by the councils. Stoker and Young (1993) argue that, despite its occasional warts, local government is the main repository of local and specialist knowledge and expertise and the only democratically elected one. They suggest that local authorities should be the lead actor and facilitator of local partnerships. Partnerships could potentially serve an important capacity building role for councils, to the extent that they are able to harness private sector expertise in identifying, appraising and prioritise economic development proposals. Peck and Tickell (1994), by contrast, are quite sceptical about the role and potential of partnerships and are careful to point out their limitations. Their main concern about the development of partnerships in Great Britain is the erosion of the power of local authorities 'away from elected local government and in favor of both the private sector and (perhaps most importantly) central government'. However, since the local economic development initiatives are a means of devolving more responsibilities to local authorities, this danger is less obvious in Northern Ireland, though the potential for private sector interests having a dominant role does exist. In order to avoid this shift in power, Peck and Tickell encourage the question, 'in what sense are new partnerships locally grown and locally accountable?' and they assert that:

> When it comes to concerns about fragmentation, about duplication, about competition for scarce resources, the problem is not solved by the creation of partnerships, it is only concealed (Peck and Ticklell, 1994: 263).

Partnerships, in their view, foster a short-term, unstrategic approach, and at best they provide a mechanism for securing consensus around regeneration strategies. They conclude by suggesting that:

> Partnerships themselves now need to be more effectively co-ordinated if local and regional goals are to be realised. The growth of them seems to exacerbate those very problems of poor co-ordination and organisational proliferation which the partnership model is supposed to solve (*ibid.*).

In the Northern Ireland context, the benefits identified from the partnership approach to local economic development, in particular a consensual approach, would represent a vast improvement. The dangers identified are less pertinent to Northern Ireland since recent initiatives actually increased the powers of local government for economic development. But the potential for poor co-ordination and organisational proliferation remains.

SOCIO-ECONOMIC AND LABOUR MARKET CONTEXT

Any analysis of the potential of local economic development strategies needs to be placed within the context of economic and social trends at district council level. In this section, a brief review of the main labour market trends is provided and some of the major issues facing councils are identified.

Relative Deprivation

The 1991 deprivation index for geographical areas in Northern Ireland (Robson *et al*, 1994) has been used by government departments and agencies as the basis for their Targeting Social Need activities (see also Chapter Seven, this volume). The index was produced at three geographical levels; district council, ward, and enumeration district. The results at district council level (Table 9.1) indicate that deprivation is mainly concentrated in Belfast and in the predominantly Catholic west and south of the region. Council areas in the Greater Belfast area and in the rural east, which are predominantly Protestant, are less deprived.

The DED and its agencies mainly use the ward level data to target policies on deprived areas. The DED has defined 215 of the 566 wards in Northern Ireland as 'deprived' for this purpose. A crude measure of the extent of deprivation is the proportion of the population living in deprived wards in a council area (Table 9.1). This ranges from zero in Castlereagh to 100% in Strabane, and averages 37% for Northern Ireland as a whole.

Labour Market Trends and Issues

The major limitation on treating district council levels as an economic planning unit is their limited size. Few of the areas may be considered as local labour markets except perhaps in respect to unskilled and low paid work. The Department of Economic Development defines Travel to Work Areas (TTWA) on the basis of commuting patterns revealed by the Census of Population, and there are twelve areas in Northern Ireland. These areas are an amalgamation of adjoining district council areas which have significant cross-boundary flows of people who reside in one area and work in a neighbouring area.

For the purposes of planning labour market services, Travel to Work Areas are the minimum size of unit which should be considered. In effect, economies of scale, significant labour market mobility between the Travel to Work Areas themselves and the distribution of industry in Northern Ireland tend to suggest that larger planning and management units are required. Hence the Training & Employment Agency regional structure is based around five geographical areas. The same general arguments holds for services to firms. LEDU, the small firms agency, has a structure based on six regional offices. In the case of larger firms, services are believed to be more effectively and efficiently delivered at an industrial sector level. Consequently LEDU, for its larger growth firms, and the IDB provide a central service from Belfast.

Table 9.1: Relative Deprivation Measures for Council Areas

	Degree of Deprivation Rank	% of population in deprived wards (DED definition)
Strabane	1	100
Belfast	2	55
Derry	3	65
Newry & Mourne	4	57
Dungannon	5	73
Fermanagh	6	62
Moyle	7	49
Cookstown	8	57
Omagh	9	55
Magherafelt	10	71
Limavady	11	52
Ballymoney	12	30
Armagh	13	39
Larne	14	19
Craigavon	15	27
Down	16	15
Antrim	17	15
Banbridge	18	6
Ballymena	19	11
Coleraine	20	26
Carrickfergus	21	10
Ards	22	10
Lisburn	23	19
Newtownabbey	24	13
Castlereagh	25	0
North Down	26	3
Northern Ireland		37

Note: The degree of overall deprivation is based on a composite index of 18 indicators covering unemployment, housing, health, education and family circumstances. Robson also produced measures of the intensity and extent of deprivation at council level but the ranking was largely consistent across all three measures.

Source: Robson *et al* (1994); Census of Population (1991).

In the planning and implementing of local economic development services there would appear to be a strong argument for district councils to co-operate and co-ordinate joint programmes. This has been a feature of several district councils' approach to the promotion of tourism over recent years. For instance, Derry, Strabane, Omagh, Dungannon and Armagh have combined to promote the 'North West Passage' as a tourist area. The consortium has recently been expanded to include parts of the North West and Midlands East regions of the South of Ireland. In respect of social and community programmes with an economic thrust, there remains a need to work with small, often isolated, communities to temper programmes to specific local needs and opportunities. The Robson (1994) analysis of deprivation in Northern Ireland, based on the 1991 Census of Population and carried out at district, ward and enumeration level, indicated that the variation of deprivation between wards within district council areas is greater than between district council areas. Hence, the creation of economic opportunities at district council level will not necessarily ensure convergence between deprived and non-deprived wards, unless access to these opportunities is improved for those living in disadvantaged areas or those marginalised from the formal labour market. District councils are therefore not a natural planning unit and they are not sufficiently large or self-contained to enable macro-planning. However, in many cases where there is good grass roots contact and a solid working knowledge of local conditions, they are small enough to understand and deliver appropriate programmes to meet local needs. They may best be viewed as a 'middle-out' approach linking regional agencies to local communities.

A number of recent studies, Gudgin (1994) and NIERC (forthcoming), have demonstrated that the divergence in economic development, and specifically unemployment, at district council level in Northern Ireland is not primarily due to variations in growth. Indeed, employment growth over the 1971 to 1993 period was higher in those district council areas in the mainly Catholic west of the region where unemployment is highest. The main problem has been that growth in these areas has not been sufficiently high to absorb the growing labour supply.

In Figure 9.1 the potential growth in the labour force over the next five years is contrasted with potential employment growth, based on past trends. The figures are shown as a proportion of the total employment base in a council area in 1993. In predominantly Catholic (defined as a 60% or more share of the population) council areas, employment would have to grow by between 10% and 15%, between 1995 and 2000 to match the growth in those who may be seeking work. Based on the experience of the past two decades, employment is unlikely to increase by more than 7%. The shortfall will be taken up by lower participation rates, more young people staying on in education, migration and unemployment. In predominantly Protestant areas, both employment[1] and labour supply growth tend to be lower, with the result that the job gap is on average significantly lower, and in some areas negative.

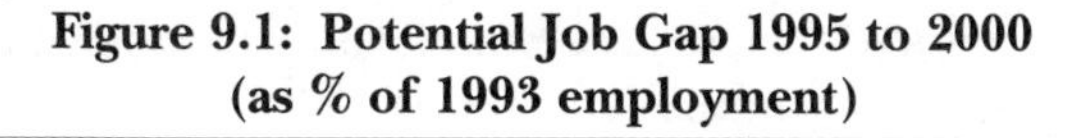

Figure 9.1: Potential Job Gap 1995 to 2000 (as % of 1993 employment)

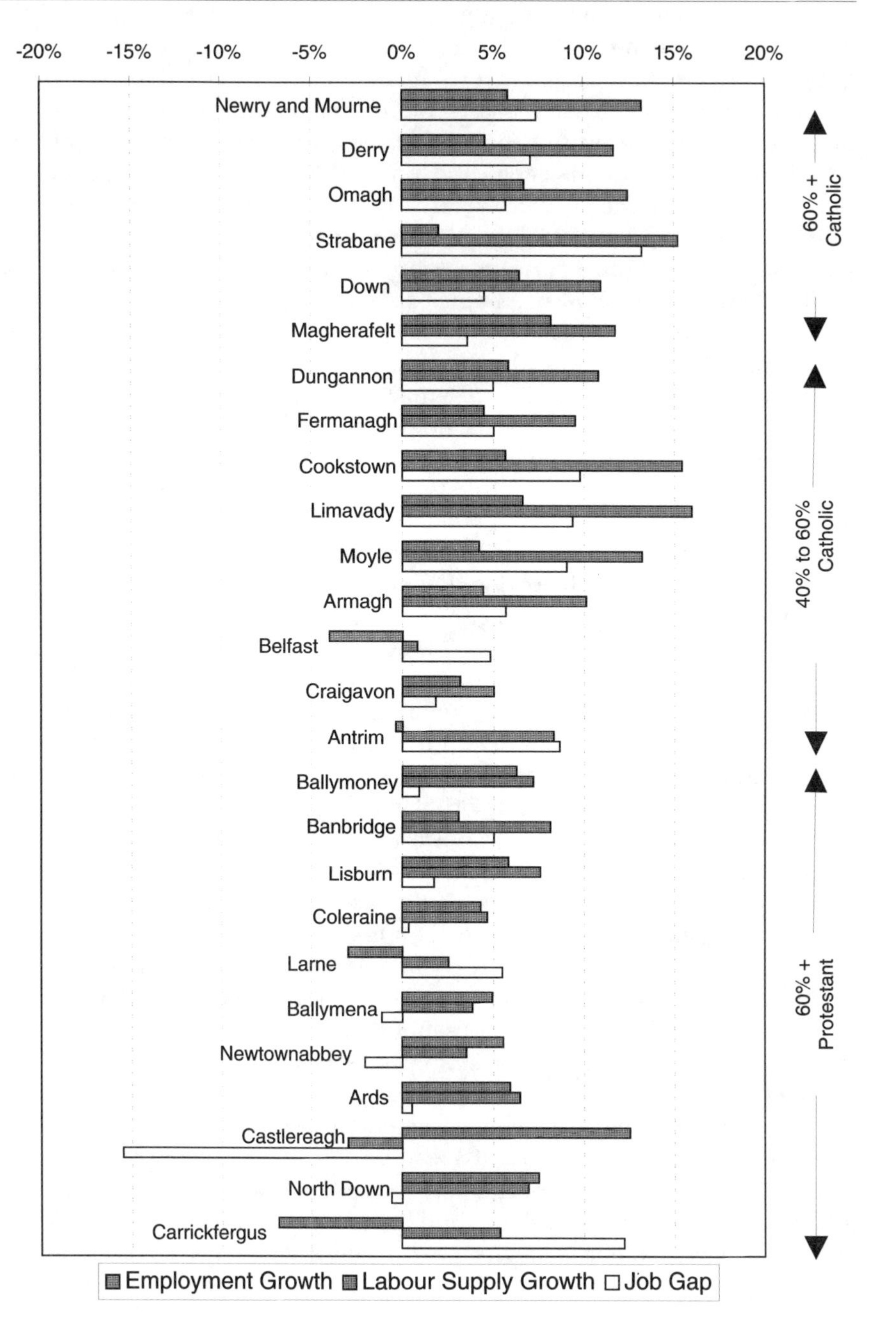

There is no guarantee that an accelerated role of employment growth will have any significant effect on the levels of unemployment, in the short-term at least. For instance, 100,000 additional jobs have been created in Northern Ireland since 1983 but unemployment has fallen by only 19,000. Gudgin and O'Shea (1993) have estimated that for every three jobs created in manufacturing, one person comes off the claimant register. The labour market adjustment process is such that participation and migration rates will adjust in line with employment and unemployment. This general ratio is likely to be larger the smaller the area considered, because of the greater possibility of migration between areas within Northern Ireland. Moreover, jobs created in an area may not necessarily be taken by residents of the area, as Shuttleworth *et al* show in Chapter Two, this volume. This is a particular problem in deprived areas with high levels of long-term unemployment; an indication that those available for work may not have the necessary confidence or skills to take advantage of any opportunities created. Community-led economic projects, however, are more likely to generate jobs which will be taken by local people.

Female employment has grown strongly (by 96,700, or 50%) while male employment has declined (by 17,500, or 6%) since 1971. This has resulted in a situation where the number of females in employment now outnumbers the number of males at the regional level and in many council areas. Female unemployment rates, whether measured by the claimant count or by the ILO definition, are now amongst the lowest in Europe. Yet there remain a number of outstanding gender equality issues. Labour market participation rates are lower for females, the quality and wages associated with female employment are generally poorer and at a local level females are often more marginalised from the formal labour market. Local economic development initiatives can help address these problems.

There is also a strong relationship between male participation and employment rates and those for females. Due to the nature of the tax-benefit system, if one spouse is not in work there is no financial advantage in the other looking for employment. The result is a growing dichotomy between households where both spouses are working and those where both are not. In addressing unemployment and poverty at local level in Northern Ireland, it is this group of 'jobless' households which should receive greatest attention. Employment and training schemes should be targeted on households where both spouses are unemployed and/or inactive and at least one partner is in long-term unemployment. The implication for councils is that economic growth will contribute to a reduction in unemployment, but only by a small proportion of the jobs created, and will not necessarily have any effect on those individuals and communities in most need. Local economic development strategies need to ensure equality of access to any employment opportunities created and correctly target training initiatives on the most marginalised.

POTENTIAL COUNCIL SPEND ON LOCAL ECONOMIC DEVELOPMENT

Council Expenditure Limits

The maximum expenditure by district councils on economic development, based on the rateable values in district council areas, in 1995/96 is estimated at £9 million. This compares with total actual expenditure on economic development by district councils in 1994/95 of £3 million. Maximum district council expenditure on economic development is equivalent to 2% of total government expenditure on mainstream economic development programmes in Northern Ireland. Assuming councils could achieve a leverage of their own to other EU, public and private funds at a ratio of 1:3 (the current EU grant rate is a maximum of 75 per cent), total expenditure on council assisted projects could be a maximum of £36 million per year. This would represent 8% of mainstream regional expenditure on economic development.

Determination of Council Expenditure

A council's expenditure limit on economic development is dependent on the rateable value in the council area. The rateable value is, in effect, the council's local tax base and it is dependent on an assessment of the market rent which could be achieved for properties in the district. A mixture of lower value properties will mean a lower tax base and a reduced ability to raise income through the district rate. Therefore, the more affluent the area, the higher the rateable value and the bigger the tax base for district rates.

This is reflected in the figures for the penny product of district council areas. The penny product represents the amount which can be raised by an additional 1p in the district rate. The penny product per head of population varies greatly between district council areas and, as a general rule, the more deprived council areas, such as Strabane, have a lower penny product per head of population than the average for Northern Ireland (see Figure 9.2). Councils with higher penny products per head of population are concentrated in more urban areas and in the east of the Province. Belfast has by far the highest level of penny product and Strabane the lowest. The degree of variation in the penny product per head ranges from -40% in Strabane to +43% in Belfast. In effect, this means that, if desired, Belfast could spend over twice as much as Strabane on economic development. Eleven of the 26 district council areas in Northern Ireland have a majority Catholic population and all of these areas have a penny product per head of population less than the Northern Ireland average. By comparison, seven of the 15 councils, which have a majority Protestant population, have a penny product per head more than the Northern Ireland average.

The system of linking district council spending on local economic development to the rateable value in the area suffers from two disadvantages. Firstly, deprived council areas are restricted to low levels of spending compared to their more affluent comparators. Secondly, deprived council

Table 9.2: Effect of Variation in Penny Product on Maximum Economic Development Spend

	Maximum Council Spend (5p in £) £	Equivalent Spend based on NI ave. £	Difference (col 1-2) £	Catholic Share of population %
Antrim	305,400	255,947	49,453	37
Ards	333,700	372,364	-38,664	13
Armagh	222,450	297,925	-75,475	49
Ballymena	346,400	325,660	20,740	20
Ballymoney	108,300	139,128	-30,828	33
Banbridge	172,050	192,507	-20,457	31
Belfast	2,298,400	1,605,488	692,912	45
Carrickfergus	183,450	188,298	-4848	8
Castlereagh	353,150	349,567	3583	11
Coleraine	339,100	289,996	49,104	25
Cookstown	128,500	184,457	-55,957	57
Craigavon	396,050	431,136	-35,086	45
Derry	526,050	548,341	-22,291	75
Down	273,750	333,520	-59,770	63
Dungannon	185,050	261,191	-76,141	59
Fermanagh	246,450	310,666	-64,216	58
Larne	159,200	169,146	-9946	25
Limavady	128,550	169,997	-41,447	57
Lisburn	573,150	571,839	1311	31
Magherafelt	148,200	208,668	-60,468	63
Moyle	68,600	85,030	-16,430	57
Newry & Mourne	344,150	476,885	-132,735	78
Newtownabbey	458,000	425,668	32,332	15
North Down	446,050	413,002	33,048	11
Omagh	202,550	263,381	-60,831	68
Strabane	130,900	207,795	-76,895	65
NI	9,077,600	9,077,600		

areas are less able to impose any additional rates or raise income from other sources. The difference between an amount equivalent to 5p in the pound on the actual rateable value in a district in 1995/96 and an amount based on the average Northern Ireland figure is set out in Table 9.2. This indicates that Strabane can spend £77,000 less per year on economic development as a result of it having a lower penny product per head than the Northern Ireland average. In contrast, Belfast could spend £693,000 more based on the Northern Ireland average. This indication of the funds available for economic development spend suggests that outcomes may result in a further divergence rather than convergence between district council areas. In practice, the actual effect will depend on how much of the potential spend councils will countenance using and the effectiveness and efficiency with which funds are employed.

THE LOCAL ECONOMIC DEVELOPMENT MEASURE

Background to the Measure

The Local Economic Development Measure of the Northern Ireland Structural Funds Plan emerged as a result of the consultation process undertaken by the Department of Finance and Personnel during 1992 and 1993, and a growing recognition by the European Commission and government in Northern Ireland that 'a local development approach can have a real impact on local employment and initiative' (EC,1994: 34). The impetus for the source of the Local Economic Development Measure was the introduction of the Miscellaneous Provisions Order 1992, which allowed councils to make payments towards the promotion of economic development in their area. This provided councils with the powers and ability to co-finance economic development projects with matching funds from the EU or elsewhere.

The need for, and desirability of, enhancing the approach to integrated community economic development was identified as a priority at a conference on 'The Structural Funds in Northern Ireland After 1995' held in December 1992. Consequently, a Community Economic Development Measure was proposed as part of the Industrial Development Sub-Programme in the consultation document on the Northern Ireland Structural Funds Plan (DFP, 1993(b)). The envisaged objectives of the Measure were primarily economic in nature, and focused on increasing the competitiveness of companies, developing strategies for local economic development, supporting the activities of Local Enterprise Agencies (LEAs), developing skills and attracting inward investment. While the implicit assumption was that the Measure would contribute to economic convergence between council areas within Northern Ireland, the potential contribution to increasing equality of opportunity and employment and to the government's more general outcome of Targeting Social Need (TSN) was not addressed.

The final decision on the Structural Funds Plan, the Northern Ireland Single Programming Document 1994-1999, incorporated some further refinement of the rationale and purpose of the Local Economic Development Measure. The measure was referred in the Single Programming Document within the context of government policies to Target Social Need, especially through community-based actions. A new emphasis was placed on a partnership approach, both between district councils and the region-wide economic development agencies and within district council areas between a wide range of local actors. The objectives of the Measure were widened to give greater scope to local initiative and to develop strategies for local economic development consistent with and complementary to the work of the IDB and LEDU; to provide support for groups pursuing local economic development objectives; and to increase the formation rate of commercially aware and suitably skilled small businesses. Examples of actions envisaged under the programme were: encouraging the development of partnerships involving a wide range of actors at local level which impact on the local economy; assisting local needs-analysis, capacity building and local area strategy development; assisting locally initiated, managed and implemented integrated actions, based on a local area strategy involving local people directed to responding to local socio-economic needs and opportunities; and facilitating collaborative effort between local authority areas and local-regional-EU linkages (EC, 1994: 35).

Structural funds allocated to the programme totalled £22 million (*ibid*: 34) over the six year period, although this allocation will be revised in 1997. The implementation of the programme is the responsibility of the Department of Economic Development (DED), with support from LEDU, the small firms agency for Northern Ireland, and other agencies. The Measure is being undertaken in three phases. In the first phase, undertaken between January 1994 and March 1995, assistance was given to councils for the development of strategies and action plans, which were the basis for funding applications submitted in subsequent phases. District councils' ability to respond quickly during this phase largely depended on the extent of their previous involvement in local economic development initiatives, their awareness and anticipation of the opportunities for European funding and the experience and expertise of council staff and elected members. The majority of district councils chose to commission consultants to assist with the development of strategies, while a significant minority chose to undertake strategic development largely in-house. The second phase of the Measure, April 1995 to March 1997, involves assistance to councils for the establishment of Local Area Partnerships (LAPs), implementation of their two year action plans and, in some cases, further development and refinement of strategies. The amount of assistance allocated under phase two of the Measure is discussed in the next section. The third phase of the measure, April 1997 to March 2000, will involve block funding for the implementation of integrated economic development plans. Details are not available of the likely allocations for this period.

Allocation of the Measure

In June 1995, the Minister for the Economy announced the allocation of EU Structural Funds under the Local Economic Development Measure for 1995/96 and 1996/97. The allocations were based on the quality of the councils' action plans, assessed in terms of their effectiveness and efficiency, and the amounts councils were committed to raising through the rates for LED.

In total, £8 million of EU Structural Funds was allocated, ranging from £70,000 in Moyle to £2.1 million in Belfast. The allocation was based on the willingness of councils to raise funds through the rates and the quality of the plans submitted. Not all decided to raise the maximum of 5p in the pound. Councils which have fared better than the Northern Ireland average, in terms of Structural Fund allocations per head of population, are Belfast, Antrim, North Down, Derry, Ballymena, Coleraine, Lisburn and Craigavon. With the exception of Derry, all are in the Belfast Travel to Work Area or in the North East of the Province. Outside the urban areas, the allocation has favoured areas with existing high employment shares and low unemployment rates. The five areas with the lowest allocation per head of population are Newry and Mourne, Dungannon, Newtownabbey, Strabane, and Cookstown. With the exception of Newtownabbey, which was a late starter in developing a strategy, these council areas are in the West, predominantly Catholic and are characterised by high unemployment levels.

The council allocation per head of population is largely in line with that indicated by the 5p in the pound limit. This is not a surprising result. Councils' plans will reflect the resources available to them and an assessment of need and opportunity in their area. Councils with greater opportunities for economic development and the ability to raise more through the rates will be more ambitious in their expenditure plans. This will result in a higher demand for co-financing from EU Structural Funds, which in turn may largely reflect the distribution of penny product between council areas. Councils which have received the highest ratio of Structural Funds to local economic development resources are Derry, Moyle, Lisburn, North Down, Omagh and Strabane. At the other end of the scale are Newtownabbey, Newry and Mourne, Castlereagh, Ards and Limavady.

The variation in structural allocations per head of population shows a similar pattern to that for the penny product rate, ranging from -40% in Dungannon to +48% in Belfast (see Figure 9.2). There are, however, some

Figure 9.2: Variation in Penny Product per head and EU Allocation per head

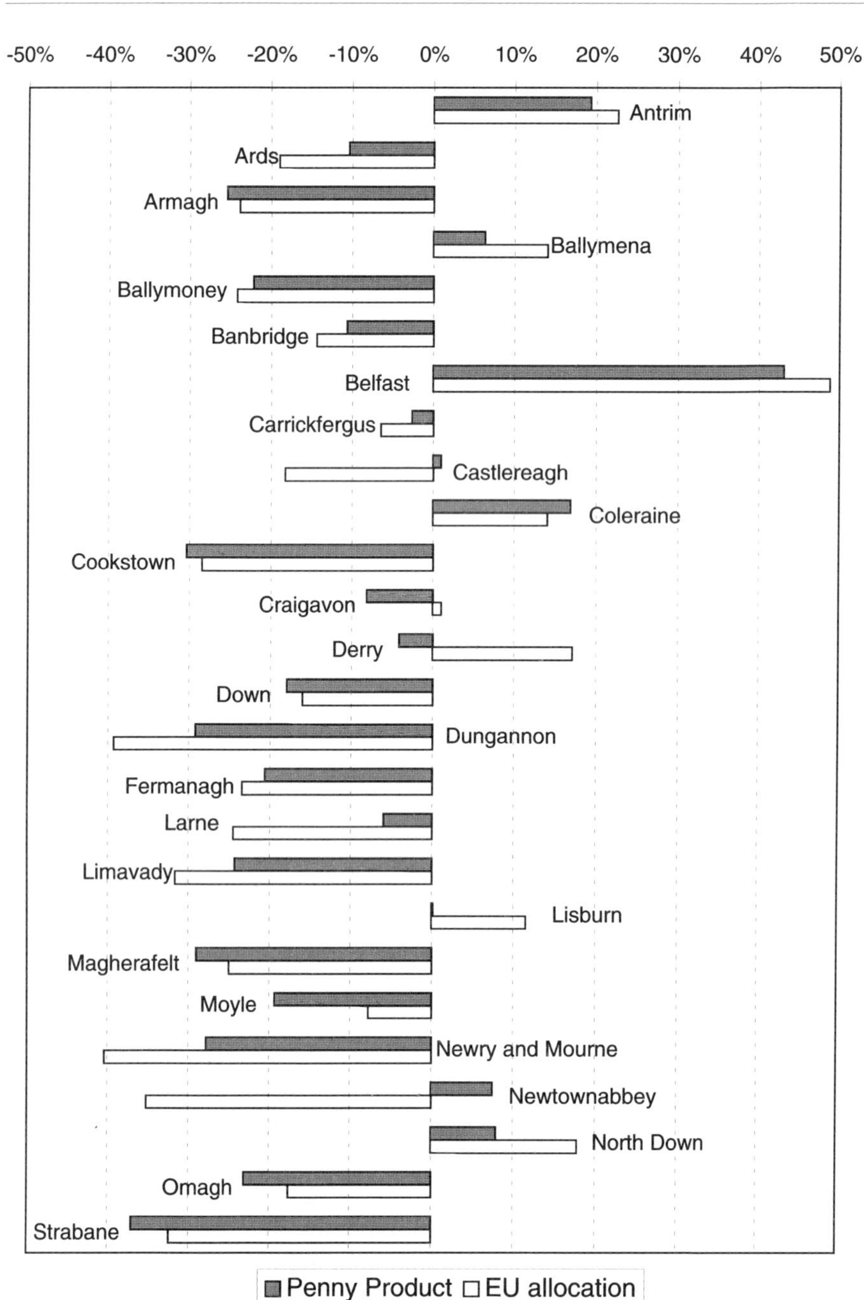

significant effects in that the allocation has favoured Derry in particular, while Castlereagh and Newtownabbey are receiving significantly less than the regional average, despite a higher than average penny product rate. The allocation of Structural Funds has tended to follow and exacerbate the inequalities resulting from linking economic development spend to the penny product. This is in marked contrast to the allocation of the District Partnership sub-programme of the EU Special Programme for Peace and Reconciliation, which has been made on the basis of need (50% of the funds) and population share (the other 50%).

A local tax related to the value of individual properties may be viewed as progressive, since, as a general rule, wealthier households will pay more while those on unemployment and income benefits will be exempt. However, any redistributive effects of such a tax will be limited to within district council boundaries. To effect a more equitable distribution of district council spending on local economic development measures would require an increase in the regional rate, which is then distributed primarily on the basis of need. The major disadvantage associated with this approach is the removal of political accountability for taxation decision, although local accountability would remain for how funds were spent.

COUNCILS' ECONOMIC DEVELOPMENT STRATEGIES

An area-based strategy provides a framework for local action to address problems and take advantage of opportunities. In the absence of a strategy, local actions may be piecemeal and un-coordinated, with the associated risk that they are less effective and efficient in achieving local economic development objectives.

Moe and Sherr (1993:74) defined strategic planning in this context as:

> A process wherein key actors agree on a limited number of goals based on a careful analysis of the wide range of strengths and weaknesses in the organisation's internal and external environment. Then develop strategies to achieve the goals and deploy resources to support the strategies.

The role of key local actors, particularly decision makers, is generally recognised as crucial. Without local leadership and support, development activities will not proceed or be ineffective. Similarly the aims and objectives should have a broad base of support and be achievable and clearly related to the needs and development opportunities of an area. Guidelines prepared by the European Commission (EC, 1992) suggest that the components of a strategy should include an analysis of problems, an audit of current activities, a review of resources, a statement of objectives, an action plan and a system for monitoring and evaluation. The process followed in Northern Ireland closely reflects this general pattern. While the presentation and structure of councils' economic development strategies differ, they all contain the above components to some degree. The structure of action plans were prescribed by the DED and required three broad elements (see Box 1).

Box 1 **Structure of Local Action Plans**	
Part A:	*Local Area Strategy* *Socio-economic analysis* *Strategic objectives and priorities* *Linkages with other programmes*
Part B:	*Local Action Plan* *Priority themes* *Technical summaries* *Partnership, management and implementation* *Financial summary*
Part C:	*Technical Details*

The economic development strategies and the subsequent action plans submitted to government for funding have been reviewed in three ways. First, the councils' plans have been assessed against a number of criteria suggested by EC and government guidelines. Second, the detailed spending plans in the councils' action plans have been analysed to assess TSN elements. Third, in-depth interviews were conducted with five district councils, selected on the basis of achieving a broad balance in terms of religion and other factors such as degree of rurality, affluence, anticipated financial leverage of council funds and location (east/west). The council areas selected were Ballymena, Belfast, Derry, Fermanagh and Magherafelt.

An analysis of the councils' economic development strategies and action plans must be qualified. First, the development of integrated economic strategies is a new departure for councils. As their role evolves and experience is gained, the strategies and planned interventions are likely to change. Second, councilors are politically accountable and must balance spending decisions against the impact of an increase in local taxation. Moreover, councils involved in large infra-structure projects, such as the new concert hall and conference centre in Belfast, may view these projects as part of their economic development effort. Third, the published strategies and action plans may not fully describe the process and decision criteria of a council and any interpretation is subjective. Finally, the district councils were not aware of how much would be allocated to them under the EU programmes and they may not have been aware of other potential sources of funding. The perceived availability of matching funds from the public and private sectors may have tempered the ambitions of some and excited the ambitions of others.

The Consultation Process

Councils appear to have undertaken widespread consultation with statutory and non-statutory agencies, the voluntary and community sector, business interests and, in some cases, academics. The plethora of community groups in Belfast and Derry posed a particular problem for the organisation of appropriate and extensive consultation. In these areas, and others, the consultation process initially took the form of workshops, each addressing particular aspects of economic regeneration. In many areas, project teams, with representatives from the various interested groups, were established to develop ideas in thematic areas such as business development, tourism and human resource development. These were often overseen by a council-led district partnership. Councils which came late to the strategic development process, such as Larne, Newtownabbey and Limavady, were in the predominately Protestant East of the Province. These areas had little experience of Local Economic Development, although similar consultative approaches have since been adopted. Many councils, through the consultation process, improved their relationship and contacts with both business and the community sector, which should have long-term implications for development of council activities as a whole. Lack of resources was frequently cited as the reason why contact with certain sectors of the local economy was not established earlier.

Feedback from interviews with representatives of the community and voluntary sector gave a mixed reaction to the strategic development process engaged in by local councils. In some areas, the process was seen as very inclusive, taking account of the views of local communities. In other areas, there was concern that the pre-eminent objective was to secure funding rather than to undertake proper planning. In Belfast, there was a perceived lack of co-ordination between the activities of the council and of agencies such as Making Belfast Work. In particular, there was some concern that the council viewed TSN as being MBW's responsibility and that the council would focus more on economic issues. However, the advent of the EU Peace and Reconciliation Fund, under which a wider Local Area Partnership would be created at regional and council level, was also viewed as an opportunity for greater community involvement in decision making processes.

SWOT Analyses

Most of the SWOT analyses produced by councils were adequate, reflecting the previous experience of some areas, such as Fermanagh, in LED and the involvement of consultants in the exercise in other areas, such as Ballymena.

Plans, however, were often insular, lacking any appreciation of the wider influences at work on local economies or comparative analysis with developments and experience elsewhere. In large part, this reflects the lack of adequate data and research at sub-regional level in Northern Ireland and the speed at which the strategies had to be produced. The SWOT analyses, whilst frequently well structured, were at best quite general and intuitive and provided few fresh insights. Nevertheless, the analyses presented an overview of the local socio-economic situation and the development problems and opportunities, which was previously not available to or recognised by local politicians and key community actors. In some cases, the exercise identified previously undetected labour shortages or skill gaps and the availability of unfilled vacancies. The degree of focus on TSN issues in the SWOT analyses varied from negligible to adequate. In the latter case, the analyses tended to take the form of references to unemployment and long-term unemployment in deprived areas. It is clear, however, that many of the councils took social issues seriously without going into any great depth on the nature and extent of social problems in their area or identifying gaps in provision by the existing agencies.

Action Plans

Unsurprisingly, as it was one of the major conditions placed by government on any funding application, the council strategies were largely designed to complement rather than compete with the Department of Economic Development's agencies. The DED agencies, particularly LEDU and the T&EA, were often directly involved in the councils' consultation and partnership building processes. The coherence between the action plans and the socio-economic analyses was weak in many cases. Action plans were frequently a collection of projects parcelled within programmes. A strong relationship with the SWOT analysis could not be made. In many cases, this was because the SWOT analysis was too general to allow comparisons with the proposed actions. Similarly, the relationship between the SWOT analysis and the action plans on TSN issues was particularly weak. For instance, in Belfast the council strategy identified the areas of West and North Belfast as economic blackspots, but there was little in the way of a TSN policy to address the identified need. As a general, rule the action plans give no indication of priorities between programmes or projects. In the event of funding not being available to carry out all of the action plan it is not clear what criteria will be applied to determine which projects are implemented first. There are some exceptions, however. For instance, Fermanagh has a clear policy of which projects and programmes should receive priority.

Implementation

Implementation and monitoring of the action plans is normally the responsibility of either a local partnership or project team for each priority area identified. In some cases, council staff, usually the economic development officer, play a more active role in implementation within a more passive partnership structure, which serves mainly as a reporting mechanism. While councils have identified potential funding sources, few have identified the required funding commitments by source. The range of required leverage of external funds to council expenditure varies greatly between councils. In several cases, councils appear to be relying solely on European Structural Funds for matching finance. Some councils, such as Fermanagh, view the 5p in the pound as an equity investment that can be used to leverage additional funds for projects from a variety of sources, while others, such as Derry, view the new funds more as 'demonstration money' to get key projects off the ground. Derry sees the main benefit of the Measure as forcing councils to focus on targeting resources more effectively and prioritising projects based on more objective criteria. Some councils have identified a series of performance indicators as benchmarks for success, while many are setting up monitoring and evaluation mechanisms based around specialised committees or the local area partnership. However, in general there is an urgent need to establish appropriate monitoring and evaluation systems on a common basis.

COUNCILS' SPENDING PLANS

The plans were examined to determine which projects are mainly designed to target social needs, that is, those likely to have a direct impact on social groups or the unemployed, and which are mainly designed to benefit business interests, that is, likely to have a more indirect impact on the unemployed. While the two are not mutually exclusive, the balance of expenditure on social compared to economic projects is an indicator of a council's attention to equality and equity issues. For the purposes of this analysis, social projects were defined in terms of the intended final beneficiaries or the nature of the activity undertaken. They included projects which targeted community groups, unemployed, socially excluded groups (women, youth, disabled), disadvantaged, schools and students/graduates. Activities classified as social projects included training, capacity building, crèche provision, housing, arts/cultural development, community relations and community businesses. Business/ physical spending includes projects providing technical assistance to businesses and the marketing of the council area itself or a specific business sector within the local economy. It also includes any physical improvement projects or physical planning activities.

Table 9.3: Summary of Proposed Spending Patterns, District Council Local Economic Development Measures, 1994-1999

District	Total Project Cost Apr 95-Mar 97	Bus./Phys. Development Budget	Social Budget	Bus./Phys spend % of total Budget	Social Spend	Sus./Phys spend per person unemployed	Social Spend per person unemployed
	£	£	£	%	%	£	£
North Down	1,546,400	704,001	842,399	46	54	42	297
Belfast	7,643,460	4,765,700	2,877,760	62	38	30	132
Derry	1,767,200	955,200	812,000	54	46	28	110
Banbridge	494,000	318,000	176,000	64	36	38	147
Fermanagh	5,810,000	3,390,000	2,420,000	58	42	207	717
Armagh	809,000	507,000	302,000	63	37	34	111
Coleraine	1,004,000	666,500	337,500	66	34	37	110
Omagh	677,000	430,000	247,000	64	36	30	88
Down	799,520	554,100	245,420	69	31	37	80
Newtownabbey	957,001	753,501	203,500	79	21	33	68
Magherafelt	1,012,500	737,500	275,000	73	27	69	134
Craigavon	1,465,000	1,228,000	237,000	84	16	41	75
Lisburn	2,361,284	1,878,069	483,215	80	20	65	111
Larne	366,000	281,000	85,000	77	23	36	57
Cookstown	294,000	220,000	74,000	75	25	30	42
Newry & Mourne	703,000	557,000	146,000	79	21	25	25
Ballymena	2,602,800	2,366,800	236,000	91	9	104	99
Limavady	592,000	469,000	123,000	79	21	65	61
Antrim	732,000	654,500	77,500	89	11	46	41
Moyle	227,000	176,500	50,500	78	22	56	48
Carrickfergus	1,649,000	1,445,500	203,500	88	12	211	138
Dungannon	423,200	377,200	46,000	89	11	28	16
Castlereagh	3,939,040	3,702,220	236,820	94	6	178	105
Ards	3,882,550	3,703,550	179,000	95	5	216	72
Ballymoney	280,502	266,702	13,800	95	5	40	11
Strabane	not available						

Table 9.3 presents summary results of the analysis. On average, councils' planned budgets for local economic development expenditure in 1995/96 and 1996/97 are roughly split three-quarters on business and physical development and one-quarter on social projects. The variations between council areas are significant, with proposed spend on social projects varying from 5% in Ards and Ballymoney to 54% in North Down.

Fourteen councils with planned social budgets of less than 25% of the total are, for the most part, in the more prosperous council areas surrounding Belfast or in the North East. These areas have low levels of deprivation, and the emphasis appears to have been placed more on economic growth than equality issues. A number of areas with higher than average unemployment, including Magherafelt and Moyle, also fall into this group. In the case of Magherafelt, the council feels that the current strength of the community sector is sufficient for the council to focus on core economic development activities. The remainder of council areas with an above average share of planned expenditure on social projects include most of the council areas in the West of the Province. Some of the highest social expenditure is planned by areas in the East of the Province, such as North Down, Banbridge and Coleraine, where social deprivation is low (Robson *et al*, 1994).

The planned business and physical development budget and social budget have been standardised, using employment and unemployment rates respectively to allow a comparison across council areas. The level of planned social expenditure per unemployed person for Northern Ireland as a whole is £125 over the two years. This figure varies from £11 per unemployed person in Ballymoney to £717 per unemployed person in Fermanagh. Fermanagh stands out as being particularly ambitious in its spending plans on all projects compared to other areas. Overly, there is no clear statistical relationship between councils' spending proposals on social projects and the extent or degree of need in council areas as indicated by unemployment or deprivation measures.

Some Issues Arising Out of Council Interviews

Some councils are already running into perceived constraints with statutory agencies who feel the district council's are invading their 'turf'. According to these councils, the major statutory agencies are not yet sensitised to the potential for councils to tailor mainstream programmes to meet local needs. They feel the statutory agencies should be more flexible in their approach to the councils in this light. Councils have different degrees of confidence in the extent of their capacity to deliver economic development programmes. This is based on their previous experience of undertaking economic development type activities. Some councils had been carrying out economic development 'through the back door,' using their existing powers to support 'voluntary organizations' to create organizations capable of delivering more mainstream economic development programmes. All of the councils interviewed, however, see their advantage in the extent to which they understand and can tailor programmes to fit local needs, provided they are given enough power to do so. Some councils are concentrating more than others on specific geographic areas and/or pockets of deprivation. In the case of Ballymena, for example, the area as a whole has an unemployment rate of 8%, but there are two communities where the rate exceeds 20%. Virtually all of their community development or 'social' programmes will go towards building up the capacity of local groups in these areas to take more proactive roles in bringing economic development to these deprived areas.

Many other councils, however, focus on specific programme areas as opposed to targeting resources exclusively to geographic areas of highest need.

Some councils are keeping Peace and Reconciliation Programme functions separate from more mainstream economic development functions. Others focus on LED with a community focus, as in the case of Fermanagh, under the assumption that 'straight economic development doesn't distribute resources effectively'. Whether or not community development functions are kept distinct from economic development functions is a key factor in how new LED resources are distributed. The institutional frameworks being set up to deliver new LED resources reflect in large part the councils' thinking on economic development, as well as their degree of confidence in their capacity to handle their new responsibilities. Councils whose institutional structures are closely tied to the funding structures supporting them have less confidence in their capacity than those that develop their own strategic vision for the community (and corresponding delivery mechanisms) separate and apart from the funding requirements.

CONCLUSIONS

The role of councils in local economic development is relatively new and still developing. Councils, other local actors and their advisors are still engaged in a learning process, and, as they gain experience, it should be expected that their strategies will be refined, if not radically revised. Most councils are too small to act in a strategic planning role because their areas tend to be part of much larger Travel to Work Areas. However, most of the councils interviewed believed they had, or could develop, strong grass roots contacts. One of the main roles of councils is likely to be to act as a co-ordinator of local efforts and mediator between the regional agencies and local communities.

The funding available to councils for local economic development is very small in comparison to total spending on economic development in Northern Ireland. The overall macro-economics impact of councils' activities is also likely to be small. For instance, the prior appraisal of the EU Northern Ireland Single Programme (1994-1999) suggests that the economic development sub-programme as a whole might create 6000 jobs. On the basis of its expenditure share, this would suggest that local economic development initiatives might create 400 jobs. In our view, these estimates are low, but they do seem to illustrate the limited impact of councils' expenditure on economic development, although this ignores the potential demonstrated by some more active councils to use local economic development resources to lever substantial funds from other sources. For instance, Fermanagh envisages utilising its own resources to raise 25 times as much from other sources.

In the longer term, as councils demonstrate their competence, it is possible that government may devolve more responsibility for delivering economic programmes to local councils. Moreover, there is undoubtedly scope for councils and local communities to contribute to an increased level of effectiveness and value for money from mainstream spending, by relating and targeting regional programmes to local needs and opportunities. There is also the danger, however, of fragmenting the economic development effort. The primary aim of the Local Economic Development Measure is to promote local economic development, rather than address equality or equity issues. In general, the councils' published development strategies and action plans demonstrate both a willingness and a capability to contribute to the economic development of districts and the region as a whole. It is not clear, however, from the socio-economic analyses of council areas and the specifics of the action plans, that all councils have yet taken TSN and equality issues into account. The emphasis on community capacity building in a number of council areas does, however, suggest that the initiative will contribute to raising these issues up the agenda in future.

The apportionment of planned spend between primarily economic and social programmes and projects indicates no clear pattern between expenditure and opportunity or need. Several of the most affluent council areas plan to spend more on social projects, while some of those council areas with high unemployment and deprivation levels plan to spend the least. This partly reflects the ability of councils to raise funds for local economic development and partly the implied balance in priorities stuck between economic growth and equality.

The main responsibility for Targeting Social Need remains with the statutory agencies. The development of local area partnerships under both the Local Economic Development Measure and the Programme for Peace and Reconciliation should have the effect of promoting TSN objectives by making the statutory agencies more responsive to local needs. However, some of the councils interviewed saw little evidence, as yet, of increased flexibility among government departments and agencies in this respect.

The link between the spending limit on local economic development imposed on councils and the penny product from the rates favour more affluent areas. As a result, those council areas with severe economic and social problems can spend less than those areas with low levels of unemployment and deprivation. The unemployed in more affluent areas are likely to benefit more than the unemployed in deprived areas under this model. The current system is, therefore, more likely to reinforce differences between council areas than to encourage convergence in socio-economic conditions between council areas. A fairer system may be to raise additional local taxation through the regional rate, rather than the district rate, and redistribute it according to need. The allocation of the EU Special

Programme on Peace and Reconciliation to district council partnerships is based on population and deprivation and may be a more appropriate allocation mechanism for the Local Economic Development measure.

ENDNOTES

1. The extension of past trends of employment growth at individual council level may be misleading for Castlereagh, Larne and Carrickfergus. The former is over estimated due to the health jobs centred on the area, but actually spread throughout the Eastern Health and Social Sevices Board area. Larne and Carrickfergus suffered from branch plant closures in the 1970s and 1980s and employment change is more likely to be positive in the short-term.

REFERENCES

European Commission (1992) *Employment Action Practical Manual,* Brussels: European Commission.

European Commission (1994) *Northern Ireland Single Programming Document 1994-1999,* Brussels: European Commission.

Department of the Environment for Northern Ireland (1992) *Circular to Clerks and Chief Executives of each District Council,* Belfast: DoE.

Department of Finance and Personnel (1993(a)) *The Structural Funds in Northern Ireland after 1993,* Conference Paper, Belfast: DFP.

Department of Finance and Personnel (1993(b)) *Northern Ireland Structural Funds Plan (1994-1999),* Consultation Draft, Belfast: DFP.

Gudgin, G. (1994) 'The Distribution of Jobs in Northern Ireland Since 1971' in *The Standing Advisory Commission on Human Rights Annual Report for 1993-94,* London: HMSO.

Gudgin, G. and O'Shea, G. (eds.) (1993) *Unemployment Forever?* Northern Ireland Economic Research Centre Report No.13, Belfast: NIERC.

Hambleton, R. and Taylor, M. (1993) *People in Cities: A Transatlantic Policy Exchange,* Bristol: School For Advanced Urban Studies.

John, P. (1993) *Local Government in Northern Ireland,* York: Joseph Rowntree Foundation.

Moe, K.J. and Sherr, I. (1993) 'Strategic Planning and the Pursuit of Reform, Economic Development and Equity' in Mier, R. (ed.) *Social Justice and Local Development Policy,* Newbury: Sage Publications.

NIERC (forthcoming) *Spatial Patterns of Employment Change in Northern Ireland for the period 1987-1991, Fair Employment,* Report to PPRU/CCRU, Belfast.

Peck, J. and Tickell, A. (1994) 'Too Many Partners: The Future for Regeneration Partnerships' *Local Economy,* November, Essex: Longman Group Ltd.

Robson, B., Bradford, M. and Deas, I. (1994) *Relative Deprivation in Northern Ireland,* PPRU Occasional Paper No.28, Belfast: PPRU.

Stoker, G. and Young, S.C. (1993) *Cities in the 1990s: Local Choice for a Balanced Strategy,* Essex: Longman.

Chapter Ten

JOB CREATION IN NORTHERN IRELAND: POLICIES AND CONSTRAINTS

John Simpson

INTRODUCTION

Unemployment has been an enduring problem in Northern Ireland. For over 60 years, the rate of unemployment has been higher than in any other region of the United Kingdom. In addition, and partly, but not only, as a consequence of fewer employment opportunities, a higher proportion of the population of working age (particularly females) remain outside the labour market than the overall UK average. As Chapter One of this volume reviews, within Northern Ireland, unemployment has been higher, and economic activity rates have been lower, amongst Roman Catholics than amongst Protestants. The 1993 Labour Force Survey (PPRU, 1994) estimated that the unemployment rate for Catholics was 18%, and for Protestants, 9%. Economic activity rates were 67% for Catholics and 74% for Protestants. Northern Ireland is usually treated as a single geographic unit and often, without differentiation, into smaller, sub-regional units. However, within Northern Ireland, unemployment rates differ significantly, with unemployment tending to be higher in the North West and in some parts of North and West Belfast. The uneven distribution of unemployment has lead to the evolution of policies aimed at the more disadvantaged areas, reviewed in Chapter Six of this volume.

The object of job creation policies is to increase employment and reduce unemployment by enhancing the advantages, and reducing the disadvantages, of Northern Ireland enterprises, so that they will add to the output of goods and services produced on a viable basis and so that new enterprises will be established.

Since Northern Ireland is, by the facts of geography, a peripheral and small region of Europe, the disadvantages of transport costs and a small home market are unavoidable. Energy costs are also higher than in other regions (and have recently become significantly higher), and freight costs for imported raw materials add further to the relative cost structures. Alongside these disadvantages, some other costs are outside local control or influence. The cost of borrowing capital is determined in the national money markets. The cost of most raw materials are set by the wider markets. The main locally determined elements in manufacturing costs are the wage and salary bill and the efficiency with which labour is used. Cost disadvantages can be offset either by lower labour costs or by higher labour productivity, or a combination of both.

It is within this context that this chapter, therefore, outlines some evidence on employment changes in recent decades, reviews the evolution of job creation policies and offers an assessment of the significance and methods of implementing recent changes as they have applied to the private sector, particularly businesses in manufacturing and tradeable services, including tourism.

IN RETROSPECT

The post-war period of full employment in Great Britain encouraged significant labour emigration from Northern Ireland and the Republic of Ireland. In addition, businesses seeking to expand had to consider where to locate new plants, taking account of labour costs and labour availability, as well as all the other factors affecting profitability. This created a more favourable peacetime opportunity for expansion, particularly in the period 1957-70, than had been experienced for several decades. In the late 1950s and the 1960s, the conjunction of these events, together with the adoption of explicit government economic development policies, both north and south, was linked with a period of accelerating growth and increased employment. In the south, the First Programme for Economic Development was adopted in 1958 and marked a period of significant recovery. In the North, the economic programme summarised in the report by Professor Wilson, published in 1965, was linked with a period when industrial output grew at twice the rate in Great Britain.

In the period 1961 to 1970, manufacturing output increased by 73% in Northern Ireland and 72% in the Republic of Ireland. By the standards of the previous decades, this was a significant improvement and was well above the increase recorded in Great Britain. Employment in manufacturing rose and unemployment in Northern Ireland fell to the then lowest level of the post-war period when it averaged 5.9% in 1966 (though unemployment in Great Britain was only 1.4%). The only year when unemployment in Northern Ireland was even lower was, perhaps surprisingly, 1974, when it fell to 5.7%. This was just before a deep recession in the United Kingdom, following the major rise in international oil prices. Also, in Northern Ireland, the impact of politically motivated violence began to affect jobs. Unemployment started a rise which reached a peak of 17.7% in 1986. Since then, unemployment has fallen to just over 11% in early 1996. Meanwhile, unemployment in the Republic of Ireland fell to its lowest level in 1971 at 6.4%, before rising steadily to 17.1% in 1986 and, after a fall and a further rise, to 15.8% in 1993. In 1994 and 1995, unemployment in the Republic fell to 13%.

Efforts to stimulate increased employment (job creation) and, as a result, reduce unemployment, in Northern Ireland have evolved over the last 50 years. Although employment, because of increases in employment-intensive services, has increased significantly in recent years, the problem of high unemployment remains a serious one. One of the easiest fallacious assumptions which can be made is that increases in employment will necessarily lead to decreases in unemployment. The caveat must be added that extra employment may also be offset by lower emigration or higher activity rates. In reality, such inter-relationships are neither stable nor always predictable.

The Effects of Violence

In the 1970s and 1980s, politically motivated violence undoubtedly reduced job opportunities, was linked to higher unemployment and interacted with periods of unusually high emigration. Measuring the precise effects of violence on the labour market is not possible, however. Arguably, unemployment in Northern Ireland has not fully reflected the economic impact of 25 years of violence. Unemployment has fluctuated broadly in line with trends which would have been expected, even without violence. Two elements have worked in opposite directions and, in terms of unemployment, have offset one another. Violence has adversely affected manufacturing employment, essentially by deterring investment or deflecting business, but it has also been linked to a major expansion in jobs in the public sector and an increase, for a period, in emigration. The former has, approximately, been offset by the two latter features.

A better indication of the effects of violence on the economy lies in a north-south comparison of changes in the manufacturing sector. In the period 1974-94, manufacturing employment in the Republic of Ireland rose by 11%; in Northern Ireland, it fell by 40%. If Northern Ireland had had the experience of the Republic, manufacturing would have employed 50,000 more people in 1994. Most of the difference emerged in the decade 1974-84 (see Table 10.1).

Table 10.1: Employment in Manufacturing in Northern Ireland and the Republic of Ireland, 1967-94

	N.I thous.	R.O.I thous.
1967	174.0	200.0
1970	179.7	213.0
1974	167.3	222.0
1979	142.2	226.7
1984	109.5	197.0
1989	106.3	185.6
1994	100.7	198.3
1967-94	- 42%	- 1%

Source: Adapted from N.I. Annual Abstract, Irish Economic Series (CSO) and Central Bank of Ireland.

Not all of the difference between north and south in manufacturing employment is attributable to politically motivated violence. The structure of manufacturing in Northern Ireland was such that, even with comparable investment in new projects, Northern Ireland would have experienced a smaller net increase in employment than the Republic. The long-term contraction in employment in shipbuilding and heavy engineering, as well as the heavier reliance on employment in textile and clothing manufacture, meant that Northern Ireland would have had to compensate for a proportionately larger loss of jobs from existing manufacturers than the Republic. Correcting for such structural differences, Northern Ireland probably 'lost' investment and business equivalent to 30-35,000 jobs because of politically motivated violence.

Another corroborative indication of the effects of political violence is that, in the last 20 years, Northern Ireland has attracted, and retained, a diminishing proportion of the investment and employment in non UK-owned enterprises in the United Kingdom. The Northern Ireland Economic Council (NIEC, 1992:30) points out that, whereas in 1973 Northern Ireland had 3.6% of this employment (well above the *pro rata* 2.7% of the population), this had fallen to 1.9% in 1989.

Competitiveness

A concern during this period of disruption to economic development was that manufacturing industry might have become less efficient with even greater significance when added to the loss of investment. For example, in a 20 year comparison, from 1974 to 1994, with the Republic of Ireland, manufacturing output increased by 245% in the Republic but increased by only 18% in Northern Ireland. However, a comparison between Northern Ireland, Scotland, Wales and the Republic of Ireland over the past decade (1984-94, see Table 10.2), confirms that the interaction of employment and output, leading to changes in output per employee, is complex.

Table 10.2: Percentage Change in Output, Employment and Labour Productivity, 1984-1994, Northern Ireland, Scotland, Wales and the Republic of Ireland

	N. Ireland	Scotland	Wales	R.o.Ireland
1984-89				
Output	+18.8	+11.4	+14.3	+49 5
Employment	-1.2	-7.4	+11.8	-5.8
Output/head	+20.2	+20.3	+2.2	+58.7
1989-94				
Output	+11.4	+7.4	+5.2	+41.5
Employment	-5.3	-11.9	-6.3	+6.8
Output/head	+17.6	+21.9	+12.2	+32.5
1984-94				
Output	+32.4	+19.8	+20.2	+111.4
Employment	-6.2	-18.4	+4.7	+0.7
Output/head	+41.2	+46.8	+14.8	+109.9

Source: Estimates from official statistical sources.

As Table 10.2 shows, whilst manufacturing output in Northern Ireland grew much more slowly than in the Republic, it increased rather more than in Scotland and Wales, which both shared similar structural adjustment problems in industries such as shipbuilding, iron and steel and coal mining. Employment rose faster in Wales than in the Republic; both did better than Northern Ireland, but Scotland did worst of the group. In terms of output per employee - a simple measure of the effects of change on productivity - Wales performed poorly compared to the others; Scotland did slightly better than Northern Ireland, but both lagged well behind the Republic.

Manufacturing Employment Monitored by the FEC

Whilst changes in employment in manufacturing in Northern Ireland have, in recent years, compared reasonably with those in Scotland and Wales but lagged behind the Republic of Ireland, an interesting feature in the context of a review of equality of employment opportunities has been a fall in the number of Protestants and an increase in the number of Catholics in manufacturing jobs. A reliable estimate of these trends can be made by using monitoring returns to the Fair Employment Commission which cover over 95% of all employment. The remaining 5% of employment is mainly in small firms or is part-time. Using the monitoring returns, which are now available for a six year period, to estimate the totals, Table 10.3 shows that from 1990 to 1995, Protestant numbers have fallen by 5600 whilst Catholic numbers have risen by 4600.

Table 10.3: Estimates of Number of Protestant and Roman Catholic Employees in Manufacturing, 1990-1995, Northern Ireland

	Protestant	Roman Catholic	Total
1990	70,900	33,900	104,800
1992	66,200	35,100	101,300
1994	64,200	36,600	100,800
1995	65,300	38,500	103,800

Source: Estimates using FEC monitoring data.

Earnings and Productivity Levels

Significantly, in terms of government concerns about competitiveness, one of the features of the past decade has been a widening of the gap between average manufacturing earnings in Northern Ireland and the rest of the United Kingdom. Average earnings in manufacturing for both men and women are now just under 80% of the UK average. In the last decade (1986-95), Northern Ireland earnings relative to the UK have dropped, especially for women, whose earnings had been 87% of the UK average in 1986. Male earnings had been 83% of the UK average in 1986. In part, these changes may reflect changes in industrial structure, but they also suggest that the labour market has produced smaller wage increases in Northern Ireland. As the earnings gap has widened, this may have enhanced the competitiveness of local operations and helped to sustain employment.

A less easily quantified variable affecting competitiveness is labour productivity. In part, this is influenced by the technology and capital equipment available: in part, it is a reflection of skill levels and effort made by employees; in part, it depends on organisational efficiency. The available evidence points to a narrowing of the productivity gap when it is measured by added-value per employee compared to Great Britain (see, for example, Roper, 1995; Gudgin, 1994). What is not clear is the extent to which added-value has been enhanced by capital investment or by improved labour productivity with existing capital assets.

A critical indication of competitiveness is the profitability of business. However, there is no information available to measure profitability in different sectors and over a period of years, which would be useful in the assessment of the success of official policies and also to influence potential investors. Two studies, (NIERC,1993(a) and 1993(b)), have pointed to the rates of return earned by local manufacturing companies before and after allowance was made for government financial assistance. Whilst trading performances vary greatly, the overall position pointed to the reliance on government support, particularly towards capital costs, in enhancing the performance of local firms.

THE EVOLUTION OF POLICY

Job creation policies must be designed with an understanding of the underlying economic trends. Unemployment has been high for many years: manufacturing jobs, despite efforts to increase the number of new jobs, have decreased sharply; labour productivity has not kept pace with changes in the Republic of Ireland; and relative earnings levels have tended to lag further behind the average for Great Britain. Nevertheless, economic policy starts from the implicit assumption that there is no inherent handicap which means that a region such as Northern Ireland should accept a permanent adverse difference in living standards or employment when compared to other west European neighbours. If business performance in Northern Ireland can be sufficiently improved, and seen to be better than or comparable with other locations, then further investment and expansion will be a logical competitive consequence. The implications are that any disadvantages should be more than offset by other advantages. Clearly this has not been the case thus far.

A Transitional Adjustment?

Given the intractable nature of the problem of unemployment, it would be helpful if there was agreement on the reasons for the failure to reduce the scale of the problem, at least relative to the position in the rest of the United Kingdom. There is, however, no consensus on the reasons why unemployment has been such an intractable problem. Consequently, there is no consensus on the appropriate response. Opinions range from those which explain the situation in terms of an excessive degree of intervention by government in ways which make business less viable and employment less likely (such as the benefits trap, where people are thought to be better off remaining unemployed instead of accepting jobs with lower pay), to those which suggest that the government does not intervene effectively enough (for example, by increasing the actions to assist businesses financially or in other ways). These differing opinions develop contrasting recommendations, ranging at one end from those who might commend less government distortion of market forces, to those who think that market forces will fail to provide acceptable answers and that (further) steps must be taken to offset market failure.

Implicitly, for many years government measures relied on an expectation that Northern Ireland's unemployment was a consequence of structural changes in industry affecting many parts of western Europe. The linen industry contracted as the demand for textiles changed and in response to competition from 'cheap imports'. Farming employment contracted as farming methods changed and young people from rural areas sought alternative employment. Similarly, shipbuilding and heavy engineering were affected by new competition and new technologies. If the problems were not due to any local disadvantage, or fault, and if the local economic infrastructure and labour supply was good enough, as was often confidently asserted, then the problem was one of transition: to accelerate a process of adaptation and change and encourage new investment. Consistent with this type of thinking, in the 1950s, manufacturers in Northern Ireland benefited from the introduction of (what became known as) Standard Capital Grants. Government repaid to investors a proportion of the capital costs of buildings, plant and equipment. The logic was that this gave an incentive for investment, and the expectation was that, once in production, businesses could operate in normal competitive markets. This was to be a direct route back to a regional economy with the characteristics of self-sustaining growth.

With hindsight, this analysis of the position in the 1950s and 1960s was naive and flawed. More fundamental problems, related to competitiveness, efficiency, productivity and training in appropriate skills, were not adequately recognised. The nature of the changes was also partly obscured by the existence of full employment in most of Great Britain. Some of the local successes of the 1960s could have been explained as a response to labour shortages elsewhere.

The evolution of policies to create jobs since the 1950s has been continuous and complex, reflecting changes in United Kingdom policies for the less prosperous regions, variations in taxation policy, public sector infrastructure commitments, labour market interventions, education and training initiatives and a wide ranging series of forms of (what is now known as) Selective Financial Assistance. Whilst these interventions were initially aimed at manufacturing activity, later in the period, tradeable services, including 'back office' activities and tourism, were also formally included. For the last two decades, the effectiveness of such changing policies has been complicated by the continuing politically motivated violence. One major uncertain factor has been the extent to which even the potentially most profitable investments may have been deterred by non-economic factors in decision making. There is at least a doubt whether any conventional policy measures could be expected to offset the economic consequences of an external perception of the effects of violence.

The government agencies can, therefore, argue that policies implemented in recent years have not been tested in normal competitive conditions. This defence should not be carried too far. For existing businesses, the reality has been that normal competitive forces have been operating and the organisational disruption stemming from violence has been minimal. There are, therefore, less valid excuses about any failures in relation to the performance of businesses already located here, than in relation to new inward investment.

Writing in early 1996, we must note a qualification to this comment about the failure to reduce the scale of the problem. In the current recovery from recession in the United Kingdom, Northern Ireland's unemployment rate, relative to the overall average, has decreased substantially. Unemployment in Scotland has also, unusually, fallen to lower than the UK average. This represents, at least, a welcome short-term development. It would not yet be safe to conclude that this is an established long-term improvement.

THE WORK OF THE MAIN JOB CREATION AGENCIES

Government efforts to encourage job creation in the private sector, mainly in manufacturing but also in tourism and tradeable services, have been directed to: improving the productivity of labour through training and education programmes; reducing the start-up costs of projects: by reducing the capital costs; by offsetting the initial labour training costs; by offsetting some of the initial employment costs; by providing space in government-owned factories at favourable rents; by offsetting part of the interest charges on borrowed funds; by making loans or taking an equity shareholding and easing the identification of potential customers: by marketing assistance; by reducing the costs of export missions etc; encouraging product and process research and development; and ensuring that the economic infrastructure of public utilities and services was adequately supportive (for example, roads, harbours, communications, electricity and water services).

The agencies which are most directly linked to the encouragement and assistance of businesses which are expected to add to local employment are the Industrial Development Board (IDB) and the Local Enterprise Development Unit (LEDU). Other Department of Economic Development agencies have specialist roles, such as the Training and Employment Agency, the Northern Ireland Tourist Board and the Industrial Research and Technology Unit.

Their primary role is to encourage expansion in firms which will add to the output of local industry or services, by providing advice and/or financial support. This should be done in a way which minimises the displacement and deadweight effects. This reduces the problems of offering assistance to businesses which would simply take business away from existing firms (displacement) and tries to avoid giving assistance to businesses to do what they would do without assistance (deadweight).

A significant exception to this general approach is allowed in the support by LEDU for self-employed people setting up in business. The incentives for these micro-businesses are not so tightly limited by these constraints.

The existence of two main agencies (the IDB and LEDU) is partly an accident of history and partly a reflection of differing needs between two sets of clients. In 1971, the then government decided that there was a need for an agency specialising in relations with smaller enterprises. LEDU was established and, without undue rigidity about the size of businesses, given responsibility for firms employing up to 50 people. The IDB was established as a separate agency in 1982. Prior to that date, relations with the larger businesses, employing over 50 people, in manufacturing and tradeable services, had been directly with the Department of Economic Development (DED), which itself had taken over the functions of the Industrial Development Organisation within the former Department of Commerce and Industry. The IDB also inherited the role of the former Northern Ireland Development Agency (previously called the Northern Ireland Finance Corporation). Both agencies operate within guidelines set by the DED, after gaining approval from government ministers and, ultimately, the Treasury. Discretionary decisions are, therefore, tightly limited by predetermined confidential criteria affecting the scope and scale of assistance which may be offered to businesses.

Results From the IDB

The IDB relates to over 440 businesses in Northern Ireland, as well as making contact with external investors who might set up businesses in the Province. Despite continuing efforts to increase the employment available from these client firms, the total employment which they generate has increased only slowly in the past decade (see Table 10.4). The operational methods of the IDB (and LEDU) changed radically in 1990-91, when a 'money for jobs' approach was replaced by the more selective 'encouragement of competitiveness' emphasis. The form of reporting by the IDB, however, still reflects the former approach, with all its inadequacies.

As Table 10.4 shows, in the last ten years (1986-95 inclusive), firms have accepted offers from the IDB linked to promises involving 81,000 jobs. Of these jobs, 41,000 were promised in new projects either from new businesses setting up in Northern Ireland or existing businesses which were planning to expand. The remaining 40,000 were described as jobs which were 'renewed' or 'maintained'. These were jobs which might have disappeared without IDB assistance. In a more normal set of commercial conditions, Government might have taken a more restrictive approach and allowed some of these firms to face difficult trading conditions without assistance. However, during the years when new projects were deterred by the perceptions of violence (particularly the late 1970s and early 1980s), government permitted the IDB to sustain and rescue some businesses which were judged to have prospects of a return to viability.

Table 10.4: Job Promotions by the IDB, 1984-1995, Northern Ireland

Year ending 31 March	Jobs promoted	Jobs renewed	Jobs maintained	Total	Jobs in client cost
1984	3556	8995	5276	17,827	n.a
1985	5267	12,037	2942	20,246	n.a
1986	2910	3661	3552	10,123	n.a.
1987	4187	6393	2122	12,702	73,496
1988	5283	3453	1620	10,356	74,133
1989	5653	1685	745	8083	77,824
1990	4731	3808	376	8915	79,079
1991	3366	3554	500	7420	85,756
1992	1991	2689	included	4680	79,885
1993	4004	1877	with	5881	80,247
1994	4886	1546	renewals	6432	81,487
1995	4095	2397		6492	82,940
1984-95 (12 years)	49,929	52,095	17,133	119,157	
1986-95 (10 years)	541,106	31,063	8915	81,084	

Source: IDB annual reports

New job promises are subject to two important characteristics. Almost invariably, some of the promises will not materialise. Experience over many years, in Northern Ireland and other regions, suggests that the average number of jobs which are actually filled will be about two-thirds of the original aspirations. The second feature is that jobs tend to be filled over a period of three to six years and then, as markets, products and technology change, the number begins to fall. Consequently, announcements in the last decade of new job promises averaging 4100 per annum have not been sufficient to be linked with a significant increase in total manufacturing employment in IDB client companies. If the transfer of Shorts and Harland and Wolff to the IDB, after privatisation in April 1991, is excluded, employment in IDB client companies in 1995 was only about 2000 larger than in 1987, although 38,000 new jobs were promised in the same period. This demonstrates the 'running hard to stand still' nature of the process of job creation.

New Job Promises Compared With Those In Other Areas

Whilst there are problems of comparability, particularly because of differences in the nature of the regional development agencies, the IDB figures can be compared roughly with those from Scotland, Wales and the

Republic of Ireland. Using an average of two recent years, and taking account of the relative size of employment in each of the areas, Northern Ireland, with 86 job promises per 10,000 existing employees, had a better expected outcome than Scotland (43 per 10,000), but less favourable than Wales (136 per 10,000) and the Republic of Ireland (123 per 10,000) (see Table 10.5).

Table 10.5: New Job Promises in the 1990s in Northern Ireland, Scotland, Wales and the Republic of Ireland

	Annual average	Jobs promised	Per 10k employees
N.Ireland - IDB	1993-95	4490	86
Scotland - Scottish E'prise	1993-95	8450	43
Wales - Welsh Digest	1992-94	12,930	136
R.of Ireland - IDA	1990-92	12,250	123

The figures in Table 10.5 need to be qualified in a number of respects. Firstly, in Northern Ireland, the results from LEDU should be added to those of the IDB. Secondly, in Scotland, the official agencies report that there are at least 2700 jobs in investments which did not apply to Locate in Scotland or the Scottish Office. An uncertain proportion of these should be added to the Scottish figure. Thirdly, the IDA figures are for that organisation before the separation of the activities of indigenous companies to Forbairt. The IDA job figures are based on its definition of 'jobs gained,' which understates the jobs promised concept by a significant margin, including the usual difference between jobs promised and jobs actually created. This alone might mean that the IDA 'jobs promised' figure would be nearer to 18,000, and the rate per 10,000 employees would rise to 180.

To return to the Northern Ireland figures, it is difficult to add an estimate of the jobs promised by LEDU client companies because LEDU no longer publishes these figures. The LEDU annual report gives information on actual changes in employment that have taken place and does not separate manufacturing jobs from those in various services. Consequently, whilst the LEDU annual report for 1994-5 shows an estimate that clients increased employment by 3500, net of closures, or 4290 before deducting employment in firms which closed (or 6400 before deducting closures or job reductions in firms where employment was reduced), this figure cannot be readily compared with the IDB jobs in manufacturing and tradeable services. The jobs created by LEDU clients include over 1300 last year which were essentially self-employed and were not significantly involved in manufacturing. Of the remaining 1100, described as 'larger start-up' businesses, no information is published on the number engaged in manufacturing. There were an extra 1820 jobs in continuing businesses; most of these would be in manufacturing. Very roughly, LEDU activities may have been linked with about 2000 extra manufacturing jobs. If these were included in the totals, Northern Ireland's performance is comparable with that in Wales, below that in the Republic of Ireland and better than that in Scotland.

Another crude comparison can be made using the estimates of the value of investment committed in each area. Some of the information is not readily available from published sources, but there is sufficient evidence to suggest that investment per promised job in Northern Ireland has been higher than in Wales and that the scale of government financial assistance has also been higher (see Table 10.6). If LEDU activities could be added, however, the overall Northern Ireland investment costs per job would be somewhat lower.

Table 10.6 Total Investment, and Financial Assistance, Per Job, early 1990s, Northern Ireland, Scotland, Wales and Republic of Ireland

	Annual average	Investment expected £m pa	Investment p.job promised (£)	Cost p.job of financial assistance (£)
Northern Ireland - IDB	1993-5	450	100,200	25,400
Scotland - LIS	1993-5	857	101,400	n.a.
Wales - Welsh Digest	1992-4	503	38,900	6500*
Rep. of Ireland - IDA	1991-2	n.p.	n.p.	13,800*

* The Welsh figure is for grants, only; the Republic of Ireland figure excludes the 'cost' of the lower tax rate on company profits.

Job Creation by LEDU Clients

The remit of LEDU is more complex than simply holding responsibility for the smaller firms which are engaged in manufacturing or tradeable services. In at least two ways, LEDU has a wider remit. First, LEDU is the agency which has the primary responsibility to encourage business start-ups, many of which are people considering becoming self-employed. The range of business activities which will attract financial support covers many business ideas outside manufacturing. Second, the concept of avoiding displacement effects can be interpreted more liberally, as many small businesses (usually the self-employed) sell in a 'home market' which is a small part of Northern Ireland, and the problems of distorting normal competitive processes are much reduced. Nevertheless, LEDU retains a list of business activities on which it is reluctant to offer significant assistance.

LEDU does not have a continuous annual record for each year over the past decade of the number of employees in client firms, nor the number of jobs promised, or created, in each year. Since 1990, however, an estimate has been made of the changes in employment in clients through a survey conducted by the Northern Ireland Economic Research Centre, on behalf of LEDU. The annual survey has been used to estimate that LEDU clients employed, at December 1994, 32,930 people. LEDU now estimate that, when part-time workers are added, the total employment by their clients is nearer to 40,000. Of this total, LEDU may have clients which employ nearly 20,000 people in manufacturing and a similar number in other sectors. In the manufacturing sector, up to 20% of the employees would be in businesses which are clients of LEDU.

Until March 1991, LEDU published annual information on the number of new jobs promised or renewed on a basis which, conceptually, was similar to the IDB (see Table 10.7). These figures are subject to the same reservations about the conversion rate to actual jobs. The number of jobs promised compared favourably with those recorded by the IDB. In three of the eight years from 1983/4 to 1990/1, LEDU published the higher figures and, measured as a possible rate of change in employment by the existing client base, LEDU figures were more than double those of the IDB. The conversion rate of job promises to actual jobs, and the duration of jobs in smaller projects, may mean that the net gain by LEDU clients differs from those in the larger IDB schemes, but limited evidence from the NIERC studies for 1986-90 does not suggest a major difference.

Table 10.7: Jobs Promoted in LEDU Assisted Clients, 1983-1991, Northern Ireland

Year	Jobs promised	Jobs renewed	Total
1983-84	3658	400	4058
1984-85	4009	274	4283
1985-86	3888	493	4381
1986-87	4201	299	4500
1987-88	4047	523	4570
1988-89	4395	402	4797
1989-90	5221	431	5652
1990-91	5501	981	6482

Source: NIAO (1992).

The employment in businesses in the survey at the end of 1990 was estimated to be 24,500. Year on year changes are not strictly comparable, because of the statistical techniques used, but the same survey estimated that total employment at the end of 1994 was 32,900. Both figures exclude part-time employees. The increase of over 8000 jobs in four years suggests that an annual net gain of about 2000 jobs has been achieved. Of the 8000 extra jobs, no information has been published yet by LEDU on the number that were in manufacturing or other sectors. Year by year there have been significant fluctuations in the rate of change (see Table 10.8). 1991 was a difficult trading period and the number of people working in LEDU client firms fell by over 600. In contrast, in 1994 (the latest information available) a net increase of 3500 was recorded. This is possibly one of the best years on record.

Table 10.8: Employment Changes in LEDU Clients, 1991-94, Northern Ireland

Year	Net change in surviving firms	New starts	Losses through closures	Net change on previous year
1991	1150	1350	-3150	-650
1992	950	1680	-1900	730
1993	405	2465	-1240	1630
1994	1820	2470	-790	3500

Source: LEDU Annual Reports

The Location of New Jobs

Whilst the primary objective of the job creation agencies is the overall growth of the Northern Ireland economy, an important consideration in terms of employment equality is the distribution of new projects and investment within Northern Ireland.

There are obvious difficulties in influencing the location of new projects when the total amount of new activity is still inadequate to meet the overall objectives, and when the people making the investment or expansion decisions are making judgements about the location which offers them the best circumstances to ensure the viability of the project. The latter means that projects are more likely to be attracted to areas which are already the favoured locations for other businesses and where unemployment may be lower, whilst social needs and a concern with equity would wish to see projects locating in areas of highest unemployment (see also Chapter Seven, this volume). In an attempt to counteract this problem, government policy has, since 1963 (Bradley *et al*, 1986), offered higher selective financial assistance to projects locating in areas of high unemployment. The businesses most likely to be influenced by different scales of assistance are those which are establishing in Northern Ireland for the first time. Existing businesses, or indigenous firms, are more likely to make investment decisions based on their existing location. Consequently, the pattern of investment decisions made by externally owned firms should reflect the success, or otherwise, of government location policies, expressed through higher rates of financial assistance or other arrangements.

The Northern Ireland Economic Council (NIEC, 1992) examined the pattern of employment arising from inward investment in 1973, 1986 and 1990. Table 10.9 ranks the 12 official Travel to Work Areas in Northern Ireland, starting with the areas with highest unemployment in 1995, and compares this to the 'location quotient' of inward investment calculated by NIEC for 1990. The 'location quotient' is calculated as employment in externally owned plants as a percentage of all manufacturing employment, compared to the overall average. A quotient of 1.0 is the equivalent of the average outcome.

The most striking feature of this comparison is that the often quoted 'blackspots' of Strabane, Newry and Londonderry emerge as gaining their 'share' of inward investment (or nearly so, for Newry), whilst the lowest figures are for Dungannon, Omagh, Magherafelt and Cookstown. Belfast and Ballymena, both of which would not usually attract the extra scale of assistance (except in West and North Belfast), gained their share. Ballymena emerged as only just better than Londonderry. When compared to the position in 1973 (just before the impact of political violence on the manufacturing base), Omagh, Cookstown and Coleraine have been hardest hit. Dungannon was at the wrong end of this league table at both dates. However, Londonderry and Magherafelt have been net beneficiaries.

Table 10.9: Importance of Inward Investment in Providing Manufacturing Jobs, 1990, Northern Ireland

	Location quotient
Strabane	1.1
Newry	0.9
Londonderry	1.6
Cookstown	0.6
Dungannon	0.1
Coleraine	0.9
Enniskillen	0.7
Omagh	0.4
Magherafelt	0.6
Belfast	0.9
Craigavon	1.2
Ballymena	1.7

Source: NIEC (1992)

This evidence on inward investment suggests that government policy on location has had some success, but needs to be qualified with a concern that some of the smaller urban centres, west of the Bann, have not gained (proportionately) as much investment as Londonderry, Strabane and Newry.

Questions which need to be addressed relating to the poor performance in these mid-Ulster towns include the scale of the differential treatment on offer (within the agreed European Union ceilings) and labour market issues, such as the possible recruitment numbers and the skills base in the localities.

The results of the NIEC study discussed above updated but did not dramatically conflict with the conclusions reached by Bradley *et al* (1986) who compared the location ratios of assisted employment in the periods 1949-63 and 1964-81, which approximate to an initial period of neutral policy on the location of investment and a later period when formal differentials were in operation. In the period 1964-81, the location ratios of Londonderry, Craigavon, Newry, Enniskillen, Dungannon and Limavady all improved and were above the average for the whole of Northern Ireland. These ratios were calculated on Employment Service Office boundaries which were smaller units than the Travel to Work Areas used in the NIEC study. The problem of the mid-Ulster towns was, however, in evidence even in this earlier study. Some of the lowest location ratios (areas which gained least new employment in industry) were Cookstown, Magherafelt, Omagh and Strabane. In the later NIEC study, Strabane had gained significantly and Dungannon had fallen back. With the enhanced scales of financial assistance, introduced in 1963, results improved in most of these mid-Ulster towns, but the improvement was less marked than in other centres. Cookstown had the poorest results - its location quotient fell.

Bradley *et al* (1986:79) concluded that:

> .... judged on the basis of population shares, areas of the Province with Roman Catholic majorities have attracted the same proportions of assisted employment as have areas with non-Roman Catholic majorities in the period 1949-81. Indeed, so far as can be determined, these areas with Catholic majorities were major beneficiaries of the period of active industrial location policy practiced between 1964 and 1981. Given these assumptions, it can be said that both Roman Catholics and non-Roman Catholics have had virtually identical probabilities of obtaining employment in government sponsored projects in the period under review.

One caution should, however, be added to these conclusions. There is a possibility that the closure rate of projects, or the rate of job loss, may have been higher in the areas of highest unemployment, which are also areas with a predominantly Catholic population. This would be consistent with these areas attracting the weaker investment projects or, possibly, these areas producing poorer results than expected, or a mixture of both. No formal study has ever been undertaken to discover whether the closures or job losses from assisted projects are correlated with location or local level of unemployment.

Poor Performance

The experience of the 30 years of job creation policies to the end of the 1980s is summed up graphically in 'Unemployment Forever':

> Following three decades of substantial government intervention in manufacturing industry, leading to a consistently higher level of investment per employee than in Great Britain, we might expect to see some strengthening of Northern Ireland's manufacturing base. Until 1989 any improvement was difficult to detect. Levels of productivity and investment, in both skills and R&D, all lagged behind Great Britain and showed little tendency to catch up (Gudgin and O'Shea, 1993:2).

The importance of this assessment is that, in the manufacturing businesses which continued to operate in Northern Ireland, measures of economic performance suggest that not only was the overall change in employment disappointing, but there were other signs of weak performances. Hitchens and Bernie (1989) reached a similar conclusion:

> Northern Ireland manufacturing (has) a level of productivity only four-fifths of that of Great Britain in the first half of the 1980s. This is a disappointing conclusion to arrive at after a large outlay of public resources to assist Northern Ireland industry.

If there was any lingering hope that the reputed work ethic, or quality of labour, or skilled labour supplies, or better management, meant that Northern Ireland enjoyed higher productivity levels which would be a source of self-sustaining expansion, these studies suggest that it has been eroded sharply. Indeed, the evidence points to these as areas of weakness, not strength. Implicitly, questions are being asked about economic performance and value for money. After a period of exceptionally heavy financial expenditure by government agencies, with considerable amounts going directly to private sector manufacturers, there was little progress to show. Of course, part of the response may be that without this expenditure, the position would have been worse. How much worse?

Contributions to Job Creation From Other Sources

This review of job creation has focused on the rationale and ability of government and government agencies to increase employment. Attention has been mainly on the exogenous sources of employment. Indigenously determined employment will be determined by market forces. For example, employment in retailing, catering services and transport vary according to competitive forces and any government intervention would be more likely to cause displacement rather than a net increase in employment.

In addition to UK government activities, both the European Union and the International Fund for Ireland have attempted to intervene in economic development. The European Union contributes, and will continue to contribute, to economic and social priorities in Northern Ireland. The Single Programme Document summarises the commitments of nearly £1billion for the period from 1994 to 1999. The Peace and Reconciliation programme will bring about £200 million extra to Northern Ireland in the three years 1995-97. Some of these funds will be directed to social and environmental issues. However, the larger part will aid economic development either through assisting with infrastructure developments, such as transport and energy investments, or labour skills enhancement through the European Social Fund, or through supplements to the work of the IDB and LEDU. Some funds will be routed through LEDU to local enterprise agencies and community projects.

The International Fund for Ireland is also a significant source of funds for development. Annually, the IFI allocates about £30 million, north and south on this island. This adds to the job creation efforts in a number of ways; in part, the IFI supplements activities that also gain government support, such as business projects, whether by grants or equity investments. Other funds encourage regeneration of smaller towns and rural areas. These provide the basic infrastructure to supplement other business activities as well as offering community support. The IFI is careful to describe its actions as being associated with investments and job creation. It is usually a partner of local groups, local enterprise agencies or government agencies in its actions.

COMPETING IN THE 1990s

Whilst EU and IFI funding will supplement other efforts to generate employment, the main expenditure comes from the existing government departments and agencies. Given the lack of dramatic progress, there is legitimate debate about whether public funds have, in the recent past, been used to sustain employment in manufacturing at the cost of eroding competitiveness rather than securing improvements. In the late 1980s, government, without offering retrospective acknowledgement of misdirected effort, accepted a need to rethink the formulation of job creation policies. Whilst there are dangers in any oversimplified statement, the change in the late 1980s might be described as a shift away from the theory that if the scale of the financial incentives (or cost offsets) was larger, then more investment and job creation could be expected: the notion that more government money would buy more jobs. In its place, government accepted that durable jobs would be more likely to come from competitive, or profitable, businesses and that the reasons for inadequate competitiveness should be more directly tackled.

A critical landmark in the evolution of job creation policies was the publication by the Department of Economic Development of 'Competing in the 1990s' (DED, 1990) and the implementation of changed policies by the various agencies. The main change of emphasis, and policy, which followed this overall review, was that, instead of directly targeting job promises and job maintenance, efforts were to be directed to enhance the competitiveness of client businesses. Job creation, it was argued, would be the consequence of improved competitiveness. Six root causes of weakness in the performance of the Northern Ireland economy were suggested by the DED. These were: the lack of an enterprise tradition; deficiencies in training and managerial competence; a small and low-income local market and a peripheral location; a small manufacturing sector coupled with a large public sector; too great a dependency by local companies on public funds, and the economic effects of continuing political instability. Given the assumptions made in the earlier periods, particularly the 1960s, the first, second and fifth of these represented a big shift in perceived wisdom. The third and fourth are factual and not easily altered and the sixth is a critical element where change involves a much larger set of problems.

Government policy, from 1990, was defined as:

> Ensuring that Government assistance, while not displacing private sector finance, is focused on obstacles to growth and will help improve the competitiveness of Northern Ireland industry; intensifying the drive for inward investment; building up management and workforce skills; stimulating the development of entrepreneurs and the growth of an enterprise culture; targeting growth areas through detailed sectoral studies ...They should also embrace certain tradeable services sectors, such as tourism, which offer good growth potential (DED,1990).

A notable feature of these policies is the emphasis on 'growth', 'enterprise' and 'competitiveness'. Whilst the aim is a stronger economy, the outcome is argued to be both higher incomes and more jobs.

One of the first conspicuous decisions, reflecting these reshaped policies, was a decision late in 1990 to lower the rate of capital grant available as part of the Selective Financial Assistance package to 30%. Previously, it had been in bands of 40%, 45% and 50%. However, for deprived areas and for attractive international inward investment, power to award a further 20% was included.

'Growing Competitively' Five Years Later

The policies adopted in 1990 will probably continue for the rest of this decade (barring a change of government). The strategy will 'continue to centre on competitiveness,' according to the official review of these policies after the first five years. One potentially significant change is the extra emphasis to be given to a policy of Targeting Social Need as part of the overall strategy. Thus, the Minister referred to the goal as 'an economy which provides worthwhile opportunities for everyone,' and added 'we intend to make real headway in tackling the problem of long-term unemployment' (DED, 1995). No acknowledgement is made of any potential clash between this social dimension and the enhancement of competitiveness.

The main weakness in the five year review was a lack of comprehensive information to demonstrate whether the new policies had made any difference. Some economic trends, or macro-economics challenges, will, of course, only become clear after a longer period. However, no short or medium-term indicators of profitability or relative competitiveness were included. The mid-term review was, thus, detailed on administrative processes but weak in confirming the effectiveness and efficiency of policies. After a five year period with the publication of little evidence, the suspicion must be that the DED, and its main job creation agencies, were not sufficiently committed to publishing adequate performance indicators. For at least three years the reassurance has always been that they were being prepared. The delay is now so great that that explanation has lost credibility.

Logically, the thrust of policies directed to 'Growing Competitively' is persuasive. However, the validity of the job creation policies and the longer-term prospects are uncertain until more information on performance is available. An important aspect of the evaluation of the effects of the recent changes will be to assess whether decisions based on competitiveness and profitability differ in their impact when compared to the former regime. If, for example, there is a more restrictive attitude to job maintenance, where redundancy threatens, this may cause short-term concern but might be a justified policy change.

CRITICAL COMMENTS ON CURRENT POLICIES AND PRACTICES

Much useful and well targeted work is undertaken by the several official agencies in stimulating enhanced competitiveness and, as a result, potentially securing extra sustainable employment opportunities. However, there are questions and issues which need to be examined to further improve the outcomes and demonstrate the effectiveness of official policies. For convenience these are presented, sometimes drawing arbitrary distinctions, as they apply to overall policy or the individual agencies. First, to return to the DED 1995 review, this was inadequate in a number of respects, including: no assessment of the instruments for the delivery of policy; inappropriate reliance on inadequate evidence on productivity; proposals for an inadequate range of monitoring indicators; and no assessment of the implications of the Targeting Social Need objective. The review avoided one of the most critical questions: the effectiveness of the instruments of economic assistance, stating that they 'are not reviewed here - they are examined on a regular basis under the Department's Policy Evaluation Programme' (DED, 1995:2). This immediately obscured one of the most important features which might have been in the review.

In effect, the DED revisited the principles justifying a policy of enhancing competitiveness, but offered no evidence on whether it was working and whether the instruments were appropriate for the purpose, although several schemes of assistance have been significantly changed to meet the new policy priorities. It was heroic to assume that they were all functioning adequately, but the DED offered no evidence. As has long been the tradition, this approach amounted to 'trust us, we know best', which is hardly consistent with claims of increased openness in public debate.

Second, the mid-term review offered no evidence which attempted to measure progress towards the stated objectives (*ibid*: 4). The evidence quoted (*ibid*: 9) on competitiveness relied on a NIERC study which offered some interesting ideas on productivity changes, but which was inadequate as a performance indicator of competitiveness. It obtained answers after adjustment for the size and structure of local firms, when questions about the need to alter these features should be part of the policy framework and because changes in productivity are not necessarily a good measure of changes in profitability or competitiveness. This suggests a lack of effort in measuring the impact of policy. At worst, the DED seems to be using improved production and productivity figures to assert that competitiveness has improved. Such a conclusion might be valid but it merits rather more careful comparative analysis.

Third, the review offered a series of macro-economics challenges for the year 2001. Presumably, progress on these challenges will be monitored and published at least annually. They are intended to include changes in: manufacturing value-added (i.e. manufacturing production); exports; manufacturing productivity; employment in manufacturing; and employment in business services. This series of indicators suggests that the DED is not preparing to publish (and possibly not even collect and calculate) information which would be closer to measuring effective competitiveness. There is no indication of why it will not publish information on trends in profitability and trends in unit wage costs. The OECD definition outlined (*ibid*:3) does not offer an operational and meaningful answer which replaces these suggestions. It seems that only partial performance measures (*ibid*:23) are being collected for publication by the IDB. Apparently, the IDB only collects measures of performance from home industry companies which accept SFA offers of assistance. Why are others excluded? There are other forms of IDB involvement with clients. In addition, the role of LEDU in collecting comparable information needs to be reopened.

Fourth, a major shift of emphasis in policy in the mid-1990s was the commitment to 'focus spending more sharply to ensure it has major impact on the most disadvantaged areas' (*ibid*:2). Before 1996, the areas of social need had two general advantages: capital grants 20% over and above the normal 30% ceiling and a preparedness to site of advance factories in these areas. Also, special groups were, and are, considering ways to encourage greater industrial development in Londonderry and in the more needy parts of Belfast through agencies such as Making Belfast Work. This is one of the most difficult questions facing those responsible for economic and social policy. The adequacy or otherwise of these partial measures can only be assessed in a wider examination of all the relevant policies, including housing, transport and the availability of skills training. The DED review did not discuss the practical questions of how job creation policy would link to the other dimensions of policy for these areas.

The Industrial Development Board

The IDB has a difficult job to do. Attracting investment against a background of political uncertainty calls for unusual skills. In 1995-6, the international image of Northern Ireland improved and the work of the IDB was easier. However, the improved perception of Northern Ireland needs to be backed up by a re-energised IDB. Some of the recent responses, for example, at the May 1995 Washington Trade conference, attracted critical comment. Unfortunately, after years of adverse publicity the IDB has created a perception of defensiveness and resistance to professional ideas for change. This can be evident in several ways: inadequacies in its Annual Reports; unwillingness to publish some more useful performance indicators; no acknowledgement of the role of EU funding; and no critical evaluation of the available instruments of assistance.

First, the IDB has not adequately conveyed to the general public and, possibly, its clients, a conviction that the early 1990s brought an important change in policy. The Annual Reports continue to give priority to the promises of new jobs contracts signed. Whilst this should continue as part of the assessment process, the absence of useful measures of overall competitive outcomes (rather than inputs) is a concern both for analytical purposes and because of what it may mean for internal activities in the IDB.

Second, the performance indicators outlined in 'Growing Competitively', all of which apply to the IDB's performance, are both very limited and overdue (see above). The IDB seems reluctant to fulfil even the limited promises it has made. The economic performance section of the most recent Annual Reports is poorly designed in relation to the new objectives. In the absence of performance indicators, no measures of relative performance (other than job promises and investment) can be made with the rest of the local economy, other regions, or other countries.

Third, although the European Union offers support to industrial development and labour market measures in Northern Ireland, the annual accounts of the IDB (and LEDU) do not give details of the impact of these receipts. Consequently, the IDB strategy for 1995-98 (IDB, 1995) can be read without taking account of the EU contribution to new investments. This might be interpreted in Brussels as either an absence of additionally or an attempt to hide the additional effects: neither would be welcome conclusions.

Fourth, neither the IDB nor LEDU offer evaluative comments on the scale, range and effectiveness of the financial and other instruments of assistance at their disposal. However, in the business community, there is a continuing debate about possible changes. There are important questions, within a UK and/or a regional context, about possible refinements to company taxation or National Insurance charges (possibly on the model used in some areas of Italy). The recent four percentage points relief on interest rates on some bank loans has introduced a new variable which, if successful, might be extended. A recurring concern in Northern Ireland is the effectiveness in the Republic of Ireland of the 10% corporate tax rate which applies to manufacturers. This has been a powerful incentive for many external investors. The IDB could not be expected to comment publicly and objectively about its significance, but such is the perception of the value of this tax regime that there is at least a possibility that Northern Ireland would attract more investment from viable companies if a similar uncomplicated version was available. Nor are the main types of current Selective Financial Assistance paid by the IDB itemised and explained. Comparing 1990-1 with 1994-5, and excluding the R&D grants which have been transferred to the Industrial Research and Technology Unit, the net totals in each year were £65.6million and £77.5million. The capital grants element of these totals at £49million and £54million, respectively, do not suggest a big change in the application of capital grants policy yet these payments might have been expected to decrease. The new feature of IDB assistance, which did not exist in 1990-91, is described as 'other revenue grants' of £5.5million. but no details of their purpose are offered. Employment grants have, however, been nearly halved: down from £14.2million to £7.7million.

Despite these particular critical comments, the IDB Strategy for 1995-98 does provide a comprehensive review of many detailed actions planned by the IDB. The criticisms should not detract from the outcome, output and input targets which the IDB has set. Some of the targets may be considered too modest. However, these now need to be monitored on an annual basis and included as part of a reshaped annual report.

Local Enterprise Development Unit

LEDU quickly adjusted its organisation in 1990 to meet the reshaped objectives which it was given. The four way division into pre-start, start-up, established businesses and growth businesses fits well with the objectives. However, LEDU has not adequately followed this through in the detail published in its Annual Reports. The new policies cannot be adequately assessed unless clear trends in each of the four divisions are presented in terms of inputs and outputs.

For the established and growth businesses, information on output (or sales), export values and changes in employment is collected as part of the NIERC survey, but no information on profitability is maintained. LEDU is to collect this information for the growth businesses. However, this raises the question: why not for all the existing businesses? In addition, these performance indicators are not yet presented in an analytical form which helps to assess sectoral and overall competitiveness. The lack of adequate databases for the development of performance indicators in LEDU was one of the 1992 criticisms by the NIAO (1992:9). Only in the last two Annual Reports has LEDU begun to offer a skeletal analysis of employment changes, and not in the form of a series allowing comparisons with earlier years.

As a whole, the annual accounts of LEDU no longer give an adequate breakdown of the purposes of its grant aid expenditure. In 'Growing Competitively' (DED, 1995), it is reported that capital grants have fallen from 50% of LEDU's spending in 1990 to 11% in 1993-4. LEDU's own reports have recently provided no breakdown of the purposes of their grants and current expenditure. Readers were informed, with no amplification, of a global total of 'expenditure related to job creation' in the years before 1994-5. In 1994-5, a useful, but overly condensed, breakdown of spending of nearly £25million on assistance to clients was given without comparison with earlier years. Neither did it fully detail the types of grant aid to business in the role of third parties. The evidence published on pre-start and start-ups (and closures) is particularly thin. This is of general importance in gaining a better understanding of this aspect of stimulating new enterprise, but would also be relevant to equality of opportunity questions. LEDU might usefully more closely integrate the cost of assistance offered and the employment gained (or lost) in separate analyses for the four separate business divisions identified in its corporate objectives.

Stimulating the development of entrepreneurs is a critical aspect of the enterprise culture. LEDU has a particular responsibility as the agency aiming to encourage the start-up of small businesses or the transition by individuals to self-employment. LEDU also links with the 36 local enterprise agencies which now exist. Readers of 'Growing Competitively' will find that, within the section dealing with LEDU's work, these are barely mentioned. A short paragraph (*ibid*; para 42) conveys the conclusion that, in terms of access to pre-start-up and start-up schemes, 'the provision was balanced in community terms' (that is, the two communities). It concludes, 'LEDU aims to build on this.' Since an important and expanding part of the network of job creation agencies are the local enterprise agencies, many of which attract support from district councils, it is surprising that the past, present and potential contribution of these agencies does not emerge as a more significant part of the review of LEDU's strategies and objectives.

Northern Ireland Tourist Board

One of the critical sectors for future development is tourism. For many years, tourism might have been described as virtually dormant. More new businesses emerged to supply the local leisure, entertainment and hotel demand but little capacity was needed for incoming tourists. This has now changed. The Tourist Board has published a macro-economics assessment of the potential for development. However, despite ambitious claims, there are critical policy questions about volume, standards, labour skills and availability, timing and facilities and their integration with local leisure industry demand which now need to be considered. The Tourist Board needs to do this recognising that the infrastructure of the tourist industry, public and private (usually accommodation, leisure facilities and travel), is jointly used by local people, business and holiday visitors. There are dangers in orienting support in ways designed to maximise the number of holiday visitors. Logically, the greater benefit to the local economy, including sustained employment, would emerge by measures to develop an extended season and attracting high spending visitors, rather than large numbers of low spending visitors in the all too short summer peaks.

The Training and Employment Agency

Building up management and workforce skills is one of the five strategic objectives set by the DED. Delivery of this aspect of government policy falls particularly on the Training and Employment Agency (T&EA), but also links to the policies and performance of the Department of Education. Of the five objectives, all of which are important and interdependent, the debate about methods of improving the availability of skills and the reshaping of educational provision for vocational and further education is, arguably, potentially the critical weak link in the chain (see also Chapters Three and Four, this volume). The T&EA is enhancing the Jobskills programme, piloting the Community Work Programme and extending and refining the Youth Training Programme, including NVQ achievement targets in the outcome assessments of the YTP. However, these programmes are no substitute for adequate provision by the education sector for all young people still within the formal compulsory education age groups. This priority has been identified and endorsed by the Growth Challenge but is, at best, understated in the priorities outlined in 'Growing Competitively'. Of all the factors contributing to differences in employment prospects for young people, this is critical and, as presently operating, likely to allow inequalities to be perpetuated.

The T&EA acknowledges the need to encourage the enhancement of management skills as part of its responsibilities. However, there is a degree of complacency in the reliance on the Company Development Programme to make effective changes linked with the contribution of management development seminars. The scale of the problems are underplayed in 'Growing Competitively,' so that, for example, there is no suggestion for the further development and expansion of an appropriately financed Ulster Business School in the University of Ulster or links with other management training providers.

CONCLUSIONS

Provided the post-1990 competitiveness strategies are executed rigorously and comprehensively, they should produce increased employment. However, the evidence so far does not meet these requirements. The combined targets for the IDB and LEDU suggest that, by 1998-9, manufacturing employment might rise to about 115,000 to 120,000 people. If this is achieved, employment will have gone back to the levels of the early 1980s. The ratio of private sector jobs outside manufacturing to those in manufacturing is rising as technology changes and incomes rise. Such an increase would mean a considerably larger increase in total employment.

Northern Ireland's job creation agencies have been operating under new guidelines since 1990. The theory, aims and objectives have not been contentious, although this may in part be a result of inadequate debate. The outcomes of the changed guidelines have not been sufficiently evaluated and, without appropriate performance indicators, may not be capable of adequate evaluation. This suggests either an unwillingness to expose the evidence to scrutiny or an unwillingness to collect the necessary evidence. Neither answer is reassuring.

REFERENCES

Bradley, J., Hewitt, V. and Jefferson, C. (1986) *Industrial location policy and equality of opportunity in assisted employment in Northern Ireland, 1949-81,* Research report No.10, Belfast: FEA.

Department of Economic Development (DED) (1995) *Growing Competitively,* Belfast: HMSO.

Deptartment of Economic Development (DED) (1990) *Competing in the 1990s - the Key to Growth,* Belfast: HMSO.

Gudgin, G. (1994) 'Pulling Ahead: Industrial Growth in Northern Ireland', *Irish Banking Review*, Summer 1994: 3-21.

Gudgin, G, and O'Shea, G. (eds.) (1993) *Unemployment Forever?*, NIERC Report No. 13, Belfast: NIERC.

Hitchens, D.M. and Bernie, J.E. (1989) *Manufacturing Productivity in Northern Ireland: a comparison with Great Britain*, Belfast: NIERC.

Industrial Development Authority (IDA) (1991-94) *Annual Reports*, Dublin: IDA.

Industrial Development Board (IDB) (1982-95) *Annual Reports*, Belfast: HMSO.

Industrial Development Board (IDB) (1995) *Industrial Development Strategy, April 1995 - March 1998*, Belfast: IDB.

Local Enterprise Development Unit (LEDU) (1990-95) *Annual Reports*, Belfast: HMSO.

Local Enterprise Development Unit (LEDU) (1995) *Making the Difference: Corporate Plan 1995-1998*, Belfast: LEDU.

Locate in Scotland (1995) *Annual Review 1994-5*, Glasgow: Locate in Scotland.

Northern Ireland Audit Office (1992) *Local Enterprise Development Unit: Review of performance*, Belfast: HMSO.

Northern Ireland Economic Council (1992) *Inward Investment in Northern Ireland*, Report 9, Belfast: NIEC.

Northern Ireland Economic Council (1990) *The Industrial Development Board: Selective financial assistance and economic development policy*, Belfast: NIEC.

Northern Ireland Economic Research Centre (1993(a)) *Manufacturing Profitability in Northern Ireland*, Belfast: NIERC.

Northern Ireland Economic Research Centre (1993(b)) *Government Grants and Manufacturing Profitability in Northern Ireland*, Belfast: NIERC.

Policy Planning and Research Unit (PPRU) (1994) *1993 Labour Force Survey; Religion Report*, Belfast: PPRU.

Roper, S. (1995) 'Manufacturing Productivity in Northern Ireland', *Economic and Social Review*, Dublin.

Scottish Enterprise (1995) *Annual Report and Accounts, 1994-5*, Glasgow: Scottish Enterprise.

Chapter Eleven

OVERVIEW AND CONCLUSIONS

Vani K. Borooah

There can be little doubt that the major problem facing Northern Ireland society is that of unemployment, and that the biggest question for public policy in Northern Ireland is how to reduce unemployment and how to alleviate its ill-effects. Chapters One and Ten provide succinct overviews of the problems surrounding unemployment in Northern Ireland. In summary, for over 60 years the unemployment rate in Northern Ireland has been higher, and the participation rate (particularly among women) lower, than any other region of the UK. Compounding these aggregate problems is the issue of how the burden of unemployment is distributed between the two communities. Generally speaking, the unemployment rate among Catholics has, historically, been approximately twice that among Protestants: the 1993 Labour Force Survey (LFS) estimated these rates as 18% and 9%, respectively. The nexus of issues surrounding the 'unemployment problem' in Northern Ireland substantially forms the theme of this book.

JOB CREATION AND UNEMPLOYMENT

As Simpson in Chapter Ten points out, high rates of unemployment cannot be blamed entirely on the political violence that has been endemic to Northern Ireland for the past quarter century. The troubles have reduced inward investment and have cost the province jobs in industry (particularly manufacturing), but they have also led to an expansion of jobs in the public sector. The net effect on jobs has, probably, been very small. Nor can the loss of manufacturing jobs be blamed entirely on the troubles: poor competitiveness, manifesting itself in relatively higher unit labour costs than in Britain, must also take some of the blame. Nevertheless, in view of Northern Ireland's poor image, the task of attracting new jobs to the Province has been an uphill one. Chapter Ten contains a very good discussion of how the IDB and LEDU have gone about this task and the degree of success that they have encountered. Simpson also argues that the location of jobs matters in terms of the impact of job creation on a particular community (see also Shuttleworth *et al* in Chapter Two of this volume for a discussion of job location). Traditional areas of high unemployment - Strabane, Newry and Londonderry - have done well out of government policy to strategically locate inward investment in Travel to Work Areas (TTWAs) where unemployment was high; however, this was at the cost of the smaller urban areas, west of the Bann, gaining little, relative to the above TTWAs.

A more fundamental problem in tackling unemployment is that job creation is not necessarily reflected in an equivalent reduction in unemployment. This is so for a number of reasons. First, it has much to do with the way unemployment is measured. As Shuttleworth *et al* (Chapter Two) discuss, if unemployment is measured by the number claiming unemployment (and unemployment-related) benefits then not all those registered as unemployed are seeking jobs; conversely, nor are all job-seekers registered as unemployed. For example, in 1991, in the UK, 890,000 persons were counted as unemployed by the Labour Force Survey (LFS) but excluded from the claimant count. Of these, 60% were women, reflecting the fact that women - because they are more likely to work part-time and to have interrupted spells of employment - are less likely than men to build up a contribution record that would make them eligible for Unemployment Benefit; at the same time, married women are often not entitled to claim Income Support (and are, therefore, again excluded from the claimant count), but instead are included in the husband's claim (if any) for means-tested benefits. However, in the same year, the claimant count included 660,000 persons who were not deemed to be unemployed on the LFS definition, either because the LFS regarded them as employed or because they failed the LFS job search/availability criteria. The LFS defines anyone working for more than an hour in the week prior to the interview as being employed. Since claimants of unemployment-related benefits are allowed to earn up to specified amounts, and since these amounts might involve them working hours in excess of the LFS threshold, they could fail the LFS 'jobless' test but yet be legitimate claimants. Hence the existence of 'employed' claimants, who comprised 40% of the 660,000 claimants excluded from the LFS count of the unemployed, is not necessarily evidence about the scale of the 'black economy'. Therefore, it should not come as a great surprise when an increase in jobs is not accompanied by a fall in registered unemployment.

Job creation should have some impact on the LFS measure of unemployment, but even here people previously not searching may emerge to take the newly created jobs leaving existing jobseekers jobless. One reason why job creation in the 1980s and 1990s has had so little impact on male joblessness is that much of the job creation in this period has been in part-time, service sector jobs which men are unwilling to take. The proportion of part-time jobs in Australia and France doubled between 1973 and 1992. Between January and September 1993, according to the LFS, the number of full-time jobs in the UK fell by 40,000, and part-time jobs rose by 100,000, with the lion's share of the new jobs being accounted for by the retailing and the hotel and catering sectors. In 1993, the 5.9 million part-time employees in the UK constituted almost a quarter of its workforce but of such employees, only 15% were men. Nor was the UK alone in having such a large share of part-time jobs. The proportion of part-time jobs in total employment was nearly 30% in Australia and Sweden and just under 20% in Japan, the USA and Germany. On average, about three-quarters of these part-time jobs were held by women (OECD, 1993).

UNEMPLOYMENT AND BARRIERS TO WORK

Over and above these broad reasons, there may be particular reasons why certain groups of jobseekers find it more difficult than others to secure jobs. One such group, constituting nearly half of the unemployed in Northern Ireland, comprises the long-term unemployed (LTU). The basic fact about the duration of unemployment is that the chances of an unemployed person finding a job decline in relation to the length of time that person has been unemployed. Roughly three million persons lose their jobs every year in the UK. Of these, most are able to find alternative employment within six months, and roughly 80% leave unemployment within a year (Nickell, 1993). Nevertheless, a significant proportion of job losers are still unemployed after a year. The problem is that the chances of a person who has been unemployed for a year finding a job are less than 20%, as compared to a nearly 60% chance for someone who has only recently become unemployed (Layard *et al*, 1991). The reason for this sharp decline in the probability of finding a job is that the long-term unemployed face greater barriers to entering the world of work than do those persons who have only been unemployed for a relatively short time.

Shuttleworth *et al* (Chapter Two) identify such barriers to entry and examine the degree to which barriers operate in the labour markets of Derry and Belfast. Within this broad context, the chapter considers several questions. First, what is the appropriate definition of unemployment? Shuttleworth *et al* note that both the claimant count measure (based on registration, discussed above) and the Census of Population measure (based on self-reporting of economic status) are flawed. To overcome difficulties inherent in both measures, they undertook a survey of 552 unemployed and inactive persons in Derry and Belfast. Of these, only 70% were 'signing on' and of those signing on, 87% were looking for a job while the remainder were 'inactive claimants'. More interestingly, more than half (57%) of those not signing on were looking for a job. These findings lend support to the earlier contention that how unemployment is measured is crucial in determining the relation between job creation and unemployment reduction and, further, that on the basis of the claimant count measure this relation could be very weak.

To analyse barriers to entry, Shuttleworth *et al* analysed the previous labour market status of appointees in five companies (with a total of 12 sites in Derry and Belfast). Over half the appointees had been employed prior to their appointment and less than 13% of appointees were drawn from the ranks of the unemployed. An important cause of this was the rather negative view that personnel managers took of the unemployed, and this finding confirms other findings of employer prejudice towards the unemployed and, especially, towards the long-term unemployed (see Layard, 1996 and Chapter Four, this volume). Overlaying this basic prejudice were, however, other ancillary attitudes operating against older jobseekers and against men seeking part-time jobs, and there was also the recognition that the geographical location of firms acts as a barrier to jobseekers from one or the other communities in Northern Ireland. This problem of geographical mobility is also discussed by Sheehan and Tomlinson in Chapter Three.

The barriers that the unemployed face in finding work, in terms of a lack of employer demand for their services, are compounded by the fact that very often they turn down job offers: Shuttleworth *et al* note that 35% of their unemployed respondents had refused a job offer, usually because of the low wages attached to such jobs but also because women job seekers had difficulties with child care arrangements. Thus, there may be a fundamental mismatch between the jobs that the unemployed are offered and the jobs they find desirable, and this only serves to exacerbate employer attitudes towards the unemployed.

Long-Term Unemployment

While the Shuttleworth *et al* chapter encompasses both the short and the long-term unemployed, Sheehan and Tomlinson, in Chapter Three, focus on the long-term unemployed (LTU). Such a focus requires little justification. The worst aspect of unemployment is that it erodes self-respect and this, in turn, generates a variety of social and psychological ailments among the unemployed, the intensity of which increases with the duration of unemployment. Recent studies (see Darity and Goldsmith, 1996) have argued that the deterioration in the emotional well-being of the unemployed involves three stages: in the first stage, the stage of shock, the individual is still optimistic; in the second stage, when efforts to secure employment have failed, the individual becomes pessimistic and suffers active distress; in the third stage, helplessness becomes acute and the individual resigns him or herself to the state of unemployment.

The heart of Sheehan and Tomlinson's first chapter involves a survey of the LTU in West Belfast. Of the 314 LTU who were surveyed, 37% reported that their health had deteriorated since they became unemployed and the most common form of ailment was depression associated with a loss of self-esteem. The mood of pessimism associated with LTU was related to the intensity with which the LTU searched for jobs: only 77% of the respondents were looking for work and the most common reason for not searching was the feeling that jobs were not available. Among those searching for jobs, there was some (but not significant) evidence of choosiness (see also the discussion of Shuttleworth *et al* above) about the type of jobs that would be deemed appropriate. A majority of respondents (only 32% of Protestant respondents, but 65% of Catholic respondents) were prepared to accept any job.

The Sheehan and Tomlinson study provides a number of major insights into the behaviour, experiences and attitudes of the LTU. The first two are in terms of the barriers to job take-up posed by violence and intimidation and by the attitudes of the LTU towards benefits and wages. The two points are related, though Sheehan and Tomlinson do not explore this. Thirty five per cent of respondents had experienced intimidation at work and, of these, 84% were Catholic. Those who point to the excess of wages over benefits conclude that the unemployed must be work-shy. However, if the price that an individual pays for work is intimidation in the work place - and 88% of Catholic males paid this price - then the monetary rewards associated with work, in terms of wages, are reduced by the psychological costs of intimidation. In that case, the difference in attractiveness between work (with wages but also with intimidation) and unemployment (with benefits and no intimidation) may not be so great, and it may be sensible for individuals to prefer the 'safe' option of unemployment rather than the more 'dangerous' option of work.

Wages and Benefits

The Sheehan and Tomlinson study (Chapter Three) explored the question of what the 'reservation' wage (that is, the minimum wage at which a person is prepared to work) of respondents was. This, at the mean, was £3.40 per hour, an amount well below the 'going' wage rate offered by most employers in West Belfast. This would suggest that inadequate wages was not the reason for unemployment. Nor was there evidence that the reservation wage was decided by benefit levels - the dominant influence in determining this wage was the expenditure needed to meet a family's basic needs. This would suggest that the LTU in West Belfast were not 'scroungers on the dole'.

So where does this leave policy towards the LTU? Both Shuttleworth *et al* and Sheehan and Tomlinson (Chapter Four) suggested negative employer attitudes towards the unemployed as a major reason for the lack of success that the unemployed had in finding jobs. These attitudes are only attenuated in the case of the LTU. As the Sheehan and Tomlinson study shows, the fact that some persons have been unemployed for a long time is not due to the fact that they have unrealistic job aspirations - a majority will take anything for very modest pay - or that they are insulated from the world of work by generous unemployment (and unemployment-related) social security benefits - most persons do not consider benefit levels in formulating their reservation wage. Rather the failure of the LTU to find jobs reflects a failure of policy to equip the LTU for the world of work and, *inter alia,* this failure embraces the welfare system.

Labour Market Policy

The main aim of a welfare system should be to encourage the unemployed back into work, even if it is in part-time work, while at the same time providing better protection for the low paid. This should include encouraging women, particularly partners of unemployed men, to work and an effective way of doing so is to remove their dependant status. For example, in Australia, the 'partner allowance', aimed at women under 40, assesses each potential wage earner separately thus allowing women to start working without eroding their partner's income support. The benefit disregards that are current in the UK, for partners of men on income support, are derisory and only serve to either keep such women at home or to 'criminalise' their paid work by making it an offence under social security rules. Benefit claimants in the LTU study suggested sums nearly four times as high as current disregards, in order to allow individuals to access some work while they, or their partners, were unemployed and on income support.

IMPLICATIONS OF PUBLIC SECTOR EMPLOYMENT FOR COMMUNITY DIFFERENTIALS

Unemployment in Northern Ireland is viewed, quite properly, to be as much of an inter-community problem as an aggregate problem. Although the Troubles did little to affect the total number of jobs in Northern Ireland, by skewing the distribution of jobs away from manufacturing towards the public sector, they did much to alter the nature of economic rewards between the communities. In 1960, estimated public sector employment in Northern Ireland was 97,000, or 22% of total employees in employment. Over 1970-74, public sector employment rose by 40% (at an average annual rate of almost 9%) and constituted, in 1974, 35% of employees in employment. Thereafter, growth in public sector employment moderated: between 1974 and 1987 it averaged 1.3% per year and between 1987 and 1991 it actually fell by about 1.5%. The latest figures show that, in 1996, 30% of total civilian employment in Northern Ireland was in the public sector.

This structural shift in Northern Ireland's economy from employment in manufacturing to employment in the public sector has had important distributional consequences both economically and politically. The major effect of the post-1971 public sector expansion, mainly of the welfare state, was not to raise the growth rate of the Northern Ireland economy or to make the economy more competitive, but rather to alter the distribution of rewards. The chief beneficiary of this expansion was the middle class, and the rise of dual-earner middle-class families with both husband and wife holding public sector jobs was a particular feature of public sector expansion in Northern Ireland. However, a large proportion of these benefits accrued to, and indeed were responsible for the rise of, the Catholic middle class. This has had the major effect of splitting the nationalist community by distancing its middle class, who had benefited greatly from Direct Rule, both economically and politically, from the dispossessed of West Belfast, South Armagh and other poor nationalist areas. The Catholic middle class, under the shelter of British public sector jobs, seemed prepared to take a more relaxed view of a united Ireland. This was precisely the kind of economic and political development which facilitated the emergence of Sinn Fein as an articulate proponent of the cause of poor Catholics, who had received only a small share of the increased prosperity that public sector expansion under Direct Rule brought, and whose alienation from the state had increased as a result of the growing (and what they perceived as the intrusive) presence of security forces in their areas of residence.

Thus over the period of Direct Rule, the middle classes of Northern Ireland felt detached from the troubles, secure in the knowledge that they were 'doing all right'. In this detachment they were, of course, helped by the fact that relative to, say, Beirut or Bosnia, it was a 'low intensity' conflict confined to working class areas and targeted on specific individuals in these areas. As noted above, the position of middle class Catholics improved considerably under Direct Rule, but the troubles also brought jobs to working class Protestants. The collapse of manufacturing in Northern Ireland in the 1970s had affected the Protestant working class (who constituted the bulk of manufacturing employees) particularly badly and the expansion of security-related jobs, as a consequence of the troubles, provided that community with an economic lifeline. Even working class Catholics, though they did not benefit from Direct Rule to the extent that other groups did, were nevertheless economically much better off under rule from Westminster than they were under rule from Stormont. The only real loser was the British tax-payer who had to subsidise the Northern Ireland show.

The scale of the dependence of Northern Ireland's economy on the largesse of the British government is reflected in the size of the British subvention. In 1993-94, this was £3.4 billion including security (£2.54 billion excluding security) amounting to 28% of Northern Ireland's GDP. There have been a number of hints from the British government that, in the context of a political settlement for Northern Ireland, the subvention issue would be handled 'sensitively'. Realistically, what this means is that Northern

Ireland can expect a 'soft' rather than a 'hard' landing - a gradual trimming of the subvention rather than an abrupt reduction. Providing that the troubles do not return with their old ferocity, we should realistically expect over the next three to five years, at a minimum, the loss of the £600 million spent, on British Exchequer account, annually on security. This could have serious implications for employment in Northern Ireland. In addition, these unemployment consequences could well be distributed unequally between Catholics and Protestants.

It is this last question - the distributional impact of public sector job losses - which is the subject of Dignan and Murphy (Chapter Seven). As they note, apart from construction, the Catholic share of employment is highest in the public sector, most notably in education and health, in which areas, compared to an overall employment share for Catholics of 37%, 43% of employees are Catholic. Using a simulation model (the basic assumptions of which are that (a) the turnover rate in jobs is higher for Protestants than for Catholics and (b) the Catholic share of applicants - due to Fair Employment law - is proportional to their share in the labour force), they conclude that, for any given rate of net employment change, the Catholic share in employment should rise. Of course, the rate at which this share changes depends upon the speed of public sector job losses and, in particular, how concentrated such job losses are on the security industry, which has always been dominated by Protestants. Their broad conclusion is that public sector job losses have, so far, not greatly affected the community balance in employment, though future changes in the speed of public sector job losses might not have such a neutral result.

LOCAL ECONOMIC DEVELOPMENT

A major employer in the public sector in Northern Ireland is the set of local government authorities. Not only are such authorities employers, but they are also empowered to undertake economic development activities which, in turn, affects the rate of job creation in their areas. Northern Ireland, as an Objective I region within the European Union (EU), is eligible for the highest level of structural funds from the EU. In turn, the Commission of the EU sees local economic development as an integral part of the economic development strategies of such Objective I regions. Against this background of the growing importance of district councils in local economic development, Scott and Hoye (in Chapter Nine) examine the capacity of district councils to undertake, and sustain, local development initiatives and review the impact of existing development projects on alleviating social need and on promoting equality in employment.

A major problem of economic development, at the district council level, according to Scott and Hoye, is that uniformly high rates of economic growth across the councils co-exist with different rates of labour force growth. Thus over 1971-93, district council areas in the mainly Catholic western part of Northern Ireland experienced high rates of economic growth, but even higher rates of economic labour force increase. It is unfortunate that Scott and Hoye have given a rather uncritical approval to the view that the economic problems west of the Bann are primarily caused by the excessively high Catholic birth rate.

Of course it is true that, in the purely short run, an addition to the labour force requires an additional job if unemployment is not to rise. But this is a purely accounting view of the labour market and ignores the dynamic that exists between population growth and job creation. Both the north and south of Ireland have population densities that are well below the Western European average. If Northern Ireland's population had grown at the Western European average growth rate, its population would today have been 1.9 million and not the 1.6 million that it is currently. Both parts of Ireland managed to achieve much higher rates of unemployment than other European countries, at a time when the populations of such countries were growing much faster than ours. As J.J. Lee put it:

> the relationship between demographic and economic variables is a highly complex one ... by mechanistically counting the number of new jobs required to provide employment for the growing population, policy makers try to impress on the public the herculean nature of the challenge they confronted - and exonerate themselves in advance from the responsibility of failure (1989: 517).

In the case of district councils, their role in promoting economic development is still relatively new and developing. The main potential for development would appear to lie in the capacity of district councils to use development resources to lever funds from other sources, since the direct funding available to councils to promote development is too small to make, of itself, much impact. In general, Scott and Hoye conclude that in promoting economic development it is not clear the councils have done a great deal towards targeting social needs or towards promoting equity in employment.

CENTRAL GOVERNMENT INITIATIVES

However, the Northern Ireland government, centrally, has been sensitive to fair employment issues and has initiated a number of policy initiatives to improve performance in these areas. These initiatives have been launched against the background of a debate on the causes of the considerable disparity in unemployment rates between Catholics and Protestants. On the one hand there are the 'structuralists', who see high Catholic unemployment rates as being the product of, to name but a few factors: poor location - Catholics do not live where industry is located; labour market segmentation - Catholics and Protestants operate in different labour markets; educational differences and differences in work commitment - with Catholics faring worse on both counts; and family size - with Catholics, due to their larger family sizes, being better off on benefits than in work because income support takes account of family size while paid employment does not. Opposing the structuralists are those who see the higher unemployment rate for Catholics being the product of either direct or indirect discrimination, in the past or in the present. Gillespie (in Chapter One) provides an excellent introduction to the main points of this debate.

This same chapter also summarises the main policy initiatives undertaken by the government under the broad rubric of 'labour market intervention', each of which are discussed in subsequent chapters. These include policies to attract new jobs to Northern Ireland (Simpson, Chapter Ten); policies to provide training to the Northern Ireland labour force so as to make the Province an attractive destination for inward investment (Caul, Chapter Five); policies to help the long-term unemployed to re-enter the world of employment (Shuttleworth *et al*, Chapter Two; Sheehan and Tomlinson, Chapter Four); the government's Targeting Social Need initiative (Quirk and McLaughlin, Chapter Seven); and policies to promote equity in public policy making and to implement equality of opportunity (Osborne *et al*, Chapter Six).

Policy Appraisal and Fair Treatment (PAFT)

The vehicle for delivering policy on this last issue has been the Policy Appraisal and Fair Treatment Initiative (PAFT), introduced in 1994, and an appraisal of PAFT, since its inception, is the subject matter of Osborne *et al* in Chapter Six. Osborne *et al* argue that a major block to community relations in Northern Ireland is the suspicion with which Catholics view policy made by a civil service in Northern Ireland that is, particularly at senior levels, Protestant dominated. In other words, irrespective of whether policy in Northern Ireland is efficient or not, Catholics perceive such policy to be inequitable and this perception itself robs policy of some of its efficiency. Against this background, the purpose of PAFT is to correct public policy for any bias that may otherwise operate for or against any of two communities. Thus, the successful implementation of PAFT would send a clear signal to both communities that, in Northern Ireland, public policy, like justice, was blind.

The formulation and implementation of policies like PAFT involve a concern with issues of equity. Unfortunately, one of the hoariest chestnuts of the social sciences is whether there is conflict between equity and efficiency so that one cannot have more of one without giving up some of the other. In the presence of this conflict, two extreme positions are possible. The first is to subsume the issue of equality within that of efficiency. On this view, there are costs to pursuing equality and these costs are worth incurring only if the efficiency benefits of equality (say from having a larger pool of potential employees to draw from) outweigh the costs of following egalitarian policies. The polar extreme of such a view is one that prizes equality for its own sake and which would sacrifice large amounts of efficiency to secure greater equality.

Most persons, when confronted with these extremes, would probably opt for a middle course, which is to tolerate a certain amount of inequality provided the mechanisms generating inequality are not unfair. Such a view would not be concerned with equality of outcomes, but rather with the processes that generate inequality. In the field of income inequality, for example, the concern would be about how income was earned and about whether a given collection of worker attributes were equally rewarded across subgroups of the population. In the labour market, the concern would be about the process by which employment was sought and offered and, once obtained, the process by which employees progressed up the promotion ladder. A longer view of fairness might complement this by arguing for measures that narrow differences between groups in attributes that determine labour market performance.

The tendency for most persons is to assume that their actions are fair and to express (genuine) surprise at anyone who might believe otherwise. To an extent, this is the result of a lack of awareness, perhaps born from a lack of experience, about the wider context in which issues of fairness should be based. To another extent, it is the result of people (and organisations) wishing to think well of themselves and being uncomfortable in the presence of others who might challenge this sense of well-being. The issue, therefore, for public policy implementation, is one of developing awareness, but in a non-threatening manner.

The Osborne *et al* study points to the importance of developing such awareness through determined, yet sensitive, leadership by an over-arching body, and suggests that the implementation of PAFT guidelines for Northern Ireland has suffered from a deficiency in this respect. A related issue is the view held by some departments of the Northern Ireland government that they simply implement policy made in Whitehall and have very little discretion in making (or even interpreting) policy. Both Osborne *et al* on PAFT and Quirk and McLaughlin (Chapter Seven) on Targeting Social Needs (TSN) point to the fact that different departments adopt this view with varying degrees of vigour. There may be good reasons for this variety and Osborne *et al* need to be more explicit about the governmental areas where they see genuine progress possible in this respect. However, the biggest stumbling block to the PAFT guidelines is that it is perceived as running counter to the dominant orthodoxy, which is that the most urgent problem facing the public sector is to be 'efficient'. Furthermore, in the search for efficiency, the public sector should divest itself of those functions which can be performed at a lower cost by the private sector. However, the cost advantage of the private sector, particularly in areas where contracting out is feasible, lies in an absence of labour market regulation. To introduce regulation - through minimum wages, or through a ceiling on working hours, or through mandatory holidays - raises costs and erodes efficiency.

In this general setting, PAFT should be seen as a form of labour market regulation, in principle no different from the items contained in the EU's Social Chapter and to which the British government is so bitterly opposed. Such regulation raises the welfare of workers, but, arguably, reduces the welfare of those prospective employees who remain unemployed, because the additional costs that regulation imposes on employers restricts the number of workers that they are prepared to take on. The final calculation on whether PAFT guidelines are to be taken seriously is, on prevailing views about the role of the public sector, ultimately a cost-benefit one. Unfortunately, the Osborne *et al* study is silent on this point. It calls for more resources to be spent in implementing PAFT but does not hint at what the opportunity costs of diverting resources towards PAFT might be. Unless one casts PAFT in the broader context of total government spending, and perhaps also makes the ancillary argument that the greater equity that might flow from a successful implementation of PAFT would have a favourable effect on efficiency, it would be difficult to get government, in these modern times where the preoccupation is with efficiency gains, to take equity issues seriously.

Targeting Social Need (TSN)

Equity issues are also paramount in designing policies to alleviate social need. Quirk and McLaughlin (Chapter Seven) discuss the problems of implementing the Northern Ireland government's set of measures for Targeting Social Need (TSN) and the problems posed by the design and implementation of such measures. The Fair Employment Act of 1989, which was the centrepiece of the government's efforts to secure greater equality of opportunity in Northern Ireland, was supplemented by TSN as an additional tool aimed at changing the policy making process. In turn, TSN was complemented by PAFT (discussed in Chapter Six). TSN stemmed from the realisation that, on all major social and economic indicators, Catholics were worse off than Protestants. In designing policies to combat this, the government was caught between the Scylla of Catholic perception of discrimination if nothing was done about their relative disadvantage, and the Charybdis of Protestant alienation if Catholics were given preferential treatment in solving problems that were common to both communities. This dilemma has bedevilled efforts to design and implement an effective TSN policy.

Quirk and McLaughlin review the implementation of TSN in Northern Ireland over 1991-95, both in terms of the adequacy of TSN and also in terms of its impact across the different departments of Northern Ireland government. Two departments within government played a critical role in the implementation of TSN: the Department of Finance and Personnel (DFP), which is the equivalent in Northern Ireland of H.M. Treasury in Great Britain, and the Central Community Relations Unit (CCRU), whose primary function was to offer advice to the Secretary of State on matters relating to community relations and 'equity' issues. Quirk and McLaughlin note that the DFP, as controller of the public purse strings, had essentially a conservative attitude towards TSN, preferring to view it more as a matter of consolidating, rather than improving or expanding, existing practice. At the same time, the CCRU, whose role it was to provoke and challenge other government departments into 'doing something' about equity issues, regarded as problematic (and therefore, undesirable) the setting of goals and timetables, in respect of TSN, for departments to follow. As a result, to employ a cricketing metaphor, the TSN ball fell between two fielders, neither of whom, it might be argued, was prepared to go for the catch. This lack of urgency towards TSN, displayed by the DFP and the CCRU, infected the attitudes of departments responsible for its implementation, most of which displayed a marked tendency to drag their feet on the issue. The moral of the Quirk and McLaughlin study (Chapter Seven) would, therefore, appear to be that for policy to be implemented effectively, it must be taken, and seen to be taken, seriously at the very apex of power.

EDUCATION AND TRAINING

No study of employment and unemployment can be complete without consideration of the education and training system within which the labour market of a country or region is embedded. This is for the simple reason that there is an intimate relation between unemployment (particularly long-term unemployment) and a lack of skills. Unskilled persons are more likely to be jobless than persons in possession of skills (see also Sheehan and Tomlinson, Chapter Three). The high level of unemployment rates, particularly among males, is largely associated with a collapse in the demand for unskilled male labour that occurred in the 1980s in most countries of the OECD, as a consequence of international competition and/or changes in technology. This fall reduced the number of unskilled jobs available and also depressed the real wages associated with such jobs. As a consequence, unskilled workers were either unemployed (that is, jobless and seeking) or they left the labour market, either because they were discouraged about the prospects of finding employment, or because they did not find employment to be sufficiently rewarding. Thus, underlying the overall unemployment figures is the phenomenon of high, and stubborn, male joblessness. Nor do the unemployment figures fully reflect the scale of this joblessness: in 1993, 13.4% of Northern Ireland working-age males were unemployed (that is, jobless and searching) but another 13% were inactive (that is, jobless and not searching).

The acquisition of skills, which has become essential to the acquisition of employment, mainly occurs in adolescence and early adulthood. However, most studies of the labour market emphasise adults, particularly males. The contribution of Caul in Chapter Five is his emphasis on school-leavers and their experiences in the belief that such experiences determine their later suitability for the world of work. Because of such an emphasis, his study is particularly valuable. The context of the chapter is as follows. Leaving aside academic high-fliers, the first preferred option of a 16 year old is to obtain a (full-time, reasonably secure and well-paying) job. Having secured a job, he (or she) may or may not receive further training (either on-the-job or off-the-job) from employers. Protestant school-leavers are more successful in getting jobs than their Catholic counterparts. Those school-leavers who do not succeed in finding employment either languish in unemployment or join a training scheme in the belief that this will improve their chances of employment - that is, that time spent on the scheme will be a good investment.

Against this background, Caul's chapter raises a number of issues. The first issue is that of 'cream-skimming'. Do employers take the best of school-leavers leaving the less able to join training schemes? In that case, training schemes contain an inherent selection bias towards the less able. Or is employment at the age of 16 and 17 a bit of a lottery, dependent on who you are, where you live and who you know rather than on what you are? This is an important issue because its answer determines the appropriate nature of the training. If there is cream-skimming, then training might have to contain a large remedial element to make up for things that should have been learnt at school but were not. In that case, the question is whether we should seek an improvement in compulsory schooling instead of investing in post-compulsory training. Caul's view is that the remedial element might have to be rather large.

The second issue is why the success rate of Protestant school-leavers in securing employment is so much better than that of Catholics. Are Protestant school-leavers better qualified both in terms of performance and subject choice? Subject choice *per se* may not matter, but subject choice may indicate the possession of, or aptitude for, more basic skills (numeracy, computer literacy) which employers find desirable. GCSE grades may not matter *per se* but good grades signal basic qualities like seriousness, reliability and motivation which are important for employers. If differences in qualifications are not important, Protestant success may be due to some of the structural factors referred to in the chapter by Gillespie (for example, the match between residence and job locations), or due to direct or indirect discrimination against Catholics, for example, through the use, by employers, of informal methods for recruiting school-leavers.

In that case, training on its own is of little value unless there are concomitant changes in non-training policy that translate trained workers into employed workers. This is particularly important since young workers are likely to be immobile, dependent on residence in the family home, so that jobs need to be brought to them rather than they to the jobs. It is also important because young workers may be the subject of workplace intimidation (discussed by Sheehan and Tomlinson in Chapter Three) so that, in terms of fair employment, the problem may be as much keeping a job as securing one. All of this is at the heart of the 'training' problem - the fact that training policy and employment policy are pursued independently so that 'training' becomes simply a way of postponing unemployment.

The third issue which Caul's chapter raises, is spare capacity in the training market. Just over a half of all training places are occupied. This suggests that either there is excess supply (demand being at the right level) or there is deficient demand, in the sense that it should be higher, but is not. In any case, action seems to be called for either in terms of reducing training resources or increasing training demand. The present situation of excess supply is the worst of both worlds.

The more general issue is that the elitism inherent in Northern Ireland's educational system is ultimately self-defeating. Hence, a starting point for reducing Northern Ireland's high unemployment levels lies in a reform of its education and training structure. Such directions for reform may be more easily mapped than traversed. The educational structure in Northern Ireland is elitist in its selection methods, being based on the out-moded British grammar school system, which identified an elite group of school children at the age of 11 and proceeded to lavish upon it educational resources; many of those not fortunate enough to pass the 11-plus exam were consigned to relatively mediocre secondary modern schools.

This binary divide continues at the level of training. At a very early stage the achievers (those who got a job at 16 or 17) are separated from the non-achievers (those who are forced onto a training scheme because they could not get a job). Hence, the non-achievers have no successful peer-models to whom they can relate. Their peers are other non-achievers and this in itself breeds defeatism. There is thus, as the Northern Ireland Affairs Select Committee (1995) recently noted, a sharp divide in Northern Ireland between those who leave education with high academic qualifications heading for professional jobs and the large numbers of school-leavers with few or no qualifications. Over one-third of employees in the industrial sector in Northern Ireland have no qualifications, as compared to 29% for Britain. If there is to be reform in Northern Ireland's educational system, it must become more egalitarian, with less emphasis on preparation for university and with more emphasis on vocational subjects and on Further (instead of Higher) Education.

FUTURE DIRECTIONS FOR POLICY

Because of the nature of its sectarian divide, policy makers in Northern Ireland have, quite properly, been as concerned with issues of distribution as with issues of growth. However, for both communities to benefit economically - rather than for one to gain at the expense of the other - economic growth is of the essence. However, this begs the question of how growth is to achieved and whether the best way for doing so is for government to adopt a 'hands-off' or a 'hands-on' policy.

The role of state intervention in development is one of the oldest issues in economics and debate on this topic has revolved around the question of when, and to what extent, governments should intervene. More recent studies, however, emphasise the quality rather than the quantity of intervention (Rodrik, 1992; Newbery, 1992). It is differences in quality, not quantity, that explain why state intervention has proved disastrous for the economies of Latin America, Eastern Europe, Africa and the Indian sub-continent, but has provided the foundation for growth and prosperity in successful economies such as Japan, Korea and Taiwan. Most importantly, one needs a proactive government (and government agencies) that will provide leadership first, by defining clearly, after general consultation, its economic goals, and second by a commitment to predictable rules of behaviour that are consistently, firmly and uniformly applied. These are, however, matters of macroeconomic policy.

At the level of social and economic policy directed specifically to the disadvantaged in society, there needs to be, as Sheehan and Tomlinson (Chapter Four) argue, 'a fresh approach to long-term unemployment and employment equity'. They trace, in Chapter Four, the outline of such an approach. In areas of high unemployment, employers need to be less preoccupied with establishing a 'balanced' workforce and need to be more concerned with drawing their employees from the ranks of the unemployed; conversely, employers in areas in which unemployment is not high need to take all measures possible to minimise workplace intimidation and employment discrimination.

More generally, work on social policy in Northern Ireland, of which the chapters in this volume are an excellent example, has done much to shed light on a range of issues facing households, including poverty, employment, health, welfare, education and housing. In particular, it has raised consciousness in Northern Ireland about poverty, deprivation and unemployment, and the general direction of this work calls for a national consensus on a strategy to tackle these issues.

However, arriving at such a consensus will not be easy. That is because the particular political ethic which created welfarism has been unravelling. Attitudes towards welfare are driven by a shift in political ideology which says 'blame a little more, understand a little less'. The problem for most governments is where to place themselves on a spectrum that extends from pure statist compassion to the most minimal of welfare safety nets. It is agreement on such a position that is essential if we are to have a coherent and agreed policy for the poor and the unemployed.

Compounding the political shift are profound changes in the nature of employment that have occurred in the past 25 years or so. Essentially, the traditional model of a single wage earning household seeking relief from temporary unemployment is no longer valid. The problem today is how to equip the unemployed for the world of work and of how to provide them with incentives to take jobs that may be only part-time or temporary. The final difficulty is of achieving a consensus, within the context of changing social conditions, which does not make excessive demands on the public purse. This last point is particularly important as Northern Ireland prepares itself to meet a possible reduction in the British subvention.

These three items, which are essential items of any consensus on poverty and unemployment, provide a fruitful research agenda. The first issue of importance is the size of Northern Ireland's potential labour force in terms of migrants from Northern Ireland who are prepared to return if jobs are available and the factors which influence migration and return migration.

The second question is the social and psychological costs of unemployment. This is an important area, to which the sociologists and psychologists (see Darity and Goldsmith, 1996, for a review of the literature) have contributed a great deal but which conventional economic analysis tends to ignore. This work could be usefully extended to include, for example, investigating the effects of psychological distress on productivity. This would give an economic dimension to this important piece of social research.

The third question relates to the behaviour and attitudes of the long-term unemployed: what jobs they are prepared to accept; the wage they would be prepared to work at; how they arrive at their reservation wage; their methods and intensity of job search; and the attitude of employers towards the long-term unemployed. It is important to have answers to these questions, since a great deal of policy towards the long-term unemployed in the UK is based on providing incentives to both the unemployed to take on work and to firms to employ them. These issues have been addressed in Chapters Two, Three and Four.

The fourth question relates to the establishment of a minimum wage. The argument against a minimum wage is that it is employment-reducing. However, there might be distributional arguments in favour of a minimum wage. What matters to unemployed people is the pay on offer for 'entry jobs' that is, jobs which provide the route back to work. Research in Britain shows that 60% of such jobs are part-time or temporary, fewer than one in five pay the average wage and over 50% of such jobs pay less than half the average wage. The plight of an unemployed person living in a 'workless' household (that is, where the partner is not working) is that he (or she) cannot afford to take such jobs. The problem may, not, therefore, be one of inadequate search but one of adverse work incentives. Thus, what might be needed is a package of measures to improve entry level wages, and this might include a sensible minimum wage, lower taxation on entry level jobs and benefit reform to ensure that benefit withdrawals do not match gains from earnings.

The nature of entry level jobs is a major reason why the old family stereotype, of a full-time male earner with a non-working wife, is no longer as relevant today as it was, say, 20 years ago. The growing number of part-time jobs has meant that an increasing number of women are working. The low wages attached to such jobs mean that they are mostly married women with employed husbands. On the other hand, it is difficult for unemployed men and their wives to take such jobs because of the adverse incentives associated with benefit withdrawal. Consequently, the distribution of work is changing, with increased polarisation between dual-earner and no-earner families.

This polarisation has considerable social costs in terms of the rise of an 'underclass'. This is a fruitful area of research which has attracted some attention in the Republic of Ireland (see Whelan, 1994). An area perhaps worth investigating are the links (if any) between unemployment (particularly youth unemployment) and crime. It is possible that in the next few years, crime, as it has already done in several other countries, will come to occupy an important position in Northern Ireland's domestic agenda.

The last question relates to the behaviour of firms. It is important to know whether firms recruit part-timers because the demand for goods and services is such that part-time work is the most effective way to respond, or if they create part-time jobs because those who wish to work part-time have desirable characteristics. Indeed, the whole nexus of attitudes of business towards labour market issues - wages, productivity, training, unemployed job applicants, the nature of job creation - is a very important area of research, and one in which the chapters in this volume by Shuttleworth *et al* and Sheehan and Tomlinson have made a very important beginning for Northern Ireland.

REFERENCES

Darity, W. and Goldsmith, A.H. (1996) 'Social Psychology, Unemployment and Macroeconomics', *Journal of Economic Perspectives*, 10: 121-39.

Layard, P.R.G. (1996) 'How to Cut Unemployment', *Centre Piece*, 1: 2-6.

Layard, P.R.G., Nickell, S. and Jackman, R. (1991) *Unemployment: Macroeconomic Performance and the Labour Market*, Oxford: Oxford University Press.

Lee, J.J. (1989) *Ireland, 1912-1985*, Cambridge: Cambridge University Press.

Newbery, D.M. (1992) 'The Role of Public Enterprises in the National Economy', *Asian Development Review*, 10: 1-34.

Nickell, S. (1993) 'Unemployment and the Benefit System', *Economic Report*, Vol. 7, London: Employment Institute.

Northern Ireland Affairs Select Committee (1995) *Employment Creation in Northern Ireland*, London: HMSO.

OECD (1993) *Employment Outlook*, Paris: OECD.

Rodrik, D. (1992) 'Political Economy and Development Policy', *European Economic Review*, 36: 329-36.

Whelan, C.T. (1994) *In Search of the Underclass: Marginalization, Poverty and Fatalism in the Republic of Ireland*, Working Paper no. 51, Dublin: ESRI.